SECOND EDITION

Introduction to Corporate Law

SECOND EDITION

Introduction to Corporate Law

By
The Philadelphia Institute
Lisa H. Warren, Esquire, Editor

West Publishing Company
St. Paul   New York   Los Angeles   San Francisco
1991

COPYRIGHT © 1978   By WEST PUBLISHING COMPANY
COPYRIGHT © 1991   By WEST PUBLISHING COMPANY
50 W. Kellogg Boulevard
P.O. Box 64526
St. Paul, MN 55164-0526

Printed in the United States of America

98 97 96 95 94 93 92 91   8 7 6 5 4 3 2 1 0

Library of Congress Cataloging-in-Publication Data

Introduction to corporate law / the Philadelphia Institute : Lisa
    Warren, editor. — 2nd ed.
      p.   cm.
    Includes bibliographical references and index.
    ISBN 0-314-80907-4
    1. Corporation law—United States.   I. Warren, Lisa.
II. Philadelphia Institute.
KF1414.I58   1991
346-73—dc20
[066]
[347.30666]   90-25204
                                                                   CIP

Composition: Northwestern Printcrafters
Copyediting: Cindi M. Gerber
Interior Design: David J. Farr, ImageSmythe Inc.

COMPUTER SERVICES/SOFTWARE MENTIONED IN CHAPTER 12.
LEXIS® and NEXIS® are registered trademarks for information products
and services of Mead Data Central, Inc. Dow Jones News/Retrieval® is a
registered trademark of Dow Jones and Company, Inc. Dialog® is a
registered trademark of Dialog Information Systems, Inc. Wordperfect® is
a registered trademark of WordPerfect Corporation. Lotus 1-2-3® is a
registered trademark of Lotus Development Company. Excel® is a registered trademark of Microsoft Corporation.

ACKNOWLEDGMENTS

This book is intended to be utilized as a course text for students studying Corporate Law. It is primarily designed for the education of legal assistants but it will be useful for anyone concerned with the structure of corporations and the manner in which corporations operate as fictitious persons.

The author of the book is The Philadelphia Institute in Philadelphia, Pennsylvania, a unique educational institution established in 1970 to train para-professionals for careers as lawyer's assistants. Thousands of people have successfully completed programs at the Institute. Of course, an institution cannot write a book—but many people connected with it have contributed their efforts in making this book possible.

Special thanks are due to Steven Haas, Esquire, Susan Freedman, Esquire, and Patricia Mangan for their authorship of the chapters on securities regulation (10), mergers and acquisitions (11), and computers (12), respectively. Thanks are also due to John Hall for providing expertise in income taxation as it appears in this edition.

LISA WARREN, ESQUIRE
THE PHILADELPHIA INSTITUTE

Philadelphia, Pennsylvania
February, 1991

PREFACE

This book is an outgrowth of materials written and published for students in the corporate law section at The Philadelphia Institute in Philadelphia, Pennsylvania. It is designed to challenge and educate students who have had little or no prior exposure to corporations and corporate law.

Hundreds of problems and questions have been added to the materials which will hopefully challenge and motivate the student. Many of the questions have intentionally not been directly answered in the book in order to promote class discussion and independent thought by the student. In addition, many of the questions raised may not have one answer, and the instructor can properly provide guidance as to these gray areas. Some questions are repeated elsewhere in the text where it is believed appropriate to tie together different concepts.

The primary purpose of the book is to be a teaching tool rather than a reference book or treatise. As a teaching tool, the book has attempted to emphasize and isolate those areas in which paralegals can be particularly useful in assisting lawyers. My experience in teaching the corporate course at the Institute for several years and in the supervision of paralegals has led me to believe that certain areas of corporate practice are most conducive to the use of paralegals. The book concentrates on these areas. The text was written on the theory that competence can only be based on understanding, not rote. The learning of concepts in a vacuum is relatively useless; the comprehension of the "why", even on an elementary level, is critical.

CONTENTS IN BRIEF

CONTENTS

CHAPTER
THREE

Qualification of Corporations in Foreign Jurisdictions 63

CHAPTER SIX

Corporate Equity and Debt Securities 151

CHAPTER
TEN

Regulation of Securities and the Securities Markets in the United States 331

SECOND EDITION

Introduction to Corporate Law

CHAPTER ONE

Introduction to Corporations

This book contains materials designed to teach students about various tasks undertaken by lawyers and their legal assistants in organizing and subsequently representing corporations. It is by no means intended to be an exhaustive study of corporate representation, but rather an overview of common corporate affairs. It is not intended as a practice manual, or "how to," but rather an analysis of the structure of corporate representation. Before discussing specific activities of the lawyers and paralegals, this chapter will provide students with a preliminary understanding of the nature of a corporation and how it is structured.

This text contains numerous statutes, forms, and formats cited as examples; the student should bear in mind that they are ever changing and hence intended as illustrations only. Also, some examples drafted go further than the minimum requirements of the form.

Chapter One is intended to provide the paralegal student with an initial exposure to corporate law which will prove useful throughout the balance of the course. Chapter One will require the student to begin working with the language and structure of state corporate laws, thereby providing a starting point for the development of skills necessary to deal with statutory materials.

LEGAL FORMATS FOR CONDUCTING A BUSINESS

People usually think of a corporation as a business enterprise. Not all business, however, is carried on by corporations. It might be helpful initially to consider some other common forms of conducting a business.

A decision must be made by the person starting a business as to the nature of the entity which will operate the business. It may be operated by one individual, by a group of individuals, or by a corporation. The choice is usually determined on the basis of several considerations: (a) the nature of the business; (b) the liabilities (obligations) to be incurred upon formation of the new business entity; (c) the complications involved in operating the entity in one form rather than another; (d) the income tax consequences of the selection of a particular entity; and (e) inheritance and estate tax implications. The decision as to the nature of the entity will be made by the lawyer and the client.

Sole proprietorship

The first form of business available is a "sole proprietorship" conducted, as the name indicates, by one person. It is a form of business in which there is one owner who receives all the income and has personal liability to pay all the debts of the business. Personal liability means that all assets of the individual, both those in the business and those that are personal, such as a savings account or a home, may be reached by business creditors for satisfaction of the obligations of the business. For example, a retail shoe store may be operated as a sole proprietorship, in which the owning individual owns all of the assets and receives all of the income derived from the store, out of which the store's expenses must be paid. The owner is personally responsible for all of the debts of the business, not only to the extent of the assets dedicated to the business, such as bank accounts and inventory of shoes, but also all other assets of the individual, including furniture, home, and personal car. Since everything is owned by one person, that person also has full authority to make all decisions concerning the operation of the store. When the owner dies, so does the business.

Partnership

Often two or more individuals about to start a business form a "partnership." A partnership is an arrangement between two or more persons to carry on a business together and to make contributions of cash, services, and property to the business and to share profits and losses therefrom.

The partnership entity, not the individual partners, holds title to the assets of the partnership. The partners have no separate interest in any partnership assets. For example, real estate acquired with partnership funds becomes partnership property. A partner's interest in a partnership is the personal property of the partner.

Although the law may differ from state to state, partnership actions generally may be taken on behalf of the partnership by any general partner. For example, a decision by one partner to buy a limousine for the partnership will bind the partner who arranged the purchase, the partnership, and the other partners to pay for the automobile.

Partners have unlimited personal liability as individuals for the debts and obligations of the partnership just as a sole proprietor does. This means that if one or more partners of the partnership incur debts or liabilities on behalf of the partnership which exceed the value of the property owned by the partnership, the assets of each individual partner will be subject to claims by creditors. A partner will be required to meet these claims out of personal assets without regard to the proportion of assets which the partner contributed to the partnership or whether the partner incurred any of the unpaid debts. Thus, each partner would be liable to the extent of all personal assets to pay for the limousine described in the preceding paragraph.

All partners have a legal right to take part in the management of the partnership. Partners can, however, give up this right or limit it in a partnership agreement signed by all the partners. For example, the right to vote on decisions of the partnership may be made to depend on the relative contribution of assets to the partnership by the partners.

When one of the partners dies or otherwise leaves the partnership, the partnership may dissolve, and the assets, after provision for the payment of all business debts, will be distributed to the remaining partner or partners.

PROBLEMS

1. If a partnership agreement between partners prohibits any one partner from buying an automobile for the partnership, can the agency selling the limousine to one partner for the partnership's benefit collect payment from all partners and the partnership if the agency did not know of the terms of the partnership agreement?

2. Assume that Smith is a sole proprietor of a shoe business. The business is worth $50,000 and, in addition, Smith owns a house worth $100,000. If Jones is injured in Smith's store, sues Smith, and recovers a judgment against Smith, how much can Jones recover from Smith? From what sources?

3. Assume that X and Y are partners in a shoe store. James slips in the store of X and Y. The partnership has assets of $100,000. X has a house worth $100,000 and Y has a house worth $110,000. If James gets a $200,000 judgment against the partnership, how much can James recover? From what sources?

Corporation

The business of the shoe store might also be conducted by a "corporation." A corporation is an entity separate and apart from its owners, thus different from either a proprietorship or a partnership. A corporation is a legal creation of the state in which it is formed, or incorporated. The principal differences between the

3

corporate form of conducting the business and the partnership or sole proprietorship forms are the following:

Liability A sole proprietor and the partners in a partnership are personally liable for the debts incurred by the business they own to the full extent of both their business and personal assets. The debts of a corporation are paid out of the assets of the corporation and neither the shareholders, directors, nor officers of the corporation are personally liable for the debts of the business enterprise if the corporation is unable to satisfy all of them. This is referred to as "limited liability."

Effect of death In the event of the death of the sole proprietor or one of the partners, the existence of the proprietorship terminates. In contrast, the death of a shareholder, director, or officer of a corporation does not terminate the corporation as a separate entity. This is referred to as "perpetual existence."[1]

Management A sole proprietorship and, in most instances, a partnership are managed directly by the owners of the business. A corporation is managed by corporate officers and a board of directors who need not be shareholders. Generally, it may not be directly managed by the shareholders who are in fact the real owners of the corporation.[2] The exception involves some "close" corporations, discussed later in this text.

Stock certificates Shareholders (sometimes called stockholders) in a corporation are issued stock certificates to evidence their ownership. In the absence of an agreement or applicable law or regulation preventing transfer, the certificates are negotiable and freely transferable.[3]

Tax treatment Corporations are subject to state and federal tax treatment which is different from that imposed on sole proprietorships and partnerships.[4] A corporation is a separate entity for taxation purposes while partnerships and proprietorships are not. The corporate entity is not ignored for federal income tax liability purposes. The income, deductions, and losses relating to the operation of the business are attributed to the corporate entity, and the corporation pays income tax at special corporate tax rates on its net income. If any net profits are distributed to the corporate shareholders as dividends, the individual shareholders pay income tax, at their respective tax rates, on the dividends they receive.

---

1. See Chapter Two for a discussion of the term of existence of a corporation.
2. See ownership and management of a corporation on p. 9.
3. See Chapter Two for a dicussion and forms of stock certificates.
4. See Taxation on p. 14 for a discussion of the tax treatment of corporations.

Partnership and proprietorship income is taxed only directly to individual partners or proprietors.

A business is usually operated in corporate form to take advantage of one or all of these corporate characteristics. In order to achieve the purpose for incorporation, the lawyer and paralegal must be certain to comply with all of the legal requirements and procedures in creating the corporation and in maintaining it.

PROBLEMS

1. Assume that X corporation has assets of $100,000. Its two shareholders, A and B, each have assets of $50,000, consisting of personal residences. If Jones (our old friend) obtains a judgment against the corporation for $125,000, how much will Jones recover? From what sources?

2. Can a corporation with only one shareholder, who is also the only officer and director, have a "perpetual existence"? Why or why not?

BUSINESS CORPORATIONS

It is possible to look at a business from several vantage points. In business school, the study of corporations normally involves a study of the means by which a corporation buys raw materials and then manufactures and sells products. The focus of such study is on the economic aspects of a business. From that point of view, it might well be irrelevant whether or not the business being considered was a corporation, as opposed to a partnership or a sole proprietorship. This is not, however, the focus of this book. You will find no mention of any specific products produced by a corporation nor how such products are produced. Rather, this book describes and defines the legal characteristics of a corporation and the legal interrelationships, requirements, and agreements which are an everyday part of its affairs.

There are corporations other than business corporations. State laws provide for the creation of nonprofit corporations such as charitable organizations, as well as municipal corporations, such as cities, townships, school districts, and other subdivisions of states, which perform governmental functions. Moreover, corporations have been created under both state and federal law for special purposes, such as the Federal Deposit Insurance Corporation which guarantees bank deposits up to certain maximum amounts. Such corporations are not the subject of this book. This book focuses entirely upon "for profit" or "business" corporations.

Authority to Organize and Operate Contained in State Law

Perhaps the most important thing to know about a business corporation is that the entity is a distinct legal person or entity formed by the authority of state law and according to the procedures set forth in such law. This means that a corporation created under the laws of Delaware will have different characteristics from a corporation created under the laws of New York or California.

Organizing the Corporation

Sections 2.01 to 2.07 of the Revised Model Business Corporation Act (MBCA)[5] set forth the procedure for creating a corporation.

Without the existence of a general authorizing corporate statute in each state, corporations could not be created except by a cumbersome procedure of a special legislative act granting authority to each proposed corporation.

State law also grants the corporations the capacity to conduct a trade or business.

Articles of Incorporation   A corporation is formed by filing "articles of incorporation" (in some states called a "certificate of incorporation" or "charter") with the designated state agency. While state law permits the formation of corporations, describes the mechanics of creating a corporation, and establishes rules and regulations applicable to all corporations formed pursuant to its terms, each corporation is also governed by its own unique articles of incorporation. The articles normally contain at least the following minimum characteristics:

   a. Name of the corporation.
   b. Location of an office of the corporation.
   c. Purpose of the corporation.
   d. The number of shares and the special characteristics, if any, of the various classes of stock which the corporation is authorized to issue.[6]

---

5. The Revised Model Business Corporation Act is an attempt by the Committee on Corporate Laws of the Section of Corporation, Banking and Business Law of the American Bar Association to establish an "ideal" state corporation law. Most states which have in recent years significantly revised their corporation laws have used the MBCA as a guide. Reference is made to the MBCA throughout the materials as a useful guide to a "typical" modern corporation law. However, the MBCA is only a model. It contains many features that older corporate statutes do not and many features that new statutes have modified or rejected. Accordingly, the reader must not assume the MBCA to be the law for any specific state. The entire text of the Revised MBCA is reproduced in this book as Appendix I. All references to the MBCA in this text are to the Revised MBCA.

6. The section covering incorporation on p. 7 contains a full discussion of articles of incorporation.

At the option of the persons filing the articles, many other provisions may be included.[7]

Bylaws In addition to the articles of incorporation, every corporation has bylaws. The bylaws of a corporation normally contain provisions for the regulation and management of the affairs of the corporation, which must be consistent with both state law and the articles of incorporation. Bylaws go into much more depth than the articles as to the operation of the corporation. The bylaws, in effect, provide some of the particular rules by which the activities of the officers, directors, and shareholders of the corporation are governed.[8]

Reasons for Articles of Incorporation and Bylaws in Addition to State Law The fact that a corporation is governed by different sets of rules may first appear both confusing and cumbersome. At the very least, however, it is necessary that each corporation establish its own separate set of rules and regulations for its own operation within the broad guidelines of state law. State law, of course, must be broad enough to accommodate a wide variety of corporate enterprises. Individual corporations are permitted under law to decide in certain aspects which rules and regulations are most appropriate for their own operation.

This does not answer the question of why there must be both articles of incorporation and bylaws, especially since it would be possible under most state laws to include within the articles of incorporation everything that is normally included in the bylaws. One reason is flexibility. The articles of incorporation of a corporation are, in effect, its constitution and a public document on file with an agency of the state. Anyone can inspect or obtain copies of the articles from the state agency. As you will see later, changes may be made in the articles of incorporation by specific filings with the state.[9] This involves expense and time for preparation and filing. In addition, and of most importance, changes in the articles of incorporation typically require approval by the shareholders of a corporation. This is sometimes, particularly in the case of a corporation with a large number of shareholders, a time-consuming and expensive process.[10] Bylaws, on the other hand, need not be filed with a state agency and may, if the bylaws (or articles of incorporation) permit, be changed by action of the board of directors alone. This makes the amendment of bylaws a more private, faster, and less expensive process than amending the articles.

7. See note 6 above.
8. See Corporate Bylaws on p. 44 for a discussion of the adoption and contents of bylaws. Note that some states spell the word as "by-laws."
9. See Chapter Four.
10. See Chapter Four.

It is worth repeating that bylaws may never permit any conduct or action by a corporation which is inconsistent with the articles of incorporation or state law, nor may the bylaws permit any action reserved by state law for inclusion in the articles of incorporation alone. In the same way, the articles of incorporation may never permit any action or conduct which is inconsistent with state law.

PROBLEMS

1. If the state law requires a corporation to have at least three directors, can the bylaws provide for two directors of the corporation? If the bylaws cannot so provide, can the articles of incorporation do so? Can the bylaws provide for four directors? How about a provision allowing for between two to five directors as may be determined from time to time by the directors?

2. If the state law says that the bylaws may be amended by the directors only if the articles of incorporation so provide, would a provision only in the bylaws allowing the directors to amend the bylaws be effective? What if the articles of incorporation state that the bylaws could be amended by the directors but the bylaws contain no such provision?

3. If the articles of incorporation of a corporation call for one director, the bylaws call for two directors, and the state law requires at least three directors, how many directors must the corporation have?

4. A state law has no requirements as to the minimum number of directors of a corporation. If the articles of incorporation call for nine directors and the bylaws for five directors, how many directors must the corporation have? Is it generally a good idea to have provisions in the articles and bylaws which are inconsistent?

State law sanctions the use of both articles of incorporation and bylaws and to some extent governs what is included in each.[11] There are circumstances where state law (a) permits certain regulations to be in either the articles of incorporation or the bylaws, (b) requires the regulation to be in the articles of incorporation, or (c) suggests that the regulation be in the bylaws.

PROBLEM

Look at Chapter 8 of the MBCA and decide whether, if at all, each section falls into (a), (b), or (c) of the previous paragraph. Why?

---

11. § 2.02, MBCA.

OWNERSHIP AND MANAGEMENT OF A CORPORATION

The three central classes of characters in corporate law are the shareholders, directors, and officers. State law defines them and the relationships among them. What follows is a summary of some of the more important characteristics, responsibilities, and rights which state law establishes for these different classes of persons. It is important to note that state law does not prohibit the same person from being a shareholder, a director, and an officer of the same corporation. As a matter of fact, in most corporations one or more individuals function in more than one role.

Shareholders and their rights

A shareholder is defined in rather simple and basic terms:

§ 1.40 Revised MBCA (1984). Act Definitions

(22) "Shareholder" means the person in whose name shares are registered in the records of a corporation or the beneficial owner of shares to the extent of the rights granted by a nominee certificate on file with a corporation.

The term "share" is defined as "the unit into which the proprietary interests in a corporation are divided.[12] Simply stated, a share is an ownership interest in the corporation.

QUESTIONS Is a share an interest in any specific asset of the corporation or in the totality of assets? If a corporation has a total of 100 shares, what interest does a holder of 60 shares have?

The shareholders are the owners of the corporation. The nature of this "ownership" can only be appreciated, however, when some of the rights granted to a shareholder under state law are examined. Some of the more important rights granted under the MBCA and most corporate statutes are as follows:

Election of Directors State law always provides that the business affairs of a business corporation shall be managed by a board of directors.[13] Directors are only elected by action of the shareholders other than in the case of filling vacancies.[14]

12. § 1.40 (21), MBCA.
13. Chapter 8, Subchapters A, B, and C, MBCA.
14. § 8.03, MBCA. Also see the discussion of shareholders' meetings in Chapter Five in this text.

Amending the Articles of Incorporation   Unless applicable law or the articles of incorporation provide otherwise, no changes may be made in the articles of incorporation of a corporation without the vote of the shareholders of a corporation.[15] This in effect means that the principal format established by a corporation, as embodied in the articles of incorporation, may not be changed without shareholder approval.

Dissolution   A corporation which has issued shares or commenced business may not decide to voluntarily dissolve and wind up its affairs without shareholder approval.[16]

Sale of Substantially All of Assets   A corporation may not voluntarily decide to sell or exchange all or substantially all of its assets without shareholder approval.[17]

Removal of Directors   Under the MBCA, shareholders may, with or without cause, remove directors of a corporation[18] at any properly noticed meeting, unless the articles of incorporation provide that directors may only be removed for cause.

Merger or Consolidation   Except for a merger with a subsidiary,[19] corporations may not merge or consolidate without shareholder approval.[20] A merger is not the same as a consolidation. A merger is a formal combination of two or more corporations where one corporation is absorbed by another, the latter of which is called the surviving corporation. In a consolidation, two or more corporations combine to create an entirely new corporation which is different from any of the absorbed corporations.

PROBLEMS

1. If X Corporation combines with Y Corporation and the result is Y Corporation, is the combination a merger or a consolidation?
2. If X Corporation combines with Y Corporation and the result is Z Corporation, what is the combination called? If X, Y, and A result in Z corporation?

Limited Liability   Except for the obligation to pay the full consideration for the shares issued by a corporation, shareholders

15. § 10.01, 10.02, and 10.03, MBCA. Also see Chapter Four in this text.
16. Chapter 14, MBCA. Also see Chapter Nine in this text.
17. § 12.01 and 12.02, MBCA.
18. § 8.08, MBCA.
19. § 11.04, MBCA.
20. § 11.01 and 11.03, MBCA.

are not liable for the debts of the corporation. This restricted liability is called "limited liability."

Does the liability of a shareholder differ from that of a sole proprietor or partner?[21] Does the corporation itself have limited liability?

Receipt of Dividends The distributions out of income with respect to shares of stock are called "dividends." Since dividends are paid on the shares of a corporation, shareholders are entitled to all dividends.[22]

The foregoing is not an exhaustive list of all the corporate attributes and the rights and privileges of shareholders. It is only intended to suggest that the characteristics of a shareholder must be defined by reference to state corporation law. The MBCA is a convenient model which has been adopted to a large degree in many states. However, it is not the form which has been adopted in its entirety in any state. The paralegal must review the relevant state law in each case to ascertain its requirements.

Directors and their powers

State law provides that a corporation be generally managed by the board of directors. The following MBCA model is an example.[23]

§ 8.01 MBCA (1984). Requirement for and Duties of Board of Directors.

(b) All corporate powers shall be exercised by or under the authority of, and the business and affairs of the corporation managed under the direction of, its board of directors, subject to any limitation set forth in the articles of incorporation.

Furthermore, state law tells us certain characteristics of a person who may be a director of a corporation:

§ 8.02 MBCA (1984). Qualifications of Directors.

The articles of incorporation or bylaws may prescribe qualifications for directors. A director need not be a resident of this state or a shareholder of the corporation unless the articles of incorporation or bylaws so prescribe.

---

21. See Legal Formats for Conducting a Business, p. 1.

22. § 6.40, MBCA. Also see Chapter Nine in this text. A "dividend" is a type of distribution (§ 1.40 [6], MBCA).

23. Chapter Five discusses generally the actions of directors.

The following is an outline of certain of the powers of the board of directors:

Election of Officers   The board of directors of a corporation elects its officers who are responsible for the day-to-day business operations.

§ 8.40 MBCA (1984). Required Officers.

(a) A corporation has the officers described in its bylaws or appointed by the board of directors in accordance with the bylaws.
(b) A duly appointed officer may appoint one or more officers or assistant officers if authorized by the bylaws or the board of directors.
(c) The bylaws or the board of directors shall delegate to one of the officers responsibility for preparing minutes of the directors' and shareholders' meetings and for authenticating records of the corporation.
(d) The same individual may simultaneously hold more than one office in a corporation.

§ 8.41 MBCA (1984). Duties of Officers.

Each officer has the authority and shall perform the duties set forth in the bylaws or, to the extent consistent with the bylaws, the duties prescribed by the board of directors or by direction of an officer authorized by the board of directors to prescribe the duties of other officers.

Issuance of Stock   The board of directors of a corporation has the power, subject to the restrictions provided by the articles of incorporation or the bylaws, to issue shares of stock and to determine the consideration (value) which must be paid for such shares of stock. It is interesting to note that this right is sometimes not spelled out directly in state law, but may be implied, as the following sample provisions from the MBCA demonstrate:

§ 6.21 MBCA (1984). Issuance of Shares.

The board of directors may authorize shares to be issued for consideration consisting of any tangible or intangible property or benefit to the corporation, including cash, promissory notes, services performed, contracts for services to be performed, or other securities of the corporation.

§ 6.01 MBCA (1984). Authorized Shares.

The articles of incorporation must prescribe the classes of shares and the number of shares of each class that the corporation is authorized to issue.

Dividends   The board of directors of a corporation may, from time to time, and within the restrictions imposed by the articles of incorporation and state law, make distributions to shareholders (i.e., pay dividends) in cash or property on the outstanding shares of a corporation.[24]

Why would the directors have the power to pay dividends rather than the shareholders?

Initiation of Certain Actions   While shareholder approval may be required in certain instances, the board of directors may initiate action under the MBCA in certain instances: (a) certain sales of a corporation's assets,[25] (b) approval of the merger of a corporation,[26] or (c) the voluntary dissolution of a corporation.[27]

Officers

State law recognizes the corporation's need to have officers who can manage its affairs on a daily basis. Normally, state law makes reference to at least a president, secretary, and treasurer. Section 8.41 of the MBCA provides a model form of statement of the role of the officers of a corporation:

§ 8.41 MBCA (1984). Duties of Officers.

Each officer has the authority and shall perform the duties set forth in the by-laws or, to the extent consistent with the bylaws, the duties prescribed by the board of directors or by direction of an officer authorized by the board of directors to prescribe the duties of other officers.

While the state law specifies certain offices and outlines the role of officers in general, the bylaws and the board of directors define the actual day-to-day functions of the officers. The board of directors sets forth the general direction of the corporation; the officers execute the individual tasks, such as hire employees, purchase inventory, sign checks, set prices of individual products, etc.

FORMAL CORPORATE DECISIONS

Method Used by Shareholders and Directors

In order for either shareholders or directors to take action, it is normally necessary for them to hold meetings to authorize the

24. § 6.40, MBCA.
25. § 12.02, MBCA.
26. § 11.01 and 11.03, MBCA.
27. § 14.02, MBCA.

action. Both state law and the bylaws of a corporation set forth a corporation's specific requirements in connection with the meetings of directors and shareholders.[28]

The specific form of the decision taken by directors or shareholders is referred to as a "resolution." A resolution is no more than a written statement of the specific authorization or approval which is agreed to by the shareholders or directors of a corporation. Normally, these resolutions are contained within the record (called "minutes") of proceedings at a directors' or shareholders' meeting or within the written consent if the action was taken by consent.[29]

Management by Shareholders

In some states it is possible to have the shareholders directly run the corporation. Such an entity is called a statutory "close corporation." A close corporation is permitted to have, in its articles of incorporation, a provision that its business and affairs will be managed by the shareholders rather than by the board of directors. If such a provision exists, the shareholders need not elect any directors, and the shareholders are deemed to be the directors of the corporation for all purposes. This right, in effect, removes one tier of the corporate hierarchy and permits the shareholders to act both as shareholders and directors. A "close corporation," however, must meet certain requirements.[30]

TAXATION

Income Tax

The federal government, nearly all state governments, and some municipal governments impose a separate tax on the income corporations earn. These tax structures change frequently, and current law must be consulted for current tax structure. This contrasts with the situation of sole proprietorships and partnerships where there is no separate entity and only the owners are taxed on income. Payment of the tax is an obligation of the corporation and not its shareholders, directors, or officers. The current federal tax rate (as of this printing) for corporations is based on a graduated table with a maximum rate of 34 percent. If a corporation pays a dividend to its shareholders, the dividend is paid out of the profits of the corporation after the payment of taxes

28. Chapter Five discusses in detail meetings of shareholders and directors and alternatives thereto.
29. See § 8.21 of the MBCA for an example of a statute authorizing written consents.
30. See Chapter Two for a description of close corporations.

(i.e., "after-tax profits") and such a dividend is taxable to the individual shareholder as income. This means that corporate earnings which are passed on to shareholders in the form of a dividend are subject to a second federal tax.[31] The fact that the corporate income was taxed and the distribution of income to shareholders remaining after such taxes was also taxed is commonly referred to as "double taxation."

QUESTION Does a partnership have "double taxation"? A sole proprietorship?

"Subchapter S" Corporations

To avoid the double federal income tax described above, Subchapter S of the United States Internal Revenue Code (IRC) allows corporations which meet certain requirements to be taxed as "small business corporations." Corporations that take advantage of the benefits of this provision of the IRC are usually referred to as "Subchapter S corporations." In order to become a Subchapter S corporation for tax purposes, all of the following requirements must be met:

1. The corporation must have authorized, issued, and outstanding only one class of stock.[32]
2. The corporation must have no more than thirty-five stockholders, and each of these stockholders must be an individual, estate, or certain trust. In addition, no shareholder may be a nonresident alien or corporation.
3. The unanimous consent of shareholders is required with the election to be taxed under Subchapter S.
4. The corporation must elect to be taxed as a Subchapter S corporation and must notify the Internal Revenue Service within a specified period of time. (Note that the size of the corporation with respect to revenues, assets, or earnings is wholly immaterial in determining whether it qualifies for taxation as a Subchapter S corporation.)
5. The corporation must be a domestic corporation that is not a member of an affiliated group.

The major tax benefit of a Subchapter S corporation is that there is no federal income tax at the corporate level. Many states also allow corporations to elect Subchapter S status for state income tax purposes.

---

31. The subject of corporate distributions is discussed in greater detail in Chapter Nine.
32. See Chapter Six for a discussion of different classes of shares of stock.

Corporate income is, therefore, except in certain limited situations, attributed directly to the stockholders in proportion to their "ownership" of the corporation and is taxed as income to them only. Any losses which the corporation incurs in its operations are also attributed directly to the stockholders, who may, except for certain limitations, use these losses to offset income from other sources. In effect, a Subchapter S corporation is treated with some variations, for tax purposes, in a manner substantially equivalent to a partnership.

An example of this situation is as follows. Assume that A and B are the shareholders in X Corporation. A owns 60 shares and B owns 40 shares. If X Corporation earns $100,000 and is not a Subchapter S corporation, it will pay federal income taxes of about $22,250, based on 1990 federal tax rates. If X Corporation declares a dividend of the remainder after taxes to A and B, A will receive cash of $46,650 and B will receive cash of $31,100. A and B will then each pay personal income taxes on these distributions. If A and B are each in the 28 percent tax bracket, A will be left with $33,588 and B with $22,392.

The situation is quite different if X Corporation has validly elected Subchapter S status. In such a case there will be no tax at the corporate level. Instead, $60,000 of income will be attributed directly to A and $40,000 directly to B. Again assuming a 28 percent personal income tax rate, A will be left with $43,200 and B with $28,000. Thus, a substantial tax saving is effected by means of the Subchapter S corporation.

State Income Taxation

States are generally permitted to tax corporations which do business within their borders. Where a corporation does business in several states, the state tax may be determined by an "allocation formula." Most allocation formulas in effect today use a three-factor formula consisting of sales, assets, and employee payroll in determining what percentage of a corporation's net income is attributed to the particular state. The diversity of allocation formulas used, however, and the inclination of state governments to devise formulas most beneficial to themselves, results in payment by many multistate corporations of state income taxes in excess of those taxes they would be required to pay if every state had an identical formula.

"Franchise" and "Capital Stock" Taxes

In addition to income taxes, most states levy a special tax on domestic corporations (corporations incorporated under the laws of the state in question). These taxes, most commonly known as capital stock or franchise taxes, are frequently based on the number of shares which a corporation is authorized to issue, the authorized capital of these shares, or some similar factors, and may be a one-time tax payable upon incorporation or an annual tax or both. Foreign corporations (corporations organized under another state law) which qualify to do business within the state are usually subjected to a similar charge.

SECURITIES LAWS

The federal government and the states have elaborate legislation regulating the offering and sale of stock by corporations, as well as other securities, evidencing a share in a corporation or a debt owed by a corporation.[33] Although such legislative schemes cover virtually all types of transactions in securities, they have the greatest impact on corporations whose securities are "publicly held," that is, owned by a large number of persons, such as Xerox, General Motors, IBM, and many smaller corporations as well. Corporations become publicly held by having a "public offering," a sale of securities to the general public in accordance with applicable federal and state laws.[34]

Paralegals should be generally aware of the existence of federal securities laws and their twofold purpose of providing prospective investors with full information about a corporation which is offering securities to the public to raise capital and of regulating a fair market for trading publicly held securities.

The opposite of a "publicly held" corporation is a "closely held" corporation which, as its name indicates, has only a few shareholders. This course will concentrate on closely held corporations, although mention will be made of publicly held corporations where appropriate.

---

33. See Chapter Six for a detailed discussion of some of the more common types of securities.
34. State securities laws are often called "blue sky laws." Each state statute differs from another, and the statute of the particular state must be consulted. A service such as the Commerce Clearing House's *Blue Sky Law Reporter* will be helpful in this regard.

CHAPTER TWO

Formation of Corporations

The impetus to form a corporation is found in the desire of one or more persons to conduct some business activity and the decision, general after consultation with counsel, that the business activity can most advantageously be conducted in the corporate form. Chapter One outlines the basic differences between corporations and other forms of business entities. This chapter will consider the initial procedures to be followed in forming the corporation ("incorporation"), including the various documents which must be prepared and filed with the state in which the entity is formed, some of the substantive factors which must be considered in the incorporation process, and other matters relating to the basic structure and operation of a corporation which must be considered at the very beginning of the corporation's existence. After the procedures relating to the incorporation and structure of corporations have been analyzed, there will be a discussion of the methods whereby the structure that has been created can be modified.

PREINCORPORATION ACTIVITY

Preparation of Worksheet

Once a decision has been made to form a corporation, it is essential to complete a worksheet listing all of the information which must be known in order to properly complete the corporation. Many of the items referred to in the following example worksheet will be more completely understood after the study of this chapter.

EXAMPLE

Information Needed for the Formation and Organization of a Corporation

1. Is this to be a regular business corporation or a close corporation?
2. Corporate name:
   Please check and/or complete one of the following:
   (Name is available)
   (Check availability of name)
   (Check availability and reserve name in following states)

3. State of incorporation:
4. Registered office:
5. Registered agent (if required by state of incorporation):
6. Mailing address for state tax purposes:
7. Term of existence:
8. Brief statement of the kind or kinds of business actually to be engaged in:
9. Purpose clause if other than general purpose clause:
10. Authorized capital (number of shares, class, and par value) (Please also include designations and preferences if other than common stock, or state whether Board of Directors is to have the power to fix, by resolution, designations and preferences):
11. Names and addresses of first directors:
12. Are directors to be named in articles or certificate of incorporation?
13. Names and addresses of officers:
14. Please circle provisions desired:
    (a) Preemptive rights for shareholders. If so, describe.
    (b) Cumulative voting for Directors.
    (c) Classification of Directors. If so, describe.
    (d) Shareholder action by less than unanimous consent in writing.
    (e) Restrictions on transfer of securities. If so, describe.

15. Number of shareholders and state of residence (for purposes of applicable state securities exemption):
16. Names of shareholders; number of shares and type and class of stock:
17. Do you want subscription agreements? If so, for whom?
18. Type of minute and stock book:
    Please check one of the following:
          (Inexpensive)   (Expensive)
19. State(s) in which to qualify corporation to do business:
20. Date of organization meeting:
21. Bank account and signatures:
21. How many signatories must sign each check?
22. Total consideration to be paid for stock to be issued: (If total is less than $500,000 disregard)
24. Fiscal Year:
25. Annual meeting date: _____ of _____
                          (day)   (month)
                          at _____ A.M./P.M.

(A nominal incorporator will be used unless advised to the contrary)
                          Lawyer: _____
                          Dated: _____

Name

Choice Before a corporation can be formed, a name must be chosen. State law imposes certain restrictions on the names of corporations. The corporate name must generally contain the word "corporation," "company," or "incorporated," or an abbreviation thereof, e. g., General Motors Corporation, American Telephone and Telegraph Company, and Aluminum Company of America. In addition, corporate names which imply a governmental activity or connection or the conduct of business which is specially regulated by statute (banks, insurance companies, public utilities, etc.) are prohibited unless special permission is obtained from the state regulatory agency directly responsible for the regulation of the particular business. Within these limitations, any name selected for the corporation is permissible, provided, however, that the name chosen may not be deceptively similar to the name of a company already incorporated or doing business within the state of incorporation. The prohibition against deceptively similar names is for the benefit of the government in avoiding confusion, not to protect the corporation's interest in its own name.

Throughout the course, reference will be made to corporate statutes to set forth examples of requirements for corporate compliance. In addition, references will be made to the Revised Model Business Corporation Act (which will be called "MBCA"). The MBCA is not a real statute which has been adopted by any state but is a model for legislation and contains many common provisions which are usual in corporate statutes. The student should always check the actual provision of the relevant state business corporation code in actual practice. The original MBCA was written by the American Bar Association Committee on Corporate Laws in 1950. It was based on the corporate statute of Illinois but has since been revised. Many states have borrowed its concepts and provisions in modifying, revising, or updating their corporate statutes. This text will utilize MBCA provisions often because of its wide applicability. The complete text of the MBCA is set forth in Appendix I.

With respect to a corporation's name, § 4.01 of the MBCA provides:

§ 4.01, MBCA. Corporate Name

(a) A corporate name:

   (1) must contain the word "corporation," "incorporated," "company," or "limited," or the abbreviation "corp." "inc.," "co.," or "ltd." or words or abbreviations of like import in another language and

(2) may not contain language stating or implying that the corporation is organized for a purpose other than that permitted by section 3.01 and its articles of incorporation.

(b) Except as authorized by subsections (c) and (d), a corporate name must be distinguishable upon the records of the secretary of state from:

(1) the corporate name of a corporation incorporated or authorized to transact business in this state;

(2) a corporate name reserved or registered under section 4.02 or 4.03;

(3) the fictitious name adopted by a foreign corporation authorized to transact business in this state because its real name is unavailable, and

(4) the corporate name of a not-for-profit corporation incorporated or authorized to transact business in this state.

What problems does this requirement of name uniqueness in each state create? Note that "limited" (implying limited liability) may be used in the name under the MBCA. A "foreign" corporation is a corporation organized under the laws of a state other than the state in question.

PROBLEMS

1. Is XYZ Corporation deceptively similar to XYZ Company? To XYZ Associates, Inc.? To X and Y, Corp.?
2. Can a corporation be formed with the following names?

   a. World Bank, Ltd.
   b. Universal Travel, Ltd.
   c. Limited Resources
   d. The World's Best Corporation
   e. United States Travel, Inc.

Note that abbreviations may be used in a name. Always be certain that the name is precisely stated as the client desires it; for instance, whether "Corporation" or "Corp." or "Inc." is used in a name is the client's decision.

Availability In order to determine if the name chosen for the corporation is available, it is normal practice to contact the Secretary of the Department of State of the proposed state of incorporation, either by telephone or letter, and ascertain the availability of the name. Many states require a written request. Check with your own state. A nominal charge is sometimes imposed for this service.

Reservation In those cases where a corporation will not be formed for some period of time, it may be desirable to "reserve" the proposed name in order to insure its availability. Many states permit the reservation of a name for a limited period (e. g., three or six months) upon the payment of a small charge.

A form for the reservation of corporate names which can be used in states which have a "reservation" procedure comparable to that set forth in the MBCA is included below.

EXAMPLE

Application for Reservation of Corporate Name

[*Date*]

FOR THE SECRETARY OF STATE
   OF THE STATE OF _____ :

Pursuant to the provisions of subparagraph (____) of Section ____ of the _____ Business Corporation Act, the undersigned applicant hereby applies for reservation of the following corporate name for a period of _____ days:

[*Corporate name*]

The name and address of the applicant is_____
_____ .

The applicant encloses a fee in the amount of $_____ to reserve the name.

_____
Applicant

[*Capacity—e. g. incorporator*]

Typically, the reservation of a corporate name will be evidenced by a document or letter from the Department of State or the Secretary of State. Such a document or letter must normally accompany the articles of incorporation (which is the incorporating document) when they are filed so that the incorporator may establish that the name for the new corporation has been reserved by the incorporator. It is also a good idea to include a copy of the confirming letter previously sent by the state.

Fictitious Corporate Names Many corporations conduct their business activities under one or more names that are different from their actual corporate name. This is a legitimate business practice. A specific name may be familiar to the public, or the corporation may be trying to develop public acceptance and awareness of the name. Another reason for using a fictitious name may be that the corporate name may be too long or cumbersome for general public acceptance. For instance, Kraftco Corporation operates under the name "Kraft" or "Kraft Foods" in the sale of its cheeses and other foods because "Kraft" has acquired a secondary meaning for the public at large. Many states have laws, separate and apart from their general corporate laws, which govern the use of such "fictitious" names by corporations. In order to introduce the student to these laws it is useful to review a typical "Fictitious Corporate Name Act."

Fictitious Name Statutes For registration purposes, a fictitious name is usually defined as any "assumed or fictitious name of the corporation using such names."[1]

QUESTIONS

Who determines whether a corporation should adopt a fictitious name? What corporate action must be taken to authorize the corporation to adopt a fictitious name?

A corporation usually is not permitted to use a fictitious name in the state unless it first registers the name with the state and/or the county of location. In Pennsylvania, for example, a fictitious name is registered by filing an application under oath with the Secretary of the State or Commonwealth.[2] The application must contain, among other things, the following information:

a. Fictitious name being or to be used by the corporation;
b. Nature of business to be conducted under the fictitious name; and
c. The full corporate name of, state and date of incorporation of, and the location of the principal place of business and the registered office of, the corporation filing the application.

PROBLEM

Locate the fictitious name registration act in your state and the forms to be filed and places to make a filing in order to register the name.

A registration fee must usually be paid to the Secretary of the State or Commonwealth and must accompany the application. When the application has been filed and the required fees paid, the Secretary will stamp the registration and return it to the corporation, thus making the fictitious name effective.

Some states require publication of the fictitious name registration by the company, usually in the county in which the principal office of the company is located.[3] Some states require the

---

1. Title 54, Pa.C.S, §301 *et seq.*

2. Some states, such as Massachusetts and Virginia, are officially called "commonwealths" rather than states.

3. For example, Title 54, Pa.C.S., § 311(g).

filing of a fictitious name registration with local authorities as well.

Amendment of Fictitious Names Corporations that have registered fictitious names are usually required to make amended filings in the event of a change in the fictitious name, the location of their principal place of business, or their registered office, among other things.[4] A corporation may file as many fictitious name registrations as it desires. These supplemental filings must usually be accompanied by additional filing fees.

When, for whatever reason, a corporation ceases to conduct business under a registered fictitious name, the corporation is required to file with the Secretary of State or of the Commonwealth a statement of cancellation and to pay the requisite filing fee. The Secretary will then issue a certificate cancelling the registration.

PROBLEM

Utilizing your state statute, make the necessary fictitious name registration documents for FUN CITY FRANCHISE CORP., a Pennsylvania corporation, to operate under the fictitious name "Fun Rides." Do you need information other than that contained in the Articles of Incorporation shown later in this chapter? If so, what information is needed?

Preincorporation Subscription

Some states require that the person or persons who will be the incorporator or incorporators (those who are forming the corporation) sign preincorporation subscriptions for one share each before the filing of articles of incorporation. A subscription is an agreement to purchase some initial stock in a corporation. A sample of such a preincorporation subscription is set forth below.

EXAMPLE

Simple Preincorporation Subscription

XYZ CORPORATION
PREINCORPORATION SUBSCRIPTION

The undersigned, intending to be legally bound hereby, subscribes for one share of the one dollar ($1.00) par value common stock of XYZ CORPORATION, a corporation to be incorporated under Pennsylvania law, at a cash price of $1.00.

Dated: _____

_____ [Seal]

---

4. For example, Title 54, Pa.C.S., § 312.

The incorporator most likely will not be a permanent shareholder of the proposed corporation. The reason for such a subscription is often to satisfy a state law requirement that the incorporator also be a "subscriber" or to have a subscriber in existence after the corporation is formed. A subscriber is defined in the MBCA at §1.40(24) as one who "subscribes for shares in a corporation, whether before or after incorporation." Once a corporation is formed, certain states specify that persons who subscribed for shares prior to incorporation are shareholders of the corporation.

As seen below, persons who sign a nominal preincorporation subscription will assign it (transfer it) to a person who will in fact be a shareholder of the corporation after incorporation has become effective. Some states do not require that incorporators subscribe for shares or become shareholders of the corporation upon incorporation.[5]

In certain cases, the incorporators desiring to form the corporation have decided what percentage of the corporation's stock ownership each will have, and the percentage will be reflected in the number of shares each incorporator will purchase. In this event, and in order to bind the incorporators to purchase stock, they will sign, prior to incorporation, a subscription agreement in which they agree to purchase a specified number of the corporation's shares of stock at a stated price. A sample form of such a preincorporation subscription agreement is set forth below.

EXAMPLE

*Preincorporation
Subscription*

I, _____ , hereby subscribe for five hundred (500) shares of the common stock of XYZ Corporation, a corporation to be organized under the laws of the State of Delaware, with an authorized capital stock of Two Thousand ($2,000) Dollars, divided into two thousand shares of common stock, par value $1.00 per share. I do hereby agree to pay for said stock the sum of Ten ($10) Dollars per share, or an aggregate sum of Five Thousand ($5,000) Dollars, in full, or in such installments and at such times as the Board of Directors may determine, on demand of the Board of Directors of the Corporation.

Dated: January 2, 19_____ .

/s/ John Doe

_____

Since the corporation will generally be formed in reliance upon this undertaking to purchase shares, most corporation statutes provide that, absent a specific provision in the subscription agree-

---

5. See, for example, Title 15, § 1309, Pennsylvania Business Corporation Law (Pa.C.S. or PBCL).

ment to the contrary, the subscription is irrevocable for a limited period of time.[6]

Once the corporation is formed, and if the preincorporation subscriptions are still binding on the subscribers, the corporation will have the power to accept the subscriptions and demand that the agreed-upon purchase price be paid.

QUESTION

What problems could arise if the formation of the corporation is later than the period of irrevocability?

Consent from Initial Directors If initial directors are named in the articles of incorporation state law may imply that a written consent be obtained from the persons so named.[7] The form of such a consent is included below.

EXAMPLE

Consent of Director

> I hereby consent to serve as a director of XYZ Corporation, a proposed Pennsylvania Corporation, and also consent to the use of my name in that capacity in the Articles of Incorporation which will be filed by an incorporator with the Commonwealth of Pennsylvania.
>
> _____
> [*Signature*]
>
> Date: _____

Some state laws require directors to be named in the articles of incorporation.

QUESTION

Where would directors be named if not in the articles of incorporation?

INCORPORATION

Many persons take part in the actual formation of a corporation, including all the organizers, counsel to the proposed corporation, a paralegal, the office of the Secretary of State, and others.[8] An existing corporation may create a corporation. This would ordinarily be called a "subsidiary," a corporation run and owned by another corporation which is called the "parent." From a strictly

---

6. For example, MBCA § 6.20 provides for irrevocability for six months, unless the subscription agreement provides otherwise.

7. Title 15, Pa.C.S., § 1306 suggests such consent may be required.

8. See § 2.01, MBCA, for a model approach.

legal standpoint the person (or entity) who forms the corporation is the "incorporator(s)" who sign the articles of incorporation[9] which are filed with the state.

PROBLEM

How many incorporators are required by your state's corporation law?

Usually one or more of the organizers of the corporation or the person preparing the articles of incorporation acts as the incorporator(s). As noted above, under the laws of many states, the incorporator is required to be a subscriber for at least one share of the corporation's stock, and the information with respect to the subscription for this share is required to be set forth in the articles. Generally, the only other qualification for serving as incorporator is the incorporator, if a natural person, be of full age.

QUESTION

What is "full age" for this purpose?

With respect to the qualifications of the incorporator, Delaware General Corporation Law ("DGCL") §101 is typical.

§ 101, DGCL.

Any person, partnership, association or corporation, singly or jointly with others, and without regard to his or their residence, domicile or state of incorporation, may incorporate or organize a corporation under this chapter by filing with the Division of Corporations in the Department of State a certificate of incorporation which shall be executed,[10] acknowledged,[11] filed and recorded in accordance with Section 103 of this title.

How Does the Corporation Become Incorporated?

Filing of Articles of Incorporation   A corporation is a creature of the state and only exists by virtue of state law. Under most modern corporation statutes, a corporation is formed and its independent existence begins either upon the filing of articles of incorporation, usually in duplicate, with the state agency designated in the

9. The articles of incorporation may be called the certificate of incorporation or charter in some states.
10. "Execution" is the act of formally signing a document.
11. "Acknowledgment" is signing a paper under oath before a public official such as a notary public.

statute, or upon the issuance of a certificate of incorporation by such state agency after receipt of the articles. Note that some states have both articles and a certificate of incorporation which are two separate documents. The articles are filed by the incorporator, and the state issues a certificate evidencing corporate existence.

For example, § 106 of the Delaware General Corporation Law provides as follows:

§106, DGCL.

Upon the filing with the Secretary of State of the certificate of incorporation, executed and acknowledged in accordance with section 103 of this title, the incorporator or incorporators who signed the certificate, and his or their successors and assigns,[12] shall, from the date of such filing, be and constitute a body corporate, by the name set forth in the certificate, subject to subsection (d) of section 103 of this title and subject to dissolution or other termination of its existence as provided in this chapter.

Note that Delaware only has one document—the certificate of incorporation.

Section 2.03 of the MBCA typifies the statutes which provide for the commencement of corporate existence when the articles of incorporation are filed:

§ 2.03, MBCA. Incorporation.

(a) Unless a delayed effective date is specified, the corporate existence begins when the articles of incorporation are filed.

(b) The secretary of state's filing of the articles of incorporation is conclusive proof that the incorporators satisfied all conditions precedent to incorporation except in a proceeding by the state to cancel or revoke the incorporation or involuntarily dissolve the corporation.

The commencement of the corporate existence means that certain legal liabilities and protections as to limited liability[13] are incurred.

Other Documents to Be Filed with Articles A particular state's corporation law may require that other documents be submitted at the same time the articles of incorporation are filed. Section 1306 of Title 15, the Pennsylvania Business Corporation Law, for example, requires the submission, with the articles of incorporation, of a docketing statement containing information about the officers and other corporate matters.

12. "Assigns" are discussed on p. 33.
13. See Chapter One in this text for a discussion of limited liability.

Incorporation Fees   All states require that a statutory fee be paid at the time the articles of incorporation are filed. Frequently the fee is calculated on the number of shares which the articles of incorporation authorize the corporation to issue and may take into consideration the par value[14] of such shares. For example, the fee may be calculated as a percentage of the dollar amount determined by multiplying the authorized number of shares by the par value per share, or it may be calculated as a dollar amount per number of authorized shares.

PROBLEM

If the fee is $\frac{1}{10}$ of 1% of the total par value of shares, what is the fee for 100,000 shares, par value $1.00 per share?

Many states assess a flat charge for filing the Articles of Incorporation and an additional "fee" (license fee or excise tax) calculated on the authorized number of shares. The MBCA, for example, at § 1.22 suggests a fixed dollar amount as the fee for filing the articles.

Other Formalities   In some states the signature(s) of the person(s) signing the articles of incorporation must be notarized.

Other Steps in the Incorporation Procedure

In addition to the preparation and filing of articles of incorporation, there are various other routine matters in forming a new corporation. The corporate law of the state of incorporation must be consulted to determine what additional steps are required. Some of the most commonly required steps are discussed below:

Publication   Several states require that the articles of incorporation be published in a newspaper of general circulation in the county in which the corporation's office designated in the articles (registered office) is located, or in some other manner. In other states, only a notice of the corporation's formation need be published. In many states, no publication at all is required. Section 1307 of the Pennsylvania Business Corporation Law illustrates a statutory notice requirement:

---

14. The "par value" is the legal minimum that must be paid for shares of stock. The corporation may set any value—$.01, $1.00, $100.00. Ordinarily a low or nominal value is set.

§ 1307, Pa.C.S. Advertisement

The incorporators or the corporation shall officially publish a notice of intention to file or of the filing of articles of incorporation. The notice may appear prior to or after the day the articles of incorporation are filed in the Department of State and shall set forth briefly:

(1) The name of the proposed corporation.

(2) A statement that the corporation is to be or has been incorporated under the provisions of the Business Corporation Law of 1988.

§ 1103, Pa.C.S.

"Officially publish." To qualify as a newspaper for publishing corporate and other association notices, general circulation in a county is sufficient, whether or not the place of publication is in the county.

This sample advertisement would satisfy the foregoing statutory requirement and would appear after the filing of articles of incorporation:

EXAMPLE

Advertisement of Incorporation

> Articles of incorporation of SMITH, INC. were filed with the Pennsylvania Department of State on July 1, 19___ . The corporation has been incorporated under the provisions of the Pennsylvania Business Corporation Law, Act of December 21, 1988, P.L. 1444, for the purpose of selling groceries at retail, and shall have unlimited power to engage in and to do any lawful act concerning any or all lawful business for which corporations may be incorporated under such law.

QUESTION

Of what value is the requirement of a legal advertisement of incorporation?

In many states service agencies place these "legal" advertisements for a nominal charge. Where these services are available, lawyers and paralegals frequently use them to save time rather than placing an advertisement with the newspaper directly. After the required advertisement appears, the newspaper in which it appeared or the service agency, if one was used, will send notarized copies of "proof of publication." These proofs will be filed in the official corporate records of the corporation.

Payment of Capital In many states, the formation of the corporation is not complete, or the corporation is prohibited from commencing business, until some minimum amount of capital contribution of money or property is paid by the shareholders.

Organization Meeting   To complete formation of the corporation, several states require an organization meeting at which action is taken to adopt bylaws, elect directors and/or officers, accept subscriptions for shares, and approve other matters,[15] is required in several states.

Recording   In several states, a certified copy of the articles of incorporation must be filed in a local office, usually in the county in which the corporation's registered office is located.

Corporate Seal, Minute Book, and Stock Certificate Book   These three items are generally referred to as the "corporate kit" and must be ordered, for each new corporation, from a local supplier who is listed under "Corporate Supplies" in the yellow pages of the telephone directory. Each law office has its own favorite supplier.

To order the corporate seal, the supplier must be told the name of the corporation and the state and year of incorporation. The use of corporate seals is discussed in Chapter Five.

The minute book will contain the written notes of proceedings at corporate meetings and official corporate documents. The only decision involved in ordering a minute book is whether it is to be an inexpensive or expensive one. When ordering the stock certificate book, the supplier must be told the name of the corporation, state of incorporation, number of shares of authorized stock and its par value, and the number of certificates to be printed. It is customary to order only twenty-five certificates for the typical corporation with a small number of shareholders. Corporations with large numbers of shareholders, such as General Motors Corporation, usually order certificates from a specialized financial printer.

Securities Law Clearance   Many states regulate the offer and sale of securities even to only a few shareholders. In some states, depending on the number of subscribers to the corporation's stock, clearance from the state securities commission, which is the state regulator of issuance of securities, will be required before any shares are actually sold. The requirements of state securities laws ("blue sky laws") are complex and vary considerably from state to state. You should become familiar with those laws relevant to your state of employment so that you are certain to comply with the statute and the regulations thereunder issued by the local blue sky commission prior to issuing securities.

Restrictions on Transfer   Prior to or shortly after incorporation, the persons organizing the corporation often agree to the imposi-

---

15. The organization meeting will be discussed in Chapter Five.

tion of some restrictions upon the transfer of the shares of the corporation for which they are subscribing and will enter into a Shareholder's Agreement.[16]

Evidence of Incorporation Sent by State

Some states acknowledge the filing of articles of incorporation by returning a duplicate copy of the articles with the signature of the Secretary of State and the filing date. The filing date is quite important because it is the date of incorporation and will be referred to later in many documents and agreements involving the corporation, such as income tax returns and contracts.

Some states, either in addition to or in lieu of the signed duplicate copy of the articles referred to above, issue a formal looking document, sometimes with the state seal attached, called a "Certificate of Incorporation." The certificate will also indicate the date of incorporation.

It may take several weeks to receive any evidence of incorporation from the state. A telephone call to the corporation bureau or department will often confirm that the articles were in fact filed. The telephone information is not official. It is advisable, if possible, not to rely on the date provided by telephone.

All evidence of incorporation received from the state should be filed in the corporate minute book.

Transfer of Preincorporation Subscription Agreement

After the articles of incorporation have been filed, any person who, while acting as incorporator, executed a preincorporation subscription agreement but who does not intend to be an initial shareholder of the corporation should assign such subscription right to one of the persons who will in fact be a shareholder of the corporation. The form of such a subscription assignment is set forth below.

EXAMPLE

Transfer of Subscription

[NAME OF CORPORATION]

TRANSFER OF SUBSCRIPTION

I, the undersigned, in consideration of the sum of One Dollar to me paid, the receipt of which is hereby acknowledged, and for other good and valuable consideration, hereby sell, assign and transfer all my right, title and interest as subscriber to an incorporator of the

---

16. The subject is covered in detail in Chapter Eight.

above named _____ corporation with respect to the shares subscribed to by me, as follows:

To _____ No. and Class of Shares

and I do hereby direct said corporation to issue certificate(s) for said shares of stock to and in the names of the aforesaid assignee(s) or his, her, their or its nominees, or assigns.

IN WITNESS WHEREOF, intending to be legally bound hereby, I have hereunto set my hand and seal this _____ day of _____ , 19__ .

_____ [Seal]

ARTICLES OF INCORPORATION

Each state requires specific information in the articles of incorporation. Section 2.02 of the MBCA, for example establishes a sample set of requirements for articles of incorporation. The individual concepts will be discussed immediately below.

The following is an analysis of certain elements generally required in the articles of incorporation.

Name

The requirements imposed upon the name of a new corporation have already been discussed.[17] Again, remember that the names must be inserted exactly in the form desired by the client.

Registered Office Within the State

All states require that corporations incorporated under their law maintain a "registered office" within the state. This provides an address to which service of process and other notices may be sent. This office need not be the executive offices of the corporation, or a principal place of business; indeed it normally need not be an actual business office of the corporation at all. For corporations which are just commencing operations, the address of the attorney forming the corporation or the residence address of one of the organizers frequently has been used as the registered office. This is not a recommended procedure, as all tax returns and other communications from the state are directed to the registered office. It is a costly and time-consuming process for the attorney to forward such papers to the client, and the papers may be lost. A

17. Beginning on p. 21 in this chapter.

corporation may choose to use a corporate service company, such as CT Corporation, for its registered office. These companies specialize in performing the service for a fee. They will be responsible for forwarding documents issued by the state to the corporation. Moreover, the law firm, perhaps, should not be the place where service of process in a lawsuit may be made. Why not?

The significant features of a corporation's registered office are the following:

a. State statutes deem it sufficient notice to a corporation for certain information to be delivered to a corporation's registered office. Legal notice, service of process in a lawsuit, tax returns, and changes in state statutes are among those things of which the corporation has notice if it has been delivered to its registered office.

b. It is generally required that certain records of the corporation be maintained at its registered office. Section 16.01 of the MBCA, for example, requires a corporation to keep, either at its registered office, its principal place of business, or at the office of its transfer agent and registrar,[18] a record of the shareholders of the corporation.

c. The location of the registered office may be relevant to determine what courts in a state have authority to handle matters relating to the corporation. Some states give authority to the court within the county in which the registered office is located to hear suits by shareholders seeking to remove a director for cause.

Registered Agent

While all states require a corporation to have a registered office or its equivalent, many do not require a registered agent. When a corporation is required to have a registered agent, the function of the agent is to permit persons to commence legal action against the corporation by notice to the agent. Consider MBCA § 5.04:

§ 5.04, MBCA. Service on Corporation

(a) A corporation's registered agent is the corporation's agent for service of process, notice, or demand required or permitted by law to be served on the corporation.

The registered agent must be a person who can be relied upon to forward documents relating to lawsuits to the corporation.

---

18. Persons appointed for the purpose of recording stock transfers for the corporation.

1. Under the MBCA, is the registered agent the sole person on whom service of process in a lawsuit may be made?
2. What if service is made on a sole shareholder?

Corporate Purpose

A corporation may engage only in the activities authorized in its articles of corporation. At one point in the development of corporate law, these purposes were required to be set forth in detail and required careful draftsmanship on the part of the incorporators. Under most modern corporation statutes, however, the corporation is generally authorized to do any lawful act concerning any or all lawful business for which corporations may be incorporated under the law of that particular state, unless the articles of incorporation otherwise provide.[19]

If, for any reason, the incorporators feel that it is desirable to limit the corporation with respect to the activities in which it may engage, the purpose clause in the articles will require careful attention in order to accomplish the desired limitation without unnecessarily restricting the corporation in the exercise of its intended business. A typical example of a "full purpose" corporation follows: "the corporation may engage in any lawful purpose."

Term of Existence

An ordinary business corporation is generally permitted to have perpetual existence. Absent very unusual and special circumstances where the incorporators know the corporate purpose will be completed at a specified time, a perpetual term is ordinarily specified in the articles when the term must be indicated. In some states, absent a contrary provision in the articles, the corporation is deemed to have perpetual existence.

Authorized Capital

The authorized capital of a business corporation consists of the total number of shares of all classes and series of stock authorized for issuance in the articles of incorporation. Many factors must be considered in each case to determine the numbers and classes of shares which should be authorized, the par value of such shares, and the relative powers, preferences, and rights of each such class.[20]

19. § 1301, Pa.C.S., and § 3.01, MBCA.

20. This subject is covered extensively in Chapter Six, "Corporate Equity and Debt Securities," beginning on p. 151.

Initial Directors

In some states, the articles of incorporation must specify the number and names of those individuals who will serve as the initial directors of the corporation. Section 2.02(b), MBCA, is permissive in nature and allows a statement in the articles of incorporation of the names and addresses of initial directors.

When a state statute requires the names of directors, it is common practice to name attorneys, paralegals, and secretaries as original directors. This is done because they are convenient for signing documents. Whenever these nominal directors are used, it is desirable to obtain their resignations in advance in the event their services no longer are available or required. A sample form of resignation is set forth below:

EXAMPLE

Resignation of Directors

[NAME OF CORPORATION]

RESIGNATIONS

We hereby resign as members of the Board of Directors of [Name of Corporation] effective immediately.

Dated: _____

/s/ _____
                    Director

/s/ _____
                    Director

/s/ _____
                    Director

In states which grant the incorporator the option of naming the initial directors, it is wise to name the initial directors in the articles only if a decision has been made as to whom they ultimately will be. Naming the initial directors eliminates the need for having both an organization meeting of the incorporators and a meeting of the initial directors.[21]

Other Provisions of Articles

Virtually any provision relevant to the operation of the corporation may, if the organizers desire, be included in the articles of incor-

---

21. See Chapter Five for a discussion of the organization meeting of the corporation beginning on p. 117.

poration. In addition, the corporation laws of many states provide that certain powers, rights, privileges, and procedures are permissible or appropriate only if provided for in the articles of incorporation. Several similar privileges or powers are conferred automatically unless expressly denied by the articles. For this reason it is essential that the specific state corporation law be considered at the outset of the incorporation procedure. Some examples of these provisions are as follows:

Shareholders' Preemptive Rights   A preemptive right is the right of a shareholder to have the opportunity to purchase shares which the corporation may desire to sell at a future date before any such shares may be sold to persons who are not then shareholders. It is designed to allow shareholders to maintain their proportionate interest in the corporation. For example, if a corporation desires to sell more stock to raise cash, preemptive rights would require that shareholders have an opportunity to purchase the stock first on a pro rata basis before the corporation sold stock to nonstockholders.

Consider how a corporation may be inhibited in acquiring a desired piece of specific real estate owned by a nonshareholder for stock if shareholders have preemptive rights. Modern corporation statutes deal with preemptive rights in one of two ways: Either the articles must expressly provide for preemptive rights, or there are no such rights; or, alternatively, preemptive rights exist unless the corporation expressly provides otherwise. The present trend is to provide that no preemptive rights exist unless expressly provided for in the articles of incorporation. This is in line with permitting corporations latitude in determining on what basis to issue stock.

The MBCA provides as follows:

§ 6.30, MBCA. Shareholders' Preemptive Rights

(a) The shareholders of a corporation do not have a preemptive right to acquire the corporation's unissued shares except to the extent the articles of incorporation so provide.

(b) A statement included in the articles of incorporation that "the corporation elects to have preemptive rights" (or words or similar import) means that the following principles apply except to the extent the articles of incorporation expressly provide otherwise:

   (1) The shareholders of the corporation have a preemptive right, granted on uniform terms and conditions prescribed by the board of directors, to provide a fair and reasonable opportunity to exercise the right to acquire proportional amounts of the corporation's unissued shares upon the decision of the board of directors to issue them.

   (2) A shareholder may waive his preemptive right. A waiver evidenced by a writing is irrevocable even though it is not supported by consideration.

(3) There is no preemptive right with respect to:
   (i) shares issued as compensation to directors, officers, agents, or employees of the corporation, its subsidiaries or affiliates;
   (ii) shares issued to satisfy conversion or option rights created to provide compensation to directors, officers, agents, or employees of the corporation, its subsidiaries or affiliates;
   (iii) shares authorized in articles of incorporation that are issued within six months from the effective date of incorporation;
   (iv) shares sold otherwise than for money.

(4) Holders of shares of any class without general voting rights but with preferential rights to distributions or assets have no preemptive rights with respect to shares of any class.

(5) Holders of shares of any class with voting rights but without preferential rights to distributions or assets have no preemptive rights with respect to shares of any class with preferential rights to distributions or assets unless the shares with preferential rights are convertible into or carry a right to subscribe for or acquire shares without preferential rights.

(6) Shares subject to preemptive rights that are not acquired by shareholders may be issued to any person for a period of one year after being offered to shareholders at a consideration set by the board of directors that is not lower than the consideration set for the exercise of preemptive rights. An offer at a lower consideration or after the expiration of one year is subject to the shareholders' preemptive rights.

(c) For purposes of this section, "shares" includes a security convertible into or carrying a right to subscribe for or acquire shares.

Cumulative Voting Cumulative voting is the right of a shareholder, voting in the election of directors, to multiply the number of votes to which the shareholder is entitled by the number of directors to be elected, and to cast the whole number of such votes for one candidate or to distribute them among any two or more candidates. The effect of cumulative voting is to enable the owners of a sizable minority of shares to elect a representative to a corporation's board of directors. This effect can be illustrated as follows:

EXAMPLE

Effect of Cumulative Voting

X Corp. has 100 shares of voting common stock issued and outstanding.[22] A and B each own 30 shares; C and D each own 20 shares. X Corp. has no other stock outstanding. There are three vacancies to be filled on the X Corp. board of directors. A and B nominate D_1, D_2, and D_3. C and D nominate D_4.

---

22. Outstanding shares are those which have been issued and are in the hands of shareholders.

1. Without cumulative voting and with one vote per share, D_1, D_2, and D_3 are elected since A and B outvote C and D 60 votes to 40 on each vacancy to be filled.
2. With cumulative voting, A and B cannot prevent C and D from electing D_4. C and D cumulate their votes (three vacancies x 40 shares equal 120 votes) and cast all votes for D_4. A and B have 180 votes available (60 shares x three vacancies). In order to cast more than 120 votes for D_1, D_2, and D_3, A and B would need a minimum of 363 votes (121 for each). Obviously, they are far short.

To determine how many shares one must hold or control under cumulative voting to insure the election of a certain number of directors, the following method may be used:

1. *Multiply* total number of shares entitled to vote by number of directors it is desired to elect.
2. *Divide* the product of (1) by a number equal to one more than the number of directors to be elected. Disregard all fractional shares in the computation.
3. *Add* one to the quotient of (2) and the result will be the least number of held or controlled shares necessary to elect the desired number of directors.

Algebraic Formula
x = shares required
a = total voting shares
c = number of directors desired to be elected
b = number of directors to be elected

$$x = \frac{ac}{b+1} + 1$$

PROBLEMS

1. What is the number of shares required to elect with cumulative voting two directors on a seven-person board of directors if there are 100 shares outstanding?
2. Can Smith be sure of electing three directors if he owns 38 shares?
3. If there is no cumulative voting can Smith be sure of electing two directors if he owns 38 shares?
4. If a corporation has 600 shares outstanding and the shareholders have cumulative voting in the election of nine directors, what is the minimum number of votes required to elect a majority of the board?
5. Can you change the formula to enable you to calculate the number of shares which must be owned to elect a specific number of directors under cumulative voting?

As in the case of preemptive rights, the modern corporate statutes deal with the question of cumulative voting in one of two ways. Either cumulative voting exists unless expressly denied in the articles of incorporation; or, if the articles are silent on the subject, no cumulative voting rights exist. In some states, however, cumulative voting is mandatory, either under statute or the state's constitution.

For example, Pa.C.S. § 1758 provides that cumulative voting exists unless abolished by specific provision in the corporation's articles.

PROBLEM

What is the status of cumulative voting in your state?

Informal Action of Shareholders Modern corporation statutes allow shareholders to take action without the necessity of a formal meeting by consenting in writing to various proposals.[23] Several states now permit informal shareholder action with less than unanimous consent. In some states, informal action with less than unanimous consent must be specifically authorized in the articles.

A sample provision to be inserted in the articles of incorporation of a corporation to permit written consents by less than all shareholders is as follows:

EXAMPLE

Sample Provision Permitting Written Consents

> Except as otherwise provided by and subject to the provisions of applicable law, any action which may be taken at a meeting of the shareholders or of a class of shareholders of the corporation may be taken without a meeting if a consent or consents in writing to such action, setting forth the action so taken, shall be (i) signed by shareholders entitled to cast a majority (or such larger percentage as may be required by law) of the number of votes which all such shareholders are entitled to cast thereon, and (ii) filed with the secretary of the corporation.

PROBLEM

Draft a provision for inclusion in the articles of incorporation of a MBCA corporation requiring the approval of two-thirds of all outstanding shares in order to amend the articles.

23. A formal meeting is generally required to take action by the directors collectively or the shareholders. The requisites of a meeting include notice, quorum, and a vote of the majority of the persons entitled to vote. See Chapter Five of this text for more information. Also see § 7.04, MBCA.

SAMPLE FORMS OF ARTICLES OF INCORPORATION

This section sets forth a sample form of articles of incorporation of a hypothetical corporation. In addition to illustrating the general makeup of the articles, this sample illustrates the importance of the corporation law of the state of incorporation as it pertains to the content of the articles. Review these articles against first the MBCA, then the PBCL, and determine their effectiveness.

EXAMPLE

Articles of Incorporation

ARTICLES OF INCORPORATION

OF

FUN CITY FRANCHISE CORP.

The undersigned, being of full age, desiring to incorporate a business corporation under the provisions of the Business Corporation Law, approved May 5, 1933, P.L. 364, as amended, does hereby certify:

1. The name of the corporation is:
   FUN CITY FRANCHISE CORP.

2. The location and post office address of its initial registered office in the Commonwealth of Pennsylvania is:
   4455 Main Street
   Philadelphia, Pennsylvania 19103

3. The purpose or purposes for which the corporation is incorporated are to engage in manufacturing and to engage in and do any lawful act concerning any or all lawful business for which corporations may be incorporated under the Pennsylvania Business Corporation Law.

4. The term for which the corporation is to exist is perpetual.

5. The aggregate number of shares which the corporation shall have authority to issue is:
   2,000,000 shares of Common Stock, par value $.01 per share.

6. The name and post office address of the incorporator and the number and class of shares subscribed by him are:

Name	Address	Number & Class of Shares
[Name and address of person preparing Articles of Incorporation]		One share of common stock

7. Unless the Board of Directors shall otherwise direct, any action which may be taken at a meeting of the shareholders or of a class of shareholders may be taken without a meeting, if a consent or consents in writing to such action, setting forth the action so taken, shall be (1) signed by shareholders entitled to cast such a

percentage of the number of votes which all such shareholders are entitled to cast thereon as is required by law for the taking of action at a meeting of the shareholders or of a class of shareholders and (2) filed with the secretary of the corporation. In no case, however, shall such percentage be less than the larger of (1) two-thirds of the total number of votes which all shareholders of the corporation or of a class of shareholders are entitled by the Articles to cast upon such action, or (2) the minimum percentage of the vote required by law, if any, for the proposed corporate action. Such action shall not become effective until after at least ten days' written notice of such action shall have been given to each shareholder of record entitled to vote thereon. This paragraph shall not be applicable to any action with respect to any plan or amendment of articles to which Section 515 of the Pennsylvania Business Corporation Law is applicable.

Signed on February 6, 19_____ .

_____
[*Signature of person named in paragraph 6*]
Incorporator

Filed in the Department of State on _____ , 19___ .

_____
Secretary of the Commonwealth

The following letter is designed to be used in transmitting the required documents and fees to Secretary of State to incorporate Fun City Franchise Corp., the hypothetical Pennsylvania corporation discussed in the text.

EXAMPLE

Letter of Transmittal

Corporation Bureau
Department of State

Re: FUN CITY FRANCHISE CORP.

Gentlemen:

Enclosed for filing for the above-named proposed business corporation are the following:

1. Articles of Incorporation in duplicate.
2. Docketing Statement in triplicate.
3. Check in the amount of $75.00 for filing fee.

Please forward the appropriate certificate and the certified copy of the articles of incorporating to the undersigned.

Sincerely,

CORPORATE BYLAWS

Introduction

The bylaws[24] of a corporation provide, in conjunction with the articles of incorporation, the standards and procedures for the legal operation of a corporation, like a corporate constitution. Those of you who have been in clubs or organizations have previously encountered bylaws as the governing rules of procedure. In many significant areas the state corporate law provides that a specific governing standard of the corporation may be set forth in either the articles of incorporation or bylaws. However, the articles may, in certain circumstances, require shareholder action for an amendment. Therefore, because the articles or bylaws absent special circumstances, can provide that the bylaws are amendable by the board of directors without shareholder approval, and, because the corporation's bylaws are not a public document which can be readily obtained by anyone (unlike the articles), it is preferable to deal with certain matters in the bylaws. The opposite would be true, however, if, for some reason, the presence of an extensive amount of management flexibility would be undesirable from the viewpoint of the shareholders of the corporation. For example, shareholders may not desire the board to issue additional stock because they desire to control the ownership of the corporation closely. In such a case, much of the material ordinarily found in the bylaws could be set forth in the articles. Any change would then require an amendment to the articles of incorporation, an action requiring shareholder approval.

If the initial directors of a corporation are named in the articles of incorporation, the bylaws will be adopted by the initial board of directors at the organization meeting.[25]

A corporation's bylaws may provide for the following:

1. **With respect to the board of directors, the bylaws generally provide for:** the number of directors which constitute the board; the procedure for the filling of vacancies on the board; the manner in which nominations to the board are made; rules on the place, frequency, and notice of directors' meetings; the formation of special committees of directors and the powers which may be delegated to such committees; the

---

24. Some states spell bylaws with a hyphen as by-laws.

25. Organization and other meetings of the corporation are discussed in detail in Chapter Five. See also § 2.05(a), MBCA.

classification of the board,[26] if any, and the term which each class shall serve; special qualifications of directors, if any; and the determination of a quorum at directors' meetings;

2. **With respect to shareholders and shareholders' meetings, the bylaws provide for:** the place, frequency, and notice of shareholders' meetings; and may also provide for shareholder procedures with respect to approval of certain corporate actions, and rights and privileges pertaining to certain classes of shareholders;

3. **With respect to officers, the bylaws define:** the positions which shall constitute corporate officers, the manner of election of officers, and the duties of officers;

4. **The bylaws describe indemnification of officers and directors of the corporation;[27]**

5. **The bylaws detail the form of stock certificates;**

6. **The bylaws set forth the procedure for amending bylaws.**

It must be emphasized that the provisions contained in the bylaws must be consistent with the articles of incorporation and the corporation law of the state of incorporation. The statute is first in order of control, followed by the articles. For example, if a corporate statute requires cumulative voting unless the articles provide otherwise, the bylaws cannot eliminate cumulative voting if the articles do not eliminate it. Similarly the bylaws cannot provide for preemptive rights if the articles deny such rights because the bylaws cannot prevail over provisions in the articles. It is important to remember that, in the absence of a specific provision in a corporation's bylaws (or articles) dealing with a particular matter, the statutory provision on the matter will "fill the void." In any event, the statute will always control unless it permits the articles or bylaws to provide otherwise, and they do so. The articles, where they comply with statutory authority, will control the bylaws.

26. Classification of directors is a method whereby some corporations provide for election of only a portion of the board each year. For example, a board of six directors might have three classes with one class consisting of two directors being elected each year. In such a case, a director will ordinarily serve for a three-year term until that class is up for reelection. Such a classification prevents a sudden takeover of corporations by outsiders by requiring several years to accomplish the election of a majority of the board.

27. Most corporate statutes permit the bylaws to provide for the corporation to defend a director or officer in a lawsuit which involves the director or officer and to pay for losses incurred by the director or officer respecting actions on behalf of the corporation if such person acted in good faith in the best interests of the corporation. See also MBCA Chapter 8, Subchapter E.

PROBLEM

Under your state law, how do you know if a quorum is present at a meeting? If no quorum exists can any action be taken at the meeting?

Form of Bylaws

The following is a *short* form of "Model Bylaws" for use in states which have enacted the Model Business Corporation Act. The numbers in brackets are references to sections in the MBCA. The student should analyze carefully the form and content to comprehend the purpose and structure of bylaws. Any law firm for which you may work probably will have its own form of bylaws.

EXAMPLE

ByLaws*

BYLAWS OF
[NAME OF CORPORATION]

Article I. Shareholders

Meetings of shareholders shall be held at the registered office of the corporation unless another place shall have been determined by the directors and stated in the notice of meeting. Annual meetings shall be held at _____ P.M. on the _____ of _____ unless a holiday and then on the next business day. [§ 7.01]

Article II. Directors

Section 1.
The number of directors shall be _____ [§ 8.03]

Section 2.
A regular meeting of the board of directors shall be held without notice immediately following the annual meeting of shareholders and at the same place. The board of directors may provide for the holding without notice of additional regular meetings. [§ 8.20, 8.22]

Section 3.
Special meetings of the board of directors may be called by the president or any two directors on 24-hour notice given personally or by telephone or telegraph, or on four days' notice given by mail. Special meetings shall be held at the place fixed by the board of directors for the holding of meetings, or if no such place has been fixed, at the principal business office of the corporation. [§ 8.20, 8.22]

Article III. Officers

Section 1.
The officers of the corporation shall be a president, a vice president, a secretary, and a treasurer, who shall be elected annually at the regular

* Numbers in [brackets] are references to sections of the Model Business Corporation Act.

meeting of the board of directors held after the annual meeting of shareholders and shall hold office only so long as they are satisfactory to the board of directors. [§ 8.40, 8.41]

Section 2.

The president shall be the principal executive officer of the corporation to put into effect the decisions of the board of directors. Subject to such decisions, he shall supervise and control the business and affairs of the corporation. He shall preside at meetings of the shareholders and directors. [§ 8.40, 8.41]

Section 3.

Subject to any specific assignments of duties made by the board of directors, the vice president, secretary, and treasurer shall act under the direction of the president. The vice president shall perform the duties of the president when the president is absent or unable to act. The secretary shall prepare and keep minutes of the meetings of the shareholders and the directors and shall have general charge of the stock records of the corporation. The treasurer shall have custody of the funds of the corporation and keep its financial records. [§ 8.40, 8.41]

Article IV. Miscellaneous

Section 1.

The board of directors may authorize any officer or agent to enter into any contract or to execute any instrument for the corporation Such authority may be general or be confined to specific instances. [§ 8.44]

Section 2.

Certificates representing shares of the corporation shall be in such form as the board of directors shall determine. [§ 6.25] Transfers of shares shall be made only on the stock transfer books of the corporation.

Article V. Action Without Meeting

Any action required or permitted to be taken by the board of directors or the shareholders at a meeting may be taken without a meeting if a consent in writing, setting forth the action so taken, shall be signed by all directors or shareholders, as the case may be. [§ 7.04, 8.21]

Article VI. Amendments

These bylaws may be altered, amended, or repeated and new bylaws may be adopted by the board of directors or by the shareholders. [§ 10.20]

The following is a long form of bylaws under the MBCA which comprehensively spells out corporate regulations:

PROBLEM

Compare the short form with the long form, and point out the most salient points of difference. Discuss the effectiveness of each form under the MBCA.

EXAMPLE

Model Bylaws—A Long Form*

BYLAWS
OF

_____

Article I. Offices

The principal office of the corporation in the State of shall be located in the City of _____ , County of _____ . The corp- ration may have such other offices, either within or without the State of _____ , as the board of directors may designate or as the business of the corporation may require from time to time.

The registered office of the corporation required by The _____ Business Corporation Act to be maintained in the State of _____ may be, but need not be, identical with the principal office in the State of _____ , and the address of the registered office may be changed from time to time by the board of directors. [§ 5.01, 5.02]

Article II. Shareholders

Section 1. Annual Meeting.
The annual meeting of the shareholders shall be held on the _____ in the month of _____ in each year, beginning with the year 19 _____ , at the hour of _____ o'clock _____ .M., or at such other time on such other day within such month as shall be fixed by the board of directors, for the purpose of electing directors and for the transaction of such other business as may come before the meeting. If the day fixed for the annual meeting shall be a legal holiday in the State of _____ , such meeting shall be held on the next succeeding business day. If the election of directors shall not be held on the day designated herein for any annual meeting of the shareholders, or at any adjournment thereof, the board of directors shall cause the election to be held at a special meeting of the shareholders as soon thereafter as conveniently may be. [Chapter 7, Subchapter A]

Section 2. Special Meetings.
Special meetings of the shareholders, for any purpose of purposes, unless otherwise prescribed by statute, may be called by the president or by the board of directors, and shall be called by the president at the request of the holders of not less than one-tenth of all outstanding shares of the corporation entitled to vote at the meeting. [§ 7.02]

Section 3. Place of Meeting.
The board of directors may designate any place, either within or without the State of _____ , as the place of meeting for any annual meeting or for any special meeting called by the board of

* Numbers in [brackets] are references to sections of the Model Business Corporation Act.

directors. A waiver of notice signed by all shareholders entitled to vote at a meeting may designate any place, either within or without the State of _____ , as the place for the holding of such meeting. If no designation is made, or if a special meeting be otherwise called, the place of meeting shall be the principal office of the corporation in the State of _____ . [§ 7.01]

Section 4. Notice of Meeting.

Written notice stating the place, day, and hour of the meeting, and in case of a special meeting, the purpose or purposes for which the meeting is called, shall, unless otherwise prescribed by statute, be delivered not less than ten nor more than fifty days before the date of the meeting, either personally or by mail, by or at the direction of the president, or the secretary, or the officer or other persons calling the meeting, to each shareholder of record entitled to vote at such meeting. If mailed, such notice shall be deemed to be delivered when deposited in the United States mail, addressed to the shareholder at his/her address as it appears on the stock transfer books of the corporation, with postage thereon prepaid. [§ 7.05]

Section 5. Closing of Transfer Books or Fixing of Record Date.

For the purpose of determining shareholders entitled to notice of or to vote at any meeting of shareholders or any adjournment thereof, or shareholders entitled to receive payment of any dividend, or in order to make a determination of shareholders for any other proper purpose, the board of directors of the corporation may provide that the stock transfer books shall be closed for a stated period but not to exceed, in any case, fifty days. If the stock transfer books shall be closed for the purpose of determining shareholders entitled to notice of or to vote at a meeting of shareholders, such books shall be closed for at least ten days immediately preceding such meeting. In lieu of closing the stock transfer books, the board of directors may fix in advance a date as the record date for any such determination of shareholders, such date in any case to be not more than fifty days and, in case of a meeting of shareholders, not less than ten days prior to the date on which the particular action, requiring such determination of shareholders, is to be taken. If the stock transfer books are not closed and no record date is fixed for the determination of shareholders entitled to notice of or to vote at a meeting of shareholders, or shareholders entitled to receive payment of a dividend, the date on which notice of the meeting is mailed or the date on which the resolution of the board of directors declaring such dividend is adopted, as the case may be, shall be the record date for such determination of shareholders. When a determination of shareholders entitled to vote at any meeting of shareholders has been made as provided in this section, such determination shall apply in any adjournment thereof. [§ 7.07]

Section 6. Voting Record.

The officer or agent having charge of the stock transfer books for shares of the corporation shall make a complete record of the shareholders entitled to vote at each meeting of shareholders or any adjournment thereof arranged in alphabetical order, with the address of and the number of shares held by each. Such record shall be produced and kept open at the time and place of meeting and shall be subject to the inspection of any shareholder during the whole time of the meeting for the purposes thereof. [§ 7.20]

Section 7. Quorum.
A majority of the outstanding shares of the corporation entitled to vote, represented in person or by proxy, shall constitute a quorum at a meeting of shareholders. If less than a majority of the outstanding shares are represented at a meeting, a majority of the shares so represented may adjourn the meeting from time to time without further notice. At such adjourned meeting at which a quorum shall be present or represented, any business may be transacted which might have been transacted at the meeting as originally noticed. The shareholders present at a duly organized meeting may continue to transact business until adjournment, notwithstanding the withdrawal of enough shareholders to leave less than a quorum. [§ 7.25]

Section 8. Proxies.
At all meetings of shareholders, a shareholder may vote in person or by proxy executed in writing by the shareholder or by his or her duly authorized attorney in fact. Such proxy shall be filed with the secretary of the corporation before or at the time of the meeting. No proxy shall be valid after eleven months from the date of its execution, unless otherwise provided in the proxy. [§ 7.22]

Section 9. Voting of Shares.
Subject to the provisions of Section 12 of this Article II, each outstanding share entitled to vote shall be entitled to one vote upon each matter submitted to a vote at a meeting of shareholders. [§ 7.21]

Section 10. Voting of Shares by Certain Holders.
Shares standing in the name of another corporation may be voted by such officer, agent, or proxy as the bylaws of such corporation may prescribe, or, in the absence of such provision, as the board of directors of such other corporation may determine. [§ 7.23]

Shares held by an administrator, executor, guardian, or conservator may be voted by him/her either in person or by proxy, without a transfer of such shares into his/her name. Shares standing in the name of a trustee may be voted by him/her, either in person or by proxy, but no trustee shall be entitled to vote shares held by him/her without a transfer of such shares into his/her name. [§ 7.22, 7.23]

Shares standing in the name of the receiver may be voted by such receiver, and shares held by or under the control of a receiver may be voted by such receiver without the transfer thereof into his/her name if authority so to do be contained in an appropriate order of the court by which such receiver was appointed. [§ 7.21]

A shareholder whose shares are pledged shall be entitled to vote such shares until the shares have been transferred into the name of the pledgee, and thereafter the pledgee shall be entitled to vote the shares so transferred. [§ 7.21]

Neither treasury shares of its own stock held by the corporation, nor shares held by another corporation if a majority of the shares entitled to vote for the election of directors of such other corporation are held by the corporation, shall be voted at any meeting or counted in determining the total number of outstanding shares at any given time for purposes of any meeting. [§ 7.21]

Section 11. Informal Action by Shareholders.
Any action required or permitted to be taken at a meeting of the shareholders may be taken without a meeting if a consent in writing,setting forth the action so taken, shall be signed by all of the shareholders entitled to vote with respect to the subject matter thereof. [§ 7.04]

Section 12. [Optional Section.] Cumulative Voting.
At each election for directors every shareholder entitled to vote at such election shall have the right to vote, in person or by proxy, the number of shares owned by him/her for as many persons as there are directors to be elected and for whose election he/she has a right to vote, or to cumulate his/her votes by giving one candidate as many votes as the number of such directors multiplied by the number of his/her shares shall equal, or by distributing such votes on the same principle among any number of such candidates. [§ 7.28]

Article III. Board of Directors

Section 1. General Powers.
The business and affairs of the corporation shall be managed by its board of directors [§ 8.01]

Section 2. Number, Tenure, and Qualifications.
The number of directors of the corporation shall be _____ .
Each director shall hold office until the next annual meeting of shareholders and until his/her successor shall have been elected and qualified. Directors need not be residents of the State of _____ or shareholders of the corporation. [§ 8.02, 8.03]

Section 3. Regular Meetings.
A regular meeting of the board of directors shall be held without other notice than this bylaw immediately after, and at the same place as, the annual meeting of shareholders. The board of directors may provide, by resolution, the time and place, either within or without the State of _____ , for the holding of additional regular meetings without other notice than such resolution. [§ 8.20]

Section 4. Special Meetings.
Special meetings of the board of directors may be called by or at the request of the president or any two directors. The person or persons authorized to call special meetings of the board of directors may fix any place, either within or without the State of _____ , as the place

for holding any special meeting of the board of directors called by them. [§ 8.20]

Section 5. Notice.

Notice of any special meeting shall be given at least two days previously thereto by written notice delivered personally or mailed to each director at his/her business address, or by telegram. If mailed, such notice shall be deemed to be delivered when deposited in the United States mail, so addressed, with postage thereon prepaid. If notice be given by telegram, such notice shall be deemed to be delivered when the telegram is delivered to the telegraph company. Any director may waive notice of any meeting. The attendance of a director at a meeting shall constitute a waiver of notice of such meeting, except where a director attends a meeting for the express purpose of objecting to the transaction of any business because the meeting is not lawfully called or convened. Neither the business to be transacted at, nor the purpose of, any regular or special meeting of the board of directors need be specified in the notice or waiver of notice of such meeting. [§ 8.22]

Section 6. Quorum.

A majority of the number of directors fixed by Section 2 of this Article III shall constitute a quorum for the transaction of business at any meeting of the board of directors, but if less than such majority is present at a meeting, a majority of the directors present may adjourn the meeting from time to time without further notice. [§ 8.24]

Section 7. Manner of Acting.

The act of the majority of the directors present at a meeting at which a quorum is present shall be the act of the board of directors. [§ 8.24]

Section 8. Action Without a Meeting.

Any action required or permitted to be taken by the board of directors at a meeting may be taken without a meeting if a consent in writing, setting forth the action so taken, shall be signed by all of the directors. [§ 8.21]

Section 9. Vacancies.

Any vacancy occurring in the board of directors may be filled by the affirmative vote of a majority of the remaining directors though less than a quorum of the board of directors. A director elected to fill a vacancy shall be elected for the unexpired term of his predecessor in office. Any directorship to be filled by reason of an increase in the number of directors may be filled by election by the board of directors for a term of office continuing only until the next election of directors by the shareholders. [§ 8.10]

Section 10. Compensation.

By resolution of the board of directors, each director may be paid his/her expenses, if any, of attendance at each meeting of the board of directors, and may be paid a stated salary as director or a fixed sum for attendance at each meeting of the board of directors or both. No such payment shall preclude any director from serving the corporation in any other capacity and receiving compensation therefor. [§ 8.11]

Section 11. Presumption of Assent.
A director of the corporation who is present at a meeting of the board of directors at which action on any corporate matter is taken shall be presumed to have assented to the action taken unless his/her dissent shall be entered in the minutes of the meeting or unless he/she shall file written dissent to such action with the person acting as secretary of the meeting before the adjournment thereof or shall forward such dissent by registered mail to the secretary of the corporation immediately after the adjournment of the meeting. Such right to dissent shall not apply to a director who voted in favor of such action. [§ 8.24]

Article IV. Officers

Section 1. Number.
The officers of the corporation shall be a president, one or more vice-presidents (the number thereof to be determined by the board of directors), a secretary, and a treasurer, each of whom shall be elected by the board of directors. Such other officers and assistant officers as may be deemed necessary may be elected or appointed by the board of directors. Any two or more offices may be held by the same person, except the offices of president and secretary. [§ 8.40, 8.41]

Section 2. Election and Term of Office.
The officers of the corporation to be elected by the board of directors shall be elected annually by the board of directors at the first meeting of the board of directors held after each annual meeting of the shareholders. If the election of officers shall not be held at such meeting, such election shall be held as soon thereafter as conveniently may be. Each officer shall hold office until his/her successor shall have been duly elected and shall have qualified or until his/her death or until he/she shall resign or shall have been removed in the manner hereinafter provided. [§ 8.40]

Section 3. Removal.
Any officer or agent may be removed by the board of directors whenever in its judgment, the best interests of the corporation will be served thereby, but such removal shall be without prejudice to the contract rights, if any, of the person so removed. Election or appointment of an officer or agent shall not of itself create contract rights. [§ 8.43]

Section 4. Vacancies.
A vacancy in any office because of death, resignation, removal, disqualification or otherwise, may be filled by the board of directors for the unexpired portion of the term. [§ 8.10, 8.43]

Section 5. President.
The president shall be the principal executive officer of the corporation and, subject to the control of the board of directors, shall in general supervise and control all of the business and affairs of the corporation. He/she shall, when present, preside at all meetings of the shareholders and of the board of directors. He/she may sign, with the secretary or any

other proper officer of the corporation thereunto authorized by the board of directors, certificates for shares of thecorporation any deeds, mortgages, bonds, contracts, or other instruments which the board of directors has authorized to be executed, except in cases where the signing and execution thereof shall be expressly delegated by the board of directors or by these Bylaws to some other officer or agent of the corporation, or shall be required by law to be otherwise signed or executed; and in general shall perform all duties incident to the office of president and such other duties as may be prescribed by the board of directors from time to time. [§ 8.40, 8.41]

Section 6. The Vice-Presidents.

In the absence of the president or in the event of his death, inability, or refusal to act, the vice-president (or in the event there be more than one vice-president, the vice-presidents in the order designated at the time of their election, or in the absence of any designation, then in the order of their election) shall perform the duties of the president, and when so acting, shall have all the power of and be subject to all the restrictions upon the president. Any vice-president may sign, with the secretary or an assistant secretary, certificates for shares of the corporation; and shall perform such other duties as from time to time may be assigned to him/her by the president or by the board of directors. [§ 8.40, 8.41]

Section 7. The Secretary.

The secretary shall: (a) keep the minutes of the proceedings of the shareholders and of the board of directors in one or more books provided for that purpose; (b) see that all notices are duly given in accordance with the provisions of these Bylaws or as required by law; (c) be custodian of the corporate records and of the seal of the corporation and see that the seal of the corporation is affixed to all documents the execution of which on behalf of the corporation under its seal is duly authorized; (d) keep a register of the post office address of each shareholder which shall be furnished to the secretary by such shareholder; (e) sign with the president, or a vice-president, certificates for shares of the corporation, the issuance of which shall have been authorized by resolution of the board of directors; (f) have general charge of the stock transfer books of the corporation; and (g) in general perform all duties incident to the office of secretary and such other duties as from time to time may be assigned to him/her by the president or by the board of directors. [§ 8.40, 8.41]

Section 8. The Treasurer.

The treasurer shall: (a) have charge and custory of and be responsible for all funds and securities of the corporation; (b) receive and give receipts for moneys due and payable to the corporation from any source whatsoever, and deposit all such moneys in the name of the corporation in such banks, trust companies, or other depositaries as shall be selected in accordance with the provisions of Article V of these Bylaws; and (c) in general perform all of the duties incident to the office of treasurer and such other duties as from time to time may be assigned to him by the president or by the board of directors. If required by the board of directors, the treasurer shall give a bond for the faithful discharge of his duties in such sum and with such surety or sureties as the board of directors shall determine. [§ 8.40, 8.41]

Section 9. Assistant Secretaries and Assistant Treasurers.

The assistant secretaries, when authorized by the board of directors, may sign with the president or a vice-president certificates for shares of the corporation the issuance of which shall have been authorized by a resolution of the board of directors. The assistant treasurers shall respectively, if required by the board of directors, give bonds for the faithful discharge of their duties in such sums and with such sureties as the board of directors shall determine. The assistant secretaries and assistant treasurers, in general, shall perform such duties as shall be assigned to them by the secretary or the treasurer, respectively, or by the president or the board of directors.[§ 8.40, 8.41]

Section 10. Salaries.

The salaries of the officers shall be fixed from time to time by the board of directors and no officer shall be prevented from receiving such salary by reason of the fact that he/she is also a director of the corporation.

Article V. Contracts, Loans, Checks, and Deposits

Section 1. Contracts.

The board of directors may authorize any officer or officers, agent or agents, to enter into any contract or execute and deliver any instrument in the name of and on behalf of the corporation, and such authority may be general or confined to specific instances. [§ 8.41, 8.44]

Section 2. Loans.

No loans shall be contracted on behalf of the corporation and no evidences of indebtedness shall be issued in its name unless authorized by a resolution of the board of directors. Such authority may be general or confined to specific instances. [§ 3.02, 8.32, 8.44, 12.01.

Section 3. Checks, Drafts, etc.

All checks, drafts, or other orders for the payment of money, notes, or other evidences of indebtedness issued in the name of the corporation, shall be signed by such officer or officers, agent or agents of the corporation and in such manner as shall from time to time be determined by resolution of the board of directors. [§ 8.44]

Section 4. Deposits.

All funds of the corporation not otherwise employed shall be deposited from time to time to the credit of the corporation in such banks, trust companies, or other depositaries as the board of directors may select.

Article VI. Certificates for Shares and Their Transfer

Section 1. Certificates for Shares.

Certificates representing shares of the corporation shall be in such form as shall be determined by the board of directors. Such certificates shall be signed by the president or a vice-president and by the secretary or an assistant secretary and sealed with the corporate seal or a facsimile thereof. The signatures of such officers upon a certificate may be facsimiles if the certificate is manually signed on behalf of a transfer agent or a registrar, other than the corporation itself or one of its employees. Each certificate for shares shall be consecutively numbered or otherwise identified. The name and address of the person to whom the shares represented thereby are issued, wtih the number of shares and date of issue, shall be entered on the stock transfer books of the corporation. All certificates surrendered to the corporation for transfer shall be cancelled and no new certificate shall be issued until the former certificate for a like number of shares shall have been surrendered and cancelled, except that in case of a lost, destroyed, or mutilated Certificate a new one may be issued therefor upon such terms and indemnity to the corporation as the board of directors may prescribe. [Chapter 6]

Section 2. Transfer of Shares.

Transfer of shares of the corporation shall be made only on the stock transfer books of the corporation by the holder of record thereof or by his/her legal representative, who shall furnish proper evidence of authority to transfer, or by his/her attorney thereunto authorized by power of attorney duly executed and filed with the secretary of the corporation, and on surrender for cancellation of the certificate for such shares. The person in whose name shares stand on the books of the corporation shall be deemed by the corporation to be the owner thereof for all purposes. [Chapter 6]

Article VII. Fiscal Year

The fiscal year of the corporation shall begin on the first day of January and end on the thirty-first day of December in each year.

Article VIII. Dividends

The board of directors may, from time to time, declare and the corporation may pay dividends on its outstanding shares in the manner, and upon the terms and conditions provided by law and its Articles of Incorporation. [§ 6.40]

Article IX. Corporate Seal

The board of directors shall provide a corporate seal which shall be circular in form and shall have inscribed thereon the name of the corporation and the state of incorporation and the words, "Corporate Seal." [§ 3.02]

Article X. Waiver of Notice

Whenever any notice is required to be given to any shareholder or director of the corporation under the provisions of these Bylaws or under the provisions of the Articles of Incorporation or under the provisions of the _____ Business Corporation Act, a waiver thereof in writing signed by the person or persons entitled to such notice, whether before or after the time stated therein, shall be deemed equivalent to the giving of such notice. [§ 7.06, 8.23]

Article XI. Amendments

These Bylaws may be altered, amended, or repealed and new Bylaws may be adopted by the board of directors or by the shareholders at any regular or special meeting.

[Optional] Article XII. Executive Committee

Section 1. Appointment.
The board of directors by resolution adopted by a majority of the full board, may designate two or more of its members to constitute an executive committee. The designation of such committee and the delegation thereto of authority shall not operate to relieve the board of directors, or any member thereof, of any responsibility imposed by law. [§ 8.25]

Section 2. Authority.
The executive committee, when the board of directors is not in session, shall have and may exercise all of the authority of the board of directors except to the extent, if any, that such authority shall be limited by the resolution appointing the executive committee and except also that the executive committee shall not have the authority of the board of directors in reference to amending the articles of incorporation, adopting a plan of merger or consolidation, recommending to the shareholders the sale, lease or other disposition of all or substantially all of the property and assets of the corporation otherwise than in the usual and regular course of its business, recommending to the shareholders a voluntary dissolution of the corporation or a revocation thereof, or amending the Bylaws of the corporation. [§ 8.25]

Section 3. Tenure and Qualifications.
Each member of the executive committee shall hold office until the next regular annual meeting of the board of directors following his/her designation and until his/her successor is designated as a member of the executive committee and is elected and qualified. [§ 8.25]

Section 4. Meetings.
Regular meetings of the executive committee may be held without notice at such times and places as the executive committee may fix from time to time by resolution. Special meetings of the executive committee may be called by any member thereof upon not less than one day's notice stating the place, date, and hour of the meeting, which notice may be written or oral, and if mailed, shall be deemed to be delivered when deposited in the United States mail addressed to the member of the executive committee at his/her business address. Any member of the executive committee may waive notice of any meeting and no notice of any meeting need be given to any member thereof who attends in person. The notice of a meeting of the executive committee need not state the business proposed to be transacted at the meeting. [§ 8.25]

Section 5. Quorum.

A majority of the members of the executive committee shall constitute a quorum for the transaction of business at any meeting thereof and action of the executive committee must be authorized by the affirmative vote of a majority of the members present at a meeting at which a quorum is present. [§ 8.25]

Section 6. Action Without a Meeting.

Any action required or permitted to be taken by the executive committee at a meeting may be taken without a meeting if a consent in writing, setting forth the action so taken, shall be signed by all of the members of the executive committee. [§ 8.25]

Section 7. Vacancies.

Any vacancy in the executive committee may be filled by a resolution adopted by a majority of the full board of directors. [§ 8.25]

Section 8. Resignations and Removal.

Any member of the executive committee may be removed at any time with or without cause by resolution adopted by a majority of the full board of directors. Any member of the executive committee may resign from the executive committee at any time by giving written notice to the president or secretary of the corporation, and unless otherwise specified therein, the acceptance of such resignation shall not be necessary to make it effective. [§ 8.25]

Section 9. Procedure.

The executive committee shall elect a presiding officer from its members and may fix its own rules of procedure which shall not be inconsistent with these Bylaws. It shall keep regular minutes of its proceedings and report the same to the board of directors for its information at the meeting thereof held next after the proceedings shall have been taken. [§ 8.25]

Article XIII. Emergency Bylaws [§ 2.07]

The Emergency Bylaws provided in this Article XIII shall be operative during any emergency in the conduct of the business of the corporation resulting from an attack on the United States or any nuclear or atomic disaster, notwithstanding any different provision in the preceding Articles of the Bylaws or in the Articles of Incorporation of the corporation or in the _____ Business Corporation Act. To the extent not inconsistent with the provisions of this Article, the Bylaws provided in the preceding Articles shall remain in effect during such emergency, and upon its termination the Emergency Bylaws shall cease to be operative.

During any such emergency:

1. A meeting of the board of directors may be called by any officer or director of the corporation. Notice of the time and place of the meeting shall be given by the person calling the meeting to such of the directors as it may be feasible to reach by any available means of communication. Such notice shall be given at such time

in advance of the meeting as circumstances permit in the judgment of the person calling the meeting.

2. At any such meeting of the board of directors, a quorum shall consist of _____ [here insert the particular provisions desired].

3. The board of directors, either before or during any such emergency, may provide, and from time to time modify, lines of succession in the event that during such an emergency any or all officers or agents of the corporation shall for any reason be rendered incapable of discharging their duties.

4. The board of directors, either before or during any such emergency, may, effective in the emergency, change the head office or designate several alternative head offices or regional offices, or authorize the officers so to do.

No officer, director, or employee acting in accordance with these Emergency Bylaws shall be liable except for willful misconduct.

These Emergency Bylaws shall be subject to repeal or change by further action of the board of directors or by action of the share-holders, but no such repeal or change shall modify the provisions of the next preceding paragraph with regard to action taken prior to the time of such repeal or change. Any amendment of these Emergency Bylaws may make any further or different provision that may be practical and necessary for the circumstances of the emergency.

It is a matter of judgment by the lawyer as to whether a long form or a short form is used. The paralegal should be able to understand both types and know how to modify them for a specific new corporation.

CLOSE CORPORATIONS

The generic term *close corporation* is usually applied to a corporation, all the stock of which is owned by a limited number of stockholders, where there is not "public" market for the stock of the corporation[28] and, often, where the transfer of stock by any stockholder is subject to restrictions imposed by agreement among the stockholders. The subject of such restrictive agreements is covered extensively in Chapter Ten of this book.

A distinction must be made between "closely held corporations" and statutory "close corporations." The former is merely a

28. A public market exists for the stock of a corporation where the stock is owned by a large number of persons and where the stock may be easily bought and sold by the public at large through stockbrokers. The stock of companies such as Xerox, General Motors, Exxon, and IBM have a public market. The trading in the stock of such companies is closely regulated by complex federal and state securities laws.

descriptive term which refers to a business corporation with comparatively few shareholders and usually no publicly held stock. However, no statutory requirements exist as to the number of shareholders or to prohibit the public ownership of stock. Further, the closely held corporation must observe corporate formalities common to widely held corporations. Failure to do so risks the "piercing of the corporation veil," that is, reaching through the corporation to hold its shareholders liable for its debts.

Several states provide for the formation of what is called a statutory close corporation which, in several respects, is treated differently under the state corporation law from corporations which do not follow the statutory requirements for a close corporation.[29] The purpose of utilizing the close corporation structure is to enable the shareholders to run the corporation more like a partnership with less formality than is required of regular corporations and to preserve the intimate relationship among the shareholders.[30]

Many states provide for the election of the statutory close corporate form directly on the form of articles of incorporation used to form a regular business corporation.

The more important features of these statutory close corporations are discussed below.

Provisions Uniquely Applicable to Close Corporations

Requisite Contents of Articles of Incorporation In states with statutory close corporations, the articles of such a corporation must state that the corporation is a close corporation. The articles may contain one or more specific provisions limiting the number of shareholders which the corporation may have. The statutes usually prohibit "public offerings" of the corporation's stock,[31] and/or impose certain restrictions on the transfer of the corporation's stock.

As an example of a close corporation statute, § 2304 of the Pennsylvania Business Corporation Law provides that, in addition to those statutory provisions applicable to the articles of an "ordinary" Pennsylvania business corporation, the articles of a close corporation must include additional information or statements.

---

29. See Pennsylvania Business Corporation Law, Title 15, § 2301 *et seq.*
30. For example, Title 15, PBCL, § 2332.
31. A "public offering" of stock is the means by which the stock of a corporation acquires a "public market." See footnote 28. *supra.*

§ 2304, Pa.C.S. Additional contents of articles of statutory close corporations.

(a) General rule—In addition to the provisions otherwise required by this sub-part, the articles of a statutory close corporation shall provide that neither the corporation nor any shareholder shall make an offering of any of its shares of any class that would constitute a "public offering" within the meaning of the Securities Act of 1933 (15 U.S.C. § 77a et seq.).

Management   The articles of incorporation of a close corporation may also provide that the corporation shall have no directors and shall be managed directly by the shareholders. In such cases, no shareholders' meeting need be called to elect directors and, generally speaking, the shareholders are considered "directors" for most corporate purposes.

Dissolution   The articles may provide that the corporation can be dissolved at the option of any shareholder, much the same as a partnership.

CHAPTER THREE

Qualification of Corporations in Foreign Jurisdictions

Depending upon the nature of its activities, a corporation may not confine its business to the state of its incorporation. In some instances the state of incorporation may have been chosen for reasons totally unrelated to the company's activities, such as favorable corporate statutes or tax laws, and no business will be conducted there.

This fact is emphasized when we consider that many of the largest corporations in the United States are Delaware corporations, yet such corporations may conduct little or no business in Delaware. When a corporation conducts affairs outside the state of its incorporation, the question arises as to what additional requirements are imposed upon such a corporation by states other than the state of incorporation. Such states are normally referred to as "foreign jurisdictions," and a corporation which was not incorporated under the laws of that state is normally referred to as a "foreign corporation" with respect to such state.[1]

A state may regulate, control, or tax a foreign corporation when the corporation is "doing business" in that state. Unfortunately there is no simple definition of what constitutes "doing business" in a foreign jurisdiction. Each state defines the term differently. In addition, the definition may vary within a single state depending upon the nature of the statutes and court decisions. "Doing business" may also mean one thing if the issue is the ability of a state to tax a foreign corporation and quite another if the issue is whether a resident of the foreign state may sue the corporation in the courts of that state.

QUESTION

Which do you think would require a greater degree of "doing business" in a state—a corporation's subjection to taxation or to suit in that state's courts?

---

1. A corporation that is incorporated in a specific state is said to be a domestic corporation with respect to that state.

Statutory law may not define the term doing business. Therefore a corporation seldom has a clear idea when it must obtain a certificate to conduct its business in the state, a procedure known as "qualifying" as a foreign corporation. Typically, the applicable law will make a general statement that it covers all foreign corporations "doing" or "transacting" business within its boundaries, and then list several exclusions from such terms.[2]

Because of the difficult issues involved in describing doing business, no attempt is made in these materials to give this concept a complete definition. A lawyer will make the decision as to whether qualification is necessary. The Supreme Court of the United States itself has often wrestled and continues to wrestle with the problem in several different contexts. It is sufficient to recognize the definitional problem and turn to an analysis of what requirements are imposed on foreign corporations, assuming that a determination has been made that the foreign corporation is doing business within the meaning of the corporate laws of a particular state.

QUESTION

If there is a doubt as to the need to qualify, why would a corporation be reluctant to do so even if the safer course would be to qualify?

Because a decision to qualify as a foreign corporation in a jurisdiction imposes obligations on the corporation, including compliance with the laws of the foreign state, the board of directors of the corporation normally must approve such a qualification. This is so even though a corporation, by virtue of its doing business in a foreign jurisdiction, is required by the laws of that state to qualify as a foreign corporation.

A typical resolution of the board of directors of a corporation, approving such qualification, is as follows:

EXAMPLE

Resolution to Qualify as a Foreign Corporation

RESOLVED, that this Company qualify as a foreign corporation under the laws of the State of Connecticut; that the President or any Vice President, and the Secretary or any Assistant Secretary of this Company be and each of them is hereby authorized and empowered to execute, verify and deliver such documents and certificates, to pay all fees and charges and to take any other action as may be necessary or desirable in connection with the qualification of this Company as a foreign corporation under the laws of the State of Connecticut.

2. See § 15.01, MBCA, for example.

Does the opening of a checking account in an MBCA-type state require a corporation to qualify to do business? Holding shareholders' or directors' meetings? Issuing a promissory note to a creditor?

QUALIFICATION

Application for Certificate of Authority

A foreign corporation is not permitted to transact business within a state until it has obtained a certificate of authority or qualification to do so. The procedure for qualification is very similar to that of incorporation in most states.

QUESTIONS Do individuals or partnerships have to qualify to do business in a state other than that of formation? Why or why not?

Section 15.03 of the MBCA describes the normal type of requirements imposed on a corporation to obtain a certificate of authority to transact business.

PROBLEM Review § 15.03 against the MBCA requirements for incorporation of a domestic corporation to identify similarities and differences between them.

Normally an application for a certificate of authority must be accompanied by (a) the corporation's articles of incorporation and all amendments to the articles, duly authenticated or certified by the appropriate official of the state of incorporation of the foreign corporation, (b) certificate attesting as to the existence and good standing of the foreign corporation from the state of its incorporation, and (c) the applicable fees and franchise taxes which are payable upon such qualification. The form of application is invariably provided by the state.

QUESTIONS What state official would be the usual certifying authority? Who would ordinarily provide such a certificate? Does it cost anything?

Form of Application

Some states may require more than one form to be filed in connection with the application for qualification.

A sample form of an application for certificate of authority under the MBCA is set forth below:

EXAMPLE

Application for Certificate of Authority

Application for Certificate of Authority

Filing fee: $ _____

APPLICATION FOR
CERTIFICATE
OF
AUTHORITY OF

_____

To the Secretary of State
of the State of _____:

Pursuant to the provisions of Section _____ of the _____ Business Corporation Act, the undersigned corporation hereby applies for a Certificate of Authority to transact business in your State, and for that purpose submits the following statement:

FIRST: The name of the corporation is _____ .

SECOND: The name which the corporation elects to use in your state is _____ .[3]

THIRD: It is incorporated under the laws of _____ .

FOURTH: The date of its incorporation is _____ and the period of its duration is _____ .

FIFTH: The address of its principal office in the state or country under the laws of which it is incorporated is_____
_____ .

SIXTH: The address of its proposed registered office in your State is _____ , and the name of its proposed registered agent in your State at that address is _____
_____ .

SEVENTH: The names and respective addresses of its directors and officers are:

Name	Office	Address
_____	_____	_____
_____	_____	_____
_____	_____	_____
_____	_____	_____
_____	_____	_____
_____	_____	_____

---

3. If the corporate name is unavailable in the new state, a new name must be selected which meets the Act requirements, § 15.03.

EIGHTH: The aggregate number of shares which it has authority to issue, itemized by classes, par value of shares, shares without par value, and series, if any, within a class, is:

Number of Shares	Class	Series	Par Value per Share or Statement that Shares are without Par Value

NINTH: The aggregate number of its issued shares, itemized by classes, par value of shares, shares without par value, and series, if any, within a class, is:

Number of Shares	Class	Series	Par Value per Share or Statement that Shares are without Par Value

TENTH: The amount of its stated capital, as defined in the Business Corporation Act, is $_____ .

ELEVENTH: An estimate of the value of all property to be owned by it for the following year, wherever located, is $_____ .

TWELFTH: An estimate of the value of its property to be located within your State during such year is $_____ .

THIRTEENTH: An estimate of the gross amount of business to be transacted by it during such years is $_____ .

FOURTEENTH: An estimate of the gross amount of business to be transacted by it at or from places of business in your State during such year is $_____ .

FIFTEENTH: This Application is accompanied by a copy of its articles of incorporation and all amendments thereto, duly authenticated by the proper officer of the state or county under the laws of which it is incorporated.

Dated _____ , 19____.

_____ 4

By _____

Its _____ President   } 5

and _____

Its _____ Secretary

---

4. Exact corporate name of corporation making the application.
5. Signatures and titles of officers signing for the corporation.

Some states do not require the designation of a registered agent in an application for a certificate of authority, but they may require that the corporation maintain a registered office. In order, however, to provide a method by which lawsuits may be initiated against a foreign corporation registered in such a state, the law requires the application for the certificate of authority to provide for the designation of the secretary of the state as its agent upon whom service of process may be served. The form above provides for such a designation.

Upon receipt of an appropriate application, the state will issue a certificate of authority. Once a certificate of authority is issued, the foreign corporation is given certain rights to operate in the state:

§ 15.05, MBCA. Effect of Certificate of Authority.

(a) A certificate of authority authorizes the foreign corporation to which it is issued to transact business in this state subject, however, to the right of the state to revoke the certificate as provided in this Act.

The certificate of authority should be filed in the minute book of the corporation.

Name

As discussed above,[6] most state laws control the name that may be used by a foreign corporation by restricting the issuance of a certificate of authority in a manner similar to that of § 15.03 of the MBCA.

PROBLEMS

What MBCA procedures allow a foreign corporation with a name deceptively similar to a domestic corporation to obtain a certificate of authority? What does the name limitation indicate that a paralegal must do if it is known that a corporation being incorporated must immediately qualify in other states?

Similarly, a foreign corporation is not permitted to change its name unless the new name would also be acceptable under state law, as in the MBCA provision at § 15.06 (e).

Since corporations with identical names can create unnecessary problems of confusion in taxing and regulatory authorities, state law attempts to control the names used by both domestic and foreign corporations. For a corporation which plans to conduct a

---

6. See the section on "Name" in Chapter Two of your text.

business in many states, such controls pose a serious problem. A corporation must (a) determine if its name is available in every state in which it may decide to transact business, and (b) reserve its name in states in which it is currently not transacting business. Normally, the availability of a name can be checked by contacting the Department of State or the Secretary of State of each state in question, either directly or by having a corporate search company conduct the check through its branch offices in each state. Reserving a name is a more difficult process. Many states have a procedure, either formally embodied in a statute[7] or established by administrative practice, to permit the reservation of a name. These procedures normally permit reservation of a name for a limited period of time (e.g., not more than three or six months).

QUESTION

For what period of time is a reservation effective under the MBCA?

_____ *120 days*

Corporations are therefore confronted with the alternatives of (a) doing nothing, in the hope that no one else will preempt a particular name, (b) attempting to qualify as a foreign corporation, even if no business activity is contemplated at present in a particular state, or (c) creating a "name-holding" corporation in the state in question whose only purpose is to protect the availability of a name. The statutes and administrative procedures of states vary on the question of whether a foreign corporation may qualify without intending in the near future to transact any business in the state. Particular care must be taken before deciding that a corporation should qualify in a foreign jurisdiction simply as a means of reserving a corporate name. As will be shown below, the obligations imposed upon foreign corporations are considerable, and qualification is not a step to be taken casually.

Registered Office

The application for a certificate of authority requires information concerning the foreign corporation's registered office and, if required, a registered agent in such state.[8] In effect, state law requires the "presence" of the foreign corporation in its jurisdiction.[9]

Changes in the registered office or registered agent of a foreign corporation require appropriate notification to the state as in the MBCA example at § 15.08.

---

7. For examples, see § 4.02 of the MBCA and p. 21 in this text.
8. Compare this requirement to similar requirements of incorporation.
9. § 15.07, MBCA.

QUESTIONS

amended certificate of authority

QUESTIONS

How is a registered agent for a foreign corporation terminated under the MBCA? How does a registered agent of a foreign corporation change an address?

Often a foreign corporation desiring to qualify in a given state will not have an office or an employee in the state suitable to act as its registered office or registered agent. For this reason, as well as for reasons of administrative convenience, a corporation often uses a specialized service company, such as CT Corporation System, to serve as its registered office and agent within foreign jurisdictions.

Advertisement

As is true of initial incorporations,[10] many state laws require a foreign business corporation to advertise its intention to apply for a certificate of authority. Under the Pennsylvania Business Corporation Act, the advertising requirements imposed upon a foreign corporation are similar to those for initial incorporations.

Under the Pennsylvania statute, a typical form of advertisement would be as follows:

EXAMPLE

Advertisement of Intention to Apply for Certificate of Authority

---

Fun City, Inc., a Delaware corporation, with its principal office in Delaware at 120 Main Street, Wilmington, Delaware, has applied for a certificate of authority under the provisions of the Pennsylvania Business Corporation Act, Act of Dec. 21, 1988, P.L. 1444, as amended, by the filing of an application for a certificate of authority with the Department of State of the Commonwealth of Pennsylvania of June 1, 19___ .

The proposed registered office of Fun City, Inc., in the Commonwealth of Pennsylvania is 1700 Market Street, Philadelphia, Pennsylvania.

Fun City, Inc., proposes to operate one or more amusement parks in the Commonwealth of Pennsylvania.

The method of placing such an advertisement in the appropriate newspaper or newspapers and the proper procedure for obtaining proof of publication of such advertisement is identical with that which has been discussed under the advertisement requirements for an initial incorporation. The proof of publication is to be placed by the paralegal in the corporate minute book.

---

10. See "Publication" in Chapter Two of this text.

CONSEQUENCES OF QUALIFICATION AS A FOREIGN CORPORATION

Service of Process

Once a foreign corporation is qualified in a given state, its registered agent, if one is specified in its application, may be served as an agent of the corporation with any process, notice, or demand required or permitted to be served by law. In effect, this means that a qualified foreign corporation becomes subject to the jurisdiction of the courts in the states in which it is qualified.

Some states provide, in addition to or in lieu of the use of a registered agent, for service of process on a foreign corporation to be accomplished by serving the Secretary of that state.[11]

QUESTIONS

Is the possibility of subjection to a lawsuit in a foreign jurisdiction a consideration for not qualifying if there is a close question as to whether qualification is necessary? Why or why not? Is it possible that a corporation may be sued in a foreign jurisdiction even if it has not qualified?

Annual Reports

A foreign corporation qualified to do business in a state is normally required to file an annual report with the state[12] in order to supply the state with enough information to determine the amount of state taxes which should be paid. The form is normally supplied by the state and must be filed within a specific period of time after the end of the appropriate calendar or fiscal year.[13] A sample form of such a report appears below:

EXAMPLE

Annual Report of Foreign Corporation

ANNUAL REPORT
OF
_____

To the Secretary of State
   of the State of _____ :

Pursuant to the provisions of Section of the Business Corporation Act, the undersigned corporation hereby submits the following annual report:

---

11. § 15.10, MBCA.
12. See § 16.22, MBCA, for a model of this type of requirement.
13. § 16.22(c), MBCA, contains such a provision.

FIRST: The name of the corporation is _____ .

SECOND: It is incorporated under the laws of _____ .

THIRD: The address of its registered office in your State is and the name of its registered agent in your State of such address is _____ .

FOURTH: If a foreign corporation, the address of its principal office in the state or country under the laws of which it is incorporated is _____ .

FIFTH: The character of the business in which it is actually engaged in your State, briefly stated, is _____ .

SIXTH: The names respective addresses of its directors and officers are:

Name	Office	Address
_____	_____	_____
_____	_____	_____
_____	_____	_____
_____	_____	_____
_____	_____	_____
_____	_____	_____

SEVENTH: The aggregate number of shares which it has authority to issue, itemized by classes, par value of shares, shares without par value, and series, if any, within a class, is:

Number of Shares	Class	Series	Par Value per Share or Statement that Shares are without Par Value

EIGHTH: The aggregate number of its issued shares, itemized by classes, par value of shares, shares without par value, and series, if any, within a class, is:

Number of Shares	Class	Series	Par Value per Share or Statement that Shares are without Par Value

NINTH: The amount of its stated capital, as defined in the_____ Business Corporation Act, as of the close of business on December 31 next preceding the date hereof, was $_____ .

Taxes

The taxes imposed upon a foreign corporation after it has qualified to do business in a given state vary enormously from state to state. The following is only a general analysis of the typical kinds of taxes levied upon qualified foreign corporations:

Initial Franchise Tax   A state may impose and collect a tax at the time that the application for a certificate of authority is filed or shortly thereafter. The tax is normally computed on the authorized number of shares of the corporation and will vary depending upon the par value of such shares, or the fact that such shares have no par value. This tax is in addition to any filing fee that relates, at least theoretically, to the cost to the state of processing the application for a certificate of authority.

Annual Franchise Tax   The annual franchise tax imposed on a foreign business corporation is normally imposed upon that portion of the business "capital" of the corporation which is present in the state. The word "capital" is a defined term, and recourse to the individual state tax law is necessary for the appropriate definition. The amount of capital which is present in a given state is typically determined by a formula.

In addition to state taxes, a foreign corporation might also be subject to taxes imposed by cities, counties, and other political subdivisions.

The subject of state and local taxation is a highly technical one which is normally the province of lawyers and accountants who are experts in the field. The foregoing discussion is intended to familiarize the student with the nature of the tax burden imposed upon a qualified foreign corporation and to suggest why corporations are sometimes unwilling to qualify to do business in a given jurisdiction if there is any remote possibility that qualification is not required by law.

Amendment of Articles of Incorporation

If a foreign corporation amends its articles of incorporation,[14] the foreign corporation is required to obtain an amended certificate of authority in the event it changes its corporate name, period of duration, or state or country of incorporation.

---

14. See Chapter Four in this text for a description of the amendment process.

CONSEQUENCES OF TRANSACTING BUSINESS WITHOUT A CERTIFICATE OF AUTHORITY

Not only does state law require a corporation doing business within the state to obtain a certificate of authority and impose requirements and obligations on such corporations, but state law also covers the contingency of a corporation which is transacting business within a state without a certificate of authority.[15] In most states a foreign corporation improperly failing to obtain a certificate of authority is denied the right to sue in the courts of that state.

QUESTION

Can an unqualified foreign corporation defend itself in a lawsuit in a state in which it has improperly failed to qualify?

Some states also impose fines and penalties on unqualified corporations which are improperly doing business in the state.

WITHDRAWAL OF QUALIFICATION

A foreign corporation which has qualified to do business within a given state may, after it has ceased doing business within that state, withdraw its qualification by filing an application for withdrawal.[16]

The proof of publication and the certificate of withdrawal should be filed in the corporation's minute book.

The following form is suggested by the MBCA for withdrawals:

EXAMPLE

Application for Certificate of Withdrawal

Filing fee: $ _____.

APPLICATION FOR
CERTIFICATE OF WITHDRAWAL
OF_____

To the Secretary of State
of the State of _____ .

Pursuant to the provisions of Section _____ of the _____ Business Corporation Act, the undersigned corporation hereby applies for a Certificate of Withdrawal from your State, and for that purpose submits the following statement:

15. § 15.02, MBCA.

16. § 15.20 of the MBCA provides a list of the information which must be contained in an application for withdrawal.

FIRST: The name of the corporation is _____.
It is incorporated under the laws of _____.

SECOND: It is not transacting business in your state.

THIRD: It hereby surrenders its authority to transact business in your state.

FOURTH: It revokes the authority of its registered agent in your State to accept service of process, and consents that service of process in any action, suit, or proceeding based upon any cause of action arising in your State during the time the corporation was authorized to transact business in your State may thereafter be made on the corporation by service thereof on the Secretary of State of your State.

FIFTH: The post office address to which the Secretary of State may mail a copy of any process against the corporation that may be served on him is _____ .

SIXTH: The undersigned or successor shall notify the Secretary of State in the future of any change of mailing address.

PROBLEM

Compare the form for withdrawal with the MBCA's suggested forms used in dissolution of a domestic corporation.[17]

If a state permitted a qualified foreign corporation to withdraw simply by filing an application for a certificate of withdrawal, the state might subsequently discover that the corporation still owed taxes from its former activities. Since a corporation would like to remove any continuing burden by withdrawing from qualification, the state considers it an appropriate time to make certain that the corporation's tax payments to the state are current. The office of the state government in which the application for withdrawal has been filed normally will not approve the application until it has received notice from the various state taxing departments that all fees and franchise taxes have been paid. This notice is usually referred to as a "clearance certificate."

PROBLEMS

In what office is the application for certificate of withdrawal (or its *SoS* equivalent) filed in your state? Does your state require a clearance certificate or similar document prior to withdrawal? *YES* How long does it ordinarily take to obtain a clearance certificate? *6 months*

17. See Chapter Nine of this text for MBCA forms of dissolution.

To obtain a clearance certificate, a corporation normally must file tax returns to the date of withdrawal and pay all taxes which the corporation may owe the state through the date of withdrawal. Only after the corporation has filed such a tax return and paid all the taxes and fees required will the state issue the clearance certificate. The accountant for the corporation ordinarily has the responsibility to file tax returns and obtain the clearance certificate.

Once a clearance certificate or its equivalent has been obtained and forwarded to the appropriate office of the state in which the application for withdrawal has been filed, the state will grant the application for withdrawal.

In some states a foreign corporation which intends to apply or applies for a certificate of withdrawal must advertise this fact.

The following is a sample of an advertisement drafted to satisfy the advertising requirement:

> Fun City, Inc., a Delaware corporation, with its principal office in Delaware located at 120 Main Street, Wilmington, Delaware, and with a registered office in the Commonwealth of Pennsylvania at 1700 Market Street, Philadelphia, Pennsylvania, has filed with the Department of State of Commonwealth of Pennsylvania, an application for a certificate of withdrawal on December 31, 19___ .

PROBLEMS

1. Does your state have an advertising requirement? If so, when and where must the advertising take place?
2. Compare the advertising requirements for a certificate with the requirements of advertising a dissolution of a domestic corporation described in Chapter Nine in this text.

QUALIFICATION PROBLEM

EXAMPLE

Memorandum Regarding Qualification

MEMORANDUM

TO: Lawyer's Assistant
FROM: Abbie Kanter

A client of ours, State Street, Inc., is a Delaware corporation formed for the purpose of selling paint at retail through its own stores. As a means of insuring supply, it has recently begun to produce its own paint, at its various locations through a wholly-owned subsidiary, State Street Paint Bank, Inc. New stores are about to be opened in Lexington, Kentucky. (Author's note: Assume that it has adopted the MBCA.)

(a) I think the corporation needs to qualify in Kentucky. Do you agree?

(b) If so, what further information do you need?

(c) Do you foresee any problems in qualifying?

(d) In any event please prepare sample resolution authorizing qualification of each corporation.[18]

QUALIFICATION CHECKLIST

A checklist of information required in qualifying a foreign corporation appears below.

Checklist of Information Required in Connection with Foreign Qualification

I. Qualification

   A. *Basic Information*

   The following information, depending on the state statute, may be required:

   1. Name of corporation.

   2. State of incorporation.

   3. Address, including street and number, of principal office in state of incorporation.

   4. Address, including street and number, of proposed registered office in foreign jurisdiction.

   5. Name and address, including street and number, of proposed registered agent in foreign jurisdiction.

   6. The statute under which the corporation was incorporated.

   7. Date of incorporation.

   8. "Purpose" clause of articles of incorporation.

   9. Actual business activity which corporation is to pursue in the state in which it wishes to qualify.

   10. Names and addresses of the directors and officers of the corporation.

   11. Number of shares which the corporation has authority to issue, itemized by classes and series, if any.

   12. Number of shares which the corporation has issued, itemized by classes and series, if any.

18. See Chapter Five "Organization Meetings."

B. *Name*

Is the name of the corporation available for use in the foreign jurisdiction? If so, must action be taken to reserve the name?

C. *Filing*

After ascertaining the appropriate state office (e.g., Department of State) in which documents must be filed, decide which of the following, and how many copies of each, must be filed:

1. Application for Certificate of Authority?
2. Any other forms?
3. Certified copy of Articles of Incorporation?
4. Good Standing Certificate?

D. *Fees*

What fees and/or taxes must be paid in connection with the application for a certificate of authority?

E. *Advertisement*

What advertising requirements, if any, must be satisfied in connection with qualification as a foreign corporation?

II. Later Requirements

A. *Annual Reports*

1. When must they be filed?
2. With whom must they be filed?
3. What information must be contained in such reports?

B. *Tax Returns*

1. When must they be filed?
2. With whom must they be filed?
3. What is the form of tax return and what information is required?

C. Report Certain Changes

If any one of the following events occur, it may be necessary to make an appropriate filing with a state in which the corporation is qualified to do business:

1. Change of Name.
2. Changes of Articles of Incorporation.
3. Change of Registered Office.
4. Change of Registered Agent.
5. Change of business activity carried on within the state.
6. Merger of Corporation.

III. Withdrawal from Qualification

When a corporation is no longer "doing" or "transacting" business within a state, it will probably desire to withdraw from qualification and thereby eliminate the various obligations imposed upon it as a qualified foreign corporation.

A. *Certificate of Withdrawal*

What information must be set forth in the certificate of withdrawal, and with whom must it be filed?

B. *Clearance Certificate*

What taxes, fees, or charges must be paid in order to obtain from the Department of Revenue a statement that all taxes, fees, etc., have been paid?

C. *Advertising*

What advertising requirements, if any, must be satisfied?

D. *Fees*

What are the filing fees for the certificate of withdrawal?

PROBLEM

Compare the foregoing checklist with the checklist for incorporation contained in Chapter Two.

CHAPTER FOUR

Amendment of Articles of Incorporation and Bylaws

AMENDMENT OF ARTICLES OF INCORPORATION

Once a corporation has been created by the filing of articles of incorporation, § 10.01 (a) of the MBCA, the corporation has the right to amend its articles of incorporation. Under § 10.02, MBCA, unless the articles of incorporation provide otherwise, the board of directors in certain circumstances may amend the articles without shareholder approval. Some amendments, however, require shareholder approval—generally, amendments which directly affect the return on or value of the shares.[1]

PROBLEMS

1. Why would a corporation want to amend its articles?
2. Would a corporation use an amendment to (a) change its name? (b) increase the number of authorized shares? (c) change the number of directors? (d) modify its fiscal year?[2] (e) adopt a different date for its annual meeting of shareholders? (f) adopt a new business purpose for the corporation? (g) adopt a new registered office?

Board Approval

An amendment which may be effected solely by the board of directors requires proper board resolution, in accordance with the appropriate notice and meeting provisions of the statute. (See, generally, Chapter 8, subchapters A and B, of MBCA).

Submission to Shareholders

In order to obtain shareholder approval when necessary, the board of directors must adopt an appropriate resolution to that effect and submit it to the shareholders for affirmative vote. Once a proposal

---

1. § 10.04, MBCA.
2. The fiscal year of a company is twelve consecutive calendar months that a corporation elects as its accounting and financial reporting year. It starts at the beginning of a month, e.g., January 1, October 1, or December 1, and ends on the last day of the twelfth calendar month thereafter.

for an amendment has been made to the shareholders, the share-holders must vote on the amendment or agree to it by written consent, if state law permits written consents in lieu of a meeting. If a meeting is desired or required, because of either state law or the impracticality of obtaining written consents where the number of shareholders is very large, shareholders must receive notice of the meeting containing certain information.

§ 10.03, MBCA. Amendment by Board of Directors and Shareholders.

(d) The corporation shall notify each shareholder, whether or not entitled to vote, of the proposed shareholders' meeting in accordance with section 7.05.[3] The notice of meeting must also state that the purpose, or one of the purposes, of the meeting is to consider the proposed amend ment and contain or be accompanied by a copy or summary of the amendment.

Note that provisions may differ by state.

Shareholder Approval

Unless the corporation's articles (or in some states the bylaws) provide for a higher percentage, proposed amendments only need be approved by a statutory percentage of votes entitled to be cast on the particular action, usually a majority or two-thirds. The MBCA stipulates a majority vote:

§ 10.03, MBCA. Amendment by Board of Directors and Shareholders.

(e) Unless this Act, the articles of incorporation, or the board of directors (act-ing pursuant to subsection (c)) require a greater vote or a vote by voting groups, the amendment to be adopted must be approved by:
   (1) a majority of the votes entitled to be cast on the amendment by any voting group with respect to which the amendment would create dis-senters' rights; and
   (2) the votes required by sections 7.25 and 7.26 by every other voting group entitled to vote on the amendment.

PROBLEM

Is there any difference between the number of votes constituting (a) a majority of the outstanding shares and (b) a majority of shares present at a duly organized meeting?

---

3. Dealing with notice of meeting to shareholders.

When more than one class of stock is outstanding, e.g., preferred and common, approval of the holders of a specified percentage of each class of stock may be required. Such approval may be necessary because of the voting rights established in the corporation's articles of incorporation. In addition, or in the alternative, approval may be required by state law.[4]

The purpose of such a provision is to give holders of a specific class of stock an opportunity to vote where a proposed amendment to the articles would adversely affect their class of stock. For example, a new class of preferred stock with priority over an existing preferred stock would adversely affect an existing class. Holders of the existing class, therefore, may have the right to vote on the amendment.

As was mentioned above, shareholder approval may be obtained at a properly called meeting pursuant to due notice or by unanimous written consent. In states in which informal consent by less than all shareholders is authorized for certain corporate actions, this method may be used to obtain the requisite shareholder approval provided that the nature of the amendment is not one for which such informal action is expressly prohibited.[5]

Articles of Amendment

Once the amendment has been adopted, whether by board or shareholder approval, articles of amendment must be prepared and executed. The contents of the articles of amendment are ordinarily limited to the text of the amendment itself. Section 10.06 of the MBCA provides for the simple contents of the articles of amendment.

These requirements include, generally, the text of the amendment, method of adoption, and any affect on shares.

The filing of the articles of amendment is necessary to consummate the amendment to the articles and makes the amendment a document of public record as are the articles. A document of public record is one which may be inspected by any person at the official office where the document was filed. Any person may obtain a copy of a public document by paying the required copying fee.

A copy of all of the documents related to the amendment should be placed in the corporate minute book.

PROBLEM

What happens if one fails to file the amendment?

_____

4. See, for example, § 242(b) of the Delaware General Corporation Law.

5. See paragraph 7 of the Articles of Incorporation of Fun City Franchise Corp. in Chapter Two for an example of such a provision.

In some states a certified copy of the articles of amendment (as was true with respect to the duplicate copy of the certificate of incorporation) must be recorded in the county in which the corporation's registered office is located.[6]

PROBLEM

If there is such a requirement, is the amendment effective if the articles of amendment are not filed in the county office?

Advertisement

Many states require publication of the filing of articles of amendment in order to notify the legal community and creditors of the corporation of the corporate action. The advertising may actually be little more than an economic benefit for the newspapers in which the advertisements are placed because few persons pay attention to them.

A sample advertisement, relating to an amendment changing the name of a corporation, which would satisfy a statutory advertising requirement is as follows:

> Articles of Amendment of FUN CITY FRANCHISE CORP., a Pennsylvania corporation with its registered office at 4455 Main Street, Philadelphia, Pennsylvania, were filed with the Department of State of the Commonwealth of Pennsylvania on July 1, 19 ___ . The purpose of the Articles of Amendment was to change the name of the corporation to "FRANCHISE MARKETING ASSOCIATES, INC."

As in the case of the initial advertisements that appeared at the time of incorporation, a proof of publication should be inserted in the corporate minute book.[7]

Fees and Taxes

Typically, a state will impose a filing fee on a corporation filing articles of amendment. In addition, if the amendment is to increase a corporation's authorized capital, states which impose a tax upon the amount of a corporation's capital initially also impose a similar levy on the amount of the increase in the capital.

Effectiveness of Amendment

As is true of the procedure for incorporation, an amendment to the articles of incorporation under modern corporation statutes is

---

6. See "Registered Office Within a State" in Chapter Two of this text.
7. See "publication" on p. 30.

generally effective either upon the filing of articles of amendment, or, if applicable, upon the issuance of a certificate of amendment by the appropriate state agency after receipt of the articles of amendment. The amendment should have no impact on the corporation's existing responsibilities.

Section 10.09 of the MBCA is typical of many statutes in providing the following:

§ 10.09, MBCA. Effect of Amendment.

As amendment to articles of incorporation does not affect a cause of action[8] existing against or in favor of the corporation, a proceeding to which the corporation is a party, or the existing rights of persons other than shareholders of the corporation. An amendment changing a corporation's name does not abate a proceeding brought by or against the corporation in its former name.

PROBLEMS

1. What does the preceding paragraph say about the effect of an amendment on third parties?
2. Can a corporation amend its articles to extinguish a debt to a third party?
3. Does the change in a corporation's name require amendments in its existing leases or other contracts?
4. Does the change in corporate name cause the corporation to lose any rights to property titled in its old name, e.g., vehicles or real estate? If not, why not?
5. Besides the filing of the articles of amendment, what must a paralegal do for a corporation that has changed its name?
6. Is there any other way that a corporation may operate under a desired name without amending its articles of corporation? (See Chapter Two.)

Amendments Prior to Issuance of Shares

Most corporate laws now establish a procedure for a corporation to amend its articles of incorporation prior to the issuance of its shares. For example, the following is the Delaware provision:

§ 241, DGCL.

(a) Before a corporation has received any payment for any of its stock, it may amend its certificate of incorporation at any time or times, in any and as many respects as may be desired, so long as its certificate of incorporation

---

8. A "cause of action" is a set of facts which can be asserted by a plaintiff sufficient to support a valid lawsuit.

as amended would contain only such provisions as it would be lawful and proper to insert in an original certificate of incorporation filed at the time of filing the amendment.

(b) The amendment of a certificate of incorporation authorized by this section shall be adopted by a majority of the incorporators, if directors were not named in the original certificate of incorporation or have not yet been elected, or, if directors were named in the original certificate of incorporation or have been elected and have qualified, by a majority of the directors. A certificate setting forth the amendment and certifying that the corporation has not received any payment for any of its stock and that the amendment has been duly adopted in accordance with the provisions of this section shall be executed, acknowledged, filed and recorded in accordance with § 103 of this title. Upon such filing, the corporation's certificate of incorporation shall be deemed to be amended accordingly as of the date on which the original certificate of incorporation became effective, except as to those persons who are substantially and adversely affected by the amendment and as to those persons the amendment shall be effective from the filing date.

The states utilizing the MBCA have a similar procedure:

§ 10.05, MBCA. Amendment Before Issuance of Shares.

If a corporation has not yet issued shares, its incorporators or board of directors may adopt one or more amendments to the corporation's articles of incorporation.

Restated Articles of Incorporation

A corporation may have many amendments to its articles, all of which are required to determine the current status of the articles, as amended. The state corporate laws usually provide for a method of allowing the amended articles to be set forth and consolidated in one document by a "restatement" of the articles. "Restatement" of the articles of incorporation may take one of two forms:

1. Setting forth a revised articles of incorporation which incorporates all changes made, including current amendments.
2. Consolidating all prior amendments in one form without making any current amendments to the articles of incorporation.

In the former case, the board of directors may decide that it would be simpler, for future reference, to amend the articles of incorporation by restating them in their entirety, rather than changing several different provisions. This is especially true when a corporation has previously amended its articles of incorporation and new additional amendments are proposed. In such cases, the procedure for restating articles of incorporation is identical to that of making any amendment to the articles of incorporation.

In the latter case, the desire is simply to "clean up" the articles of incorporation by consolidating the original articles and all amendments into a single document: the restated articles of incorporation. States which follow the MBCA approach permit this restatement without shareholder approval as set forth in § 10.07 of the MBCA.

If no such provision existed, restatement of articles of incorporation (even though no substantive change was intended in the articles) would still require the same procedure as required for any current amendment to the articles of incorporation.

PROBLEM

Utilizing (a) the articles of FUN CITY FRANCHISE CORP. in Chapter Two and (b) the amendment to change its name that you made earlier in this chapter, restate the articles in their entirety in one document.

AMENDMENT OF BYLAWS

As indicated above, a corporation's articles of incorporation or its bylaws may provide for amendment of the bylaws by the board of directors. For example, § 109 (a) of the Delaware General Corporation Law provides that:

§ 109, Delaware General Corporation Law.

(a) The original or other bylaws of a corporation may be adopted, amended or repealed by the incorporators, by the initial directors if they were named in the certificate of incorporation, or, before a corporation has received any payment for any of its stock, by its board of directors. After a corporation has received any payment for any of its stock, the power to adopt, amend or repeal bylaws shall be in the stockholders entitled to vote, or, in the case of a non stock corporation, in its members entitled to vote; provided, however, any corporation may, in its certificate of incorporation, confer the power to adopt, amend or repeal bylaws upon the directors or, in the case of a non stock corporation, upon its governing body by whatever name designated. The fact that such power has been so conferred upon the directors or governing body, as the case may be, shall not divest the stockholders or members of the power, nor limit their power to adopt, amend or repeal bylaws.

PROBLEM

Can a Delaware corporation provide for amendment of the bylaws by the directors under the foregoing provision if the bylaws so provide but the articles are silent?

Some states, such as Pennsylvania, permit either the articles or bylaws to vest power to amend the bylaws in the board of directors, subject to numerous statutory exceptions which reserve amendment power to the shareholders.

Procedure

When shareholder action is not required, the board of directors may amend the bylaws by resolution adopted at a duly constituted meeting or by unanimous consent in writing without a meeting when this type of informal action is permitted under the corporation law of the state of incorporation.[9] A form of board resolution adopting an amendment to the bylaws by unanimous consent is as follows:

EXAMPLE

Board of Directors Approval of Amendment to Bylaws

[NAME OF CORPORATION]

ACTION BY UNANIMOUS CONSENT IN WRITING
OF THE
BOARD OF DIRECTORS

The undersigned, constituting the entire Board of Directors of [Name of Corporation], a [State of Incorporation] corporation, in accordance with the authority contained in the [State of Incorporation] Business Corporation Law, and in accordance with the bylaws of this corporation, without the formality of convening a meeting, hereby unanimously consent to the following action of this corporation:

RESOLVED: that Section 2.3(a) of the Corporation's bylaws be amended so as to read in its entirety as follows:

"(a) *Place*. Meetings of the board of directors shall be held at the corporation's executive offices located at 1700 Market Street, Philadelphia, Pennsylvania, unless another location is designated in the notice of the meeting."

Dated: _____

[Signature lines for all Directors]

Filed with the undersigned on _____ , 19 ___ .

/s/ _____
Secretary of [Name of Corporation]

9. See Chapter Five for a fuller discussion of actions by unanimous consent by the directors.

When shareholder action is required, a meeting of shareholders, or informal action of shareholders without a meeting, is required.[10]

PROBLEM

Amend Article III, Section 2 of the long form of bylaws on page 51 of Chapter Two to provide for a classified board of 6 directors with three classes of 2 directors each. Designate the three classes as A, B, and C. (Refer to footnote 26 of Chapter Two for an explanation of classification of a board of directors.)

Restatement of Bylaws

Generally, no specific procedure is established by statute for the restatement of a corporation's bylaws since the bylaws are not usually a matter of public record. Since restatement is a method of amendment, bylaws may be restated in the same manner that they may be amended, i.e., by the board of directors, if properly permitted by the articles of incorporation or bylaws, or by the shareholders.

---

10. The procedures for such meetings or actions are discussed in Chapter Five of this text.

Shareholders' and Directors' Meetings

Adherence to "formalities" is essential if the existence of a corporation is to withstand challenge. Cases exist which have held that the shareholder of a corporation cannot benefit from the corporation's limited liability if no efforts were made to operate the corporation "as a corporation" with the requisite meetings and actions by shareholders and directors. The authority of a corporation's officers to act on behalf of the corporation may have to be verified by reference to minutes of directors' and shareholders' meetings.

Despite the importance of accurate and complete records of actions by shareholders and directors, the proper maintenance of such records and the proper followup to insure timely corporate action may be neglected by lawyers as a result of the pressure of immediate problems. As a consequence, a lawyer's assistant is often charged with the responsibility of insuring the accurate and timely preparation of corporate minutes and of being certain that all corporation represented by the law firm are current in their shareholders' and directors' meetings and minutes.

In Chapter One the role of directors and shareholders of a corporation was outlined.[1] In the discussion of the powers of directors and shareholders, certain facts must be noted: (a) when a corporation has more than one director, a single director has no authority or rights relating to the management of the corporation in the director's individual capacity; rather, such authority and rights are vested in the "board of directors" and any action undertaken by directors must be taken collectively as an action of the board of directors; and (b) no matter what the number of directors or shareholders, any action taken by the directors or shareholders must satisfy the formal requirements prescribed by state law and the articles of incorporation and bylaws of the corporation. This chapter will examine the formal requirements imposed on the actions of shareholders and directors and provide examples of some of the more common types of actions.

---

1. The basic roles of directors and shareholders are outlined in Chapter One.

REQUIREMENTS OF MEETINGS

Historically, all actions by the directors and shareholders of a corporation were required to be taken at meetings. The following is a discussion of the customary statutory requirements which must be satisfied by such meetings and the methods of conducting meetings in order that any action approved at a meeting be properly authorized. Preparation of notices, ballots and other meeting documents, including minutes, are tasks of paralegals. The forms included herein are only examples. The paralegal always must remember to make forms fit the matter at hand, not to try to make the matter at hand fit the forms! Forms are only useful tools, not a final product. Using them is no substitute for understanding the matter.

Shareholders' Meetings

Location   State law normally leaves it to the bylaws to specify the place at which shareholders' meetings are to be held. The Model Business Corporation Act sets forth a requirement which has been adopted in many states.[2]

§ 7.01 (b), MBCA.

(c) Annual shareholders' meetings may be held in or out of this state at the place stated in or fixed in accordance with the bylaws. If no place is stated in or fixed in accordance with the bylaws, annual meetings shall be held at the corporation's principal office.

PROBLEM

What is the principal office of the corporation?[3]

An example of a possible bylaw provision giving latitude to the board of directors to specify the location of a shareholders' meeting is as follows:

> Meetings of the shareholders shall be held at such place as may be designated by the board of directors from time to time.

Time and Calling of Meeting   Normally, state law requires that there be at least one regular meeting of the shareholders of the corporation each year (commonly called the "annual meeting") at which meeting the directors of the corporation must be elected.

---

2. See Chapter Two, p. 21, for an explanation of the MBCA.
3. See Chapter Two if you need help.

PROBLEM

How does a shareholder go about calling a meeting under the MBCA if the corporation fails to do so in a calendar year? Who besides the board of directors and shareholders can call a shareholders' meeting under the MBCA?

The bylaws of a corporation will ordinarily specify the time for the annual meeting. For example, a provision such as the following may be utilized:

> *Annual Meeting.* An annual meeting of the shareholders for the election of directors and for other business shall be held at such time as may be fixed by the board of directors, on the first Monday in March of each year (or if such is a legal holiday, on the next following business day), or on such other day as may be fixed by the board of directors.

QUESTIONS

What time of the year should the annual meeting occur? Immediately before the end of the fiscal year?[4] Immediately thereafter? Three months thereafter? Why?

In addition to annual meetings, there may also be special meetings of the shareholders. For example, the MBCA suggests the following provision:

§ 7.02, MBCA. Special Meeting.

(a) A corporation shall hold a special meeting of shareholders: . . .
    (2) if the holders of at least 10 percent of all the votes entitled to be cast on any issue proposed to be considered at the proposed special meeting sign, date, and deliver to the corporation's secretary one or more written demands for the meeting describing the purpose or purposes for which it is to be held.

Often, a bylaw provision will grant to the president of the corporation the right to call a special meeting of the shareholders:

> *Special Meetings.* Special meetings of the shareholders may becalled at any time by the president, or the board of directors, or the holders of at least one-tenth of the outstanding shares of stock of the Company entitled to vote at the meeting.

PROBLEMS

1. Why would a special meeting ever be necessary?

---

4. See footnote 2 of Chapter Four for an explanation of the meaning of "fiscal year."

2. How do shareholders call a meeting?

Notice Virtually every state provides some statutory procedure for giving notice of meetings of shareholders, to shareholders, including the time and place of the meeting. In the case of the annual meeting, the purpose of the meeting generally need not be given, but as a matter of practice and courtesy, most notices of shareholders' meetings do contain some description of the business to be transacted at the meeting. In the case of special meetings, the notice must often specify the purpose for which the meeting was called. Sections 7.05 (a) and (c) of the MBCA are fairly typical of the statutory notice provisions that states have adopted:

§ 7.05, MBCA.

(a) A corporation shall notify shareholders of the date, time, and place of each annual and special shareholders' meeting no fewer than 10 nor more than 60 days before the meeting date. Unless this Act or the articles of incorporation require otherwise, the corporation is required to give notice only to shareholders entitled to vote at the meeting.

(c) Notice of a special meeting must include a description of the purpose or purposes for which the meeting is called.

A paralegal will often be asked to prepare the notice of the shareholders' meeting. Examples of notices for an annual meeting of shareholders and a special meeting of shareholders are found below.

EXAMPLE

Notice of Annual Meeting of Shareholders

FUN CITY MARKETING, INC.
1700 Market Street
Philadelphia, Pennsylvania 19103

May 1, 19 ___

NOTICE OF ANNUAL MEETING
OF SHAREHOLDERS

To Our Shareholders:

Notice is hereby given that the Annual Meeting of shareholders will be held at the Corporation's offices located at 1700 Market Street, Philadelphia, Pennsylvania at 10:00 A.M., on May 26, 19___ , for the purpose of considering the following matters:

1. To elect five Directors pursuant to the bylaws of the Company. The following individuals have been nominated for election as directors by management in accordance with the Corporation's bylaws:

Joan Smith
James Green
Richard Thomas
William Jones
Susan Gray

2. To ratify certain purchases and contracts made and entered into by the board of directors.
3. To transact such other business as may properly come before the meeting.

/s/James Green
Secretary of FUN CITY MARKETING, INC.

EXAMPLE

Notice of Special Meeting of Shareholders

[NAME AND ADDRESS OF CORPORATION]

[Date]

NOTICE OF SPECIAL MEETING
OF SHAREHOLDERS

To Our Shareholders:

Notice is hereby given that a Special Meeting of Shareholders will be held at _____ at _____ M., on _____ , for the purpose of considering the following matters:

1. To consider and act upon a proposal to adopt an Amendment to the Articles of Incorporation to change the corporation's name to _____ .

2. To transact such other business as may properly come before the meeting.

Secretary of [Name of Corporation]

PROBLEM

XYX Corporation is calling a special meeting of shareholders on January 5, 19 __ , at 10:00 A.M. for purpose of increasing the authorized capital of the corporation to 100,000 shares, par value $1.00 per share. The meeting will be held at the corporate headquarters at 125 Market Street, Milwaukee, Wisconsin. Draft a notice of the meeting.

An affidavit of the Secretary of a corporation establishing that notice of a shareholders' meeting was mailed to all shareholders is set forth below:

EXAMPLE

Affidavit of Mailing

I, James Green, Secretary of Fun City Marketing, Inc., a Delaware corporation (the "Corporation"), being duly sworn to depose and say that I caused notice of the annual meeting of the shareholders of the said Corporation, a copy of which is hereto attached and is hereby made a part of this affidavit, to be deposited in the United States Post Office at the City of Dover, Delaware, in a sealed envelope, postage prepaid, duly addressed to each shareholder of record of the said Corporation at his or her last-known post office address as the same appeared on the books of the Corporation.

/s/James Green
Secretary of FUN CITY MARKETING, INC.

BE IT REMEMBERED that on this 11th day of July, 19 ___, personally appeared before me, a Notary Public for the State of Delaware, James Green, who, being duly sworn, did depose and say that he is the Secretary of Fun City Marketing, Inc., and that the facts stated in the above Affidavit are true.

GIVEN under my hand and seal the day and year aforesaid.

/s/John Doe
Notary Public

[*Seal*]

PROBLEMS

What is an affidavit? Why is it necessary here? What is a notary public? Is it necessary or advisable to have a notary public execute all legal documents?

The Securities Exchange Act of 1934, a federal statute, imposes substantial additional requirements on notices of shareholders' meetings given by certain corporations whose stock is publicly held.[5]

Who Is Entitled to Notice? The names of the shareholders entitled to notice of a shareholders' meeting is complicated because the identity of the shareholders of a corporation may change as

---

5. See Chapter 10 for a discussion of the federal securities laws and "publicly-held corporations."

shares of stock are transferred from individual to individual. Therefore, corporate laws generally provide for the board of directors either to (a) select a specific date (the "record date") before the meeting for determining the identity of the corporation's shareholders who are entitled to notice of and to vote at the meeting or (b) to close the transfer books to prevent changes in ownership from a specified date to the date of the meeting. For example, § 7.07 of the MBCA provides for the fixing of a record date, either in the bylaws or by the board of directors.

PROBLEM

If the meeting date is to be October 1, what obligations under the MBCA do the directors have for determining the shareholders entitled to notice of and to vote at the meeting?

Stock exchanges impose certain additional requirements relating to the timing of the record date with respect to corporations whose stock is publicly held and traded on national stock exchanges. First of all, stock exchanges prohibit closing of the books. This is because stocks which are actively traded on exchanges, such as General Motors, should not be impeded or prevented from trading by closing of the transfer books. Additionally, the stock exchanges require prior notice of any record date, whether it be to determine shareholders entitled to vote at a shareholders' meeting, to receive dividends, or to exercise some other right in their capacity as shareholders. Thus, when a board of directors of a corporation whose stock is listed on an Exchange intends to call a meeting of shareholders, it must, in establishing the record date and meeting date, take into consideration not only the notice requirements of state law and the corporation's bylaws, but also the rules of the Exchange requiring sufficient notice of the record date.

It is also necessary to determine which classes of stock are entitled to vote on a particular matter.[6] Holders of common stock are generally entitled to vote on any matter for which shareholder approval is required. On the other hand, there are situations and particular matters on which another class of stock or all other classes of stock may have voting privileges. For example, if dividend rights or rights on dissolution of the corporation of a preferred class of stock were to be changed by an amendment to the articles, that preferred class would have the right to vote on the amendment. Since preferred usually has no voting rights, absent this special issue, that class would not ordinarily have such a right.

Generally, the corporation's articles or bylaws will indicate which classes of stock are entitled to vote on any given question.

---

6. See Chapter Six for a discussion of different classes of stock.

However, if the holders of any class of stock could be uniquely affected as a class by certain corporate action, such an elimination of that class's dividend rights, they are entitled to have notice of the meeting and to vote on that matter, notwithstanding the fact that their stock is termed nonvoting by the corporation's articles or bylaws.[7] The purpose of such a right is to grant fairness to such shareholders and prevent the loss of rights without their consent.

Maintenance of Shareholders List   State laws require the officers of corporations to make available to the shareholders, at or prior to a meeting, a list of all shareholders at the record date who are entitled to vote at the meeting. The MBCA § 7.20 requires the provision of a voting record of shareholders entitled to vote. The requirement of producing a list before the meeting will enable shareholders who oppose management to contact the shareholders to campaign for their position. It will also permit shareholders to verify, independently of management, who is entitled to vote at the meeting and their voting strength.

Paralegals often attend meetings, tally votes, and take roll of shareholders present. In the case of corporations which have many hundreds or thousands of shareholders, the shareholder list usually consists of a computer printout. In such cases the record of shareholders' ownership is on computer programs.

Proxies   State laws permit shareholders, who are not able to be present at a shareholders' meeting, to have their shares voted on their behalf by others by the use of "proxies."

A proxy is a written authorization to the person or persons named to vote shares at a shareholders' meeting with the same effect as if the holder of the shares were present in person at the meeting. The MBCA suggests the following:

§ 7.22, MBCA. Proxies.

(a) A shareholder may vote his shares in person or by proxy.

(b) A shareholder may appoint a proxy to vote or otherwise act for him by signing an appointment form, either personally or by his attorney-in-fact.[8]

(c) An appointment of a proxy is effective when received by the secretary or other officer or agent authorized to tabulate votes. An appointment is valid for 11 months unless a longer period is expressly provided in the appointment form.

---

7. § 10.04 of the MBCA provides a sample of a statutory provision regarding voting rights of classes other than common stock.

8. An attorney-in-fact is a person who has been granted a power of attorney by another person. A power of attorney is a writing which authorizes a person to act for the person signing the writing as described in the writing. It is the creation of a formal "agency" relationship.

A form of proxy appears below:

EXAMPLE

Proxy Form for Annual Meeting of Shareholders

FUN CITY MARKETING, INC.

ANNUAL MEETING OF SHAREHOLDERS
JULY 31, 19 ___

KNOW ALL PERSONS BY THESE PRESENTS, that the undersigned shareholder of Fun City Marketing, Inc., hereby appoints John Jones, William Smith and Ephraim Too and each of them to the true and lawful attorney or attorneys of said shareholder, with full power of substitution and revocation to each of them (the action of a majority of them or their substitutes present and acting or, if only one be present and acting then the action of such one to be in any event controlling) for and in the name of the undersigned to vote all shares of stock which the undersigned would be entitled to vote if personally present at the annual meeting of the shareholders of said corporation, called to be held on Friday, July 31, 19 ___, and at any adjournment or adjournments thereof, with all the powers the undersigned would possess if personally present: 1. for the election of directors; 2. for the appointment of a firm of certified public accountants to act as auditors of the corporation; and 3. for the transaction of such other business as may come before the said meeting.

The undersigned hereby acknowledges receipt of the notice, dated July 1, 19 ___, of such annual meeting of shareholders and hereby revokes any proxy or proxies heretofore given.

_____
[Date]

_____
[Name of Registered Shareholder]

Shares_____

(Signature should correspond with name typed on the reverse hereof. No witness is required.)

Return proxies to FUN CITY MARKETING, INC.,
Philadelphia, Pennsylvania 19103

PROBLEM

Using the above form, draft a proxy card for XYZ Corporation to be used at its January 15, 19 ___, meeting where (a) auditors are being appointed and (b) a proposal to amend the articles of incorporation to change the corporate name to ABC Corporation is to be considered. (Don't forget the general authorization provision.)

The only way to obtain a sufficient number of votes (a "quorum")[9] to hold a valid shareholders' meeting for publicly held corporations with a large number of shareholders is for the management of the corporation to solicit proxies. The federal securities laws impose requirements on such corporations when they solicit proxies from their shareholders.

PROBLEMS

Can a shareholder give a proxy and later revoke it by sending another proxy with different instructions prior to the voting at the meeting? By revoking it and electing to vote in person? Can such revocation be effective if received by the corporation after the first proxy has been voted in accordance with its instructions?

A proxy card for companies with large numbers of shareholders is usually merely a printed computer card which may be addressed to shareholders and tallied by the computer.

Quorum   No action may be taken at any meeting of shareholders unless a quorum is present. The MBCA provision is set forth in § 7.25.

PROBLEMS

Using § 7.25 of the MBCA, compute how many shares constitute a quorum if 1,000,000 shares are outstanding if the articles of incorporation are silent on the subject.

If the minimum required number of shares for a quorum is present, how many shares must vote affirmatively on a matter to approve the action?

Normally, the determination that a quorum exists is made by the secretary of the corporation. However, when there are judges of election, they will perform this function.

Judges of Election   Many corporation statutes provide for use of inspectors or judges of elections. They may be employees of the corporation who are not standing for election as directors of the corporation, or, if a company is large enough to have employed a separate transfer agent that keeps records of shareholders, an employee of the transfer agent may serve. These inspectors or judges, when utilized, are charged with and have the authority to determine officially the number of shares entitled to vote at the meeting, the shares represented (in person or by proxy) at the

9. "Quorum" will be discussed shortly.

meeting, the presence of a quorum, and to tabulate and determine the outcome of all shareholder votes. They are ordinarily only utilized by corporations which have a substantial number of shareholders or a corporation with a few shareholders when there is an election contest. Section 1765 of the Pennsylvania Business Corporation Law, Title 15, is typical in setting forth the authority and responsibility of judges of election and the circumstances when their use is required or optional:

§ 1765, Title 15, PBCL.

Unless otherwise provided in a bylaw adopted by the shareholders:

(1) **Appointment.** — In advance of any meeting of shareholders of a business corporation, the board of directors may appoint judges of election, who need not be shareholders, to act at the meeting or any adjournment thereof. If judges of election are not so appointed, the presiding officer of the meeting may, and on the request of any shareholder shall, appoint judges of election at the meeting. The number of judges shall be one or three. A person who is a candidate for office to be filled at the meeting shall not act as a judge.

(2) **Vacancies.** — In case any person appointed as a judge fails to appear or fails or refuses to act, the vacancy may be filled by appointment made by the board of directors in advance of the convening of the meeting or at the meeting by the presiding officer thereof.

(3) **Duties.** — The judges of election shall determine the number of shares outstanding and the voting power of each, the shares represented at the meeting, the existence of a quorum, the authenticity, validity and effect of proxies, receive votes or ballots, hear and determine all challenges and questions in any way arising in connection with the right to vote, count and tabulate all votes, determine the result and do such acts as may be proper to conduct the election or vote with fairness to all shareholders. The judges of election shall perform their duties impartially, in good faith, to the best of their ability and as expeditiously as is practical. If there are three judges of election, the decision, act or certificate of a majority shall be effective in all respects as the decision, act or certificate of all.

(4) **Report.** — On request of the presiding officer of the meeting, or of any shareholder, the judges shall make a report in writing of any challenge or question or matter determined by them, and execute a certificate of any fact found by them. Any report or certificate made by them shall be prima facie evidence of the facts stated therein.

The corporation pays the judges who are appointed by the board of directors. Note that the MBCA has no provision similar to the above Pennsylvania provision.

QUESTION

Does this mean that a shareholders' meeting in an MBCA state could not have judges of election appointed?

Normally, the judges of election are required to execute an "oath" which is filed with the minutes of the meeting. A form of Oath of Judge of Elections is set forth below:

> We, John Able, Joan Baker and James Charley, duly appointed Judges of Election of Fun City Marketing, Inc., do solemnly swear that we will faithfully and impartially perform our duties as Judges of Election at the annual meeting of shareholders of the above named corporation to be held on July 31, 19 ___ , and that we will fairly and diligently canvass the votes cast at such election and honestly and truthfully report the result of said election.
>
> /s/John Able
> —————————
> John Able
>
> /s/Joan Baker
> —————————
> Joan Baker
>
> /s/James Charley
> —————————
> James Charley
>
> SWORN TO AND SUBSCRIBED BEFORE ME THIS 31st day of July, 19 ___ .
>
> /s/John Doe
> —————————
> Notary Public

Voting The simplest method of voting, and one that is only practical in corporations with a few shareholders, is for the shareholders present at the meeting, along with persons holding proxies for shareholders who are not present at the meeting, to indicate by voice or hand their approval or disapproval for any proposal presented and for the person presiding at the meeting to record which shareholders are for or against the proposal and the number of shares voted by each shareholder. If judges or inspectors are elected, they will tally the vote.

The more common method of voting is by ballot, even when not required by state law. Many states, however, require that the election of directors be conducted by ballot. For example, Delaware law provides as follows:[10]

§ 211 (e), Delaware General Corporation Law.[11]

All elections shall be by written ballot, unless otherwise provided in the certificate of incorporation.

10. Compare the Pennsylvania Business Corporation Law at § 1758 (b), which does not require a ballot unless the bylaws otherwise provide.

11. Note that a Delaware corporation can avoid the necessity of a ballot only if the certificate of incorporation so provides. Even such a provision in the bylaws is not effective. This points up the necessity of reading the statute of the state of incorporation.

Ballots normally make specific reference to the matter to be voted upon so that no confusion can exist in their use. Sample forms of ballots for use by a shareholder voting his or her own stock and by a person voting stock pursuant to a proxy are included below:

EXAMPLE

Ballot for Shareholders

XYZ CORPORATION

ANNUAL MEETING OF SHAREHOLDERS
HELD JULY 1, 19 ___

BALLOT

The undersigned, the holder of record on July 1, 19 ___ , of ___ shares of the Common Stock of XYZ Corporation, a Pennsylvania corporation (the "Company"), and entitled to vote such shares at the above-mentioned meeting of shareholders of the Company, does hereby, for and on behalf of himself or herself, vote said shares with respect to the election of directors and the adoption of proposals attached hereto as follows:

Proposal 1—Election of Directors

Names of Directors	Number of Shares For	Number of Shares Against
1.	_____	_____
2.	_____	_____
3.	_____	_____
4.	_____	_____
etc.		

Proposal 2—Amendment of "Purpose" Clause

Number of Shares For _____ Number of Shares Against _____

Proposal 3—Elimination of Cumulative Voting

Number of Shares For _____ Number of Shares Against _____

Proposal 4—Approval of Auditors

Number of Shares For _____ Number of Shares Against _____

_____ (Signed)

_____ (Printed)
[Name of Registered Shareholder]

EXAMPLE

Ballot for Proxies

XYZ CORPORATION

ANNUAL MEETING OF SHAREHOLDERS
HELD JULY 31, 19 __

MANAGEMENT PROXY BALLOT

The undersigned, as attorneys and proxies of shareholders of XYZ Corporation, a Pennsylvania corporation (the "Company"), acting pursuant to written proxies executed by holders of record of an aggregate _____ shares of the Common Stock of the Company entitled to vote at the above-mentioned meeting of shareholders of the Company, which proxies have been filed with the Secretary of the Company, do hereby, for and on behalf of said shareholders, vote said shares with respect to the election of directors and the adoption of proposals attached hereto, as follows:

Proposal 1—Election of Directors

Names of Directors	Number of Shares For	Number of Shares Against
1.	_____	_____
2.	_____	_____
3.	_____	_____
4.	_____	_____
etc.		

Proposal 2—Amendment of "Purpose" Clause

Number of Shares For _____ Number of Shares Against _____

Proposal 3—Elimination of Cumulative Voting

Number of Shares For _____ Number of Shares Against _____

Proposal 4—Approval of Auditors

Number of Shares For _____ Number of Shares Against _____

_____
[Name of Proxy]

_____
[Name of Proxy]

It should be noted that there must be a separate ballot or section of a ballot for each proposal that will be voted upon at the meeting.

Once all of the shareholders and holders of proxies who are present at the meeting have voted by ballot, the judges of election, if they have been appointed, or the secretary of the meeting, if he or she is serving as the judge, will prepare a report setting forth the results of the voting. A sample form of report of voting is found below:

EXAMPLE

Report of Judge of Elections

> XYZ CORPORATION
>
> ANNUAL MEETING OF SHAREHOLDERS
> HELD JULY 31, 19 ___
>
> REPORT OF JUDGE OF ELECTIONS
>
> The undersigned, duly appointed and qualified Judge of Election at the Annual Meeting of Shareholders of XYZ Corporation (the "Company") held on July 31, 19 ___ , American Trust Bank Building, Southwest Corner of Broad Street and 7th Avenue, New York, New York, does hereby certify:
>
> 1. Before entering upon the discharge of my duties as Judge of Election at said Meeting, I took and subscribed to an oath to execute faithfully the duties of Judge of Election with strict impartiality in accordance with the best of my ability.
> 2. At said Meeting, I examined the list of holders of the Common Stock of the Company as of the close of business on July 1, 19 ___ , the record date for said meeting, and the written proxies and ballots presented to me; and I determined that the holders of record of _____ shares of the Common Stock of the Company are represented in person or proxy at the Meeting, out of a total of 1,000,000 shares of Common Stock which are outstanding. Therefore, there were represented in person or by written proxies ___ % of the Common Stock of the Company entitled to vote at the Meeting, which percentage constituted a quorum pursuant to the requirements of law.
> 3. The result of a vote taken by ballot and conducted by me as Judge of Election on the resolutions and proposals attached hereto, duly moved and seconded at said Meeting, was as follows:
>
> **Proposal 1—Election of Directors**
>
> **Votes Cast in Favor of Nominees for Directors**
>
> | Names of Directors | Number of Shares For | Number of Shares Against |
> |---|---|---|
> | 1. | _____ | _____ |
> | 2. | _____ | _____ |

```
3.                              _____      _____

4.                              _____      _____

etc.
```

Proposal 2

Number of Shares For _____ Number of Shares Against _____

Proposal 3

Number of Shares For _____ Number of Shares Against _____

Proposal 4

Number of Shares For _____ Number of Shares Against _____

A majority of the outstanding shares of Common Stock having been voted at this Meeting, at which a quorum was present, in favor of all proposals and for the nominees for directors, such proposals have been duly adopted and such nominees have been duly elected directors of the Company.

IN WITNESS WHEREOF, I have made the foregoing report and subscribe my name hereto this 31st day of July, 19 ___ .

```
                              _____
                              [Name of Judge of Election]
```

Minutes   At every shareholders' meeting a record of the meeting is made and later placed in the minute book. The minutes are a summary of the proceedings and contain any formal resolutions of the shareholders.[12]

The minutes are not a transcription of the meeting but only a summary. They are often initially written by the paralegal and reviewed by the attorney in charge and corporate officials. The styles of preparing minutes vary greatly, and the law firm or corporation with which the paralegal is affiliated will have its own style and preferences as to form.[13]

Resolutions, whether those of shareholders or directors, must do two things: (a) authorize the corporation to take an action and (b) designate those officers or other persons who are entitled to consummate the transaction on behalf of the corporation and the amount of discretion that such persons shall have in consummating the transaction. Unless corporate resolutions carefully do those two things, it is not clear what the corporation is to do or who is to

---

12. The form of resolution will follow the format of directors' resolutions discussed below under "Directors Meetings."

13. See the example of a form of minutes of a meeting of a corporation under "Minutes" near the end of this chapter.

do it on behalf of the corporation. A corporation can only act through designated authorized persons.

PROBLEMS

How does the requirement of formal resolutions for a corporation differ from the method of operation of a partnership or sole proprietorship?[14] Are minutes and resolutions necessary to authorize actions of the partnership or proprietorship? Why or why not? Can partners or proprietors act on behalf of the business without specific authorization by resolution?

Summary The following is a checklist of tasks for a paralegal prior to and after a shareholders' meeting.

1. Prepare notice of meeting (waiver of notice if possible), including

   a. Location
   b. Place
   c. Time
   d. Actions to take place
   e. Setting of record date

2. Prepare shareholders' list
3. Mail to shareholders

   a. Notice of meeting
   b. Annual report to shareholders
   c. Proxy statement and proxies (if solicited or required)

4. Prepare script of meeting
5. Attend meeting

   a. Make notes of proceedings
   b. Identify formal and informal actions

6. Prepare draft of minutes and formal resolutions

Directors' Meetings

As previously discussed, directors can only act as a body. The action of an individual director is meaningless unless there is only one director. This is done by statute at meetings or by written

---

14. See Chapter One for a discussion of partnerships and sole proprietorships.

consent.[15] In contrast to shareholders' meetings, state laws normally impose fewer rigid requirements on directors' meetings, leaving the details to the bylaws of the corporation. This is because the directors' meetings are ordinarily attended by fewer persons and the meetings are less formal in order to encourage free and open discussion. This absence of specific formalities will be evident in the discussion which follows.

Location Normally, state law does not indicate the location of directors' meetings. Typically, the bylaws of the corporation will allow the directors themselves to decide upon the location of their meetings. A common type of bylaw provisions follows:

> *Place.* Meetings of the board of directors shall be held at such place as may be designated by the board or in the notice of the meeting.

When State law does not impose any requirement for the frequency of directors' meetings. The bylaws of most corporations permit the board to designate a regular meeting as in the following example:

> *Regular Meetings.* Regular meetings of the board of directors shall be held at such times as the board may designate by resolution. Notice of regular meetings need not be given.

Acting under the authority given to it in the bylaws, the board of directors will adopt a resolution, such as the one that follows, specifying when regular meetings will be held:

> RESOLVED, that regular meetings of the board of directors of this Company shall be held at the executive offices of the Company on the first Monday of the months of February, April, June, August, October, and December, or, if such date shall be a legal holiday, on the next succeeding day which is not a legal holiday.

PROBLEM

Must regular meetings be provided for in the bylaws? Does the MBCA require them?

In addition to regular meetings, bylaws will also provide for special meetings as the following example shows:

> *Special Meetings.* Special meetings of the board of directors may be called at any time by the president and shall be called by the president upon the written request of one-third of the directors. Notice (which need not be written) of the time and place of each

---

15. Consents are discussed on page 113.

special meeting shall be given to each director at least two days before the meeting.

Notice Absent statutory requirements, it is typical to provide in the bylaws for no notice in the case of regular meetings and for a short notice period in the case of special meetings. This distinction is illustrated in the bylaw clauses above, relating to regular and special meetings.

PROBLEM Must the purpose for a special meeting be stated in the notice? Why or why not?

Who Is Entitled to Notice? As indicated in the bylaw clause relating to the special meetings of directors above, each director is entitled to notice of a special meeting of directors.

PROBLEM What if one director of seven is not properly notified before a meeting is held? Is action by the other six directors valid? If not, can the defect in notice be remedied? What if the director who was not properly notified is present at the meeting? Use the MBCA in formulating your answers.

Quorum While state laws do not impose many requirements in connection with directors' meetings, they normally do impose quorum requirements, such as that suggested by the MBCA.

§ 8.24, MBCA. Quorum and Voting.

(a) Unless the articles of incorporation or bylaws require a greater number, a quorum of a board of directors consists of:

  (1) a majority of the fixed number of directors if the corporation has a fixed board size or

  (2) a majority of the number of directors prescribed, or if no number is prescribed the number in office immediately before the meeting begins, if the corporation has a variable-range size board.

(b) The articles of incorporation or bylaws may authorize a quorum of a board of directors to consist of no fewer than one-third of the fixed or prescribed number of directors determined under subsection (a).

(c) If a quorum is present when a vote is taken, the affirmative vote of a majority of directors present is the act of the board of directors unless the articles of incorporation or bylaws require the vote of a greater number of directors.

PROBLEM

If X corporation has nine directors, and the bylaws and articles are silent as to a quorum at a directors' meeting, how many directors are required to do business at a directors' meeting under the MBCA statute? What is the minimum number of directors that can possibly take affirmative action at such a meeting?

The bylaws may also contain a clause covering quorum requirements, but this clause will not normally depart from the statutory requirement. A sample bylaw provision follows:

> *Quorum.* A majority of all the directors in office shall constitute a quorum for the transaction of business at any meeting and, except as otherwise provided herein, the acts of a majority of the directors present at any meeting at which a quorum is present shall be the acts of the board of directors.

Proxies Since statutes do not permit directors to be represented at directors' meetings by written proxies, directors must meet to be able to vote on the matters considered at the meeting. The reason for prohibition of proxies is that directors are "fiduciaries"[16] of a corporation and as such have been imposed with certain obligations. Therefore, they cannot delegate away their obligations to a proxy and must act personally.

Voting No requirements are imposed by statute on the method by which directors vote. Normally voting is done by a voice vote with one person, who is keeping the minutes of the meeting, keeping a record. As discussed earlier, it is often the paralegal who will be keeping the minutes.

Minutes A paralegal often will make the initial draft of minutes which record the proceedings and resolutions of a meeting.[17]

PROBLEMS

Why are minutes needed? Do partnerships hold meetings of partners to authorize partners to act? Can partners act without such meetings?[18] Can corporations act without such meetings? Must a directors' meeting be held to authorize every corporate action? Only major actions? If so, which major actions? If a corporation is in the business of selling real estate, must every sale of land be preceded

---

16. A "fiduciary" is a person in a position of trust with respect to another person such as the relationship of a director to the corporation. The law imposes duties on a fiduciary so that the director must not take advantage of the position or the law will make the director answerable for damages. There are many other fiduciary relationships on which the law imposes obligations and duties. For example: attorney-client, physician-patient, trustee-trust, spouse-spouse, parent-child. Can you think of others?

17. The discussion of minutes above is applicable to directors' meetings as well.

18. See Chapter One for a discussion of differences between partnerships and corporations.

by a directors' resolution? How about a sale of land by a manufacturing company? How about the sale of a corporation engaged in the sale of real estate of all its real estate at one time to one purchaser?

Often the directors will be asked to approve a transaction which has already taken place, perhaps because there was inadequate time to prepare for a directors' meeting. For example, the president of the company may enter into a lease on behalf of the corporation without board approval and later seek approval of the board. The process of confirming a previous act done on behalf of a corporation is called "ratification." Ordinarily any action that could have been authorized in advance by the directors can be ratified by them after the fact. An example of a resolution ratifying a lease is as follows:

> RESOLVED, that the entry into a lease in the form attached hereto between XYZ Corporation and this Corporation pursuant to which this Corporation shall lease Blackacre for a period of one year for $10,000, be and is hereby ratified, approved, confirmed and adopted.

PROBLEM

Can shareholders similarly ratify actions which have previously taken place?

Summary   Following is a summary of actions that paralegals may do prior to or after a directors' meeting:

1. Prepare notice of meeting (waiver of notice if available), including

   a. Location
   b. Place
   c. Time
   d. Actions to take place at meeting

2. Mail notice to directors
3. Attend meeting

   a. Take notes of proceedings
   b. Identify formal and informal actions

4. Prepare draft of minutes and formal resolution

111

Other Matters

Waiver of Notice Under the corporate laws of many states, a "waiver of notice," signed by the person entitled to receive notice, is deemed to be the equivalent of actual notice. A waiver of notice may be used for both shareholders' and directors' meetings. Section 1705 (a) of the Pennsylvania Business Corporation Law typifies this approach:

§ 1705, Title 15, PBCL.

(a) Written waiver.—Whenever any written notice is required to be given under the provisions of this subpart or the articles or bylaws of any business corporation, a waiver thereof in writing, signed by the person or persons entitled to the notice, whether before or after the time stated therein, shall be deemed equivalent to the giving of the notice. Except as otherwise required by this subsection, neither the business to be transacted at, nor the purpose of, a meeting need be specified in the waiver of notice of the meeting. In the case of a special meeting of shareholders, the waiver of notice shall specify the general nature of the business to be transacted.

A form "waiver of notice" is set forth below:

EXAMPLE

Waiver of Notice

> We, the undersigned, being shareholders of _____ , a corporation organized under the laws of the State of _____ , do hereby waive any and all notice required by the laws of the State of _____ , or by the Articles of Incorporation or Bylaws of said Corporation, and do hereby consent to the holding of a _____ (insert "annual" or "special") meeting of shareholders of said Corporation, on _____ , 19 ___ , at _____ .M., or any adjournment or adjournments thereof, at the principal office of the Corporation, _____ , for the purpose of _____ .
>
> We do further consent to the transaction of any business, in addition to the business herein noticed to be transacted, that may come before said meeting.
>
> Dated at the City of _____ , State of _____ , this _____ day of _____ , 19 ___ .
>
> *[Signature for all shareholders]*

Special Method of Participation at Meetings Traditionally, for a shareholder or director to participate in and vote at a meeting, it was necessary to be physically present at the meeting or, in the case of a shareholders' meeting, to be represented by proxy. In recent years, some states such as Pennsylvania have permitted persons to be present at meetings by way of telephone:

§ 1708, Title 15, PBCL.

One or more persons may participate in a meeting of the incorporators, the board of directors or the shareholders of a business corporation by means of conference telephone or similar communications equipment by means of which all persons participating in the meeting can hear each other. Participation in a meeting pursuant to this section shall constitute presence in person at the meeting. Title 15 Pa. C.S. Section 1708.

Appropriate bylaw provisions to permit conference telephone participation are as follows:

DIRECTORS:

Participation

One or more directors may participate in a meeting of the board or a committee of the board by means of conference telephone or similar communications equipment by means of which all persons participating in the meeting can hear each other.

SHAREHOLDERS:

Participation

One or more shareholders may participate in a shareholders' meeting by means of conference telephone or similar communications equipment by means of which all persons participating in the meeting can hear each other.

PROBLEMS

Why is it important that all persons at the meeting hear each other? Is a quorum determined the same way at a telephone meeting as at a meeting in one place? If the corporate laws of the state of incorporation are silent about the use of conference telephone calls for meetings, is a meeting valid if the articles or bylaws have authorized conference telephone meetings?

WRITTEN CONSENTS

For most corporations, the necessity of having a meeting in order for directors and shareholders to take action can prove cumbersome. The logistics of getting people together on a regular basis may be difficult. To eliminate the necessity of having an actual meeting, some state laws have created a procedure by which action may be taken if consented to in writing by all of the directors or shareholders. The MBCA suggested approach is set forth in § 8.21 as to directors and § 7.04 as to shareholders.

Forms of unanimous written consents by the board of directors and shareholders of a corporation are set forth below:

EXAMPLE

*Unanimous
Written Consent of
Directors*

[NAME OF CORPORATION]

ACTION BY UNANIMOUS CONSENT IN WRITING
OF THE
BOARD OF DIRECTORS

The undersigned, constituting the entire Board of Directors of [name of corporation], a [name of state] corporation, in accordance with the authority contained in Section _____ of the _____ Business Corporation Law, without the formality of convening a meeting do hereby unanimously consent to the following action of this corporation.

RESOLVED, that

[Set forth action taken]

Dated: _____

[Signature lines for all directors with their names
under the respective signature lines]

Filed with the undersigned on _____, 19 ___.

_____
Secretary of [Name of Corporation]

EXAMPLE

*Unanimous
Written Consent of
Shareholders*

[NAME OF CORPORATION]

ACTION BY UNANIMOUS CONSENT IN WRITING
OF THE SHAREHOLDERS

The undersigned, being all the shareholders of [name of corporation], a [name of state] corporation, in accordance with the authority contained in Section _____ of the _____ Business Corporation Law, without the formality of convening a meeting do hereby unanimously consent to the following action of this corporation:

RESOLVED, that

[Set forth action taken]

Dated: _____

[Signature lines for all shareholders with their names
under their respective lines]

Filed with the undersigned on _____ , 19 ___ .

_____
Secretary of [*Name of Corporation*]

It must be noted that the written consent is the action itself. Therefore, until it has been *fully executed* by all of the consenters (directors or shareholders) no action has taken place.

QUESTIONS

How does this contrast with a meeting of directors or shareholders where the action is effectuated and the minutes of the meeting are later drawn up? Are the minutes of the meeting the action itself or only evidence thereof?

Under some state laws, shareholder action may be taken by a written consent signed by fewer than all of the shareholders in certain circumstances. For example, Delaware provides the following:

§ 228, DGCL.

(a) Unless otherwise provided in the certificate of incorporation, any action required by this chapter to be taken at any annual or special meeting of stockholders of a corporation, or any action which may be taken at any annual or special meeting of such stockholders, may be taken without a meeting, without prior notice and without a vote, if a consent in writing, setting forth the action so taken, shall be signed by the holders of outstanding stock having not less than the minimum number of votes that would be necessary to authorize or take such action at a meeting at which all shares entitled to vote thereon were present and voted . . .

(d) Prompt notice of the taking of the corporate action without a meeting by less than unanimous written consent shall be given to those stockholders . . . who have not consented in writing. In the event that the action which is consented to is such as would have required the filing of a certificate under any other section of this title, if such action had been voted on by stockholders . . . at a meeting thereof, the certificate filed under such other section shall state, in lieu of any statement required by such section concerning any vote of stockholders . . ., that written consent has been given in accordance with the provisions of this section, and that written notice has been given as provided in this section.

This provision allows fewer than all shareholders to consent in writing to an action.

PROBLEM

What if a Delaware corporation follows this procedure but fails to notify other shareholders of the action within a reasonable time?

A suggested form for use by paralegals evidencing written consent by fewer than all of the shareholders of a Delaware corporation and a special form of notice of such action which is required to be sent to all shareholders pursuant to Delaware law are included below:

EXAMPLE

Less Than Unanimous Written Consent of Shareholders (Delaware)

[NAME OF CORPORATION]

ACTION BY CONSENT IN WRITING
OF THE SHAREHOLDERS

The undersigned, being the holders of shares entitled to cast more than two-thirds of the votes which may be voted in approval of the corporate action hereafter set forth, and in accordance with the authority contained in Section 228 of the Delaware General Corporation Law, without the formality of convening a meeting do hereby consent to the following action of this corporation:

RESOLVED, that

[Set forth the action taken]

Dated: _____

[Signature lines for all shareholders whose consent will be obtained with names under their respective lines]

Filed with the undersigned on _____ , 19 ___ .

_____
Secretary of [Name of Corporation]

EXAMPLE

Notice of Informal Action by Less Than Unanimous Consent of Shareholders (Delaware)

[NAME OF CORPORATION]

[ADDRESS OF CORPORATION]

[Use the Corporation's stationery if available]

TO ALL SHAREHOLDERS:

Pursuant to the provisions of Section 228 of the Delaware General Corporation Law, notice is hereby given of the following corporate action:

[*Set forth action taken*]

This action was approved by the [Board of Directors on _____ [1], and by the] holders of _____ [2] of the Corporation's _____ [3] voting shares in a written consent dated _____ [4], and filed with the Corporation on _____ [5].

Sincerely,

_____
Secretary of [*Name of Corporation*]

1. Date of Board action, if Board approval was required.
2. Number of shares represented by the shareholders' written consent.
3. Number of voting shares outstanding.
4. Date of shareholder action by written consent.
5. Date shareholders' written consent was filed with Secretary.

ORGANIZATION MEETING

General

The first meeting in a corporation's history is called the "organization meeting." At this meeting certain matters are transacted which permit the corporation to proceed with its intended business. In most states, the requirement of an initial meeting of directors (if they are named in the articles) or incorporators (if no directors are named in the articles) is expressly set forth in the corporate law, and the provisions of the law also indicate some of the matters that will be the subject of the meeting. The MBCA provides the following:

§ 2.05, MBCA. Organization of Corporation.

(a) After incorporation:

  (1) if initial directors are named in the articles of incorporation, the initial directors shall hold an organizational meeting, at the call of a majority of the directors, to complete the organization of the corporation by appointing officers, adopting bylaws, and carrying on any other business brought before the meeting.

  (2) If initial directors are not named in the articles, the incorporator or incorporators shall hold an organizational meeting at the call of a majority of the incorporators:

      (i)   to elect directors and complete the organization of the corporation: or

      (ii) to elect a board of directors who shall complete the organization of the corporation.

(b) Action required or permitted by this Act to be taken by incorporators at an organizational meeting may be taken without a meeting if the action taken is evidenced by one or more written consents describing the action taken and signed by each incorporator.

PROBLEMS

In view of the requirement of § 2.05 of the MBCA, is a waiver of notice in lieu of notice of the organization meeting valid? Can the meeting be by unanimous written consent in lieu of a meeting?

Section 1310 (a) of the Pennsylvania Business Corporation Law (which Act does not require that the initial directors be named in the articles) provides the following:

§ 1310, Title 15, PBCL.

(a) **General rule.**—After the corporate existence begins, an organization meeting of the initial directors or, if directors are not named in the articles, of the incorporator or incorporators shall be held, within or without this Commonwealth,[19] for the purpose of adopting bylaws which they shall have authority to do at the meeting, of electing directors, if directors are not named in the articles, and the transaction of such other business as may come before the meeting. A bylaw adopted at the organization meeting of directors or incorporators shall be deemed to be a bylaw adopted by the shareholders for the purposes of this subpart and of any other provision of law.

If state law permits directors to act by written consent,[20] the "organization meeting" can ordinarily be effected by such a written consent. If a meeting must be held, it is common to have a waiver of notice signed by all of the participants rather than waiting for the period required in the notice provision of the law.

One or Two Organization Meetings

If the articles of incorporation have named directors, and if such persons are intended to serve as the actual directors of the corporation after operations have commenced, then only one organization meeting is necessary to transact all the required

---

19. Note that Pennsylvania (and a few other states such as Massachusetts and Virginia) are formally referred to as a "commonwealth" rather than a "state." This is a formality only, not a matter of legal significance.

20. See discussion under "Written Consents" earlier in this chapter.

business. Sometimes, however, "nominal" directors, such as para-legals, attorneys, or other employees will be named as directors. This is done to expedite formation of the corporation where the directors who are going to act after operation of the corporation have commenced either are unavailable or undetermined. If the named directors are not intended to serve as directors of the corporation after operations have commenced, then it is necessary to provide for their resignation and for the election of new directors. This can be done in one of two ways:

1. After the organization meeting, and after shares have been issued, the nominal directors may resign and the shareholders of the corporation, either at a meeting or by a written consent, elect new directors; or

2. At the organization meeting, nominal directors resign one at a time and new directors are elected to fill each of the vacancies at that meeting.

The following is an example of resolutions which would be used if this latter approach is utilized:

RESOLVED, that the resignation of John Smith as a director of this Company be and hereby is accepted, effective immediately.

RESOLVED, that Jennifer Jones be and hereby is elected a director of this Company to fill the vacancy created by the resignation of John Smith accepted in the preceding resolution and to serve in accordance with the Bylaws of this Company until the next annual meeting of this Company and her successor shall have been elected; and that Jennifer Jones be and hereby is requested to participate in this meeting of the Board of Directors.

Similar resolutions would be adopted for each other resignation and replacement.

It should be noted that a majority of the directors who are elected must participate in the meeting to insure that a quorum will continue to exist throughout the meeting.

If no directors are named in the articles of incorporation, then two organization meetings may be necessary: the first, a meeting of incorporators to elect directors and, if permitted by state law, to approve the bylaws, and the second, a meeting of directors, to take all other appropriate action. Some states, however, permit incorporators to elect themselves as directors and then proceed with the meeting of directors.

Included below is a set of minutes of an organization meeting of incorporators at which the bylaws are adopted and directors are elected.

EXAMPLE

*Minutes of
Meeting of
Incorporators*

[NAME OF CORPORATION]

MINUTES OF MEETING OF INCORPORATORS

A meeting of the incorporators named in the Certificate of Incorporation of _____, a [state] corporation, was held at _____ at _____ o'clock ___ .M. on _____, pursuant to the foregoing waiver of notice.

The following persons were present, namely:

[Names of all Incorporators]

being all of the incorporators of the Corporation.

_____ called the meeting to order, and upon motion duly made and seconded, was chosen to act as Chair of the meeting and _____ was chosen to act as Secretary thereof. The Secretary presented the waiver of notice of the meeting, and, there being no objection, the Chair ordered that such waiver be filed with the records of the Corporation.

The Secretary reported that the Certificate of Incorporation had been filed in the Office of the Secretary of the State of _____ on _____, and that a certified copy thereof had been recorded in the Office of the Recorder of _____ County in said State, being the County in which the principal office of the corporation in said State is located. There being no objection, the Chair ordered that the Secretary cause a copy of the Certificate of Incorporation to be inserted in the Minute Book of the Corporation.

The Secretary presented a copy of the proposed bylaws for the regulation of the Corporation's affairs and such proposed bylaws having been read, the same were, upon motion duly made and seconded, adopted and in all respects approved and confirmed as and for the bylaws of the Corporation. The Secretary was directed to cause a copy of the bylaws to be inserted in the Minute Book of the Corporation.

The Chair then stated that it was in order to elect Directors of the Corporation as contemplated in the bylaws, and upon motion duly made and seconded, the following, namely:

[Names]

were duly nominated as Directors of the Corporation to hold office, subject to the provisions of the bylaws, until their respective successors shall be elected and qualify.

There being no other nominations, a ballot was then taken, and, all of the incorporators having voted, the Chair canvassed the ballots and declared that _____ had been duly elected, by unanimous vote of all the Incorporators, as Directors of the Corporation to hold office, subject to the provisions of the bylaws, until their respective successors should be elected and qualify.

Upon motion duly made and seconded, the following resolution was then unanimously adopted:

RESOLVED, that the Board of Directors of this corporation be and it hereby is authorized in its discretion, subject to the provisions of law and the Certificate of Incorporation and bylaws of this Corporation, to issue from time to time shares of the capital stock of this Corporation in such amounts and for such consideration permitted by laws as said Board shall from time to time determine.

There being no further business to come before the meeting, it was, upon motion duly made and seconded, adjourned.

_____
Secretary of the Meeting

A form of minutes of an organization meeting of directors at which all necessary initial action is taken follows:

EXAMPLE

Organization Meeting of Directors (Following Incorporators' Meeting)

[*NAME OF CORPORATION*]

MINUTES OF FIRST MEETING
OF
BOARD OF DIRECTORS

The first meeting of the Board of Directors of the above corporation was held at _____ o'clock ___ .M. on _____ at _____ pursuant to due notice.

The following directors, constituting all of the directors, were present, namely:

[*Names*]

_____ called the meeting to order and upon motion duly made and seconded was chosen to act as Chair of the meeting and _____ was chosen to act as Secretary of the meeting.

The Secretary then presented the Minutes of the Meeting of the Incorporators of the Corporation held at ___ o'clock ___ .M., reciting that the Articles of Incorporation had been filed in the office of the Secretary of the State of _____ on _____ .
The Secretary also presented a copy of the Bylaws of the Corporation

adopted at said Incorporators' meeting and, upon motion duly made and seconded, the following resolution was unanimously adopted:

RESOLVED, that the minutes of the meeting of the Incorporators of this Corporation presented to this meeting, be and hereby are in all respects approved; and that the bylaws adopted at said meeting of Incorporators be and hereby are in all respects also approved and adopted by the Board of Directors as the bylaws of this Corporation for the regulation of its business and affairs.

The Chair then stated that it was in order to proceed to the election of officers of the Corporation, and upon motion duly made and seconded, the following persons were duly elected to the offices set forth below opposite their respective names, each to serve, subject to the provisions of the bylaws, until their respective successors are elected and qualify:

Thereupon, upon motion duly made and seconded, the following resolution was duly adopted:

RESOLVED, that the proper officers of this Corporation be and they hereby are authorized and directed for and on behalf of the Corporation and under its corporate seal, if required, to make, execute, and file any certificates or reports required by law to be filed in any State or States in which the officers of the Corporation shall find it necessary or advisable to file them in order to authorize the Corporation to transact business in such State or States, or for any other lawful purpose whatsoever.[21]

The Secretary presented a proposed corporate seal for the Corporation to the meeting, and upon motion duly made and seconded, the following resolution was duly adopted:

RESOLVED, that the seal in the form presented to this meeting, bearing the inscription "_____ Corporate Seal 19 ___ State of _____" be and hereby is approved and adopted as the corporate seal of this Corporation.

The Chair then presented a form of proposed stock certificate of the Corporation and a specimen copy thereof was directed by the Chair to be filed with the records of the meeting. Thereupon, upon motion duly made and seconded, the following resolutions were duly adopted:

---

21. A corporation, unlike individuals, cannot operate outside its state of incorporation, unless it "registers" or "qualifies" to do business in the other states in which it is doing business. This resolution authorizes such qualification in other states. A corporation is called a "foreign" corporation by states other than its state of incorporation. See Chapter Two, "Corporate Bylaws."

RESOLVED, that the form of stock certificate for shares of capital stock of this Corporation, presented to this meeting, be and hereby is approved and adopted as the stock certificate of this Corporation, and that stock certificates in such form appropriately filled in, may be signed by the President or any Vice President and the Treasurer or any Assistant Treasurer or the Secretary or any Assistant Secretary of this corporation.

RESOLVED, that all of the authorized common stock of this Corporation, none of which is now outstanding, shall be issued pursuant to the following Plan in accordance with the provisions of Section 1244[22] of the Internal Revenue Code of 1954, as amended: namely, that this Board of Directors, in its discretion, shall offer out of the Corporation's authorized common stock, during the period beginning with the date of this resolution and expiring not later than two years from the date hereof, all or any part of such shares to the full amount or number authorized by the Articles of Incorporation, in such amounts and for such consideration, consisting of money or property (other than stock or securities), as it from time to time determines and as may be permitted by law, provided that the maximum consideration to be received for all such shares shall not exceed $500,000.

RESOLVED, that the appropriate officers of this Corporation are each authorized to execute and file with the State of _____ Securities Commission and the corresponding regulatory bodies of other states and the District of Columbia, such applications or documents as may be required by applicable law.

RESOLVED, that the Corporation accepts the offers of the following persons to purchase the number of shares of the common stock of the Corporation at the prices indicated opposite their names, and the appropriate officers are authorized to issue certificates therefor upon payment of the total purchase price in cash as soon as the appropriate applications or documents have been filed and, if required, approved by the State of _____ Securities Commission or any corresponding regulatory body:

Name	No. of Shares	Total Purchase Price

Upon motion duly made and seconded, the following resolution was unanimously adopted:

RESOLVED, that this Board of Directors does hereby adopt in their entirety the resolutions set forth in the certified copy of banking resolutions directed to The New Banking and Trust Company, a copy of which was presented to this meeting.

22. § 1244 plans are discussed later in this chapter.

RESOLVED, that the Treasurer of this Company be and hereby is authorized and empowered to pay and discharge all taxes, fees, and other expenses heretofore incurred or to be incurred in connection with the organization of this Corporation and to reimburse the officers of this Corporation and all other persons for all expenditures heretofore made by them in such connection.

RESOLVED, that the Secretary of this Corporation be and hereby is authorized and empowered to procure the necessary corporate books and records and to open and maintain stock transfer books in accordance with the laws of the State of _____ as well as any other applicable laws.

RESOLVED, that the President, any Vice President, the Treasurer, or the Secretary of this Corporation be, and each of them hereby is, authorized and empowered to sign for and on behalf of this Corporation and in its corporate name all documents necessary to be signed by this Corporation in the ordinary course of its business; and that the Secretary or any Assistant Secretary of this Corporation be, and hereby is, authorized and empowered to affix the corporate seal of this Corporation to any such document when so signed, to sign in attestation of such seal on all documents to which such seal is affixed, and to certify under such seal and issue copies of this or any other resolution adopted by the Board of Directors or shareholders of this Corporation.

There being no further business, on motion duly made and seconded, the meeting adjourned.

_____
Secretary of the Meeting

The minutes of an Organization Meeting in the form of a Written Consent in lieu of a meeting is set forth below:

EXAMPLE

Organization Meeting by Written Consent (Directors Named in Articles of Incorporation)

[NAME OF CORPORATION]

ACTION BY UNANIMOUS CONSENT IN WRITING
OF THE
BOARD OF DIRECTORS

The undersigned, being all of the directors of _____ , a [name of state] corporation (the "Company"), hereby adopt, by this unanimous consent in writing in accordance with Section _____ of the [name of state] Business Corporation Law, the following resolutions with the same force and effect as if they had been unanimously adopted at a duly convened meeting of the board of directors of the Company:

RESOLVED, that the bylaws, a copy of which is attached hereto and incorporated herein by reference, are hereby approved and adopted as the bylaws of this Company;

RESOLVED, that the following persons are elected to the offices of this Company set opposite their respective names, to serve in accordance with the bylaws of this Company and at the discretion of the board:

1. James Allen — President
2. Laura Bond — Vice President
3. Emmet J. Charles — Vice President
4. Raymond Dent, Jr. — Treasurer and Assistant Secretary
5. Joan Edwards — Secretary and Assistant Treasurer

RESOLVED, that the seal impressed on the margin of this page is hereby adopted as the seal of this Company;

RESOLVED, that the form of share certificate for the common stock of this Company attached hereto and incorporated herein by reference is approved and adopted and that share certificates in such form, appropriately filled in, may be signed by the President or any Vice President and the Treasurer or any Assistant Treasurer or the Secretary or any Assistant Secretary of this Company.

RESOLVED, that this Company's fiscal year will end on December 31 of each year;

RESOLVED, that the Treasurer of this Company be and hereby is authorized and empowered to pay and discharge all taxes, fees, and other expenses heretofore incurred or to be incurred in connection with the organization of the Company and to reimburse the officers of this Company and all other persons for all expenditures heretofore made by them in such connection.

RESOLVED, that the Secretary of this Company be and hereby is authorized and empowered to procure the necessary corporate books and records and to open and maintain stock transfer books in accordance with the laws of the State of [name of state] as well as any other applicable laws.

RESOLVED, that the President, any Vice President, the Treasurer or the Secretary of this Company be, and each of them hereby is, authorized and empowered to sign for and on behalf of this Company and in its corporate name all documents necessary to be signed by this Company in the ordinary course of its business; and that the Secretary or any Assistant Secretary of this Company be, and hereby is, authorized and empowered to affix the corporate seal of this Company to any such document when so signed, to sign in attestation of such seal on all documents to which such seal is affixed, and to certify under such seal and issue copies of this or any other resolution adopted by the Board of Directors or stockholders of this Company.

RESOLVED, that the following Plan for offering common stock under § 1244 of the Internal Revenue Code is adopted:

PLAN FOR OFFERING COMMON STOCK

Adopted on [*date*]

The common stock ("Stock"), none of which has yet been issued, of the Company will be offered for sale only in accordance with the following plan, and no other stock of the Company will be offered for sale while this plan is in effect.

1. Stock will be offered for sale commencing [*date*] at such price (payable in cash or property other than stock or securities) not less than the par value per share and not in excess of an aggregate of $500,000 as the board of directors of the Company may from time to time determine.
2. Proceeds of the sale of Stock under this plan will be used by the Company for its general corporate purposes.
3. This plan will terminate on [*date—2 years from adoption*], unless sooner withdrawn by the board of directors, and no Stock will be issued under it after that date.
4. This plan is adopted under Section 1244 of the Internal Revenue Code of 1954, as amended.

RESOLVED, that this Company accepts the offer of Mr. Bryan Good to purchase 250 shares of the common stock of this Company, par value $1 per share, at the price of $100 per share.

RESOLVED, that this Company issue and deliver to Mr. Bryan Good 250 shares of its common stock, par value $1 per share, against receipt of the full consideration for said shares, namely, $25,000; that the proper officers of this Company be and hereby are authorized and empowered to execute a common stock certificate representing said 250 shares of common stock, registered in the name of Mr. Good, to affix thereto the seal of this Company, and to deliver same to Mr. Good against payment therefor; and that said 250 shares of this Company's common stock, when issued to Mr. Good, shall be fully paid and nonassessable common stock of this Company.

RESOLVED, that this Company open a bank account with Northern-Penn National Bank; and that the resolutions attached hereto and incorporated herein by reference relating to such bank account be and hereby are adopted and approved.

_____

[*Name of Director*]

_____
[*Name of Director*]

_____
[*Name of Director*]

Dated: _____

Business Conducted at Organization Meeting

The following points will be covered in resolutions adopted at an organization meeting of the directors who were named in the articles of incorporation. The paralegal will often be assigned the task of preparing them as part of the original organization package.

Approve Articles of Incorporation While it is not essential to do so, the minutes of many organization meetings will reflect the filing of the articles of incorporation, the issuance of a certificate of incorporation from the state agency, the approval of the articles of incorporation, and a statement that the articles and certificate should be filed in the minute book of the corporation as set forth in the following resolution:

> RESOLVED, that the Articles of Incorporation of this Company, having been filed with the Department of State of the State of New Jersey on June 26, 19 __ and a Certificate of Incorporation having been issued by said Department of State, be and hereby are approved, and that the Secretary of this Company be and hereby is instructed to file said Articles of Incorporation and Certificate of Incorporation in the minute book of this Company.

Adopt Bylaws The bylaws of the Company will be adopted and approved in a manner similar to that set forth below:

> RESOLVED, that the bylaws in the form presented to this meeting are approved and adopted as the bylaws of this Company, and are to be filed and maintained in a current status in the minute book of the Company.

Elect Officers Officers of the corporation will be elected as the following example indicates:

> RESOLVED, that the following persons are elected to the offices of this Company set opposite their respective names, to serve in accordance with the bylaws of this Company and at the discretion of the board:

1. James Clark	President
2. Mary Dodd	Vice President
3. Helen Edwards	Vice President
4. John Frank	Treasurer
5. Jessica Good	Secretary

Approve Corporate Seal   A corporate seal for the corporation will be approved:

> RESOLVED, that the seal presented to this meeting, an imprint of which is affixed below, be and is hereby adopted as the seal of this Company.

It might be appropriate to digress for a moment to discuss the function of the corporate seal. The corporate statutes of all states authorize a corporation to have a corporate seal. The example in the MBCA declares:

§ 3.02, MBCA. General Powers

Unless its articles of incorporation provide otherwise, every corporation has perpetual duration and succession in its corporate name and has the same powers as an individual to do all things necessary or convenient to carry out its business and affairs, including without limitation power ...

(2) to have a corporate seal, which may be altered at will, and to use it, or a facsimile of it, by impressing or affixing it or in any other manner reproducing it;

While a corporation may have a seal, most statutes do not require the use of a seal for the validity or effectiveness of any contract or agreement to which the corporation is a party. The following Pennsylvania provision is typical:

§ 1506, Title 15, PBCL.

(a) General Rule. — Any form of execution provided in the articles or by-laws to the contrary notwithstanding, any note, mortgage, evidence of indebtedness, contract or other document, or any assignment or endorsement thereof, executed or entered into between any business corporation and any other person, when signed by one or more officers or agents having actual or apparent authority to sign it, or by the president or vice president and secretary or assistant secretary or treasurer or assistant treasurer of the corporation, shall be held to have been properly executed for and in behalf of the corporation.

(b) Seal unnecessary. — The affixation of the corporate sale shall not be necessary to the valid execution, assignment or endorsement by a corporation of any instrument or other document.

Similarly, the Internal Revenue Service no longer requires corporate seals to be affixed to corporate tax returns and other filings.

Corporate laws may require the use of the corporate seal on share certificates[23] and for certain filings by the corporation with the state. In certain states, the corporate seal may be required on certain documents executed by a corporation; for example, documents required for the proper execution by a corporation of a mortgage or a deed conveying real estate. Such requirements may not be found in the state corporate laws but rather in those state laws relating directly to mortgages, real estate deeds, etc. In addition, institutions such as banks may require a seal on documents even though they are not legally required. Be sure to check with the party on the other side of a transaction as to whether a corporate seal will be necessary.

QUESTIONS

What happens if a statute requires a seal in a particular case and it is not affixed to a document? What happens if the bylaws require a seal but it is not affixed to a document? Is the document binding on the corporation anyway? On the other party?

While corporations are not required to use their corporate seals except in certain limited areas, the use of corporate seals is common, and agreements which are of significance to the corporation may have the corporate seal impressed. In the typical case, the board of directors, in approving the execution of an agreement, will specify in a resolution the following:

> RESOLVED, that the President or any Vice President be and each of them hereby is authorized and directed to execute in the name and on behalf of this Company the XYZ Agreement; and that the Secretary or any Assistant Secretary be and each of them hereby is authorized and directed to affix thereto and attest[24] the corporate seal of this Company.

Note again that the resolutions do two major things: (a) authorize the corporation to do a specific act and (b) designate those persons who may effectuate the act on behalf of the corporation.[25] Since a corporation can only act through designated individuals, resolutions must do both things. Where so authorized, the corporate seal will be affixed to the agreement and the secretary or assistant secretary of the corporation will sign, attesting to the fact that the seal affixed on the agreement is in fact the corporate seal of the corporation.

---

23. For example, § 6.25, MBCA.

24. In the strictest sense, "attesting" means formally acting as a witness to the execution by another officer.

25. Resolutions were discussed earlier in this chapter.

Approve Form of Share Certificate   The form of share certificate may be approved by the following type of resolution:[26]

> RESOLVED, that the form of share certificate for the common stock of this Company presented to this meeting is approved and adopted and that share certificates in such form, appropriately filled in, may be signed by the President or any Vice President and the Treasurer or the Secretary of this Company.

Establish Fiscal Year[27]   The fiscal year (financial accounting year) for keeping the corporation's financial records may be established by resolution:

> RESOLVED, that this Company's fiscal year will end on November 30 of each year.

Note that a corporation may adopt a fiscal year other than the calendar year, e.g., July 1 to June 30, but it must ordinarily start at the beginning of a month and end at the end of a month.

Adopt Bank Resolutions   Since the corporation will need to open and maintain a checking account at a bank for deposits and paying bills, it must adopt resolutions authorizing the bank account and establishing which persons will have authority to sign for the corporation with respect to the account. The form of resolutions to open the account are normally prescribed and supplied by the bank in which the account will be opened and maintained, and corporations typically adopt bank resolutions in the form established by the bank:

> RESOLVED, that this Company open a bank account with First National Bank of Iowa; and that the resolutions presented to this meeting relating to such bank account be and hereby are adopted and approved.

Below is a typical form of resolution required by a bank:

EXAMPLE

*Banking
Resolution*

AUTHORITY FOR CORPORATION TO OPEN A BANK ACCOUNT, BORROW MONEY, GUARANTEE LETTERS OF CREDIT, AND PROVIDE SECURITY
CERTIFIED COPY OF RESOLUTION(S)[28] OF
Fine Art, Inc.

---

26. The statutory requirements for share certificates are discussed in Chapter Two.

27. Chapter Three shows that the bylaws may provide an alternative method of establishing the fiscal year.

28. Note that this form is the certificate of the secretary of the corporation to be presented to the bank stating that the resolution has been adopted. See Problems following this form.

130

AUTHORIZING: (1) OPENING AND KEEPING A BANK ACCOUNT,
(2) THE BORROWING OF MONEY,
(3) GUARANTEE OF LETTERS OF CREDIT, AND
(4) PROVIDING SECURITY.

I, the undersigned Secretary of Fine Art, Inc., a Corporation duly organized and existing under the laws of Iowa, having its place of business at 211 S. Broad St., Des Moines, Iowa, hereby certify that the following is a true copy of certain Resolution(s) duly adopted by the Board of Directors of the Corporation in accordance with the Bylaws at, and recorded in the minutes of, a duly convened meeting of the said Board on July 21, 19 ___ , and not subsequently rescinded or modified:

RESOLVED

1. "That an account of deposit and discount be opened and maintained with First National Bank of Iowa, the said account to be subject to the rules and regulations set forth in the deposit receipt folder furnished by the Bank, as well as to the rules and regulations of the Iowa Clearing House Association, to the regulations and operating letters of the Federal Reserve System and the Federal Reserve Bank of Chicago, to the Uniform Commercial Code (Ia.), and to such amendments to any of the foregoing as may hereafter be made.

    That funds of this Corporation on deposit with the said Bank be subject to withdrawal by checks, notes, drafts, bills of exchange, acceptances, orders and/or other instruments made in the corporate name, when signed by any ____two____ of the following:[29]

    (insert number)

President: _____

Any Vice-President: _____

Secretary: _____

Treasurer: _____

(Type or print title(s) of officer(s) or name(s) of person(s) authorized
to sign; it is suggested that title(s) only be inserted)

and all such checks, notes, drafts, bills of exchange, acceptances, orders and other instruments signed by the Corporation as aforesaid drawn upon said Bank, as drawee or made payable at the Bank, including instruments drawn to cash or bearer or to the individual order of any officer of the Corporation (whether signed by such officer or otherwise), shall be honored and paid by the said Bank and charged to the account of this Corporation, without any obligation upon the Bank to make any inquiry thereabout whatever.

---

29. See Problems following this form.

That any and all checks, drafts, notes, and other orders and items of every kind deposited or to be deposited for the account of this Corporation for credit or for collection or otherwise, requiring endorsement in the name of this Corporation, shall be sufficiently endorsed when they bear the name of the Corporation stamped or in writing endorsed thereon, without any signature or countersignature thereto affixed."

2. "That the officers of this Corporation are hereby authorized from time to time to borrow money and to obtain credit for this Corporation from the said Bank on such terms as may seem to them advisable and to make and deliver notes, drafts, acceptances, assignments, agreements, and/or any other obligations of this Corproation therefor in form satisfactory to the said Bank, any of said obligations to be signed by any ____two____ of the following:
(insert number)

President: _____

Any Vice-President: _____

Secretary: _____

Treasurer: _____

(Type or print title(s) of officer(s) or name(s) of person(s) authorized to sign; it is suggested that title(s) only be inserted)

3. "That the officers of this Corporation are hereby authorized to execute on behalf of this Corporation its guarantee of Letters of Credit issued or to be issued at its request and on its behalf by or through said Bank and also to execute on behalf of this Corporation any and all agreements relating to drafts drawn under such Letters of Credit, said guarantee and agreements to be signed by any ____two____ of the following:
(insert number)

President: _____

Any Vice-President: _____

Secretary: _____

Treasurer: _____

(Type or print title(s) of officer(s) or name(s) of person(s) authorized to sign; it is suggested that title(s) only be inserted)

4. "As security for money borrowed and credit obtained, and as security for said Letters of Credit, the aforesaid officers of this Corporation, and any one or more attorneys-in-fact appointed by them in writing for such purpose, are hereby authorized to pledge, assign, transfer, endorse, and deliver, either originally or in addition or substitution, any stocks, bonds, bills receivable, accounts receivable, contracts, bills of lading, warehouse receipts and commodities covered thereby, trust receipts and commodities and/or chattels covered thereby, mortgages, deeds to real property, policies of life insurance, other choices in action or evidence

132

thereof, and/or any other property of this Corporation; with full authority to the officers of this Corporation having authority to sign or countersign notes, and to any such attorney-in-fact, to endorse and/or assign the same in the name of this Corporation, to execute trust receipts, security agreements, financing statements, and generally to execute any other documents or do any other act that may be necessary or required in connection with the Corporation's account or dealings with the said Bank, including the sale, discount, or rediscount of any and all commercial paper, bills receivable, and other instruments and evidences of debt at any time held by this Corporation, and to that end to endorse, transfer, and deliver the same."[30]

5. That the foregoing resolutions shall continue in full force and effect until written notice of revocation, duly signed by any officer of this Corporation in the name of the Corporation, or a certified copy of a subsequent resolution of the Corporation pertaining to matters herein contained, shall have been received by the said Bank."

I further certify that the foregoing resolutions are fully in accord with and pursuant to the Bylaws of this Corporation.

I further certify that the following persons have been duly elected to the offices of this Corporation set opposite their respective names and now hold said offices respectively:

1. James Hill   President
2. Delores Coburn   Executive Vice President
3. Oliver Sinclair   Financial Vice President
4. T. Baird Silton   Secretary
5. Jennifer Simpson   Treasurer

IN WITNESS WHEREOF I have hereunto set my hand, and affixed the Corporate Seal of this Corporation this 2nd day of August, 19 ___ .

/s/**Jennifer Simpson**
_____
(Manual Signature)   Secretary

[*Corporate Seal*]   /s/ _____
(If the Secretary is authorized to act alone by any of the foregoing resolutions and such Secretary signs this certification, the President must also sign manually)

PROBLEMS

1. [Footnote 28] Why is the certificate of an officer as to adoption of the resolution required? How else would the bank know that the resolution was adopted?

2. [Footnote 29] What if only one officer signs a check on Fine Art's bank account? Can the bank honor it? What if the bank does honor it?

30. This paragraph permits the officers of the corporation to pledge or otherwise provide collateral of the corporation (generally, money or property put up to back up the promise of the corporation to pay) to secure any borrowing from the bank.

Adopt Section 1244 Plan   Section 1244 of the Federal Internal Revenue Code provides special tax treatment to certain shareholders of a corporation that has satisfied all of the requirements of such Section. When such a plan has been adopted, eligible shareholders may treat any loss (up to a specified maximum amount) realized upon the sale of the corporation's stock or when the stock becomes worthless as an "ordinary" loss for federal tax losses, and not a "capital" loss (which a sale of stock would ordinarily be). An ordinary loss may be used to offset other ordinary income of a taxpayer (e.g., wages, interest, income, dividends) for the purposes of computing taxable income while a capital loss may be generally used only to offset capital gains (e.g., sales of other stock) and, to the extent there are more capital losses than capital gains, the excess loss may be offset against ordinary income to the extent of $3,000. The remaining loss can be called forward. For example, if a shareholder of a corporation with a Section 1244 Plan has a salary of $25,000 and a loss in the same year on a sale of his Section 1244 stock of $15,000, the taxable income of such shareholder for federal income tax purposes will be reduced to $10,000 for that year. However, had the loss on the sale of the stock not been 1244 stock the taxable income would have been approximately $22,000 because of the limitations in offset of capital losses against ordinary income.

The corporation might want to adopt a Section 1244 Plan on a timely basis before the issuance of stock. Ordinarily *all* new corporations should establish a Section 1244 Plan as part of their initial minutes even if their shareholders may not qualify for Section 1244 treatment. It costs nothing to adopt the Plan. A form of resolutions adopting such a Plan may be as follows:

RESOLVED, that the following Plan for offering common stock under Section 1244 of the Internal Revenue Code is adopted:

Plan for Offering Common Stock
Adopted on July 1, 19 ___

The common stock ("Stock"), none of which has as yet been issued, of SMITH CORPORATION (the "Company"), will be offered for sale only in accordance with the following plan, and no other stock of the Company will be offered for sale while this plan is in effect.

1. Stock will be offered for sale commencing July 1, 19 ___ at such price (payable in cash or property other than stock or securities) not less than the par value per share and not in excess of an aggregate of $500,000[31] as the board of directors of the Company may from time to time determine.
2. Proceeds of the sale of Stock under this plan will be used by the Company for its general corporate purposes.

31. No more than $500,000 in stock may be issued under a valid Section 1244 Plan.

3. This plan will terminate on June 30, 19 ___ ,[32] unless sooner withdrawn by the board of directors, and no Stock will be issued under it after that date.

4. This plan is adopted under Section 1244 of the Internal Revenue Code of 1954.

This plan need not be filed with the Internal Revenue Service, but it should be filed with the minutes of the corporation.

Authorize Issuance of Stock At the organization meeting, the directors will authorize the issuance of stock to designated persons at a specified price. The board may set any price for issuance of stock.

QUESTIONS

Use the MBCA as a model statute for your answers.
1. Can stock be issued for property? What method should directors use to value property received in exchange for stock?
2. Can stock be issued for services?

Stock should not be issued for less than its "par value," if any.[33] However, the shares may, and often are, issued at greater than par value. The par value may be designated at any amount in the articles of incorporation. The example which follows assumes that there will be only one shareholder of the corporation:

> RESOLVED, that this Company accepts the offer of John Smith ("Smith") to purchase 250 shares of the common stock of this Company, par value $1 per share, at the price of $100 per share.
>
> RESOLVED, that this Company issue and deliver to Smith 250 shares of its common stock, par value $1 per share, against receipt of the full consideration for said shares, namely $25,000; that the proper officers of this Company be and hereby are authorized and empowered to execute a common stock certificate representing said 250 shares of common stock, registered in the name of Smith, to affix thereto the seal of this Company, and to deliver same to Smith against payment therefor; and that said 250 shares of this Company's common stock, when issued to Smith pursuant to this resolution, shall be fully paid and nonassessable[34] common stock of this Company.

General Authorization to Officers The following resolutions provide for ongoing general authorization to certain officers of the

---

32. The stock must be issued within two years after adoption of the Plan.

33. "Par value" is the minimum that may legally be paid in for stock upon issuance. Par value is discussed in Chapter Six of this text.

34. Nonassessable stock is stock which has been issued for not less than par value, if any, and the owner cannot be charged for any further amount. This confers limited liability on the shareholder.

corporation, as well as authorization to pay expenses in connection with the formation of the corporation:

> RESOLVED, that the Treasurer of this Company be and hereby is authorized and empowered to pay and discharge all taxes, fees, and other expenses heretofore incurred or to be incurred in connection with the organization of this Company and to reimburse the officers of this Company and all other persons for all expenditures heretofore made by them in such connection.

> RESOLVED, that the Secretary of this Company be and hereby is authorized and empowered to procure the necessary corporate books and records and to open and maintain stock transfer books in accordance with the laws of the State of Iowa as well as any other applicable laws.

> RESOLVED, that the President, any Vice President, the Treasurer, or the Secretary of this Company be, and each of them hereby is, authorized and empowered to sign for and on behalf of this Company and in its corporate name all documents necessary to be signed by this Company in the ordinary course of its business; and that the Secretary or any Assistant Secretary of this Company be, and hereby is, authorized and empowered to affix the corporate seal of this Company to any such document when so signed, to sign in attestation of such seal on all documents to which such seal is affixed, and to certify under such seal and issue copies of this or any other resolution adopted by the Board of Directors or stockholders of this Company.

Form of Resolutions   It is important to note that when the above resolutions refer to the corporate seal, the form of share certificate, etc., the reference makes it clear that the items are being presented to the meeting. In such an event the attending persons would physically observe such documents and objects. If the same resolutions were adopted by a unanimous written consent, the items should be physically attached to the minutes. Each resolution should then state that the document is "attached hereto and incorporated herein by reference as if set forth herein in full," or, in the case of the seal, "imprinted hereon," and such items should in fact be attached to or imprinted on the written consent. For example, the following would be used for ratifying the form of the share certificates by unanimous consent:

> RESOLVED, that the form of share certificate for the common stock of this Company attached to these minutes and incorporated herein as if set forth herein in full is approved and adopted and that share certificates in such form, appropriately filled in, may be signed by the President or any Vice President and the Treasurer or Secretary of this Company.

PROBLEM   Prepare an approval of the corporate seal in appropriate form for unanimous written consent.

CONDUCT OF MEETINGS

Introduction

While state laws impose many requirements on the shareholders' and directors' meetings and specify certain voting procedures, they contain no guidelines on the actual mechanics of the meeting itself. Corporate laws do not address themselves to such questions as who should preside at a meeting, what should be the order of business, what are the rights of persons to participate in the meeting, etc. In some instances, the bylaws of a corporation will answer some of these questions but very seldom all of them. The mechanics are largely determined by general rules of "parliamentary procedure" and by standards of a "reasonable" method of conducting a meeting.

The following sections provide a discussion of some of the more usual procedures used in conducting shareholders' and directors' meetings.

Chair and Secretary of the Meeting

Someone must preside over a meeting of shareholders and directors and someone must record the business transacted. The function of "presiding" is normally performed, in the absence of any bylaw provision, by the senior officer of the corporation, who is usually the president. The "recording" function is normally performed by the secretary of the corporation.

Some corporations have bylaw provisions indicating which officers of the corporation preside and keep minutes of the meetings. If the corporation has designated a "chairperson of the board," that person will typically, as the title would suggest, serve at least as chair of all directors' meetings and perhaps as chair of all shareholders' meetings. An example of bylaw provisions governing this subject follow:

(a) The Chairperson of the Board, if elected or appointed, shall preside at all meetings of the shareholders and of the Board of Directors and shall have such powers and duties as the Board may prescribe.

(b) The President shall be the chief executive officer of the corporation and shall have general charge and supervision of the business of the corporation and shall exercise or perform all the powers and duties usually incident to the office of President. In the absence of the Chairperson of the Board, the President shall preside at all meetings of the shareholders and of the Board of Directors, shall from time to time make such reports of the affairs of the corporation as the Board may require and shall annually present to the annual meeting of the shareholders a report of the business of the corporation for the preceding fiscal year.

(c) The Secretary shall attend all sessions of the Board and all meetings of the shareholders and act as clerk thereof, and record all the votes and minutes thereof in books to be kept for that purpose; and shall perform like duties for the executive committee of the Board of Directors when required. The Secretary shall give, or cause to be given, notice of all meetings of the shareholders and of the Board of Directors, shall perform such other duties as may be prescribed by the Board or by the President, shall keep in safe custody the corporate seal of the corporation, and may affix the same to any instrument requiring it and attest the same.

Order of Business

Both shareholders' and directors' meetings are held for specific purposes—normally, the approval of corporate action or the election of officers or directors.

PROBLEMS

1. Who elects the directors?
2. Who elects the officers?
3. Who would vote on an amendment to the articles to change the corporate name?

Before such meetings are held, the person who will act as chair of the meeting will usually have an agenda (a list) of the specific matters to be considered at the meeting. In addition, in the case of shareholders' meetings, the agenda may list those procedural requirements which must be satisfied in order for any action to be properly approved (e.g., determination that proper notice has been given, that a quorum exists, etc.). In deciding upon the order, most corporate officers rely upon general rules of "parliamentary procedure." The following is a summary of the events which might occur in a routine meeting:

Shareholders' Meeting

1. Chairperson calls the meeting to order.
2. Chairperson designates secretary of the meeting and Judge of Election, if appropriate.
3. Chairperson determines whether proper notice for the meeting was given.
4. Secretary (or Judge of Election) reports on number of shares entitled to vote at meeting and number of shares

represented at the meeting to determine if a quorum is present.

5. Minutes of last meeting read or a motion is adopted to dispense with reading.

6. Proposal for action presented to the meeting.

7. Discussion of proposal.

8. Voting on proposal.

9. Report of Judge of Election.

10. Adjournment.

Directors' Meeting Directors' meetings are more informal than shareholders' meetings. There are usually fewer persons in attendance and they have more familiarity with each other. Many times, a meeting of directors will review generally the business operations of the corporation and no specific proposal will be acted upon. When a specific proposal is to be acted upon, the following might represent a summary of the meeting:

1. Chairperson calls the meeting to order.

2. Chairperson designates the secretary of the meeting.

3. Minutes of last meeting read or dispensed with by motion.

4. Proposal for action presented to the meeting.

5. Discussion of proposal.

6. Voting on proposal.

7. Adjournment.

Bylaw Provision If a corporation deemed it desirable to do so, it might include a provision in the bylaws covering the order of business at a shareholders' meeting. A sample of such a bylaw provision follows:

The following order of business shall be observed at all meetings of stockholders, unless otherwise determined by the holders of a majority of the outstanding stock entitled to vote, present in person or represented by proxy; or unless the Chairperson of the meeting determines that this order is impracticable or inconsistent with the purposes of the meeting, in which event the Chairperson may make appropriate changes in this order of business, which changes shall be announced by the Chairperson upon the determination of a quorum:

1. Call meeting to order.

2. Appoint temporary secretary, if necessary.

3. Appoint Judges of Election, if necessary.

4. Present proof of notice of the meeting.

5. Present list of stockholders.

6. Determine that a quorum is present.

7. Read minutes of last previous meeting.

8. Reports of officers and committees.

9. Elect directors, if the meeting is an annual meeting or a meeting called for that purpose.

10. All other business that must be considered.

11. Adjourn.

Script of Meeting

Prior sections in this chapter have given a bare outline of the events at a shareholders' or directors' meeting. A more complete picture may be obtained by reading a sample "script" of a shareholders' meeting, set forth below.

EXAMPLE

Script of Shareholders' Meeting

XYZ CORPORATION

ANNUAL MEETING OF SHAREHOLDERS
JULY 31, 19___

North Trust Bank Building
Southwest Corner of Ninth Street
and South Henry Square
Sacramento, California

Mr. Anderson (President and Chairperson): This annual meeting of the shareholders of XYZ Corporation is now called to order.

On behalf of your board of directors and officers, I wish to express my sincere thanks to the shareholders who mailed their proxies, as well as to those of you who are here today, for their interest in the affairs of the Company.

I shall now ask Ms. Brown, the Secretary of the Company, to report whether the requirements for the holding of this meeting have been fulfilled.

Ms. Brown (Secretary): In compliance with the provisions of the bylaws of the Company, the board of directors of the Company by resolutions adopted on June 25, 19___, called this annual meeting of shareholders and established July 1, 19___, as the record date for the determination of shareholders entitled to notice of and to vote at this meeting.

At least 10 days prior to the date fixed for the holding of this meeting, there was mailed to all shareholders of record on July 1, 19___, a notice of meeting, a proxy statement, and a proxy.[35] My affidavit indicating that such mailing occurred has been filed with the Company.

---

35. A proxy is a piece of paper designating another person to vote in the absence of the first from the meeting (discussed earlier in this chapter). This is in contrast to a "proxy statement" which is a document that public companies mail to their shareholders which describes the actions to be taken at the meeting, in attempt to solicit their proxy to vote.

An alphabetical list of the shareholders of the Company, showing the name, address, and number of shares held by each shareholder as of the record date is now on file at this meeting for reference and has been available for inspection at the principal office of the Company for at least the last ten days.[36]

Of the 1,000,000 shares of Common Stock of the Company which were outstanding on the record date for this meeting, there are proxies on file with the Company representing 800,000 shares of such stock, or 80% of the total number of shares outstanding. This constitutes a quorum for the transaction of business.[37]

Mr. Anderson: Thank you Ms. Brown. Since requirements for calling this meeting have been duly observed and there is represented here considerably more than the necessary number of shares of the outstanding stock of the Company to constitute a quorum, I hereby declare this meeting to be duly constituted for the transaction of all business. Are there any additional proxies to be submitted to the Secretary of the Company at this time? (Pause)

I hereby designate Mr. Charles of the North Trust Bank to act as judge of election for this meeting. Mr. Charles has already signed an Oath of Judge of Election and presented it to the Secretary of the meeting. The Secretary is instructed to file it with the minutes of this meeting.

As I am sure you recognized from the proxy material which was sent to each shareholder of the Company, there are a number of things to be considered by the shareholders of the Company at this meeting, and I propose that we now take up the matters listed in the proxy statement in the order in which they are listed. In order to expedite matters, we will defer discussion and voting on any of the proposals until all of the proposals have been presented. After the proposals have been presented, I will endeavor to answer all questions which you might have.

The first matter set forth in the proxy material is the election of five directors to serve until the next annual meeting of shareholders and until their respective successors shall be elected and have qualified. I would like now to introduce to you the management nominees for directors of the Company, who are all present today: Ms. Kay, Mr. Mark, Mr. Nocks, Mr. Brown, and me. Are there any other nominations for the board of directors?

Shareholder in Audience: I move that the nominations for directors be closed.

Second Shareholder in audience: I second the motion.

Mr. Anderson: Will all those in favor of the motion to close the nominations for directors please so indicate. Will all those opposed please so indicate. The motion is carried, and nominations for directors of the Company are closed.

---

36. For the reason for this procedure, see the discussion on "Maintenance of Shareholders List" earlier in this chapter.
37. How does Ms. Brown know that 80% is enough for a quorum?

As I indicated, we are postponing the voting on this and other matters until all management proposals are before this meeting.

The second proposal before us is the amendment of Article III of the Articles of Incorporation of the Company in order to modernize the Articles to conform to current corporate practice of giving to the Company the greatest authority permitted under state law to engage in all forms of lawful business activities.

The following resolutions are hereby offered to amend Article III of the Articles of Incorporation of the Company and have been recommended by the Board of Directors for adoption by the shareholders:

RESOLVED, that Article III of the Articles of Incorporation of the Company shall be restated in its entirety to read as follows:
"The Company shall have unlimited power to engage in and to do any lawful act concerning any or all lawful business, including manufacturing, processing, research, and development, for which corporations may be incorporated under the Act under the provisions of which the Company was incorporated.[38]

RESOLVED, that the proper officers of this Company be and each of them hereby is authorized and empowered to take all such action as any one of them may deem necessary or desirable to effect said amendment of the Articles of Incorporation of the Company.

The next proposal to be submitted to this meeting is the proposal to amend the Articles of Incorporation and bylaws of the Company to eliminate cumulative voting in the election of directors.[39] At present, directors of the Company are elected by cumulative voting and today's election of directors will be so conducted. Under cumulative voting, each shareholder has that number of votes in the election of directors equal to the number of shares owned by him multiplied by the number of directors to be elected. Each shareholder is entitled to cast the whole number of such votes for one candidate or to distribute them among any two or more candidates. The candidates receiving the highest number of votes are elected. Upon the elimination of cumulative voting, shareholders of the Company will only be entitled to one vote per share in the election of directors and it will therefore require the vote of a majority of the outstanding shares represented at annual meetings of shareholders to elect a person to the board of directors.

The following resolutions are offered to effect the elimination of cumulative voting.

RESOLVED, that paragraph B of Section 5 of Article Fifth of the Articles of Incorporation of this Company shall be restated in its entirety to read as follows:
"B. Such voting rights of the Common Stock shall be noncumulative on all matters submitted to the shareholders, including the election of directors."

RESOLVED, that Section 3–09 of the bylaws of the Company shall be amended and restated in their entirety to read as follows:

---

38. As the reader can tell from comparing this form to the form in Chapter Two, there is no magic in the exact style of the purpose clause.

39. See Chapter Two for a discussion of cumulative voting and its consequences.

"Election of Directors. Noncumulative Voting. Elections for directors need not be by ballot except by written demand by shareholders at the meeting and before the voting begins. In all elections for directors, each shareholder entitled to vote shall have the right by person or by proxy to one vote for each share standing in the name of the shareholder on the record date."

RESOLVED, that the proper officers of this Company be and each of them hereby is authorized and empowered to take such action as any one of them may deem necessary or desirable to effect the foregoing amendments to the Articles of Incorporation and bylaws of this Company.

The final management proposal to be considered at this meeting is the ratification of the recommendation of the Board to appoint Jones & Co. as auditors for the Company. Jones & Co. has been acting as auditors for the Company since May 1, 19__, is familiar with the affairs of the Company, and has been of great assistance to us in our period of growth. The following resolution is offered in connection with the approval of the appointment of Jones & Co. as auditors of the Company:

RESOLVED, that the appointment of Jones & Co., independent certified accountants, as auditors for the Company in connection with the fiscal year of the Company beginning May 1, 19__, and ending April 30, 19__, be and hereby is approved.

Shareholder in audience: I move that Messrs. Anderson, Mark and Nocks and Ms. Brown and Kay be elected directors of the Company and that all of the resolutions just presented to this meeting by Mr. Anderson be adopted.

Second Shareholder in audience: I second the motion.

Mr. Anderson: I will now attempt to answer any questions which are asked by shareholders at our meeting today. (Entertain questions)

If there are no further questions, I suggest that we proceed to a vote on these matters. As I indicated to you, the election of directors shall be by cumulative voting.[40] The proposals for Amendment of the Articles of Incorporation require the affirmative vote of the holders of a majority of the outstanding stock to be approved.[41] The proposal for the approval of Jones & Co. as the Company's auditors requires only the affirmative vote of the holders of a majority of the shares present in person or proxy at this meeting to be approved.[42] The voting shall be by ballot, and separate votes may be cast on each proposal before this meeting. Ballots are available and anyone so wishing to vote by ballot should now so indicate so that he or she may receive a ballot. All persons voting by ballot should deliver their ballots to our Judge of Election.

40. Would it have been possible to vote on the amendments to the Articles *before* the election of directors and, if the amendments passed, elect directors by noncumulative voting?

41. Note that the correct way of expressing the vote required is *not* the "affirmative vote of a majority of the outstanding stock" but rather "the affirmative vote of *holders* of a majority of the outstanding stock."

42. How does the required number of votes for approval of Jones and Co. differ from that required for the Amendment to the Articles of Incorporation?

Are there any persons who wish to vote and who have not had an opportunity to do so?

If there are no persons who have not yet voted, I hereby declare the polls closed and request the Judge of Election to determine the votes cast and to submit his report.

While waiting for the results of the voting, I would like to take this opportunity to discuss the results of the Company's operations for the last year (brief report of results). I now have the report of the Judge of Elections covering all of the proposals presented to this meeting, and I would like to summarize it for you.

I am happy to announce that the holders of 790,000 shares voted for the election of each of Messrs. Anderson, Mark and Nocks, and Ms. Brown and Kay as directors of the Company. Since more than a majority of the shares were voted in favor of the election of each nominee, I am happy to announce that these persons will continue to serve your Company as directors for the ensuing year.

The second proposal, which concerned the revision of the purpose clause of the Articles of Incorporation of the Company, was approved by a vote of the holders of 795,000 shares in favor of such amendment and 5,000 shares against such amendment.

The shareholders of the Company have also approved the proposal which provided for the elimination of cumulative voting in the election of directors by a vote of the holders of 790,000 shares for the proposal and 10,000 shares against the proposal.

Finally, the shareholders of the Company have approved the appointment of Jones & Co. as auditors of the Company, by a vote of the holders of 800,000 shares for the proposal and no shares against the proposal.

Since shares constituting more than 79% of the outstanding stock of the Company were voted in favor of all the matters presented to this meeting, I therefore declare that all of the resolutions presented to this meeting have been duly approved by the shareholders of this Company. The report of the Judge of Elections will be filed in the Company's minute book by the Secretary of the meeting.

If there is no other business, I would entertain a motion that this meeting be adjourned.

Shareholder in audience: I move that this meeting be adjourned.

Second Shareholder in audience: I second such motion.

Mr. Anderson: All in favor so indicate. All opposed please so indicate. Ladies and Gentlemen, thank you for your cooperation at this meeting, and I declare this meeting to be adjourned.

Normally scripts are prepared *prior* to meetings to be used when there are a large number of shareholders expected to be present. Lawyers or paralegals will prepare the script for use at the meeting, and the chairperson of the meeting will not depart from it to any degree. The script provides for certain persons to make and second motions and helps insure a smooth flow of business at the meeting. Participating persons are invariably asked in advance to perform these functions, and they, too, will have a copy of the "script." Note that the script is very different from the minutes of the meeting, which is a summarized record of events occurring at the meeting.

MINUTES

The record of events that occur at meetings of shareholders and directors are maintained in the form of minutes. State laws generally require such records as set forth in the following MBCA example.

§ 16.01, MBCA. Corporate Records.

(a) A corporation shall keep as permanent records minutes of all meetings of its shareholders and board of directors, a record of all actions taken by the shareholders or board of directors without a meeting, and a record of all actions taken by a committee of the board of directors in place of the board of directors on behalf of the corporation. ...

(d) A corporation shall maintain its records in written form or in another form capable of conversion into written form within a reasonable time.

Corporate minutes are usually written by lawyers and paralegals. The language used follows a characteristic form but will vary somewhat from lawyer to lawyer. Unlike the script of the meeting, informal activities are not placed in the minutes. However, informal discussion of corporate matters should be reported. Examples of minutes of shareholders' and directors' meetings are included below:

EXAMPLE

Minutes of Directors' Meeting

FUN CITY MARKETING, INC.

SPECIAL MEETING OF THE BOARD OF DIRECTORS
MAY 26, 19___

A special meeting of the Board of Directors of Fun City Marketing, Inc. was held at the offices of the corporation, located at 1700 Market Street, Philadelphia, Pennsylvania, on May 26, 19___, at 10:00 _____A.M.
The following directors were present:

Joan Smith   William Jones
James Green   George Gray
            Richard Thomas

being all of the directors of the said corporation.
Joan Smith, the Chairperson of the meeting, announced that a quorum of the directors was present and that the meeting was ready to proceed with its business.

James Green, acting as Secretary of the meeting, presented a Waiver of Notice[43] to the meeting that had been signed by all directors. The Chairperson directed that a copy of the signed waiver of notice be affixed to the minutes of this meeting.

Upon motion duly made, seconded, and unanimously passed, the reading of the minutes of the last meeting of the board was waived and the minutes were deemed approved.

There were no reports of officers or committees scheduled to be given at the meeting. Instead, the Chairperson informed the directors that Roger Kent, the President of the Company, had resigned as of May 15, 19___. The Chairperson then suggested that the board consider nominations for the office of President of the corporation. After discussion, the name of James Green was placed in nomination. No other names being proposed, the Chairperson declared that nominations be closed and a ballot taken. The Chairperson announced the result of the balloting to be four votes in favor of Mr. Green's election and none opposed, Mr. Green not having voted. Mr. Green thereupon accepted the office to which he was elected.

The Secretary announced that there was no unfinished business pending. The Chairperson asked if there was any new business to be brought before the board. As there was no new business, and no further business to be conducted, the meeting was, on motion duly made, seconded, and unanimously carried, adjourned.

/s/James Green[44]
Secretary of the Meeting

Attest:
/s/Joan Smith[45]
Chairperson

FUN CITY MARKETING, INC.

ANNUAL MEETING OF SHAREHOLDERS
MAY 26, 19___

Time and Place[46]
The annual meeting of the shareholders of Fun City Marketing, Inc. was held at its principal office at 1700 Market Street, Philadelphia, Pennsylvania, on May 26, 19___, at 10:00 A.M., pursuant to notice given by the Secretary.

---

43. Discussed earlier in this chapter.

44. Often the only person to sign the minutes will be the Secretary without a cosigner.

45. The "/s/" that you often see is the method of conforming a document to an executed (signed) document to indicate that, while it is not a manually signed document, it is a true and correct copy of the executed document.

46. The centered headings are for the convenience of the student only and do not constitute a part of the minutes.

Chairperson and Secretary

Pursuant to the bylaws, Ms. Joan Smith, Chairperson of the Board of Directors of the Corporation, presided over the meeting and Mr. James Green, Secretary of the Corporation, acted as Secretary of the meeting.

Shareholders List

The Chairperson announced that the transfer books and the stock books of the Corporation, together with a full, true, and complete list in alphabetical order of all the shareholders entitled to vote at the ensuing election, with the residence of each, and the number of shares held by each (which list has been on file at the office of the Corporation continuously since May 15, 19__ ,[47] were before the meeting and would remain open for inspection during elections.

Quorum

Upon the Chairperson's request, the Secretary reported that, of the 225,000 shares of the Corporation's common stock entitled to vote at the meeting, the holders of 150,000 shares were present in person and the holders of 50,000 shares were represented by valid proxies.

Thereupon the Chairperson announced that holders of stock in excess of the amount necessary to constitute a quorum were present in person or represented by proxy.

The proxies presented were ordered to be filed with the Secretary of the meeting.

Notice of Meeting

The Secretary presented an affidavit, duly certified by himself as Secretary of the Corporation, to the effect that notice of the meeting had been mailed to each shareholder entitled to such notice, addressed to such shareholder at his address set forth on the shareholder ledger, postage prepaid, as required by the bylaws of the Corporation. The affidavit was approved and ordered attached to the minutes of this meeting.

Upon motion duly made and seconded, Messrs. Able, Baker, and Charley (none of whom were candidates for the office of director)[48] were duly appointed Judges of Election pursuant to the bylaws, and their oaths as such Judges, duly subscribed by them, were handed to the Secretary.

Minutes of Prior Meeting

The Secretary then presented the minutes of the most recent meeting of stockholders which had been held on May 15, 19__. The minutes were read and approved.[49]

Thereupon the Chairperson presented to the meeting the following papers and documents, all of which were laid upon the table and were publicly declared by the Chairperson to be open for inspection by any shareholder:

---

47. Why is this necessary? See "Maintenance of Shareholders List" discussed early in this chapter.

48. Can a candidate for director be a judge of election?

49. Often the chairperson will entertain a motion to dispense with the reading of minutes to expedite the meeting.

1. The minutes of the Board of Directors, covering all purchases, contracts, contributions, compensations, acts, proceedings, elections, and appointments by the Board of Directors, since the annual meeting held on May 15, 19___.
2. The 19___ annual report, a copy of which had been mailed to every shareholder of record as of the record date.

Ratification of Past Actions

Upon motion duly made and seconded, the following resolution was unanimously adopted:

RESOLVED, that all purchases, contracts, contributions, compensations, acts, proceedings, elections, and appointments by the Board of Directors since the Annual Meeting of Shareholders of the corporation on May 15, 19___ , and all matters referred to in the Annual Report to Shareholders for the fiscal year ended March 31, 19___ , are hereby approved, ratified, confirmed, and adopted.[50]

Election of Directors

The meeting then proceeded to the election of five directors constituting the entire board of directors, to hold office until the next annual meeting of shareholders and until their successors shall be elected and shall qualify.

The Chairperson reported that the following named individuals had been nominated by management in accordance with the bylaws:

Joan Smith	William Jones
James Green	George Gray
Richard Thomas	

There were no other nominations.

Upon motion duly made, seconded, and unanimously carried, the nominations were closed.

Mr. John Doe then asked that a ballot be taken upon the foregoing nominations, and on motion duly seconded, it was so ordered.[51]

The Chairperson, before declaring the polls open, asked if there were any other nominations. Hearing none, she thereupon declared the polls open at 10:45 o'clock A.M., and stated that they would remain open for fifteen minutes for the receipt of ballots upon the nominations made.

At 11:00 o'clock A.M., the Chairperson stated that the polls had now been open for fifteen minutes, and she inquired whether there were any shareholders who had not voted and who desired to vote. As no one requested further opportunity to vote, the polls were then declared closed.

The Judges of Election thereupon inspected the proxies, counted the ballots, and submitted their report. Upon motion duly made and seconded, the report of the Judges of Election was unanimously approved, and the Secretary was directed to file the original report.

---

50. Does this resolution exonerate directors and officers from any future challenges for wrongdoing in the prior year by a complaining shareholder? If the shareholder had personally voted for the resolution?

51. Often a ballot will not be required by the bylaws or will be dispensed with on motion.

The Chairperson thereupon declared that Ms. Smith and Messrs. Green, Thomas, Gray, and Jones had been duly elected directors of the Corporation, to serve until the next annual meeting, and until their successors shall be elected and shall qualify.

Documents To Be Attached To Meeting Minutes
The Secretary was directed by the Chairperson to insert copies of the following in the Corporation's minute book:

1. Notice of meeting and the affidavit stating that the notice had been deposited in the mail
2. Form of proxy
3. Certificate of the Secretary as to the regularity of the powers of attorney and the number of shares represented by proxies
4. Judges' oath and report

Adjournment
No other business coming before the meeting, it was, on motion duly made and seconded, adjourned.

/s/James Green
Secretary of the Meeting

Attest:
/s/Joan Smith
Chairperson

MINUTE BOOKS

Minutes of shareholders' and directors' meetings and written consents of shareholders and directors are normally kept in a minute book. Because the minute book serves as a record of the "legal" history of the corporation and the actions taken by the directors and shareholders, it is typical to include the following in a minute book:

1. Certificate of Incorporation and Articles of Incorporation
2. All Certificates of Amendment and Articles of Amendment
3. Bylaws and all bylaw amendments
4. Fictitious name filings
5. Certificate of authority to do business in a foreign state
6. Certificates of Merger and Articles of Merger
7. Duplicate originals of any other filings with the state required by corporate law (such as Annual Reports in some states, i.e., New Jersey)

8. Proof of all publications required by state corporate law

9. All minutes of shareholders' and directors' meetings, all written consents and all notices and waiver of notices of meetings

As in the case of certain matters acted upon at the organization meeting, there are many instances when the board of directors will approve an agreement or instrument "in the form presented to this meeting." When this occurs, it is important to include within the minute book a copy of the document, such as a lease or purchase agreement, for example, actually presented to the meeting. In some cases, only a draft of the document will be available for approval at the meeting. In such a case, that draft should be attached. The document should also be marked to indicate the meeting at which it was presented. Otherwise, a person reading the minute book will be unable to determine what document was approved, an unfortunate situation which could create a question as to whether the execution of a specific form of agreement was in fact authorized by the board of directors.

CHAPTER SIX

Corporate Equity and Debt Securities

Chapter Six is intended to introduce the vocabulary and principal characteristics of debt and equity securities. With such background knowledge, a lawyer's assistant will be better able to perform a variety of tasks, including preparing minutes, reviewing articles of incorporation, arranging for transfers of stock with transfer agents and registrars, obtaining information from loan agreements, assisting in the registration of securities for public sale, and in preparing closing agenda and binders. In drafting minutes or forming a new corporation, the student is expected to master all aspects of the course materials and develop substantial competence in performing tasks. However, the student is not expected to develop the expertise to create all of the terms of complicated debt or equity securities.

This chapter provides a comprehensive description of the principal types of securities a corporation may issue. Corporate securities fall into two categories: (a) a security which evidences a person's ownership interest in a corporation and (b) a security which evidences the corporation's/debtor's obligation to pay money to another person. The former type is called an "equity" security and the latter is referred to as a "debt" security. Each of these types of securities will be discussed in detail.

EQUITY SECURITIES

Class and Series

State corporate laws permit the creation of various types of equity securities. The basic unit of equity securities is called a share, which is defined under the MBCA to mean "the units into which the proprietary interests in a corporation are divided.[1] Statutes do not limit a corporation to issuing one type of share. Some states differentiate by "classes" and others subdivide classes into a further category of "series." Other states do not make a clear distinction of this nature. The statute of the state of incorporation of the company in question must be reviewed for the permitted characterization of shares.

1. § 1.40 (21), MBCA.

For example, § 6.01 of the MBCA permits a corporation to divide its shares into one or more classes.

In addition, § 6.02 of the MBCA permits certain classes of stock to be further divided into "series" which may vary from other series of the same class only in certain characteristics, and in all other respects must be identical to other series in the same class.

Corporations are creatures of state statute, and the state laws governing this area vary from state to state. Some statutes may not be as rigid in limiting the characteristics of shares as to which different series of a specific class may differ from each other. Still other corporate statutes may not even contemplate a series subdivision of classes.

Certificates

Equity securities are usually, but not always, tangibly represented by "certificates." Certificates are pieces of paper *evidencing* shares; they are not the shares of the corporation itself which cannot tangibly be separated out of the mass of corporate assets. Remember that a share is an undivided interest in the corporation; a certificate is merely the physical evidence of a share. Section 6.25 of the MBCA has language similar to other state statutes describing some of the features of a certificate.

QUESTIONS

What does § 6.25 of the MBCA do to prevent the officers from being required to execute all certificates manually? What alternative does the corporation have to listing all rights of all classes on the certificate?

It should be noted that the statutory language would differ in a state where there was no specific designation of series as part of a class and that merely viewed *any* difference in characteristics of shares as a separate class or category. For most purposes, the difference is one of semantics.

If state law (such as the MBCA example) permits, most corporations that have more than one class of stock authorized do not set forth on their certificates a full statement of the relative rights and preferences of all authorized classes of stock, the variations between series of each class of stock, and the authority of the board of directors to fix and determine the relative rights and preferences of additional series of stock. This is because of both the considerable expense of printing certificates with all of the terms spelled out in full and the need to reprint certificates of any change in preferred stock terms occurs. Instead, the following

EXAMPLE   *A Sample of a Certificate (front and back)*

PHOTO WORLD LTD.

INCORPORATED UNDER THE LAWS OF THE COMMONWEALTH OF PENNSYLVANIA

Authorized Shares 1,000   Par Value $1 Per Share

This Certifies that _____ is the owner
(SEE REVERSE FOR CERTAIN DEFINITIONS)

of _____ Shares of

PHOTO WORLD LTD.

full paid and non-assessable, transferable only on the books of the Corporation in person or by Attorney upon surrender of this Certificate properly endorsed.

In Witness Whereof, the said Corporation has caused this Certificate to be signed by its duly authorized officers, and its Corporate Seal to be hereunto affixed this _____ day of _____ A.D. 19____

M BURR KEIM PHILA.   SECRETARY   PRESIDENT

[B6694]

The following abbreviations, when used in the inscription on the face of this certificate, shall be construed as though they were written out in full according to applicable laws or regulations:

TEN COM — as tenants in common
TEN ENT — as tenants by the entireties
JT TEN — as joint tenants with right of survivorship and not as tenants in common

UNIF GIFT MIN ACT — _____ Custodian _____ under
(Cust)   (Minor)
Uniform Gifts to Minors Act _____
(State)

Additional abbreviations may also be used though not in the above list.

For Value Received, _____ hereby sell, assign and transfer unto

PLEASE INSERT SOCIAL SECURITY OR OTHER
IDENTIFYING NUMBER OF ASSIGNEE

Shares represented by the within Certificate, and do hereby irrevocably constitute and appoint _____ Attorney
to transfer the said Shares on the books of the within named Corporation with full power of substitution in the premises.
Dated _____ 19____

In presence of

NOTICE: THE SIGNATURE OF THIS ASSIGNMENT MUST CORRESPOND WITH THE NAME AS WRITTEN UPON THE FACE OF THE CERTIFICATE, IN EVERY PARTICULAR, WITHOUT ALTERATION OR ENLARGEMENT, OR ANY CHANGE WHATEVER.

[B6695]

is an example of the statement which will normally appear on all certificates representing all classes of stock of the corporation where state law permits:

> The Corporation shall furnish to any shareholder of the corporation, upon request and without charge, a full statement of (a) the designations, preferences, limitations, and relative rights of the Common Stock and Preferred Stock that the Corporation is authorized to issue, (b) the variations in the relative rights and preferences between series of the Preferred Stock as the same have been fixed and determined, and (c) the authority of the board of directors to fix and determine the relative rights and preferences of subsequent series of Preferred Stock.

Observe that the specific language of the foregoing statement would be used where appropriate; that is, where there were two classes authorized—Common Stock and Preferred Stock—and where the board of directors was permitted by its articles of incorporation to divide the Preferred Stock into series and to determine the relative rights and preferences of each series. As is always the case, the paralegal must review the state statute and the articles and bylaws of the specific corporation to determine the appropriate language to use in a specific case. Forms are only general guides and examples. The mere existence of a provision in a form never excuses one from truly understanding that provision. Be sure to make forms fit the case at hand; don't try to make the case at hand fit forms.

PROBLEM

Using the general form of statement set forth above, draft language for a corporation which has Class A Common Stock, Class B Common Stock, and Preferred Stock where the board of directors has no authority to authorize series of Preferred Stock.

Par Value and No Par Value Stock

Shares of stock are often described as either par value stock or no par value stock. Whether par value or no par value is used by a corporation in a specific case depends on a variety of factors including, for example, what the state law permits and how state taxes are imposed differently on the two types. One of the more important factors is the predilection of the lawyer for whom the paralegal is creating the corporation. There is no set procedure about whether par value or no value is used. Some states, like Pennsylvania, have even done away with concepts of par value, stated capital, capital surplus, and treasury stock.[2]

If the stock is to be par value stock, it is important to note the amount per share of the par value. The par value[3] of shares places a bottom limit on the consideration which a corporation must receive for each share stock. For this reason, the par value should be nominal, e.g., $10 or $1.00, to insure that sufficient consideration will be paid for the shares.

Corporate Distributions As will be discussed later in this chapter, the law restricts the amount of assets which a corporation may distribute to its shareholders. One of the significant limitations is that, under many state statutes, a corporation cannot pay a dividend out of the par value it has received for the sale of its stock. The idea is to protect creditors of the corporation from unwarranted and excessive distributions to shareholders with the possibility of stripping the corporation of assets needed to pay debts.

What Shares May Be Sold?

In order for a corporation to issue any shares of stock, the shares must be "authorized." Section 6.01 of the MBCA provides that a corporation has the authority to issue the number of shares stated in its articles of incorporation. As you saw in Chapter Two, the articles of incorporation always specify the number of shares which the corporation may issue.

When shares have been issued, (that is, sold by proper corporate action to a shareholder and the required consideration received by the corporation) and are held by someone *other* than the corporation (and, therefore, outstanding), these shares are referred to as being "issued" and "outstanding." The reason for this dual description is that a corporation may, subsequent to the issuance of shares, reacquire these same shares. (see § 6.31, MBCA). In that case, when the shares are held by the corporation itself, they are sometimes termed "treasury shares" and are deemed to be "issued" but *not* "outstanding." A corporation may resell treasury shares and, when sold, such shares will once again become outstanding. Treasury shares are not voted and do not share in dividends or other corporate distributions, due to the fact that they are not outstanding.

---

2. § 1524 (c) and § 1551, Title 15, PBCL.

3. Par value is a legal term for the minimum amount that may legally be paid for shares of stock with par value. It is not the "intrinsic" value, "market" value, or any other value of the shares. It is simply the legal minimum that must be paid for shares to be validly issued. "No par value" stock has no legal minimum which must be paid for the shares except that amount determined by the board of directors. There is no magic about the amount of par value. Ordinarily where shares have par value, it is one cent, ten cents, or one dollar; that is, a small amount. Why?

QUESTIONS Are treasury shares treated as an asset? If treasury shares are cancelled, are a corporation's net assets changed?

The distinction between "authorized" but "unissued" shares, on the one hand, and "treasury shares" on the other, is relevant because a corporation may not issue "authorized" and "unissued" shares for a consideration which is less than the par value. In the absence of par value, the directors determine whether the consideration which has been paid for shares is adequate.[4]

Concept of "Fully Paid and Nonassessable"

Corporate statutes normally define the phrase fully paid and nonassessable in a manner similar to this MBCA definition:

§ 6.21 (d), MBCA.

When the corporation receives the consideration for which the board of directors authorized the issuance of shares, the shares issued therefor are fully paid and nonassessable.

Most corporate laws impose certain liabilities upon shareholders unless the shares which have been issued to them are fully paid and nonassessable. (For examples, see § 6.22, MBCA and § 1526, Pennsylvania Business Corporation Law.) These liabilities may include assessment for unpaid amounts on subscription agreements against the holder of the stock.[5] Stock certificates represent that the shares which they evidence are fully paid and nonassessable. It is unclear whether a good faith purchaser for value[6] of such shares would be liable if such shares were not really fully paid and nonassessable.

Since limited liability for shareholders is one of the purposes of incorporation,[7] it is important for the lawyer and paralegal to know what is required in order to achieve limited liability.

---

4. The reason is that even though the treasury shares are not outstanding, they have been issued; therefore, par value was paid for them when they were first issued. Accordingly, they may be resold for less than par inasmuch as par has already been paid in for such shares. Can treasury shares with a par value of $1.00 be sold by a corporation for $.50 a share? Can authorized but unissued shares with a par value of $1.00 be sold for $.50? Also see § 6.21, MBCA.

5. See Chapter Two for an example of subscription agreements.

6. A "good faith purchaser for value" is a person that may be protected by the law in certain circumstances where such person might otherwise be liable. Generally "good faith" means that the person brought the stock (or other asset) without any knowledge or reason to know of any problems with respect to the title to the stock, e.g., that it is not fully paid and nonassessable or subject to other offsets. This concept of protecting an innocent purchaser has application in other areas of law, such as title to real estate.

7. See discussion in Chapter One.

An analysis of these statutes indicates that a fourstop factual review is necessary to determine when shares are fully paid and nonassessable.

1. **What Was the Consideration for the Shares?**
   Since the board of directors establishes the consideration (the value received for the shares) to be paid for shares, the first step is to determine what consideration was fixed by the board of directors for shares which have been issued. Normally this is done by an examination of the minutes of directors' meetings.[8]

2. **Was the Consideration Legally Adequate?**
   For the purpose of deciding whether the shares are fully paid and nonassessable, it is irrelevant that the directors might have sold the shares for more. The legally relevant question is whether the amount of consideration for shares (other than treasury shares) is less than the required minimum per share.[9] The articles of incorporation must be reviewed to determine the required consideration. (For example, see § 6.21, MBCA.)

3. **Was the Consideration Received?**
   A review must be made to see if the consideration specified by the board of directors has been paid for the shares. Normally this involves examining the books and records of the corporation to find out what has in fact been received by the corporation.

QUESTIONS

What books and records would disclose this fact? Would the minute book or stock book disclose this? How about financial records?

4. **What Type of Consideration Was Received?**
   State law also establishes the type of consideration which is acceptable for the issuance of shares, such as the following MBCA requirements:

§ 6.21 (b), MBCA.

The board of directors may authorize shares to be issued for consideration consisting of any tangible or intangible property or benefit to the corporation, including cash, promissory notes, services performed, contracts for services to be performed, or other securities of the corporation.

8. See discussion of minutes in Chapter Five.
9. See footnote 3 for a definition of "par value."

§ 6.21 (e), MBCA.

The corporation may place in escrow shares issued for a contract for future services or benefits or a promissory note, or make other arrangements to restrict the transfer of the shares, and may credit distributions in respect of the shares against their purchase price, until the services are performed, the note is paid, or the benefits received. If the services are not performed, the note is not paid, or the benefits are not received, the shares escrowed or restricted and the distributions credited may be cancelled in whole or part.

QUESTIONS Under the MBCA, could shares of stock be issued for a patent? For a promissory note of the prospective shareholder?

If the board of directors authorized the issuance of shares for a legally unacceptable type of consideration, even if the consideration were paid to the corporation, the shares might not be deemed fully paid and nonassessable. It should be noted that most courts have interpreted a prohibition against promissory notes to mean only the promissory note issued by the person buying the shares. If the person buying the shares gives the corporation a promissory note made by another, it is deemed to be payment, because such a note is "property" (an asset) of the person buying the shares.

Common Stock

In passing, Chapter Two mentioned the existence of several types of stock. Common stock is the most usual type of equity security. Common stock may be defined as that class of stock which is created when the articles of incorporation provide for a class of stock without any special features. In such case, state corporate law will describe the characteristics of common stock. Relevant sections of the MBCA define these characteristics.

Voting Rights Subchapter B of Chapter 7 of the MBCA sets forth the voting rights of holders of common stock. Note that the MBCA permits the articles to exclude voting rights in certain cases.

QUESTION If a certificate for 100 shares of X corporation has been issued to A for only a portion of the total purchase price for such shares, can A have full voting rights with respect to such shares under the MBCA?

When it comes to voting for the election of directors, some states provide for cumulative voting unless the articles of incorporation provide otherwise, while other states only have cumulative voting if the articles specifically include it.[10]

Preemptive Rights When a shareholder has preemptive rights, the shareholder has the right to purchase a pro-rata share of a new issue of common stock, or securities convertible into common stock, which the corporation proposes to issue.[11] Management may not desire preemptive rights because management wants flexibility to issue shares without first offering them to other shareholders. For example, many times management desires to issue shares in exchange for consideration other than cash, e.g., property or stock of another company. Could management do this if preemptive rights exist? In recent years, most state laws have denied shareholders preemptive rights unless the articles of incorporation specifically provide otherwise.

Dividend Rights Corporate laws generally give the board of directors the power to declare and pay dividends, which are distributions to shareholders of cash, property, or stock out of earnings of the corporation, such as in the following MBCA provision:

§ 6.40 (a), MBCA.

A board of directors may authorize and the corporation may make distributions to its shareholders subject to restriction by the articles of incorporation and the limitation in subsection (c).

The board of directors is not required to declare a dividend. Even if the board wanted to declare a dividend, there are two restrictions on the right of common stockholders to receive dividends:

   a. Preferred stockholders[12] may have priority if dividends are paid. The effect of this priority is that no dividends may be paid on common stock until preferred stockholders have received all dividends to which they are entitled.
   b. In order to protect creditors who may not be able to collect a corporation's debts from its shareholders because of the corporate characteristics of limited liability, dividends may not be paid if the payment would make the corporation insolvent or would deplete the corporation's net worth below a certain minimum level.[13]

---

10. See Chapter Two for a discussion of cumulative voting.
11. See Chapter Two for a discussion of preemptive rights.
12. Preferred stock will be discussed more fully later in this chapter.
13. Dividend rights will be discussed shortly.

Liquidation Rights   A corporation that desires to liquidate (wind up its affairs and distribute remaining assets) is required by state law to pay, or adequately provide, first, for the payment of all liabilities and obligations then outstanding and to distribute the remainder of its assets, either in cash or in kind, among its shareholders according to their respective rights and interests.[14]

When the only class of stock outstanding is common stock, the holders will share in the remainder of the corporation's assets in proportion to their relative ownership of the corporation's common stock. If there is outstanding any preferred stock which has priority in liquidation, then the holders of common stock will not receive any payments in the corporate liquidation until the rights of the preferred stockholders have been satisfied.

Obligations of Common Stockholders   Section 6.22 of the MBCA succinctly states the only basis for shareholder liability to the corporation or its creditors:

§ 6.22, MBCA. Liability of Shareholders—

(a) A purchaser from a corporation of its own shares is not liable to the corporation or its creditors with respect to the shares except to pay the consideration for which the shares were authorized to be issued (section 6.21) or specified in the subscription agreement (section 6.20).

(b) Unless otherwise provided in the articles of incorporation, a shareholder of a corporation is not personally liable for the acts or debts of the corporation except that he may become personally liable by reason of his own acts or conduct.

Once a shareholder has paid the agreed price for the shares, the shareholder generally has no further financial responsibility of any sort with respect to the corporation. This statement, however, requires one slight qualification. A few states still have a provision in their corporate law which makes some or all shareholders liable for certain wages due to employees. For example, § 630 of the New York Business Corporation Law imposes such an obligation on the ten largest shareholders of a corporation, unless the shares are "publicly held," i.e., held by a large number of shareholders as designated in the statute.

Different Classes of Common Stock

Some corporations have two classes of common stock, which may vary in one or more of the following respects:

---

14. § 14.05, MBCA.

Voting Rights One reason for the existence of two classes of common stock is to insure certain persons that they will be in control of a corporation even though they do not own a majority of the outstanding common stock.

What corporate document would create two classes of common stock?

_____

The persons in control may own voting common stock while other shareholders own nonvoting common stock. In such a case, the holders of nonvoting common stock will not be entitled to vote in any matter which requires shareholder approval (e.g., election of directors, mergers, or consolidation) unless state law otherwise requires such a vote. Another way of accomplishing the same result is to have one class of common stock with a greater number of votes per share than the other class. In either event, persons who control a small fraction of the total number of outstanding shares of common stock will have control of the corporation.

Normally, a corporation creates two classes of common stock with different voting rights both when the shareholders wish to preserve their control but recognize the need to issue a large number of shares in the future to the public, or when the corporation does not wish to create stock with preferred rights.

QUESTION

Why would a corporation have a need to issue a large number of shares?

_____

The "insiders" or current shareholders in such a case are issued voting common stock, and the corporation is then in a position to issue nonvoting or common stock with lesser voting power to new shareholders.

The two classes of common stock will be provided for and described in the articles of incorporation. Typical provisions, as they might appear in the articles, follow:

EXAMPLE

Two Classes, One Voting, One Nonvoting

> The Corporation shall have an authorized capital of 1,000,000 shares, divided into 200,000 shares of Class A Common Stock, par value $1.00 per share, and 800,000 shares of Class B Common Stock, par value $1.00 per share. Shares of Class A Common Stock and Class B Common Stock shall be identical in all respects except that the holders of Class A Common Stock shall be entitled to vote on all matters submitted to a vote of shareholders and holders of Class B Common Stock shall not be entitled to vote on any matter submitted to a vote of shareholders.

EXAMPLE

Two Classes, One Entitled to One Vote Per Share, One Entitled to Fifteen Votes Per Share

> The Corporation shall have an authorized capital of 1,000,000 shares of Class A Common Stock, par value $.01 per share, and 100,000 shares of Class B Common Stock, par value $.01 per share. Shares of Class A Common Stock and Class B Common Stock shall be identical in all respects except that the holders of Class A Common Stock shall be entitled to one vote per share and the holders of Class B Common Stock shall be entitled to fifteen votes per share on all matters submitted to a vote of shareholders.

It should be noted again that, while the articles of incorporation may deprive the holders of any class of stock of all voting rights, state law requires that such persons be entitled to vote on certain matters.[15]

Dividend Rights   Two classes of common stock may differ in their priority with respect to dividends. Normally such an arrangement is described in the articles in a manner similar to the following:

> The Corporation may not declare and pay a dividend in cash or property on shares of Class B Common Stock without declaring and paying an equal dividend on shares of Class A Common Stock. The corporation may declare and pay a dividend on shares of the Class A Common Stock without declaring and paying any dividend on shares of the Class B Common Stock.

In such a situation the Class B Common Stock will usually be owned by the persons in control of the corporation while the Class A Common Stock will be publicly held. The holders of Class A Common Stock are assured that, if any dividends are paid, they will at least receive the same amount per share as the holders of Class B Common Stock, and it is possible that they may receive more. The holders of Class B Common Stock (i.e., the persons in control of the corporation) may be more interested in paying dividends to the Class A stockholders in order to increase the value of the Class A Stock than they are in receiving dividends themselves. This interest in the value of Class A Stock is seldom altruistic. The Class B Common Stock is usually convertible into Class A Common Stock. After helping to create a higher market price for Class A Stock, the Class B shareholder will convert the stock to Class A.

Conversion   Often the class of common stock with the lesser rights—that is, without voting rights or with a lower priority in the payment of dividends—will be convertible, either immediately or

15. "Voting Rights" will be discussed later in this chapter.

at some future date, on a share-for-share basis into the other class of common stock. In the case of classes of common stock which differ as to voting rights, provisions to convert the nonvoting common stock into voting common stock may reflect the judgment that in the long run it is inappropriate to deprive shareholders of voting rights. In the case of classes of common stock with different dividend rights, the holders of the class with the lesser dividend rights (who are normally the persons in control of the corporation) will normally want the right to convert into the publicly held common stock with the superior dividend rights so that their shares may be made more attractive to potential buyers and therefore command a higher purchase price when sold.

When conversion on a share-for-share basis from one class of common stock to another class of common stock is permitted, it is necessary to provide in the articles that no changes by way of a stock dividend[16] or stock split[17] may occur with respect to one class of common stock without the same changes being made to the other class of common stock. This is commonly called an antidilution provision because it prevents a class from having its interest reduced by such events.

An example of articles of incorporation which provide for two classes of common stock and for the right of conversion from one class to the other is set forth below:

EXAMPLE

Capital Stock Description (Two Classes of Common Stock) Excerpted from Articles of Incorporation

Any holder of Class B Common Stock may, at his or her option, convert all or any part of such Class B Common Stock into Class A Common Stock at the rate of one (1) share of Class A Common Stock for each share of Class B Common Stock, upon presentation and surrender to the Corporation at its principal office, or to any agency maintained for the transfer of Class B Common Stock, of the certificates for such Class B Common Stock so to be converted, duly endorsed for transfer; and thereupon the holders of such Class B Common Stock shall be entitled to receive in exchange therefor, a certificate or certificates for fully paid and nonassessable shares of Class A Common Stock. The Class B Common Stock shall be deemed to have been converted and the person converting the same to have become a holder of record of Class A Common Stock for the purpose of receiving dividends and for all other purposes whatsoever, as of the date when the certificate or certificates for such Class B Common Stock are presented and surrendered to the Corporation as aforesaid, provided, however, that no share of Class B Stock surrendered for conversion after the date of declaration of and before or on the record date for a dividend on Class A Common Stock shall be converted into Class A Common Stock during such period.

16. A distribution of additional stock by a corporation rather than money. It involves a transfer of accumulated profits to capital stock by giving shareholders additional stock.

17. An increase in outstanding shares by dividing shares into a greater number of shares, usually by an amendment to the articles. The result is that each shareholder holds more shares but with a proportionately reduced value per share.

> The Corporation shall, so long as any of the Class B Common Stock is outstanding, reserve and keep available out of its authorized and unissued Class A Common Stock, solely for the purpose of effecting the conversion of the Class B Common Stock, such number of shares of Class A Common Stock as shall from time to time be sufficient to effect the conversion of all shares of the Class B Common Stock then outstanding. The Corporation shall, from time to time, if necessary, amend its Articles of Incorporation to increase its authorized capital stock and take such other action as may be necessary to permit the issuance from time to time of shares of Class A Common Stock as fully paid and nonassessable shares, upon the conversion of the Class B Common Stock as herein provided.

Preferred Stock

"Preferred stock"[18] is a generic term used to describe any class of stock which has a priority vis a vis common stock with respect to the assets of the corporation. There is no such thing as a typical preferred stock, and the only effective limit on the types of preferred stock which may be created is in the imagination of lawyers and their corporate clients.

The characteristics of preferred stock are found in the corporation's articles of incorporation. Section 6.01 of the MBCA specifically states that a corporation may issue shares of preferred or special classes "which must be described in its articles of incorporation." Unfortunately this is somewhat misleading. If a corporation never intends to have more than two classes of stock outstanding—a common stock and a preferred stock—and does not intend to have series of preferred stock, then the articles of incorporation will contain all of the provisions governing both classes of stock. In recent years, however, companies have found it desirable to be able to issue different types, or "series," of preferred stock. Why? Modern state statutes have permitted corporations to issue these series of preferred stock without amending the articles of incorporation each time a new series of preferred stock was to be issued by resolution of the board of directors. A full discussion of this will be set forth under "Creation of Preferred Stock" later in this chapter.

A description of some customary provisions which may be found in preferred stock follows.

Dividends As discussed previously in connection with common stock,[19] a corporation is never under an obligation to pay divi-

---

18. Preferred stock was mentioned earlier in this chapter.
19. Discussed earlier in this chapter.

dends. A dividend is only paid by the corporation after the board of directors has declared the dividend and there are sufficient assets, as determined by state law, available for the payment. These legal limitations on available assets apply not only to dividends on common stock but also to dividends on preferred stock.

Although preferred stockholders do not have a "right" to require the corporation to pay a dividend, normally they are entitled to receive a dividend in a specified amount and at specified times before any dividends are paid by the corporation on any class of stock "junior" to the preferred stock. Common stock is "junior" to preferred stock in most cases insofar as the payment of dividends is concerned.

QUESTION

Can one class of preferred stock be "junior" to another class?

The priority to dividends may either be "cumulative" or "noncumulative." If it is cumulative, the corporation must pay to the preferred stockholders all dividends specified in the terms of the preferred stock from the date the dividends begin to cumulate through to the current dividend before it pays any dividends on junior classes of stock.

QUESTIONS

Could a corporation have two classes of common stock, one with a preference only as to dividends, rather than a class of preferred stock and a class of common stock? Is there really any difference between the two types of classes other than their names?

The terms of the preferred stock may provide, for example, that the payment of dividends shall be at a rate of $1.00 per share, per annum, payable quarterly, that such dividends shall be paid prior to the payment of any dividend on shares of common stock, and that such shares are cumulative from the date of issue. If this class of preferred stock has been outstanding for three years and no dividends have been paid on the stock (called a "dividend average"), then the corporation must pay the preferred stockholders a dividend of $3.00 (covering the period during which the shares were outstanding) before it can pay any dividend to the common stockholders. For each additional year that no dividends are paid on the preferred stock, another $1.00 would cumulate to be paid before any dividends may be paid on the common stock.

QUESTIONS Can the preferred stock ever get more than $1.00 per share dividend per year? Must such a payment be provided for in the articles?

If the preferred stockholders were not entitled to cumulative dividends, then the corporation would only be required to pay them a dividend of $.25 per share for the then current quarter-year period prior to the payment of any dividends on the outstanding shares of common stock.

It is usual for preferred stock to contain the following dividend terms:

1. specified annual rate,
2. specified time of payment,
3. the first payment date,
4. if the dividends are cumulative, when the accumulation begins, and
5. specification that no dividends may be paid on the common stock (other than dividends payable in common stock rather than cash or other property[20]) unless all dividends due to preferred stockholders have been paid.

EXAMPLE

Preferred Stock Description from Articles of Incorporation

> Each share of Preferred Stock shall entitle the holder of record thereof to receive, out of funds legally available therefor, when and as declared by the Board of Directors, dividends in cash at the annual rate of $1.00 per share, which shall be payable in equal quarterly installments on the first day of January, April, July, and October of each year, beginning with July 1, 19___. Cash dividends on each share of Preferred Stock shall be cumulative, whether or not earned and whether or not surplus would be available therefor, and shall commence to accrue and accumulate from the first dividend payment date following the issuance thereof, such accumulation to include, if not paid, the full quarterly dividend payable on such first dividend payment date. Such cash dividends shall be declared and set apart or paid before any dividends (other than dividends payable in shares of Common Stock) shall be paid on the Common Stock.

An analysis of the terms in the sample provision follows:

1. A beginning date for dividend payment: July 1, 19___. This is desirable so that it is clear what date dividend arrearages commence if the corporation fails to pay a dividend to the preferred stockholders.

---

20. These are stock dividends. See footnote 16 of this chapter.

2. It provides, as is normally the case, that dividends are cumulative even if, as a matter of state law, the corporation is not legally permitted to pay dividends.

3. In determining the amount of accrued but unpaid dividends, the dividend payable on the first payment date is a full quarterly dividend, no matter how soon before such date the preferred stock was issued. If the sample provision provided for the accumulation of dividends from the date of issue, then the corporation would not be in arrears if, on the first dividend payment date following issuance, it paid to the preferred stockholders a portion of the regular quarterly dividend pro rated on the basis of the number of days of the quarter during which the stock was outstanding.

QUESTION

If the first quarterly dividend date is April 1, 19 __ , and the stock is issued March 1, 19 __ , what payment would a preferred shareholder be entitled to receive if no provision is made for a full payment for the first dividend?

_____

4. Since a dividend in common stock to existing common stockholders does not deplete the corporation of any assets[21] or impose any additional obligations on the corporation, a stock dividend is permitted even if the corporation is in default in the payment of dividends on preferred stock.

The dividend preference is meaningful for three reasons. First, a corporation will generally be considered to be in poor financial shape if it fails to pay preferred stock dividends, and the board of directors, to avoid this impression, will normally want to keep these dividends current. Second, if the board of directors wants to declare dividends to common stockholders, dividends must not be in arrears on cumulative preferred stock. Third, the value of the preferred stock (and the common stock) may be severely depressed by passing up dividends.[22]

Liquidation Rights Preferred stock provisions will also indicate what rights, if any, the preferred stockholders have upon the

21. Why are assets not depleted by such a dividend? See footnote 16 of this chapter.

22. The depressed price may result from reluctance of investors to invest in stock of a company unwilling or unable to meet its preferred stock dividends.

liquidation or dissolution[23] of the corporation. While the holders of preferred stock are not guaranteed that they will receive anything upon the liquidation of the corporation (as is true of any investor in the corporation), they are normally given the right to receive a specified amount (if available for distribution), plus any dividends which have accrued but have not been paid, prior to any payments to holders of junior stock.

EXAMPLE

Preferred Stock Dissolution Description for Articles of Incorporation

> In the event of any dissolution, liquidation, or winding up of the affairs of the corporation, and after payment or provision for the payment of the debts and other liabilities of the corporation has been made, the holders of the Preferred Stock shall be entitled to receive, out of the net assets of the corporation, $10.00 per share, plus an amount per share equal to accrued but unpaid dividends, whether or not earned or declared, on each such share up to the date fixed for distribution and no more before any distribution shall be made to the holders of the Common Stock. If the net assets of the corporation are not sufficient to pay such amounts in full, holders of all shares of Preferred Stock shall participate ratably in the distribution of assets in proportion to the full amounts to which they are entitled.

The foregoing provision is reasonably self explanatory.

QUESTIONS

If there were 1,000,000 shares of the above preferred stock outstanding, how much would preferred shareholders receive upon liquidation? How much would be received for each preferred share if only $7,000,000 were available for distribution on liquidation to holders of preferred stock?

It should be noted that it is important to spell out in such a provision that the holder of preferred stock is entitled to a certain dollar amount "and no more." Otherwise, a question might arise as to whether the holders of preferred stock were entitled, after receiving a specified amount, to participate with the holders of common stock in any remaining assets of the corporation.

QUESTION

Is there ever a "liquidation price" established for common stock?

Redemption Rights   A corporation does not, unless it is specifically spelled out in the terms of a class of stock, have the right to

---

23. Dissolution is the formal termination of corporate existence, whereas liquidation may wind up the business without formal dissolution, e.g., where the shareholders wish to keep the name for possible future use.

require the holders of such stock to sell all or any part of their shares to the corporation. Such a right is called a "right of redemption." Redemption provisions are frequently present with respect to a preferred stock.

QUESTIONS

Why would the corporation ever want to redeem preferred stock? Is common stock redeemable?

A redemption provision must establish the terms of the forced sale by the preferred stockholders and the procedures which must be followed by the corporation when it invokes its redemption right. In some instances, the redemption terms may be the most complicated of the preferred stock provisions. A sample provision is set forth below. The sample provision, which is less complex than many provisions may be, might typically be found in the terms of a preferred stock which has been issued to one or two persons.

EXAMPLE

Simple Notice of Redemption; Specification of Method of Payment and Effect

> Shares of Preferred Stock are subject to redemption by the corporation, at the option of its board of directors, in whole or in part, at any time and from time to time, upon 30 days prior written notice to the registered holders thereof, at the addresses of such holders as the same appears on the corporations's records, at the price of $10.00 per share, plus an amount equal to the accrued and unpaid dividends thereon to the date of said redemption. In case of the redemption of a part only of the shares of Preferred Stock at the time outstanding, the corporation may select by lot, or in such other equitable manner as the board of directors may determine, the shares of Preferred Stock so to be redeemed. If such notice of redemption shall have been duly given and if, on or before the redemption date specified in such notice, the funds necessary for such redemption shall have been set apart, so as to be and to continue to be available therefor, then, notwithstanding that any shares of Preferred Stock called for redemption shall not have been surrendered for cancellation, such shares of Preferred Stock shall no longer be deemed outstanding; and all rights of the holders of such shares of Preferred Stock so called for a redemption shall forthwith on such redemption date cease and terminate, except only the right of the holders thereof to receive the redemption price as specified above.

In analyzing the sample provision, the following considerations should be noted:

    a. The corporation has the right to redeem all or any part of the preferred stock at any time. The determination of when to cause the redemption and the number of shares to be covered is at the sole discretion of the board of directors.

b. In order to redeem stock, it is necessary for the corporation to give notice to all preferred stockholders who are affected. The notice must be given at least 30 days prior to the date set for redemption and must specify the redemption date. If less than all of the shares of preferred stock are being redeemed, the notice must also contain a statement of the number of shares of preferred stock being redeemed from each holder.

c. The amount payable upon redemption has two components: a fixed dollar amount and an amount equal to all accrued and unpaid dividends on the shares of preferred stock being redeemed.

d. In order to protect the preferred stockholders, the corporation is required to set aside funds sufficient to pay the redemption price for all shares called for redemption. If the corporation fails to do this, then the redemption is not effective, and the shares of preferred stock called for redemption will still be deemed outstanding.

e. The corporation will pay the redemption price only when the stock certificates representing the preferred stock are surrendered to the corporation for cancellation. There is no time limit on the surrender of the certificates. However, any preferred stockholder will be penalized if his shares have been called and the shareholder does not act promptly, because the redemption price does not include any interest from the proposed date of redemption to the date of payment.

QUESTION

If there is a dividend arrearage of $3.00 per share on a cumulative preferred stock and the redemption price is $10.00 per share, what does the holder of such preferred stock receive upon redemption?

Many state corporate laws place some limitation on the right of the corporation to redeem stock. In Pennsylvania, for example, the right to redeem is contingent upon the corporation's continued ability to pay its debts as they become due, or resulting "balance sheet insolvency."[24] The purpose of the limitations is to prevent redemptions of stock where the corporation may not have adequate funds to pay creditors.

State law may require a statement to be filed with the appropriate state agency with respect to the redemption of shares of stock.

---

24. § 1103 and § 1551 (a), (b), PBCL. See also § 6.40, MBCA.

QUESTIONS

Is common stock required to be cancelled upon redemption? In a state adopting a provision such as § 6.31 of the MBCA, could a corporation hold preferred stock for reissuance?

_____

A sample statement of cancellation appears below:

EXAMPLE

Statement of Cancellation of Shares

Filing fee: $_____

STATEMENT OF
CANCELLATION OF REDEEMABLE SHARES
OF

_____

To the Secretary of State
   of the State of _____:
   Pursuant to the provisions of Section _____ of the _____ Business Corporation Act, the undersigned corporation submits the following statement of cancellation by redemption or purchase of redeemable shares of the corporation:
   FIRST: The name of the corporation is _____

_____

   SECOND: The number of redeemable shares of the corporation cancelled through redemption or purchase is _____, itemized as follows:

Class	**Series**	**Number of Shares**

   THIRD: The aggregate number of issued shares of the corporation after giving effect to such cancellation is _____, itemized as follows:

Class	**Series**	**Number of Shares**

   FOURTH: The amount of the stated capital of the corporation after giving effect to such cancellation is $_____.

   FIFTH: The number of shares which the corporation has authority to issue after giving effect to such cancellation is _____, itemized as follows:

Class	**Series**	**Number of Shares**

Dated _____, 19___.

_____ (Note 1)

By_____
   Its _____ President

and_____
   Its _____ Secretary

} (Note 2)

Add Verification Form A)

NOTES: 1. Exact corporate name of corporation making the statement.
        2. Signatures and titles of officers signing for the corporation.

Voting Rights   If there were no provision in the terms of preferred stock dealing with voting rights, a state law similar to the MBCA would grant to the preferred stockholders the same voting rights as the holders of common stock:

§ 7.21 (a), MBCA.

Except as provided in subsections (b) and (c) or unless the articles of incorporation provide otherwise, each outstanding share, regardless of class, is entitled to one vote on each matter voted on at a shareholders' meeting. Only shares are entitled to vote.

Even when the holders of preferred stock are specifically denied general voting rights in the articles of incorporation, the articles may grant them the right to vote, as a class, on certain types of proposed actions such as:

a. the creation of another class of stock ranking prior to or on a parity with the preferred stock as to dividends or liquidation,

b. an increase in the authorized number of shares of preferred stock,

c. any change in the preferences and special rights of the outstanding preferred stock, or

d. any other action which would adversely affect the rights of the holders of preferred stock.

QUESTION   Would a grant of voting rights to preferred stock by the bylaws be effective under § 7.21 of the MBCA?

Even if the terms of a preferred stock did not grant to the holders special voting rights in connection with certain corporate actions, state law would grant comparable rights, irrespective of what was set forth in a corporation's articles of incorporation.[25]

QUESTIONS   Why do some corporate statutes grant voting rights to holders of preferred stock in connection with amendment to the articles of incorporation even if the articles deny such preferred stock all voting rights? Which prevails in such a case: the statute which grants the preferred voting rights, or the articles of incorporation which denies such rights?

---

25. For example, see § 10.04 of the MBCA.

When an applicable provision of state law covers the subject of voting rights accorded holders of preferred stock, the natural question is why the matter should be covered in the terms of the preferred stock. The answer is that the terms of the preferred stock may provide greater protection to the preferred stockholders by establishing greater voting rights than the statute accords holders of preferred stock.

QUESTION

Why would management ever want to give greater voting rights to holders of preferred stock than those provided by law?

In addition, the terms may provide for the relative rights between two or more series of the same preferred stock. Still another reason for including voting terms is that state law can change, without any ability of the corporation or holders of preferred stock to control the change, while the terms of a preferred stock can be changed only by a majority of preferred stockholders.

Holders of preferred stock are often granted the right to elect a specified number of directors if certain conditions should occur. Under most circumstances, preferred stockholders do not vote in the election of directors, or, if they do, their votes may be counted with the common stock in the election, and in the latter case they do not vote separately as a class. Therefore, they may not have an effective voice in the management of the corporation. This lack of control is critical when a corporation has failed to pay dividends on preferred stock for a period of time, for this failure indicates either unprofitable operations or a decision by the board of directors not to pay dividends. Under such conditions, the terms of the preferred stock normally grant the right to the holders of preferred stock to elect a specified number of directors for as long as the failure to pay dividends continues. Such rights would appear in the place where the preferred stock is authorized (either the articles or the authorizing resolution of the board of directors).

EXAMPLE

Voting Rights for Preferred Stock When Dividends are in Arrears

If and whenever, and as often as, dividends on any Preference Shares[26] shall be in arrears in an aggregate amount of at least $10.00 per share, the holders of Preference Shares shall have the additional right, voting separately as a class (without losing any other voting rights), at each meeting of shareholders thereafter held for the election of a Board of Directors, to elect two of the total number of Directors to be elected at such meeting. Such additional right shall continue in the Preference

26. Sometimes preferred stock may be referred to as "preference stock," merely as a different name.

> Shares until such time as all accumulated dividends on Preference Shares have been paid or declared and set aside for payment, whereupon such right shall cease until such time, if any, as such right shall again accrue as hereinabove provided. In the event of any vacancy occurring in the case of the two Directors elected by the Preference Shares voting as a class as aforesaid, unless (at the time when such vacancy shall have occurred as aforesaid) all accumulated dividends on Preference Shares shall have been paid or declared and set aside for payment, a special meeting of the holders of Preference Shares shall be called promptly to fill any such vacancy, which meeting shall be within thirty (30) days after such call, and at a place and upon notice as provided for the holding of meetings of shareholders, except that no such special meeting shall be required to be called if any such vacancy shall occur less than ninety (90) days before the date fixed for the annual meeting of shareholders. As to each meeting held as aforesaid while the Preference Shares have the right, voting separately as a class, to vote for the election of the two Directors, or to fill any vacancy, a majority of the outstanding Preference Shares shall be required to constitute a quorum for the election of such Directors or to fill any such vacancy at any such meeting. The Directors so elected shall serve until the next annual meeting or until their successors shall be elected and shall qualify; provided, however, whenever, during the term of office of such Directors all accumulated dividends shall have been paid or declared and set apart for payment, the term of office of such Directors shall forthwith terminate.

The above provision says that the holders of the class of Preference Stock can elect two directors when dividends are in arrears in a certain amount.

QUESTIONS

What does it provide if a vacancy occurs in one of the two directorships elected by the holders of the Preference Stock? What happens to the Directors elected by holders of the Preference Stock if the dividend arrearages are eliminated?

The special voting rights which arise when preferred dividends are in arrears may be granted irrespective of any general voting rights the preferred shareholders may have under state law. The sample provision set forth above clearly reflects the fact that such voting rights are in addition to any other voting rights.

If the terms of a preferred stock grant special voting rights in the election of directors, there may be a provision included which requires a special meeting at which the holders of preferred stock may exercise these rights.

Sinking Fund   Under the terms of the typical preferred stock, the shares will remain outstanding until the corporation's liquidation or dissolution, unless the corporation decides to exercise its right to redeem all or any part of the preferred stock. Holders of preferred stock have no assurance of the existence of a fund for any payments from the corporation.

Prospective purchasers of preferred stock sometimes require as a condition to such purchase, that a "sinking fund" provision be included within the terms of the proposed preferred stock. Basically, a sinking fund provision states that the corporation shall, out of funds available according to state corporate law, and after all cumulative dividends have been paid, either (a) redeem a specified number of shares of preferred stock each year or (b) place each year a specified sum of money in a separate account, out of the control of the corporation (such as a separate trust account where the corporation is not the trustee) to be used only for retiring the preferred stock at a specified date. Unless the specified number of shares have been redeemed or the required sum set aside, no dividends or other distributions (other than stock dividends payable in common stock) may be declared or paid on any shares of common stock and no shares of common stock may be purchased or otherwise acquired by the corporation. This provision grants the preferred stockholders some assurance that payments will be made to them periodically to repurchase their stock so long as the corporation has sufficient assets available.[27]

EXAMPLE

Sinking Fund Provision; Credit against Sinking Fund for Other Preferred Stock Purchases

Out of any funds of the corporation legally available therefor after cumulative dividends in full on all outstanding shares of Preferred Stock for all quarterly dividends periods up to and including the then current dividend period have been paid or declared and a sum set apart for payment, and before any dividends or other distributions may be paid or declared and set apart for payment in respect of any shares of Common Stock or any shares of Common Stock may be purchased or otherwise acquired for consideration, the corporation shall set aside, as and for a sinking fund for the Preferred Stock, on the twentieth day of February, May, August, and November, beginning November 20, 19___, the sum or sums sufficient to redeem on or before the next March 1, June 1, September 1, and December 1, respectively, 2000 shares of Preferred

Stock at $10.00 per share plus an amount equal to all accrued and unpaid dividends, whether or not declared or earned, provided that the amount to be so set aside need never exceed the amount sufficient to redeem at such price plus such dividends all shares of Preferred Stock then outstanding. Sums so set aside for the sinking fund shall be applied to the redemption of Preferred Stock.

---

27. For example, § 6.40, MBCA.

QUESTIONS What amount of money does the above provision require to be set aside per year for the sinking fund? How much must be set aside if only 1,000 shares of preferred stock are left outstanding?

_____

As the above example indicates, the sinking fund operates as a means of forced redemption and ties in with the redemption provisions of the preferred stock terms.

Conversion Rights   A holder of preferred stock who has "conversion rights" is able to exchange preferred stock for common stock of the same corporation at a specified exchange rate. Convertible preferred stock permits the holders to enjoy the protection of having a "senior" security, that is, one entitled to preference as to dividends and on liquidation or dissolution, while still being able to benefit from any increase in the market value of the corporation's common stock. Such right is often called an "equity kicker" because the preferred has the additional possibility of increase in value as the price of the common stock goes up. Investors are usually willing to pay more for a preferred stock with such a "kicker."

The advantage of having convertible preferred stock can best be appreciated by examining the factors which contribute to the value of preferred stock without any conversion rights. The value of such a preferred stock will be determined largely by the size and profitability of the issuing corporation (because a profitable corporation is more likely to pay the dividend on preferred stock), the preferred stock's liquidation and redemption prices, the existence of a sinking fund and, most important, its fixed dividend rate. Anyone purchasing a straight preferred stock has, as the most immediate concern, the amount of the dividend which is payable on each preferred share. If the annual dividend per share is $1.00, then a prospective purchaser has to decide how many dollars to pay in order to justify investment in a preferred stock yielding a dividend of that amount. If the purchaser expected a 10% return on such an investment, then the purchaser would be willing to pay $10.00 a share for the preferred stock.

QUESTION How much would such an investor be willing to pay for such a preferred stock if the investor required a return of 5%?

_____

A prospective purchaser would, as indicated above, also consider the liquidation price and redemption price. The liquidation price, however, is only of major significance if the corporation intends or is likely to liquidate in the near future. This is not a normal occurrence because a corporation only liquidates at the termination of its business activities. Therefore, the liquidation price normally has little effect on the price of the stock. The redemption price is only relevant in the board of directors is likely to decide to redeem outstanding preferred stock. Since redemptions are again not a normal occurrence in the absence of a schedule of redemption in the terms of the preferred stock, the redemption price will also not have a significant effect upon the value of the preferred stock.

As the value of preferred stock is dependent primarily upon a fixed dividend rate and the ability of the corporation to continue to make dividend payments, the value is not likely to change much, if at all, if the corporation is able to meet the dividend adequately when it becomes more profitable. The only change in value (assuming the corporation has continued to pay the required dividends) that is likely to take place results from a change in the collective judgment of investors regarding a satisfactory rate of return on preferred stocks, e.g., a desire to earn 10% rather than 5%.

When preferred stock is convertible into common stock, however, a new factor is introduced into the valuation of the preferred stock. If, for example, one share of preferred stock is convertible into one share of common stock, and if the preferred stock pays dividends at an annual rate of $1.00 per share, it is unlikely that the value of the preferred stock will be affected when the market price of the common stock is, for example, $5.00 per share if investors demand a rate of return for such preferred stocks of 10%. Why? At such time, it would not make economic sense for the holder of preferred stock, who could sell that preferred stock for $10.00 per share (assuming investors are willing to accept a 10% return on such preferred stocks), to convert it into a security which has a market value of only $5.00 per share. If, however, the common stock of the company had a market value of $30.00 per share, then a holder of preferred stock would be able to realize $30.00 for each share of preferred stock by converting it to common stock. Under such circumstances, the preferred stock would no longer have a price primarily established by the relation to the dividend rate but instead would have a price established almost exclusively as a result of its ability to be converted into common stock. The market value for the preferred stock at such a level will then fluctuate almost directly in relation to the market value of the common stock.

PROBLEM

If a preferred stock has a dividend rate of $2.50 per year and the investor demands a return of 8%, what would be the likely market price of such preferred stock? Assume that such preferred stock is convertible into common stock on the basis of one share of preferred stock for each two shares of common receivable on conversion. If the market price of the common stock is $12.00 per share, what is the likely price of the preferred stock if the required rate of return is 8%? If the required rate of return is 10%? What if the required rate of return is 8% and the price of the common stock is $18.00 per share? $20.00 per share?

QUESTIONS

If a preferred stock has both a redemption feature and a conversion feature, can the call for redemption of the convertible preferred force holders to convert into common stock? What relation between the preferred stock redemption price and common stock market price is likely to force conversions? Should the right to convert terminate with the notice of redemption of the convertible preferred stock?

The principal components which may be found in the conversion terms of a convertible preferred stock are set forth below. These components will appear in the articles of incorporation if the preferred stock is authorized in the articles.

QUESTION

Where would these conversion terms appear if the board of directors has the power to authorize the series?

Conversion Rate Provision   The terms of the preferred stock will specify the number of shares of common stock into which each share of preferred stock is convertible.

EXAMPLE

Conversion Rate Provision

> Shares of Preferred Stock may be converted at any time or from time to time into shares of Common Stock at the rate of two (2) shares of Common Stock for each share of Preferred Stock, such conversion rate to be subject to adjustment as hereinafter provided.

Method of Conversion   Preferred stock terms will usually set forth the specific procedure which must be followed by the holder of preferred stock in order to convert into common stock.

178

EXAMPLE

Effective Date of Conversion; Effect of Subscription Rights of Preferred Stock

> Any holder of shares of Preferred Stock who elects to convert them shall surrender the certificate therefor at the principal office of the Corporation, with the form of written notice on such certificate endorsed to reflect his election to convert them. The conversion privilege shall be deemed to have been exercised and the shares of Common Stock issuable upon such conversion shall be deemed to have been issued, upon the date the Corporation receives for conversion the certificate representing such shares with the requirements for conversion satisfied, except that as to any shares of Preferred Stock which are surrendered for conversion on a date which is less than five business days preceding the date fixed for the determination of holders of Common Stock entitled to receive rights to subscribe for or to purchase shares of Common Stock or other securities of the Corporation convertible into Common Stock, the conversion privilege shall have been deemed to have been exercised on the business day next succeeding the date fixed for such determination. Each person entitled to receive the Common Stock issuable upon such conversion shall from the same date be treated as the record holder of such Common Stock, and the person who surrenders such shares for conversion shall on that date cease to be treated as the record holder of the shares surrendered.

Such provisions to establish the date on which the conversion becomes effective contain language which delays the effective date if certificates are not surrendered to the corporation a specified number of days before the record date[28] fixed to determine the common stockholders entitled to receive subscription rights. As the name implies, subscription rights are rights granted to shareholders to purchase the corporation's common stock at a specified price during a specified period of time. Such rights are valuable because the purchase price is normally below the then current market price for the common stock in order to encourage the shareholders to exercise the right. The corporation can then raise a substantial portion of the money it desires from a new stock issuance from among its existing shareholders and reduce the selling effort to outsiders. The reason for the delay in the effective date of conversion is to permit the corporation to know, before the record date, exactly how many shares of common stock will be outstanding as of the record date.

Treatment of Fractions Normally corporations do not issue fractional shares of common stock because of the inconvenience and expense involved. If, in connection with a conversion of a preferred stock into common stock, the holder of preferred stock would otherwise be entitled to a fractional share, a procedure is usually

---

28. The record date is the specific date set by the board of directors to determine the name and number of record shareholders entitled to the right.

established to pay the converting shareholder an appropriate cash value for the fractional share.

In cases of corporations which do not have a public market (and, therefore, an easily ascertainable market value) for the shares of their common stock, appropriate provision must be made to value one share of common stock for the purpose of determining the value of the fractional share. One way around the problem is to give the board of directors the responsibility of determining the fair value of one share of common stock.

Adjustments to Conversion Rates Perhaps the most difficult terms in any convertible preferred stock have to do with the method of adjusting the conversion rate in the event of certain actions by a corporation. These are called "antidilution" provisions because they preserve the value of the preferred stock in certain events, such as a stock dividend, stock split, reverse stock split, or other change in capitalization.[29]

These provisions are very complex and may take an infinite number of forms. A paralegal is rarely asked to draft a complex antidilution provision from scratch. Such provisions would appear in the articles, if that is the place where the preferred stock is authorized, or in the resolutions of the board of directors if it has the power to authorize series preferred stock provisions.

Documenting Changes in Conversion Rights In order that the interested parties know of a change in the conversion rate of a preferred stock and the events which gave rise to the change, the board of directors normally is required to give notice to all preferred stockholders and to the applicable transfer agents who effect transfers of the preferred and common stock on the books of the corporation.

EXAMPLE

Adjustment Provision

Whenever the conversion rate is required to be adjusted, (a) the Corporation shall file a certificate setting forth such adjusted conversion rate and the facts upon which the adjustment is based with the Transfer Agents for the Preferred Stock and Common Stock and, thereafter (until further adjusted), the adjusted conversion rate shall be as set forth in such certificate, and (b) the Corporation shall mail notice of such adjusted conversion rate to each holder of shares of Preferred Stock.

If there were no transfer agents, the provision could be simplified by ignoring the notice to transfer agent.

Reservations of Adequate Number of Shares of Common Stock When a corporation has outstanding a convertible preferred stock, the corporation must have available at all times a sufficient number of

---

29. See Chapter Nine for a discussion of such changes.

shares of authorized stock to permit conversion of all outstanding shares. Typically, a corporation by a resolution of its board of directors undertakes to reserve an adequate number of shares from its authorized and unissued shares of common stock or treasury stock.

QUESTION

As a review, what is the difference between "authorized but unissued" stock and "treasury" stock?

EXAMPLE

Reservation Provision

> So long as any shares of the convertible Preferred Stock remain outstanding, and the holders thereof have the right to convert them into shares of Common Stock, the corporation shall reserve from the authorized and unissued shares of its Common Stock a sufficient number of shares to provide for such conversion.

Creation of Preferred Stock

As briefly discussed above, the articles of incorporation may contain all provisions regarding preferred stock. However, if a series of preferred is allowed by corporate law and is authorized in the articles of incorporation, amendment of the articles may not be necessary for authorizing a new preferred stock.[30]

States that have adopted statutes similar to MBCA § 6.02 permit shares of any class of preferred stock to be divided into series. Section 6.02 additionally permits the articles of incorporation to authorize the board of directors to fix the relative rights and preferences of all series into which any class of preferred stock may be divided.

If a corporation in a MBCA-type state is willing to have different types of preferred stock that differ in only the above-mentioned ways, it can, by having the appropriate provisions in its articles of incorporation, enjoy the flexibility of having different series of preferred stock issuable by action of its board of directors alone.

QUESTIONS

Why is such flexibility useful? What is the alternative method for establishing preferred stock?

Before discussing the specific terms of a class of preferred stock which may be divided into series by action of the board of

---

30. See "Preferred Stock" earlier in this chapter.

directors, we should review the difference between a "class" of stock and a "series" of a class of stock. (This discussion is *only* true for states which have adopted a scene similar to the MBCA's § 6.02 as to series and classes of preferred stock.)

What kinds of classes are there?

Section 6.02 also permits classes of preferred stock or special classes to have terms which are different from common stock in the areas of dividends, assets distributed upon liquidation, redemption, and conversion, and it requires that the holders of different series of stock within the same class are on a parity with each other except in certain areas. The differences between the series of the same class, therefore, are primarily differences either in numbers (e.g., the divided rate) or in certain characteristics which do not affect their relative rights to the assets of the corporation (e.g., voting rights and conversion rights).

While the MBCA establishes reasonably precise differences between classes and series of stock, and limits the ways in which series of stock may vary, certain state laws permit the corporation greater latitude in creating series of stock. For example, the Delaware General Corporation Law provides in part:

§ 151, DGCL.

(a) Every corporation may issue one or more classes of stock or one or more series of stock within any class thereof, any or all of which classes may be of stock with par value or stock without par value and which classes or series may have such voting powers, full or limited, or no voting powers, and such designations, preferences and relative, participating, optional or other special rights, and qualifications, or restrictions thereof, as shall be stated and expressed in the certificate of incorporation or of any amendment thereto, or in the resolution or resolutions providing for the issue of such stock adopted by the board of directors pursuant to authority expressly vested in it by the provisions of its certificate of incorporation. . . . The power to increase or decrease or otherwise adjust the capital stock as provided in this chapter shall apply to all or any such classes of stock.

From the standpoint of statutory construction, Delaware law has minimized the differences between classes and series of stock. In effect, different series of the same class of stock must be identical only in their par value or lack of par value.

Why does Delaware have this scheme rather than that of the MBCA? Who benefits most from the broad Delaware-type provision?

Board of Directors' Resolutions When the articles of incorporation grant authority to the board of directors to establish a series of preferred stock, the board must adopt resolutions, if it proposes to issue the stock, setting forth the terms of the series as in the following example:

> RESOLVED, that this Company hereby establishes 50,000 shares of its authorized Preferred Stock, par value $1.00 per share, as a series of such Preferred Stock which shall be designated as the "7% Convertible Preferred Stock."
>
> RESOLVED, that the terms of the 7% Convertible Preferred Stock in the respects in which the shares of such series may vary from the shares of other series of the Preferred Stock shall be as follows:
>
> *[Terms of Series]*
>
> RESOLVED, that the President or any Vice-President and the Secretary or any Assistant Secretary of this Company be and each of them hereby is authorized and empowered to execute in the name of and on behalf of this Company a statement setting forth the terms of the 7% Convertible Preferred Stock in the form presented to this meeting, which form is hereby approved, with such changes therein, if any, as may be approved by the officers of this Company executing same, as conclusively evidenced by their execution thereof; and that the proper officers of this Company be and each of them hereby is authorized and empowered to file said statement with the office of the Secretary of State of the State of New York, to pay such taxes and fees and to take any such other action as may be necessary or desirable, in the opinion of any one of such officers, to cause the foregoing terms of the 7% Convertible Preferred Stock to become validly established and fixed under applicable law.

A sample form of the statement required to be filed in a state in order to fix the terms of a series of preferred stock established by the Board of Directors is included below:

EXAMPLE

Statement of Creation of Series of Preferred Stock

Filing fee: $_____

STATEMENT OF
RESOLUTION ESTABLISHING SERIES OF SHARES
OF

To the Secretary of State
of the State of _____:
   Pursuant to the provisions of Section 16 of the _____ Business Corporation Act, the undersigned corporation submits the following statement for the purpose of establishing and designating a series of shares and fixing and determining the relative rights and preferences thereof:
   FIRST: The name of the corporation is _____

   SECOND: The following resolution, establishing and designating a series of shares and fixing and determining the relative rights and preferences thereof, was duly adopted by the board of directors of the corporation on _____, 19__:

[*Insert copy of resolution*]

Dated _____, 19__.

_____ (Note 1)

By_____

Its _____ President

(Note 2)

and_____

Its _____ Secretary

(Add Verification Form A)

NOTES: 1. Exact corporate name of corporation making the statement.
2. Signatures and titles of officers signing for the corporation.

Transfer Agents and Registrars

State law requires a corporation to keep a record of the names and addresses of all shareholders and the number and class of shares held by each, as in the following example:

§ 16.01 (c), MBCA.

A corporation or its agent shall maintain a record of its shareholders, in a form that permits preparation of a list of the names and addresses of all shareholders, in alphabetical order by class of shares showing the number and class of shares held by each.

The statute above recognizes that corporations may use transfer agents and registrars (which are normally banks or companies that specialize in the business of acting as transfer agents) to keep records of the shareholders of the corporation, but does not describe their function. Surprisingly, most state corporate laws do not define the duties of transfer agents and registrars, either.

Many companies do not have separate transfer agents and registrars. In these cases, one bank usually performs both functions, by preparing stock certificates and keeping records of the outstanding certificates.

When a corporation has a transfer agent and a registrar, the board of directors must, in its resolutions authorizing the issuance of additional shares of stock, provide for appropriate instructions to the transfer agent and registrar. An example of such resolutions is included below:

ISSUANCE OF NEW SHARES OF COMMON STOCK
INVOLVING AUTHORIZATION TO THE
TRANSFER AGENT AND REGISTRAR

RESOLVED, that this Company issue 10,000 shares of Common Stock, par value $1.00 per share, of the Company (the "Common Stock") to John Smith against payment therefor of a price of $10.00 per share, or an aggregate price of $100,000, payable in cash; that, upon the receipt of said aggregate price of $100,000, the First National Bank, as Transfer Agent for the Common Stock, be and hereby is authorized and directed to countersign for original issue, and to deliver to John Smith when registered by The Trust Company, Registrar for the Common Stock, one certificate for 10,000 additional shares of Common Stock registered in the name of John Smith; and that The Trust Company, as Registrar for the Common Stock, be and hereby is authorized and directed to register and countersign, when presented to it for such purpose by the Transfer Agent, the certificate for said additional 10,000 shares of Common Stock.

RESOLVED, that the President, any Vice President, the Secretary, or the Treasurer of this Company be and each of them hereby is authorized and empowered to give such instructions to the Transfer Agent and Registrar of the Common Stock and to take such other action as any one of them may deem necessary or desirable to effect the issuance and delivery of the 10,000 shares of Common Stock to John Smith, against payment therefor, in accordance with the foregoing resolution.

RESOLVED, that the Board of Directors of this Company declares that the 10,000 additional shares of Common Stock, when issued, sold, paid for, and delivered in accordance with the foregoing resolutions shall be fully paid and nonassessable shares of the Common Stock of this Company.

DEBT SECURITIES

Introduction

A person is a creditor of a corporation when the corporation owes that person money, generally because of a loan, but possibly as a result of the sale of property to the corporation or the performance of services for the corporation on credit. The corporation's debt is usually evidenced by some written instrument,[31] which is referred to as a "debt security." Debt can also exist without a formal document, such as an account payable for goods purchased by a corporation. A security is represented by a writing, however.

In contrast to equity securities, the holder of debt securities will have no right to (1) participate in the control of the corporation by electing directors, (2) receive all or a portion of the corporation's surplus or profits, or (3) share in its assets upon any

31. A formal written document.

185

dissolution (except to the extent of any unpaid portion of said debt). Instead, the holder of debt securities will have the right to receive money from the corporation at stipulated times, together (generally) with interest. "Interest" is the charge which the corporation pays for the use of money over time. The corporation, as a debtor, at the request of the creditor often undertakes certain additional obligations in the operation of its business when it issues debt securities. These obligations are usually part of the written agreement or "deal" with the corporation's creditors. The terms may be set forth in the debt security itself or in a separate document. Such obligations may act to prohibit or limit dividends, other debt, change in business operations, expansion, and other matters. The obligations do not arise out of state law or the provisions of the articles of incorporation but out of the agreement of the debtor corporation and its creditor. However, they may be very restricting on a corporation and its management and may severely limit certain types of corporate actions in order to increase the likelihood of repayment of the debt. The consensual relationship between debtor and creditor is a contractual one and, hence, governed in the first instance by state contract law.

The rest of this section will discuss some of the more common types of debt securities. The variations in debt securities are almost limitless, and it is the ingenuity of the parties and their relative bargaining positions rather than any statute which will determine their rights.

Types of Debt Securities

Simple Note A "note" represents the simplest form of debt security. An installment note will contain at least the following elements:

1. A statement of the amount borrowed, referred to as the "principal" or the "principal amount"
2. A promise by the corporation to repay the principal to a specific person or bearer[32] at a certain time or times, in certain amounts, and at a certain place
3. A promise to pay interest at certain times, rates, in certain amounts, and at a certain place, or a statement that no interest is to be paid
4. Signature of the obligor (the person making the note)
5. Date of issuance

---

32. A "bearer" is one in possession of the note who presents the note for payment.

A "demand note" is distinguished from other types of simple notes in that the time that the principal is to be paid by the corporation is not stated. Instead, the holder of the demand note has the right to require the payment of the outstanding principal amount of the note together with accrued interest at any time after making demand for payment.

EXAMPLES

Installment Note and Demand Note

Installment Note:

$1,000,000   NOTE   July 1, 19___

Jones Corporation, a Delaware corporation, herein called the "Corporation," hereby promises to pay to the order of Sam Smith the sum of $1,000,000 on December 31, 19___, and to pay interest thereon from the date hereof at the rate of 9% per annum, payable monthly commencing on the first day of the month next following the month in which this Note is dated. The principal and interest shall be payable when due at the principal office of Sam Smith in San Francisco, California.

Jones Corporation

By: _____
       Samuel Jones, President[33]

Demand Note:

$250,000   NOTE   July 1, 19___

Jones Corporation, a Delaware corporation, herein called the "Corporation," hereby promises to pay to the order of Tammy Katman the sum of $250,000 upon demand made in writing to the Corporation at its principal office in Philadelphia, Pennsylvania, together with interest thereon from July 1, 19___, to the date of payment at the rate of 10% per annum.

Jones Corporation

By: _____
       Samuel Jones, President

The above demand note is different from the installment note in that it provides for the payment of interest at the time the principal of the note is paid.

PROBLEM

Draft a promissory note payable to Jessica Amy Smith issued on January 15, 197___, to X Corporation with interest at 12% per annum payable quarterly. The amount is $150,000, and Henry Johnson is President of X Corporation. The note is due on January 15, 19___. Ms. Smith lives in Cherry Hill, New Jersey.

---

33. Note the form of signature of a corporation. The corporate name is given with a line for the executing officer.

The following form sets forth a note which is more complicated and has additional characteristics:

EXAMPLE

Multiple Interest Rate Note

$30,000.00   NOTE   _____, 19__

FOR VALUE RECEIVED, Macro Electric Vehicle Corporation, a Delaware corporation (hereinafter called "Maker"), promises to pay to the order of _____ (hereinafter called "Holder"), the principal sum of Thirty Thousand Dollars ($30,000) in lawful money of the United States of America, together with interest calculated at the following rates per annum on the outstanding principal balance from time to time.

1. During the period commencing with the date of this Note and terminating one (1) year from said date, to one-half of one percent (½ of 1%) in excess of the "prime rate" (as hereinafter defined) in effect on the date of this Note:

2. During the period commencing one (1) year and one (1) day from the date of this Note and terminating two (2) years from the date of this Note, at one percent (1%) in excess of the "prime rate" in effect one (1) year and one (1) day from the date of this Note;

3. During the period commencing two (2) years and one (1) day from the date of this Note and terminating three (3) years from the date of this Note, at one and one-half (1½%) percent in excess of the "prime rate" in effect two (2) years and one (1) day from the date of this Note.

"Prime rate" is herein defined to mean the average interest rate charged by the following New York City banks for short-term unsecured loans to their most creditworthy borrowers—Chase Manhattan Bank, Citibank, and Chemical Bank—publicly announced from time to time as the "Prime Rate."

Interest shall be paid on the first day of each month after the date hereof until the principal amount hereof is paid in full.

The unpaid principal balance of this Note, together with accrued interest thereon, shall be paid in full three (3) years from the date of this Note.

All or any portion (in multiples of $10,000 only) of the outstanding principal balance of this Note from time to time may be paid on any interest payment date without penalty; provided, however, that said payment must be accompanied by the interest payment due on said date. All payments of principal and/or interest hereunder shall be first applied to unpaid interest which has accrued to the date of said payment and then to the unpaid principal.

Both the unpaid principal and accrued interest of this Note shall bear interest at the rate of 15% per annum after the date when due.

Upon the occurrence of any "Event of Default" (as hereinafter defined), Holder shall have the right, after seven (7) days written notice to the Maker, to declare the entire unpaid balance of the principal, together with the accrued interest thereon, immediately due and owing, anything herein to the contrary notwithstanding, and payment of said principal sum and interest may be collected at once, provided that prior to the expiration of the said seven (7) days, the Maker shall not have cured all Events of Default set forth in Holder's notice to Maker.

"Event of Default" is herein defined as any one or more of the following:

1. Failure to make any payment of principal or interest hereunder after the same shall have become due and payable;
2. The filing of any petition or the commencement of any proceedings against Maker, if consented to or acquiesced in by Maker or not dismissed within thirty (30) days, (a) under the Bankruptcy Code as amended, (b) for the appointment of a receiver; or (c) seeking other relief under any bankruptcy, reorganization, insolvency, dissolution, or liquidation statute of the Federal or any state government.
3. The institution by Maker of a general assignment for the benefit of Maker's creditors.
4. The suspension of Maker's business or the commission of any act by Maker which can reasonably be construed as a business failure.

The Maker hereby empowers the prothonotary, clerk or any attorney of any court of record within the United States or elsewhere to appear for the Maker and, with or without one or more declarations filed, to confess a judgment or judgments against the Maker in favor of the holder hereof as of any term for the unpaid balance of principal and interest hereof with costs of suit and an attorney's commission of 5% for collection, with release of all errors and without stay of execution, and inquisition and extension upon any levy on real estate is hereby waived and condemnation agreed to, and the exemption of all property from levy and sale on any execution thereon, and exemption of wages from attachment, are also hereby expressly waived, and no benefit of exemption shall be claimed under or by virtue of any exemption law now in force or which may hereafter be enacted.[34]

MACRO ELECTRIC VEHICLE CORPORATION

Attest: _____   By: _____

An analysis of the foregoing note follows:

Interest Rate Tied to "Prime Rate" The "prime rate" of interest is that rate of interest charged by banks to their most creditworthy borrowers for short-term unsecured debts. This rate "floats" with the market and will vary over time and from time to time. The rate varies from bank to bank, and, as set forth above, the prime rate of a specific bank or banks should be designated.

Rights Upon Default Notes will often contain provisions which specify under what circumstances the obligor is in default and the remedies available to the holder of the note in the event of default. One such remedy may be the right of the holder to "confess

---

34. This paragraph, which is typically referred to as a confession of judgment clause, is taken from a note used in a transaction in Pennsylvania. Each state's law must be followed in drafting a provision for use in that state. Many states do not allow use of such a provision. Does your state?

judgment" against the obligor. A confession of judgment clause in the note, where permitted, allows a court procedure pursuant to which the holder of the note, without obtaining the obligor's consent or approval, may obtain an immediate judgment from a court against the obligor and enforce the judgment by levy and execution on the obligor's property in accordance with state law. However, many states prohibit its use absolutely, and, even in those states where the procedure is permitted, it has been severely reduced in effectiveness in recent years on constitutional grounds. Care must be taken to review the current law in the specific state to ascertain its applicability.

Secured Debt   The note described above is an "unsecured debt" of the corporation. In such a case the creditor only has a claim against the general assets of the corporation. The holder has no special rights to any particular asset of the corporation. Rather, the holder's only recourse is to sue for payment and run the risks inherent in any piece of litigation, including inability to prove the debt or unavailability of assets to satisfy a judgment. In contrast, if there is a default on a debt and the holder of a debt security has the right to require the sale of a designated asset and to use the proceeds of such sale to pay the corporation's debt to the holder, then the debt is considered "secured."

Mortgage   Where the asset securing the debt is an interest in land and/or buildings or other real estate improvements, the instrument which grants these rights is referred to as a "mortgage" and the debtor corporation is called a "mortgagor." The mortgage does not create the debt itself but rather grants certain rights to a creditor holder of the mortgage, the "mortgagee," in the event of a default in the underlying debt obligation. The note secured by the mortgage is designated a "mortgage note." The mortgage note will refer to the mortgaged real estate and the mortgage and will normally impose certain obligations upon the mortgagor to protect and preserve the assets which secure the note. The mortgage note usually requires the mortgagor, among other things, to keep the mortgaged property adequately insured, to maintain the property in good order and condition, and to pay all taxes due respecting the mortgaged property.

A person who holds a corporate debt which is secured by a mortgage wants to be certain that no one else will be able to obtain any rights to the mortgaged property that are superior to or in a parity with his rights. Obviously, the mortgage would not provide good security for the debt if the corporation could sell or transfer the property to someone else and if, as a result of the transfer, the property was no longer securing the debt owed by the corporation. Such a result can occur if the party to whom the property was transferred did not have notice of the existence of the mortgage.

190

State laws provide a procedure by which mortgages are to be "recorded," thereby providing a public record which notifies all other parties of the secured interest of the lender. Anyone who desires to purchase the property must check the public records to ascertain the state of the title to the real estate. With limited exception relating to foreclosure, defined below, no transfer of the property subject to such notice can cut off the lender's interest in the security. Further, since any mortgagee has the right to force the sale of the mortgaged property in order to satisfy a defaulted obligation secured by the mortgage (called "foreclosure"), mortgagees quite often will not permit junior encumbrances or liens created with respect to the mortgaged property.

The subject of mortgages is generally within the field of "real estate" law and is not covered by state corporate statutes.

Security Agreements Every state in the United States (except Louisiana) has adopted the Uniform Commercial Code. Like the MBCA, the Code, while "uniform," varies in each state in many respects. Article 9 of the Code establishes a procedure by which individuals and corporations may secure debts with "personal property." Personal property is a catchall phrase that encompasses all non-real estate assets, whether tangible or intangible. Personal property includes machinery, equipment, inventory, raw materials, and furniture (tangible assets) as well as general intangibles and accounts (intangible assets).

In order for a creditor to secure a corporate debt with designated personal property, and thereby acquire a "security interest" in the property, Article 9 requires that a "security agreement" exist. With limited exceptions, the security agreement must be in writing and be signed by the debtor. It must also contain minimum information in order to be valid, including a list of the assets which secured the debt, generally called the "collateral." In addition, at the very least, it must contain language granting the security interest. It usually goes much beyond the minimum requirements. The following is a sample agreement granting the security interest and protecting the rights of the "secured party" in the assets securing the debt.

EXAMPLE

Security Agreement

SECURITY AGREEMENT

SECURITY AGREEMENT made this 1st day of July, 19___, between XYZ CORPORATION, 1700 Market Street, Philadelphia, Pennsylvania, a Pennsylvania corporation ("DEBTOR"), and THE ABC INSURANCE COMPANY, Five Penn Center, Philadelphia, Pennsylvania, a Pennsylvania corporation ("SECURED PARTY"):

WITNESSETH:

On this date SECURED PARTY shall advance to DEBTOR the principal sum of $1,000,000, to be repaid together with interest, all as

191

provided in and evidenced by a Note ("Note") of even date herewith, in the face amount of One Million Dollars ($1,000,000).

NOW, THEREFORE, to induce the SECURED PARTY to lend the sum of $1,000,000 to DEBTOR, DEBTOR and SECURED PARTY, intending to be legally bound hereby, agree as follows:

1. DEBTOR hereby grants to SECURED PARTY a security interest in all of the interest of DEBTOR in the property described in Exhibit A hereto, whenever acquired, wherever located, together with all parts, accessories, attachments, and equipment at any time installed therein or affixed thereto and all accessories thereto and additions and replacements thereof, and all proceeds and products of any of the foregoing (collectively referred to as the "Collateral"):

2. This security interest is given as security for the repayment of the aforementioned loan in accordance with the terms of the Note. DEBTOR, for itself and any subsequent owner, will at DEBTOR'S expense execute and deliver for filing all financing and other statements and take or join with SECURED PARTY in taking any other action requested by SECURED PARTY to perfect and continue perfected SECURED PARTY'S secured interest throughout the term of the Note.

3. All of the covenants and agreements in the Note to be performed by DEBTOR thereunder are incorporated herein by reference, and all of the remedies provided for herein may be exercised concurrently with the remedies provided for in the Note.

4. Until default DEBTOR shall be entitled to possession, use and enjoyment of the Collateral. A default under the Note shall also constitute a default to this Agreement. Under such circumstances SECURED PARTY may exercise all rights and remedies of a SECURED PARTY under the Uniform Commercial Code of Pennsylvania.

IN WITNESS WHEREOF, the parties have executed this Agreement as of the day and year first above written.

THE ABC INSURANCE COMPANY	XYZ CORPORATION
By: /s/George Green	By: /s/Leonard Low
Vice President	President
Attest: /s/ William White	Attest: /s/ Eileen Ajax
Secretary	Secretary

Depending upon the nature of the collateral, Article 9 also requires the filing of "financing statements" to publicly notify all persons of the existence of the security interest. This is similar to the recording of a mortgage as discussed above. The filing of a financing statement is called "perfection" of the security interest. It gives the secured party added assurance of prevailing over competing creditors for the collateral. A standard type of financing statement used in many states follows:

EXAMPLE

Financing Statement

This FINANCING STATEMENT is presented to a Filing Officer for filing pursuant to the Uniform Commercial Code.	No. of Additional Sheets Presented:	Maturity Date 3. (optional):	
1. Debtor(s) (Last Name First and Address(es):	2. Secured Party(ies): Name(s) and Address(es):	4. For Filing Officer: Date, Time, No. Filing Office	
XYZ Corporation 1700 Market Street Philadelphia, PA	The ABC Insurance Company Five Penn Center Philadelphia, PA		

5. This Financing Statement covers the following types (or items) of property:

All property on Exhibit A attached hereto.

6. Assignee(s) of Secured Party and Address(es)

☒ Proceeds —   ☐ Products of the Collateral are also covered.

7. ☐ The described crops are growing or to be grown on:*
☐ The described goods are or are to be offered to:*
* (Describe Real Estate below).

8. Describe Real Estate Here:

9. Name(s) of Record Owner(s):

No. & Street	Town or City	County	Section	Block	Lot

10. This statement is filed without the debtor's signature to perfect a security interest in collateral (check appropriate box)

☐ already subject to a security interest in another jurisdiction when it was brought into this state, or
☐ which is proceeds of the original collateral described above in which a security interest was perfected:

XYZ CORPORATION   ABC INSURANCE COMPANY

By _____   By _____
        Signature(s) of Debtor(s)   Signature(s) of Secured Party(ies)

Leonard Low,   President   George Green, Vice President

(1) FILING OFFICER COPY – NUMERICAL
FORM DSCB:UCC-1 (Rev. 8-72)—Approved by Department of State of the Commonwealth of Pa.

[B6697]

A financing statement has, at the minimum, the following requirements:

1. Name and address of debtor
2. Name and address of secured party
3. Designation of collateral covered
4. Signature of debtor
5. Signature of secured party

Note that some states only permit the official state-approved financing statements to be filed or charge a higher fee for nonapproved forms. In all cases a paralegal must ascertain the state filing requirements before preparing the forms. The proper offices for filing against a specific debtor must be carefully ascertained in every case. Various legal services exist to assist the paralegal in this research.

QUESTION

Where is a financing statement properly filed in your state?

_____

As in the area of mortgages, security interests are not covered in state corporate statutes. The Uniform Commercial Code, although found among a state's statutes, is not within the corporate statutes.

Trust Indenture The debt securities discussed in the preceding sections involve only two parties: the corporation as the debtor and the person to whom the corporation is obligated and who may have the advantage of a mortgage or security agreement covering certain real or personal property of the corporation. In many instances, however, there is a third party—a trustee—which acts on behalf of several individual holders of a debt security. A trustee is usually a bank.

When a corporation or municipality proposes to issue a debt security, whether secured or unsecured, to more than one person, it may decide (or by law be required) to designate one person, the trustee, to act on behalf of all holders of the debt security in case of default by the debtor. This avoids the necessity of dealing with many individual creditors in the event of a default. The corporation will execute a trust indenture with a trustee prior to the issuance of debt securities. The trust indenture will contain all of the terms and conditions of the securities, and, pursuant to its terms, the corporation will be permitted to issue bonds or debentures. (Normally, the term "bonds" is used to describe secured debt and the word "debentures" is used to describe unsecured debt.) In certain instances, where the debt is a large amount to be held by many persons, the use of a trustee is required by the Federal Trust Indenture Act of 1939. A trust indenture normally will contain complex provisions designating the trustee and its responsibilities, the form of the debt instrument, the events of default, certain obligations of the corporation as to its operation, and the mortgage or security interest, if any.

Common Provisions in Debt Securities

Certain of the more common substantive provisions of debt securities will be discussed now. These provisions, for the most part, are the counterpart for debt securities of provisions found in equity securities. The only new concept which is introduced is "subordination." In simple terms, subordination is an agreement by the holders of one type of debt security that they will not be entitled to receive any interest or principal payment from the debtor if the debtor has not paid one or more other types of debt securities or if the holders of another type of security have not been paid in full. In effect, the subordination of debt establishes relative priorities between various debt securities of a corporation.

QUESTION Why would the holders of debt securities ever agree to be subordinate to another type of indebtedness?

Redemption Most holders of debt securities are unwilling to permit the debtor to redeem debt before its maturity date. The reason for this is that the holder of the debt security desires some minimum period of time during which the holder can expect to receive the bargained-for interest on the debt security even if interest rates have declined and the debtor would be able to borrow money at lower interest rates. Therefore, debt securities often provide for a period of time after the issuance of the debt during which no redemption can take place. After this period has elapsed, the debtor may redeem the debt but in many cases will have to pay a premium. The premium usually declines as the maturity date of the debt approaches. The rationale of such an arrangement, once again, is to assure the holders of the debt security that they will receive the anticipated interest for a certain period of time. This is accomplished by discouraging the debtor from redeeming the debt with money borrowed at a lower interest cost if interest rates should decline.

EXAMPLE

Redemption at Premium

This note and the notes of this issue are subject to redemption by the Corporation, at the option of its Board of Directors, in whole or in part, at any time after July 1, 19___, and from time to time thereafter and until maturity, upon thirty (30) days prior written notice to the registered holder at the address of such holder as the same appears on the Corporation's records, at the following redemption prices (expressed in percentages of the principal amount), together in each case with accrued interest to the date fixed for redemption:

Time	Percentage of Principal Amount
July 1, 1985 to June 30, 1986	106%
July 1, 1986 to June 30, 1987	105%
July 1, 1987 to June 30, 1988	104%
July 1, 1988 to June 30, 1989	103%
July 1, 1989 to June 30, 1990	102%
July 1, 1990 to June 30, 1991	101%
July 1, 1991 to maturity	100%

In case of the redemption of a part only of the notes of this issue at the time outstanding, the Corporation may select by lot, or in such other equitable manner as the Board of Directors may determine, the notes so to be redeemed. The Board of Directors shall have full power and authority, subject to the limitations and provisions herein contained, to prescribe the manner in which, and the terms and conditions upon which, the notes shall be redeemed from time to time. If such notice of redemption shall have been duly given, and if, on or before the redemption date specified in such notice, the funds necessary for such redemption shall have been set apart so as to be and continue to be available therefor, then, notwithstanding that any notes called for redemption shall not have been surrendered for cancellation, the notes shall no longer be deemed outstanding; the right to receive interest thereon shall cease to accrue from and after the date of redemption so fixed; and all rights with respect to such notes so called for redemption shall forthwith on such redemption date cease and terminate, except only the right of the holders thereof to receive the redemption price therefor, together with accrued interest to the date fixed for redemption.

If a corporation has the above provision in its debt security, what price must it pay if the security is to be called in its entirety as of August 1, 1988 and $10,000,000 is outstanding?

Sinking Fund As briefly mentioned before, a sinking fund provision in a debt security is designed to minimize the burden on the debtor of paying the entire principal amount of the debt at maturity. It does this by providing for a regular procedure for retiring part of the debt periodically before maturity or setting aside money in a separate account outside of the control of the debtor for the purpose only of retiring the debt.[35] The holders of the debt security are likely to favor such a provision because the lessened burden to the debtor will increase the likelihood of repayment.

Why might the holders dislike such a provision? (Hint: See the immediately preceding subsection relating to redemption.)

Sinking fund provisions may be very complex when the debt has been issued under a trust indenture because of the role of the trustee.

Conversion Corporate debt securities are frequently convertible into equity securities. This "equity kicker" is designed to make the security more attractive to prospective purchasers. The terms of the conversion and the mechanics for carrying it out must be set forth in detail. The form should be similar to those for preferred stock with respect to "antidilution provisions."[36]

Subordination When holders of a debt security agree to "subordinate" that debt to other debt which the debtor may then or at some future time have outstanding, they are agreeing to permit the holders of other debt securities to have a prior right to the debtor's assets in the event that the superior debt is not paid. The following

35. See the discussion earlier in this chapter of sinking funds with respect to preferred stock.
36. See the discussion earlier in this chapter of conversion with respect to preferred stock.

is a sample of a relatively simple form of subordination provision. Note how carefully the terms are defined and spelled out.

EXAMPLE

Subordination Provision

> The notes of this issue are subordinate and junior in right to payment, as to principal only, to any and all indebtedness which is now due or which in the future may become due by the Corporation, hereinafter called "Senior Debt,"[37] except to the extent that any such indebtedness is evidenced by notes of this issue. The holder of this note, by acceptance hereof, agrees to such subordination and junior right to payment, and, in furtherance thereof also agrees: (1) that, in the event of liquidation of the Corporation, in dissolution (voluntary or involuntary), bankruptcy, any other insolvency proceedings, or otherwise, not to receive any amount on account of the principal of this note unless and until all Senior Debt is first paid in full, and the holder hereof agrees to and does hereby assign all claims against and rights to share in the assets of the Corporation in any such liquidation, arising from the principal of this note, pro rata to holders of the Senior Debt, to the extent necessary to assure payment in full of all Senior Debt prior to any payment in such liquidation of any of the principal hereof; and (2) if, at the maturity of this note, the Corporation is in default with respect to any Senior Debt, the maturity of this note shall be extended without notice until such time as there shall be no default by the Corporation with respect to any Senior Debt; and (3) that, in the event the holder of this note obtains a judgment for the principal hereof, not to enforce collection of such judgment while Senior Debt is in existence, and to make on or insert in the record of such judgment the fact that such judgment is subordinate and junior in right to payment to Senior Debt as herein defined. The foregoing agreements are expressly and solely for the benefit of holders of Senior Debt and nothing herein shall impair the obligation of the Corporation to the holder hereof under the terms hereof.

QUESTION

Why is it extremely advantageous to the corporation to have some of its debts subordinated?

In deciding whether the purchase of senior debt securities is a good investment, a purchaser can basically ignore the amount of subordinated debt outstanding because the senior debt must be paid in full before the subordinated debt receives any payment. For that reason, however, the subordinated debt itself is less attractive to investors. Subordinated debt is usually salable only if the debt security has some other feature which compensates for its inherent disadvantage (e.g., higher interest rate, conversion feature, favorable redemption terms). It may be purchased by an existing shareholder of the corporation who wants to supply the corporation with additional cash without adversely affecting the corpora-

---

37. Note again the importance of using a shorthand definition for a complicated term or concept.

tion's ability to borrow money from other sources. Such a shareholder would, at the same time, perhaps want to have rights to the corporation's assets which are superior to that of a common stockholder. By making the shareholder a lender, even on a subordinated basis with respect to the new injection of money, the corporation makes the shareholder prior in right of payment to shareholders.

QUESTIONS

Is the shareholder's status as a shareholder affected with respect to the money already invested as a shareholder by becoming a subordinated lender? How?

It should be noted that, with the agreement of the lender, debt may be subordinated after its creation. That situation may occur where the debtor is in a period of financial hardship and cannot fully repay the original debt. The holders of the debt securities might believe that, with further borrowed capital, the debtor would have a chance to recover. Accordingly, they may be willing to subordinate their right of repayment to the new borrowing.

QUESTIONS

Can a debt security be subordinate to some debt and superior to other debt? Who must agree to such an arrangement if it is possible to create it?

CHAPTER SEVEN

Employment Agreements

Since lawyers are often called upon to prepare employment contracts for their clients, and since there are common elements in most of these contracts, it is natural to expect that lawyers' assistants may be expected to prepare initial drafts of employment contracts. Chapter Seven is intended to provide the necessary training for this purpose. It is also designed to further refine the drafting skills of a lawyer's assistant and to introduce the lawyer's assistant to the typical format of legal agreements.

GENERAL CONSIDERATIONS

Purpose

The purpose of an employment agreement is rather obvious—to set forth in writing the terms on which an employment relationship is entered into, and the rights, duties, and obligations of the employer and employee. The terms of an employment agreement may vary substantially from one agreement to another depending upon the nature of the job, the duration of the agreement, the amount of compensation involved, and numerous other factors. However, every well-drafted employment agreement will contain provisions dealing with the basic components of the employment relationship. These basic components are listed below and will be individually discussed and analyzed.

Employment Relationships Without Written Agreements

The majority of employment relationships are never documented by written agreements. Employees performing relatively routine services who do not have special skills which would make replacement difficult normally perform without an employment agreement. The employment relationship of such employees is governed in accordance with compensation provisions and other rules and regulations developed by the employer and with applicable federal and state laws establishing wage and hour requirements and requirements as to working conditions systematically applied to the class of employee involved. The rights of employees who are members of an organized union are normally governed exclusively by the union agreement. It is unusual for such an employee to have an individual employment agreement.

General Benefits and Burdens of Written Employment Agreements

Written employment agreements are commonly entered into with persons who occupy key managerial and executive positions, salespeople, research and development personnel engaged in projects which may be entitled to legal protection (such as a patent, copyright, or trade secret protection), and other employees bringing special skills to their jobs. However, even with respect to these types of employees, many employers strongly resist or, as a matter of policy, refuse to enter into written employment agreements. This attitude is based on the fact that in many cases an employment agreement establishes legal rights and security for the employee without providing comparable benefit to the employer.

Fundamentally, an employee, upon entering into an employment agreement, makes a commitment to render certain services for a certain period of time, and the employer, in return, commits itself to pay the agreed compensation and provide other benefits during that period. If the employee comes to dislike the employment, either because of the rate of compensation, the coworkers, or the opportunity to get a better job, the employee can simply leave the employment and, as a practical matter, incur no liability to the employer by the decision to leave.

While an employment agreement may extend for a specified period of time (e.g., three years), the employer has no legal right to force an employee to remain in its employ for such period; all that can happen if an employee leaves is for the employer to terminate the benefits payable to the employee under the contract. An employer cannot require an employee to perform as agreed because such a requirement would be involuntary servitude in violation of federal and state constitutions; and, according to a general principle of contract law, a contract for personal services may not be specifically enforced.

On the other hand, the employer cannot terminate the employment of an employee who is under contract without remaining financially liable to the employee, unless the employer can demonstrate, as an objective factual matter, that the employee has failed to perform the duties under the agreement or has otherwise violated a provision of the agreement. If no oral or written agreement existed, an employment relationship could be terminated by the employer at will, without legal consequences or continuing financial responsibility to the employee. Absent union provisions, employment with the ability of the employer to terminate at will is the situation existing in most employment relationships.

QUESTION

If an employee does not have a written employment contract but was hired on the understanding that the employee would be compensated "at $200,000 per annum," is such employee assured of at least one year of employment?

The principal legal obligations incurred by an employee in signing an employment agreement are to perform as required by the agreement and to comply with the "restrictive covenant," one of the basic components of employment agreements. A restrictive covenant exists where an employment agreement provides that if the employee terminates the employment in violation of the agreement, or upon the termination of employment through expiration of the agreement itself, the employee will be legally barred for a period of time thereafter from engaging in activities competitive to the business activities of the employer. Such a restrictive covenant is intended to prevent an employee from breaking the relationship for the employee's own economic self-interest to the detriment of the employer or to use business secrets or customer lists obtained during the employment. However, legal and practical considerations limit the effectiveness of restrictive convenants in many employment agreements.

General Statement of Basic Components and Structure of Employment Agreements

The basic components of an employment agreement are as follows:

1. Mutual agreement to employ and to perform duties
2. Capacity and duties to be performed by employee
3. Term of employment and termination
4. Compensation and other economic benefits to employee

   a. Basic compensation
   b. Incentive compensation
   c. Other benefits
   d. Expense reimbursement

5. Restrictive covenants, trade secret protective clauses, and related provisions

Each of these basic components of an employment agreement will be separately analyzed. Depending upon the general complexity of the agreement, the nature of the employment, and other considerations, one of the basic components listed above may not appear as a single section or paragraph of an agreement but, rather, may be covered in numerous different sections or paragraphs. Alternatively, a single section or paragraph of an employment agreement may deal with certain aspects of two or more of such basic components. The structure of an employment agreement will become evident from the form provisions and form agreements contained in these materials.

ANALYSIS OF BASIC COMPONENTS OF EMPLOYMENT AGREEMENTS

Mutual Agreement to Employ and Perform Duties

Form Provision   The following clause is a typical example of this normally short and simple provision. It contains the operative bilateral contractual promises, commonly the initial provision of an employment agreement:

Company hereby employs Employee as its sales manager, and Employee hereby accepts said employment, subject to all of the terms and conditions of this agreement.

Discussion   This provision is intended to do nothing more than express the basic undertaking of each party to the other. It has legal significance because, as a general principle of contract law, an agreement must contain obligations or benefits running to or from both parties in order to be binding. It has become a matter of common practice to have such a general expression of mutual obligation at the outset of any agreement, whether employment or otherwise.[1]

Capacity and Duties

Form Provisions   The following are two typical examples of employment agreement provisions setting forth the capacity and duties of the employee:

---

1. Look at the form agreements at the end of this chapter for variations on this type of provision.

EXAMPLE

*Employment
Agreement
Provisions
Form 1*

(a) Employee is employed as the executive officer of Corporation in charge of production, and to assist the chief executive officer of Corporation in the operation and management of the business and affairs of Corporation, subject to the supervision and direction of Corporation's Board of Directors, and to perform such other technical, managerial, and executive functions and services for Corporation as Employee may from time to time be requested to perform by the President or the Board of Directors of Corporation.

(b) During the period of employment hereunder, Employee agrees to devote Employee's time, energy, skill, and best efforts to promote the business and affairs of Corporation, and to perform faithfully to the fullest extent of Employee's ability all the duties which relate to Employee's position as may be requested of Employee by Corporation's Board of Directors or President. Employee agrees that during the original term of this agreement and any renewal terms, Employee will not be employed by, participate or engage in, or be a part of in any manner, directly or indirectly, the affairs of any other business enterprise or occupation which would interfere with the performance of Employee's full time duties hereunder.

EXAMPLE

*Employment
Agreement
Provisions
Form 2*

Employee shall serve as a salesperson in the territory comprising the states of Pennsylvania, New Jersey, and Delaware (herein called the "Territory"). Employee agrees to devote Employee's entire time, energy, skill, and attention to the sale of products fabricated or sold by Employer, to the exclusion of all other business interests, and in that connection to solicit orders actively for the sale of said products of Employer, to generally promote the business and affairs of Employer, and to perform such other duties as may from time to time be assigned to Employee by the officers of Employer. Employee shall travel throughout the Territory, and give it thorough coverage in accordance, and in compliance, with the instructions and directions from Employer, which shall include the time or times when Employee shall travel in the aforesaid Territory and the duration of the trips. Employee shall submit periodic itineraries, reports, and other data, as required, in accordance with Employer's sales program.

Discussion

General While the above examples state the employee's duties in rather summary fashion, they are typical of provisions on the subject included in agreements with executives, high level supervisory personnel, and sales personnel. When an employee's work is more specialized or unique, the agreement is more likely to detail the specific function. Such a detailed description is sometimes included even in common employment situations.[2] The provisions dealing with capacity and duties are of great legal importance. In the event an employee asserts a claim based on an alleged improper termination of employment, the employer's defense usually will be that the employee failed to carry out the prescribed duties.

Note carefully that, as is true of form utilization in all cases, a paralegal must modify forms to fit the matter at hand, not try to make the matter at hand fit an available form. Moreover, agreements are not drafted in a vacuum; they have a point of view and perspective. If a paralegal is drafting an employment agreement for the employer, it will look far different than if the paralegal were drafting it for the employee in the same transaction.[3]

Principal Elements

1. Breadth of Coverage

Regardless of the extent to which duties are specifically designated, it is desirable from the employer's point of view to have catchall language which provides that the employee shall perform such other duties as may be requested by higher ranking officers of the company or by the company's board of directors. From the employee's point of view, it is important that the agreement at least indicate that the other duties which may be requested shall be "reasonable" and be related to the principal duties which are to be performed. The form provisions above are favorable to the employer in that they do not clearly specify such limitations. While a court interpreting these provisions might conclude, in the event of a dispute, that such limitations are implicit, the employee would have been well-advised to ask for express language, and the employer would not be likely to refuse such a request.

2. Time Commitment

It is important to the employer that the capacity and duties provision state that the employee's commitment is a full-time one, if that is in fact the understanding. When dealing with executives, it is not unusual for the employee to insist that the agreement specify that the employee shall, nevertheless, be permitted to have investments in other companies, to serve on boards of directors of other noncompeting companies, to participate in civic and charitable organizations, or other similar activities.[4]

2. See, for example, paragraph 1 of Form Agreement 1 and paragraph 2 of Form Agreement 2 near the end of this chapter.
3. In this connection, consider the difference in detail of job description that would be drafted from an employer perspective rather than an employee perspective. Which side (employer or employee) is more likely to desire a very detailed description of the job?
4. See, for example, paragraphs 2(c) and 8 of Form Agreement 2.

3. Title of Employee

An employee is often quite concerned about a title. Although it may be contemplated that an executive will be the president or vice president of the employer, the employment agreement should, from the employer's point of view, designate the employee's capacity as that of chief executive or as a senior executive rather than as president or vice president. This is because corporate officers, as a matter of law, are elected in each year by the company's board of directors, and the corporation cannot properly make a contractual commitment on a subject which the directors have the right and obligation to determine.[5]

4. Other

Depending upon the nature of the employment, the capacity and duties provisions may specify the place of employment,[6] may have particular provisions as to hours, may specify the amount of vacation to which the employee is entitled,[7] may put maximums on the portion of time that the employee can be required to travel, or deal with any number of other particulars.[8]

Restrictions on Employee's Authority   In establishing the capacity and duties of an employee, the employment agreement will in some instances set forth specific limitations on the employee's authority. For example, the following provision or some comparable language commonly appears in an agreement with a salesperson.[9]

> Employee's authority to act for Employer is limited strictly to the solicitation of orders, and all orders received as a result of Employee's solicitation shall be subject to acceptance or rejection by Employer at its principal office in Philadelphia, Pennsylvania. Employer may refuse or reject, either in whole or in part, any order received as a result of Employee's solicitations, and may cancel any such order, either in whole or in part, after acceptance. Employee agrees in all respects to observe the rules and regulations of Employer as to price, terms, and other conditions of sale, and Employee shall have no power to authorize returns or offer special prices, terms, or conditions unless special written instructions are given to Employee by Employer.

5. The provisions of paragraphs 2(a), 7(b), and 8 of Form Agreement 2 recognize that the employee has no contractual right to be elected an officer but gives the employee certain termination rights if not so elected. Such provisions are rare and represent good provisions from the employee's perspective.

6. See paragraphs 1 and 3 of Form Agreement 3.

7. See paragraph 2(b) of Form Agreement 2.

8. Again, the detail as to which particulars are covered depends on the item, which side is being represented, and the results of negotiations.

9. See also Form 2 on p. 238.

Another express limitation might specify a dollar ceiling on the size of contracts which the employee is permitted to enter into on behalf of the company without prior approval by a higher officer or the company's board of directors, for example, a limit on the dollar amount of raw materials which may be ordered by a production manager. The purposes of such provisions are twofold: (a) to make clear to the employee the limits of authority, and (b) to provide support to the employer in justifying that it is not "doing business" within a particular state even if one of its salesperson-employees is soliciting sales or performing certain other functions in that jurisdiction.[10]

PROBLEM

Which of the following is the better provision in an employment contract from the employer's standpoint? Why?

Alternative 1.

Employee will carry out such business activities as may be requested by the Board of Directors from time to time during the term of this Agreement.

Alternative 2.

Employee will perform as a sales executive and in such other sales supervisory positions as may be requested by the Board of Directors from time to time during the term of this Agreement.

Term of Employment; Termination

Form Provision   The following is a typical provision setting forth the duration of the obligations of the parties under an employment agreement:

> This agreement shall be for a term of three (3) years, commencing on the date hereof, and thereafter shall automatically be renewed from year to year, unless either party shall give notice to the other no less than ninety (90) days prior to the end of the initial term or of any renewal term of such party's intention to terminate the agreement at the end of said term.

Discussion

General   In the absence of an employment agreement, the employment relationship is terminable at the will of either party. If a written employment agreement does not specify the term of the

10. Certain burdens are assumed by a corporation which is "doing business" in a state other than its state of incorporation, and it must, therefore, qualify to do business in such state. Under § 15.01 of the MBCA, a foreign corporation is not deemed to be transacting business within the state so as to require qualification if all it does is solicit or procure orders "where such orders require acceptance without this state before becoming binding contracts." A restriction of the type found in the preceding form will support the position that a corporation need not qualify as a foreign corporation and thereby subject itself to additional regulatory and tax burdens.

agreement, the agreement is assumed to be for a term which is reasonable in the light of the circumstances. That doctrine leaves so much uncertainty that it is basic to every employment agreement that a term be specified.

Does an employer guarantee that an employee will stay in the employ for the specified term by execution of an employment agreement? Does the employee guarantee employment for that period of time? Which party benefits more?

If, as in the above form provision, renewals of the employment term are automatically assumed, a notice period must be specified to provide for the mechanics of termination of the agreement by either party. The notice period is not necessarily the same for both parties although it usually is. The appropriate length of the notice period varies depending upon the nature of the employment, with more specialized and unique employees properly calling for longer notice periods because of the difficulty of finding suitable employment and/or replacement.[11]

Employment agreements sometimes do not have automatic renewal provisions but are simply for a specified term. In such a case, neither party has an obligation to continue the employment relationship after the term has expired or to notify the other party of termination.

Termination Many employment agreements do not have any express provisions dealing with what acts or omissions provide justification for the other party to terminate the agreement. However, it is implicit in every employment agreement that, if one party breaches or fails to perform the agreement, the other party has the right to terminate without further liability or obligation. As indicated in the discussion of capacity and duties, a dispute about whether termination by the employer was proper will usually turn on whether or not the employee property performed, which is an inherently factual matter that frequently cannot be adequately dealt with by written standards in an agreement, no matter how well drafted. Some agreements do spell out specific grounds for termination, such as the employee's being convicted of a crime or committing an act involving moral turpitude.[12]

11. The mechanics of form and place of notice are dealt with by a notice provision which is one of the routine provisions near the end of every employment agreement. See, for example, paragraph 7 of Form Agreement 1, paragraph 9 of Form Agreement 2, paragraph 14 of Form Agreement 3, and paragraph 10 of Form Agreement 4.

12. See, for example, paragraph 7(c) of Form Agreement 2.

In the case of executives, continuation of employment is sometimes made dependent on the attainment of certain sales increases or profit levels, although it is more common to set lower fixed compensation levels and provide for bonuses or another form of incentive compensation based on sales or profit targets. Disability which causes an inability of the employee to work for more than a specified period of time and death are other reasons for termination.[13]

Special drafting becomes necessary when an employment agreement provides for incentive compensation. For example, if the agreement gives the employee the right to a bonus of 5% of the employer's profits for a given year, the agreement should set forth what happens if employment is terminated during the course of that year.[14]

Compensation

The compensation arrangements in an employment agreement can range from a simple straight salary or straight commission arrangement to a complex combination of various incentive compensation arrangements, fringe benefits, and expense allowances coupled with a salary. The discussion of compensation arrangements will, therefore, be divided into several subsections dealing with these matters.

Basic Compensation

Form Provisions The following are two typical examples of employment agreement provisions setting forth basic compensation arrangements, the first establishing a straight salary arrangement and the second a straight commission arrangement, with a "draw":

EXAMPLE

Compensation Provisions Form 1

> Corporation shall pay to Employee, as basic compensation for all services rendered by Employee during the employment hereunder, a salary at the rate of $20,000 per annum, payable in such weekly, biweekly, or monthly installments as shall be in accordance with Corporation's prevailing payroll arrangements.

13. See the sample clause on page 244, which provides for termination after a specified period of disability.

14. See the sample forms under "Incentive Compensation" to be discussed shortly in this chapter.

EXAMPLE

Compensation Provisions Form 2

As sole compensation for Employee's services as a salesperson, Employer shall (subject to the withholding provisions of all applicable federal, state, and local employment taxes) pay Employee the commissions hereinafter set forth on all orders which are obtained by Employee and filled by Employer, for which full payment is received. In the event of returns by, or credits or allowances to any customer, Employee's commission account will be charged for any commissions previously credited or paid pertaining to such merchandise or account.

The commission on merchandise sold at regular prices will be paid at the rate of 5% of net sales of Employer from orders obtained by Employee. The commission paid on merchandise sold below regular wholesale price (or with special terms and/or conditions) will be 2% of net sales of Employer based on orders obtained by Employee, except if otherwise specified by Employer prior to such offering of merchandise (Employee shall be authorized to solicit orders below regular wholesale price or with special terms and/or conditions only when expressly permitted to do so by Employer). Furthermore, no commission shall be paid with respect to merchandise sold 33⅓% or more below regular wholesale price, except as otherwise specified by Employer prior to such offering of merchandise.

Employer agrees that Employee shall have the right to make a weekly draw of $200 against future commissions, such drawings to be deemed on account of, or advances against commissions to be earned by Employee and to be charged and deducted from commissions earned as and when such commissions shall be payable to Employee.

Employer agrees to furnish Employee with a copy of all invoices covering any goods shipped into Employee's territory and to furnish Employee with a statement on or before the 25th day of each month covering the amount of sales represented by such shipments for the previous month and the amount of commission due Employee, which amount shall be paid at the time said statement is delivered.

Discussion

1. Salary

Form 1 above provides for a straight salary and is simple and self-explanatory. The provision indicates the amount of compensation and the frequency with which the compensation is to be paid. Straight salary provisions will sometimes have escalation arrangements, for example, a salary of $20,000 during the first year, $22,000 the second year, and so forth, or a rate of escalation based upon a certain percentage of the initial year's compensation.[15] The presence of a fixed compensation amount or schedule does not, of course, prevent the parties from agreeing to

15. See paragraph 3 of Form Agreement 1.

209

a change in salary arrangements during the term of the agreement, by an amendment to the agreement.[16]

2. Commission

Form 2 above sets forth a complex commission arrangement involving numerous issues, such as which sales are included, at what point in the course of processing a customer's order for goods the commission on that order has been earned, varying commission rates on sales at different prices, and the right of the sales representative to make draws against commission. It is critical, however, to spell out all of these aspects with clarity so that there is no ambiguity in the provision. Without attempting to illustrate all the possible variations on each of these issues, it is sufficient to point out that each of the issues can be resolved in numerous ways. For example, the commission clause above states that the commission on a particular order is earned only at such time as full payment therefor has been received from the customer. It is probably more common (particularly in a seasonal or special order business in which goods may not be shipped, billed, or paid for for several months after an order is placed) for a commission to be earned at the time that the goods are shipped, with a subsequent charge against the employee's commission account if the customer fails to pay. In some cases, the commission is earned regardless of payment and the risk of uncollectibility is borne by the employer.

3. Effect of General Legal Principles When Agreement is Silent

The commission provision in Form 2 above may be considered deficient in at least one respect. It establishes the right of the employee to make a weekly "draw" which is an advance against future commissions earned. This means that commission payments are reduced by the amount previously drawn by the employee, but the clause does not spell out what the result will be if the salesman does not earn an amount equal to or greater than what he has drawn. In some states the law on this point is that the draw is a minimum compensation to which the employee is entitled regardless of commissions earned. In other states, the employer would have the right to recover from the employee the amount by which the draw exceeded commissions earned. Since the laws of different states vary on this point, and since the law in many other states is unclear, it is important to recognize this problem at the time the agreement is being prepared and deal with it expressly in the agreement when it is feasible to do so. If disputes or questions arise in the course of the employment relationship,

---

16. Language in an agreement such as that of the last clause of paragraph 4 of Form Agreement 4 stating that compensation is subject to adjustments which may be mutually agreed upon, is often desired by employees but has no legal effect. In the absence of an actual amendment to the agreement which must be agreed upon, the specified compensation amount remains applicable, without the employee's having any right to adjustments.

the lawyer will be called upon to interpret the agreement for his client, and the lawyer's task will be simplified to the extent that the point in issue is covered by clear language in the agreement, rather than by general principles of law which may not be well-defined and will, in any event, require time-consuming and expensive research.

A client may sometimes prefer that an agreement be silent on a certain point, rather than raise a sensitive issue, even at the risk of weakening the client's legal position if a dispute arises. In the case of the draw provision, for example, most employers would probably be very hesitant to present an agreement to an employee that states that the employee may be obligated to repay certain amounts previously paid to him. It is the responsibility of the paralegal to highlight the issue to the lawyer for presentation to the client, so that the lawyer may advise the client of the implications of the silence of the agreement on the issue. In the absence of clear law on the subject in the jurisdiction involved, unless there is persuasive evidence that the agreement was thoroughly negotiated, an issue on which the agreement is silent is likely to be resolved in favor of the employee.

QUESTION

Why do you suppose that this is the case?

_____

Incentive Compensation

General The concept underlying any incentive compensation arrangement is that all or some portion of the employee's compensation should be dependent upon the success of the employee's and employer's efforts. The theory is, of course, that the employee will strive to make the employer successful when the employee will directly share in this success. An incentive compensation arrangement may take almost unlimited possible forms. There may be payments in cash or in stock of the employer corporation, payments based on the sales or profits of the corporation or the market value of the corporation's stock, payments which are made currently, or payments which are deferred for a short period or until retirement. The incentive compensation may be based upon the performance of an entire company or upon the performance of a particular subsidiary or division of a company or even upon the company's success with respect to a particular product.

The paralegal ordinarily will not frame the incentive compensation arrangement. However, the paralegal must understand the possibilities in order to draft a provision that has been negotiated.

211

The basic idea of incentive compensation usually is to have the arrangement relate to the employee's functions. Therefore, a person who is a sales manager is likely to have an incentive compensation arrangement based on the company's sales or increases in sales over what they were before the manager joined the company. If the employee is a sales manager for a particular territory, a sales-based incentive compensation arrangement normally would relate to sales performance in that territory. In the case of an executive whose duties are not principally in the sales area, the arrangement would be more likely to be based upon the company's profits or profit increases.

Because of the wide variety of incentive compensation arrangements, the discussion will be divided into several subcategories.

Cash Incentive Compensation

1. Form Provisions

As mentioned above, the basis and method of computing incentive compensation can have many variations. The following are two typical examples of incentive compensation arrangements, the first being based upon the net income of the division of the employing company for which the employee works, and the second being based upon increases in the sales revenues of the employing company over sales revenues for the previous year:

EXAMPLE

Incentive Compensation Provisions Form 1

In addition to the fixed salary specified above, Employee shall be entitled to a bonus, as follows:

(a) For each of the first two years of employment under this Agreement, five percent (5%) of the net income of the Fletcher Division during each fiscal year of the Company.

(b) For each year of employment under the Agreement thereafter, two and one-half percent (2½%) of the net income of the Fletcher Division during each fiscal year of the Company.

Said bonus shall be payable within thirty (30) days following the receipt by Company and Employee of the statement of profit and loss for the fiscal year prepared by Company's independent certified public accountants. For the purposes of this paragraph:

(i) The "net income" of the Fletcher Division shall be determined by the Company's independent certified public accountants in accordance with generally accepted accounting principles consistently applied (except for adjustments expressly specified in the subsequent subparagraph of this paragraph), based upon the separate records and books of account maintained for the Fletcher Division, and said determination shall be conclusive and binding on the parties to this Agreement;

(ii) No charge against the income of the Fletcher Division shall be made for any federal or state taxes paid or payable by Company which are determined or measured by the amount of the income of Company or of the Fletcher Division;

(iii) Gains or losses resulting from the disposition of assets other than inventory and any other extraordinary gains or losses shall be excluded from the computation of the net income of Company and the Fletcher Division;

(iv) All transactions between the Fletcher Division and other divisions of the Company or between the Fletcher Division and the parent corporation of the Company or other subsidiaries of said parent corporation shall be at the going rates then in effect for those transactions, in accordance with overall policies established by the parent corporation of the Company;

(v) For any period less than a full fiscal year of Corporation during which Employee is employed hereunder, the portion of the Fletcher Division's net income with respect to which Employee shall be entitled to a bonus shall be the Fletcher's Division's net income for that portion of the fiscal year during which Employee was employed.

EXAMPLE

Incentive Compensation Provisions Form 2

(i) In addition to the fixed salary above, Employee shall be entitled to incentive compensation, to be paid within ninety (90) days after the end of the fiscal year in question, computed by multiplying the amount by which the "Adjusted Net Sales" (as hereinafter defined) of Employer for said year exceed Employer's "Net Sales" (as hereinafter defined) for the fiscal year immediately prior to said year, by the applicable percentage set forth in subparagraph (ii) hereof.

(ii) For the purposes of the preceding subparagraph hereof, the percentages applicable to the amount by which the Adjusted Net Sales of Employer during the fiscal year in question exceeds the Net Sales of Employer for the immediately preceding fiscal year are as follows:

Up to $250,000 of excess net sales...........................½%
More than $250,000 and up to $500,000 of excess net sales ...¾%
More than $500,000 of excess net sales.......................1%

(iii) For the purpose of this Agreement, "Net Sales" shall mean the gross sales of Employer, less all returns, allowances, credits, and discounts, as set forth on the income statement prepared by Employer's independent accountants for the fiscal year in question. For the purpose of this Agreement "Adjusted Net Sales" shall mean Net Sales, reduced by the portion of Net Sales revenues attributable to increases in average unit prices over the average unit prices of the previous year, it being the understanding of the parties that Employee's incentive compensation is to be based upon increases in the number of units sold rather than increases in Net Sales revenues arising from price increases.

(iv) If Employee ceases to be employed hereunder on a date other than the last day of the fiscal year of Employer, then Employee shall be entitled to a portion of the incentive compensation which would have been payable to Employee if Employee had been employed throughout said fiscal year, determined by computing the full amount of incentive compensation which would have been payable and multiplying said amount by a fraction, the numerator of which shall be the number of working days of said fiscal year during which Employee was employed, and the denominator of which shall be the total number of working days in that fiscal year.

2. Discussion

Every well-drafted cash incentive compensation provision should deal with each of the issues discussed below:

Frequency and Specific Time of Payment

Each of the form provisions above provides for a single annual incentive compensation payment. This arrangement has the advantage of requiring computations only once per year and also facilitates reliance upon the accountants engaged by the employer for making the computations, since most companies have annual financial statements prepared by independent accountants. There are other forms of incentive compensation arrangements which provide for monthly, quarterly or semiannual payments, particularly when the incentive compensation represents a substantial portion of the employee's overall compensation. In such cases it is common to provide that the first payment to be made after the end of the company's fiscal year will be adjusted if the payments made during the year aggregate an amount different from what would have been paid based on a single payment made on the basis of the company's performance throughout the year. The need for such a provision arises from the fact that many accounting determinations which may significantly affect the company's financial results (for example, the taking of inventory by a physical count on the last day of the fiscal year) are made accurately only once a year, with estimates being made in the interim.

In addition to the matter of frequency of payments, the specific time of payment also should be set forth. With annual payments, it is normal to specify a date which can reasonably be expected to be an early date after the completion of the financial statements by the accountants. The first form provision expressly ties in with the annual financial statements by stating that the payment date is to be thirty days after receipt of the financial statements by the company. The second form provision specifies a payment date ninety days after the end of the fiscal year. This date is intended to tie in with the company's yearly financial statements, but the provision leaves itself open to the possibility that the financial statements may be delayed beyond the payment date.

Who Makes Determinations

Both of the above forms provide that the independent accountants engaged by the company shall make the determinations which in turn establish the amount of the incentive compensation. When the company engages independent accountants to certify that the statements they have prepared are true and correct, without qualification (called "certified" or "audited" statements), it is customary to have their determinations be conclusive on all parties. Reliance on accountants' computations is common even when certified statements are not being prepared, but, since the accountant is engaged and paid by the employer, there may be some risk to the employee of an unfavorable determination in such circumstances, and the risk may be still greater if the determinations are being made by a company officer. In such circumstances the employee may be wise to insist that the provision merely state that net income or net sales shall be determined in accordance with generally accepted accounting principles, consistently applied, leaving it open for assertion with respect to any particular computation that in fact the computation was not in accordance with a consistent application of such principles.

Accounting Questions and Definitions

Regardless of who is making the determinations, it is always necessary to consider whether there should be any variations from generally accepted accounting principles for purposes of computing incentive compensation. In Form 1 there are several express deviations from the general definition of net income. The theory behind these definitions is simply that unusual occurrences in the company's operation should be disregarded for purposes of determining compensation of an employee who has no control over nor anything to do with such occurrences. Note that such exclusions can favor or disfavor the employee depending upon whether the unusual transaction was beneficial or disadvantageous to the company.

It will be necessary to define certain terms in order that the accounting provisions as well as other terms are well-drafted. The general form used by lawyers to define terms in agreements, including parties, concepts, places, and the like, is to define the term and place the defined term in quotations. Look at the first paragraph in Form Agreement 1 setting forth the parties, and notice the method of defining "Employer" and "Employee." The terms "Employer" and "Employee" (as well as other defined terms) are capitalized to indicate that for purposes of the agreement they are proper nouns. The importance of defining terms at the earliest possible point in the agreement is that the person drafting the agreement then has a shorthand, precise method of utilizing the term later in the agreement. If "Net Sales" or "Adjusted Net Sales" were not defined terms, the person drafting would repeatedly have to restate the concept. In doing so, variations and errors would creep into the term, as well as unnecessary repetition of the concept and great lengthening of the agreement. To avoid confusion and ambiguity, once a term is defined, only that term should be used.

As illustrated by both of the above form provisions, the definitions for accounting terms frequently involve simply making it clear that generally accepted accounting principles will be applicable except for specific inclusions or exclusions which might not be taken into account in accordance with generally accepted accounting principles. However, just as it is true that general legal principles are sometimes uncertain, so are generally accepted accounting principles sometimes uncertain. Therefore, when the parties have in mind a clear idea of what the method of computation is to be, it is ordinarily worthwhile to set that forth, even though it may be that the same result would be reached by the accountants in applying generally accepted accounting principles.[17] When a payment is to be based on "profits or "income," it is always important to make clear whether the reference is to profits or income before or after income taxes.[18]

If the incentive bonus depends upon the performance of a subsidiary or a division of a corporation, then it is important to deal with those transactions between a parent corporation and its subsidiary or between the corporation and its division[19] which might affect the performance result.[20] In addition, it would be prudent to indicate that some part or none, as the parties may agree, of the parent corporation's overhead is to be included as a charge against net income for the purpose of calculating the incentive bonus.

Form 2 illustrates an incentive compensation arrangement based on changes in sales from one year to the next. In such circumstances it is particularly important for the paralegal to focus on elements which could cause changes with which the employee has nothing to do and no control and which should, therefore, be eliminated in making the comparative computations.[21]

Termination During Fiscal Period

The possibility of termination of employment during a period with respect to which incentive compensation is being earned must be dealt with expressly in the agreement since, in the absence of an express provision, there are many methods of determining what, if any, compensation has been earned by the employee for the partial period of employment. The two form provisions illustrate two of the possibilities. In Form 1 compensation is computed upon the company's performance during the portion of the year in which the employee worked. Form 2 provision takes into account the performance of the company throughout the fiscal period and makes the payment a pro rata portion of what would have been paid if employment had continued throughout the period.

17. See, for example, the definition of "Net Sales" in the Form 2 above.

18. See, for example, subparagraph (ii) of the Form 1 above.

19. A division is merely part of the corporation's operations which is segregated for corporate and financial purposes by product, location, function, or some other logical basis of differentiation. A subsidiary is a separate corporation, all or a portion of the stock of which is owned by another corporation called its "parent."

20. See subparagraph (iv) of the Form 1 above.

21. The distinction between "Net Sales" and "Adjusted Net Sales" in subparagraph (ii) of the Form 2 illustrates a method of making this elimination.

While at first glance these two provisions may seem essentially the same, they may well not be, and they present different problems. When the employer is in a business which is seasonal—for example, sales of toys which are concentrated at the end of the calendar year—and the approach of making the incentive compensation payment is based upon the period of actual employment, the employee may do very well or very poorly. The performance would depend upon whether the portion of the year in which the employee worked has the high yield portion or the low yield portion. This contrasts with what the employee would have received on the basis of a prorated portion of an entire year's performance. Proration based upon the entire year's performance eliminates the need for making special midyear computations, but it also defers payment until the end of the year, although the employment may have been terminated a substantial time prior to the end of the year. Proration also means that the compensation received by the employee will be affected favorably or unfavorably by the performance of a successor during the balance of the year.

Incentive compensation provisions sometimes specify no adjustment for short periods—that it, that no incentive compensation will be paid unless the employee remains in the employ throughout the entire period in question. If this is the desired result, it should be expressly stated because of the likelihood that an ambiguity in the agreement will be resolved in favor of the employee.

This discussion illustrates the importance of covering all issues in the employment agreement. At the time of entering into an employment agreement, the parties would be unlikely to consider the fiscal period as related to employee termination and in most cases would accept almost any provision dealing with this subject. Yet, in the event of termination, this issue is almost certain to arise and will be disputed if not dealt with clearly in the agreement. One of the principal purposes of an employment agreement is to eliminate the possibility of such disputes.

Stock Options

1. Discussion

It has been common to provide employee incentive compensation by giving employees an ownership interest in the company through the issuance to the employee of shares of stock or rights to purchase shares of stock of the company. The theory of such an incentive arrangement is that if, through the employee's efforts, the company's profits improve, the improvement is likely to be reflected in an increase in the value of the company's stock and, therefore, an increase in the value of the employee's stock or stock rights.

A stock option is a right to purchase stock during a certain period of time at a certain purchase price, regardless of the market price of the stock at the time the option is exercised. The option may be granted at the present market value of the stock or above or below present market value. The option is or becomes valuable when the market value of the employer's stock is higher than the purchase price specified in the employee's option. If the market value is not higher the employee will probably not exercise his option as there is no obligation or incentive to do so.

2. Form Provision

The grant of stock options to an employee may or may not be a part of that employee's employment agreement. The following is a typical example of an employment agreement provision covering the right of an employee to receive stock options:

> Corporation, by action of its Board of Directors at the next regularly scheduled meeting of the Board of Directors, shall grant to Employee an option exercisable at any time or times within five years after the date on which said option is granted, to purchase from Corporation up to a total of 10,000 shares of its Common Stock at a purchase price per share equal to the greater of $1.00 or the fair market value of Corporation's Common Stock on the date of grant. The option to be granted hereunder shall be evidenced by an instrument in writing containing all of the terms and conditions which are included in the form Stock Option Agreement which was approved by the Board of Directors of the Corporation.

QUESTIONS
What if the Board of Directors does not grant the option as required? Is it obligated to do so?

3. Economic Comparison

A stock option is the grant of a right to the employee to purchase a specified number of shares at a specified purchase price per share during a specified period of time. A stock option is similar to a cash incentive payment arrangement in that its worth is likely to depend on the success of the employer. However, it differs from a cash arrangement in a number of ways.

First, the market value of the stock and, hence, the value of the option may increase or decrease based on general market fluctuations, regardless of the success of the employer. Second, the benefit to the employee is usually not immediate because the right to exercise the option may be deferred until a future date and, in any event, will produce "spendable" income only after the option has been exercised and the stock has been sold. Third, there are restrictions on the exercise and sale or transfer of the stock purchasable under the option, both to satisfy the requirements of the federal and state securities acts and to permit treatment of any gain at more favorable capital gains tax rates. Because of these restrictions, the benefits which may be derived from the option may disappear before the stock can be sold.

Other Benefits

Form Provision   The following are typical examples of provisions providing other employee benefits (often referred to as "fringe benefits"):

EXAMPLE

Fringe Benefits Provisions Form 1

> Throughout the term of Employee's employment hereunder, Employee shall be entitled to participate in Employer's Profit Sharing Plan, Pension Plan, Group Insurance Plan, and Long Term Disability Protection Insurance Plan, and such other employee benefit plans as may hereafter be instituted by Employer, in the same manner and to the same extent as may from time to time be provided for other employees of Employer who are department heads.

EXAMPLE

Fringe Benefits Provisions Form 2

> Employee shall be entitled to the benefits of the Company's accident and sickness policy and disability income plan underwritten by Provident Life and Accident Insurance Company. Benefits payable are $1,100/month lifetime for accident and $1,100/month for sickness disability to age sixty-five. Employee shall be entitled to receive the following life insurance coverage with benefits payable to beneficiaries designated by Employee:
>
> | | |
> |---|---|
> | Group Life | —$40,000 upon death $80,000 upon accidental death |
> | Key person life[22] | —$75,000 upon death, provided that Employee is insurable at regular rates |
> | Travel group policy | —$60,000 upon accidental death |

Discussion

1. General

   The provision of Form 1 is simple and is applicable when the employer has well-established employee benefit arrangements. In such cases, the employer normally will have a brochure describing the benefits which will be furnished to the employee. Since these benefits may change from time to time, due to the employer's switching from one group insurance plan to another, or discon-

---

22. "Key person" insurance is a separate policy specifically on the life of a valuable individual employee as contrasted with "group life" which is for all employees or all employees of a specific class.

tinuing certain plans, or because of cancellation of a plan by the insurer, the language "as may from time to time be provided" in Form 1 is important to the employer in order to avoid being held responsible to an employee for benefits described in the brochure which may not exist at the time that the employee becomes entitled to such benefits.

The Form 2 provision illustrates benefits which, at least with respect to the life insurance arrangements, may not be part of an overall plan but rather represent insurance coverage for a particular employee, with greater or lesser coverage, or no such coverage, being provided to other employees

2. Pension and Profit Sharing Plans

Pension and profit sharing plans represent the most common form of deferred compensation—that is, compensation which vests in the employee during the employee's years of service with the employer, but the receipt of which is deferred until retirement. There is nothing to prohibit an employer and an employee from entering into an agreement which would provide that for each year of employment a specified sum will be "earned" which will be payable to the employee or the employee's heirs upon retirement or death. However, such arrangements are normally entered into as part of an overall plan applicable to a class of employees because certain tax advantages can be obtained through adoption of such plans. Furthermore, the Employee Retirement Income Security Act of 1974 (ERISA), as amended, imposes many restrictions on employers with respect to such plans. Such plans must meet certain technical requirements in order to achieve the desired tax advantages.

From the employee's point of view, language such as that in Form 1 above covering "such other employee benefit plans as may hereafter be instituted by employer" is particularly important in employment situations with a young, growing company which may not have adopted significant benefit arrangements at the time that employment commences but which is likely to institute such plans with the passage of time. Even without such language, however, the employee will automatically get the benefit of any tax-qualified profit sharing plan or pension plan adopted by the employer for any employees of the same general class or level, since such plans must be implemented on a nondiscriminatory basis—that is, on a basis which gives large classes of employees equal rights to participate.[23]

3. Disability

Both of the above form provisions include insured disability benefit plans. When such insured plans have not been imple-

---

23. ERISA and income tax regulations require such nondiscrimination.

mented by the employer, the employment agreement will frequently establish certain arrangements respecting disability, the following provision being typical:

> If Employee should become unable to perform Employee's duties hereunder, because of partial or total disability or incapacity due to illness, accident, or other cause, Corporation shall continue Employee's salary at the full rate set forth in this agreement for a period of six months. If Employee is still unable to perform the duties hereunder at the end of said six-month period, Corporation shall have the right at any time thereafter to terminate Employee's employment upon ten (10) days' written notice to Employee, in which event Corporation shall have no further liability or obligation under this Agreement.

Needless to say, such a contractual provision is no substitute for long term insured disability protection.

QUESTIONS Would an employee desire the foregoing sample provision? What changes might be reasonable to request in such a provision?

4. Automobile

Certain executive and sales positions normally carry with them the use by the employee of a company car. A typical clause follows:

> During Employee's employment hereunder, Company will provide Employee with an automobile having a manufacturer's suggested retail price of not less than $10,000 for Employee's use in connection with the performance of duties hereunder, and Employee shall be entitled to a new automobile of such value every two years during such employment.

QUESTION What problems from an employee's point of view can result from the foregoing method of determining the automobile to be supplied?

Frequently, the contract provision on this subject will simply provide for a "suitable automobile" and will not specify the frequency with which the employee will be entitled to a new automobile.[24] If such issues can be readily resolved at the outset, however, it is desirable to do so in order to avoid possible disagreements at a subsequent date.[25]

---

24. See paragraph 6 of Form Agreement 4.
25. See paragraph 11 of Form Agreement 3 for the treatment of a related issue.

Expense Reimbursement

Form Provision A typical general provision for reimbursement of expenses is as follows:

> During Employee's employment hereunder, Employer will reimburse Employee for all ordinary and necessary business expenses incurred by Employee in connection with the business of Employer. Such payment shall be made by Employer upon submission by Employee of vouchers itemizing such expenses in a form satisfactory to Employer.

Discussion

1. General

The words "ordinary and necessary" are quite important from the employer's point of view. An employer would normally expect that any expenses incurred by an employee which are reimbursable under the employment agreement would be deductible by the employer on its income tax returns. From a federal income tax point of view, only business expenses which are "ordinary and necessary," as that term is defined in the Internal Revenue Code and the regulations promulgated thereunder and in judicial decisions interpreting the term, are properly deductible.

The employee may desire that this provision make clear that the reimbursable expenses include expenses for entertainment, automobile, travel, and other items, to avoid any implication to the contrary. In some instances an employee is granted an expense allowance permitting expenditures up to a specified amount of dollars monthly or annually without the requirements to make any specific accounting. When the employee is to bear certain of the expenses, which is often the case with territorial sales personnel, it is advisable that the employer so specify in the agreement, to avoid a contrary implication.[26]

2. Moving Expenses

Under certain circumstances of employment, particular provisions may cover moving expenses or allowances. For example, when an employee is moving from one geographical area to another, moving expenses are frequently reimbursed by the employer pursuant to a clause such as the following:

Company shall reimburse employee for the reasonable moving expenses (up to a maximum of $6,500) incurred by employee in moving employee's family residence from Chicago, Illinois, to the San Francisco, California, area.

Internal Revenue Service provisions may limit the amount an employer will be willing to pay for moving expenses because of

---

26. See, for example, paragraph 10 of Form Agreement 3.

limitations on deductibility of moving expenses as "ordinary and necessary" business expenses.[27]

3. Product Allowances or Discounts

When the employer is in the business of producing consumer goods, the employee may contract for the right to select, free of charge or at a specified discount, up to a certain dollar amount of such goods during each year. An example of such a clause follows:

> Employee shall be entitled to select, free of charge, clothing manufactured by Employer to the extent of five hundred dollars ($500.00) per annum, said amount being based upon Employer's regular wholesale prices less ten percent (10%) thereof.

Restrictive Covenants, Trade Secret Protective Clauses, and Related Provisions

General Considerations As stated in the introductory portion of these materials, the provisions of an employment agreement falling within this category are those which represent the most significant advantage to the derived by the employer from an employment agreement. Although the variety of such clauses have much in common and are frequently dealt with in a single section of an employment agreement, various provisions within this category differ greatly in their importance, legal enforceability, and legal effect as compared to the legal effect which would flow if the employment agreement did not contain such a clause. Therefore, various types of provisions coming within the general category of employer protection and employee restriction will be discussed separately.

Trade Secrets Protective Provisions

Form Provisions The following is a typical example of a clause designed to protect the employer from the employee's appropriation of trade secrets:

> Employee covenants and agrees that Employee will not, during the term of employment or thereafter, for any reason or purpose whatsoever, use for personal benefit, or disclose, communicate, or divulge to, or use for the benefit, direct or indirect, of any person, firm, association, or corporation other than Corporation,[28] any information as to business methods, business policies, systems, procedures, techniques, computer programs, research or development projects

---

27. See the preceding subsection for a discussion of "ordinary and necessary" business expenses.
28. Note the differentiation in this clause of *the* Corporation (a capitalized defined term) and *a* corporation in general (with a lower case "c").

or results thereof, trade secrets, inventions, knowledge and processes used or developed by Corporation, any forms, names and addresses of customers or clients, data on or relating to past, present, or prospective customers or clients, or any other information relating to or dealing with the business operations or activities of Corporation, made known to Employee or learned or acquired by Employee while in the employ of Corporation.

Discussion

1. Underlying Legal Principles

Even in the absence of an employment agreement or a provision such as the form provision above, employers are generally entitled to protection against the appropriation by an employee or former employee of "trade secrets." A basic legal dictionary definition of a trade secret may be "a plan or process, tool, mechanism or compound known only to its owner and those of its employees to whom it is necessary to disclose it." The theory underlying this protection is that a process, technique, or method developed by an employer or by its employees during the course of employment is, in effect, "property" of the employer, and, therefore, the employer is entitled to be protected from having the employee learn or become acquainted with the "trade secret" and thereafter use it for the employee's own economic interests or those of another employer.

Although the law provides protection for trade secrets, such protection is not freely given by the courts. Just as copyright or patent rights are available only if the party desiring to assert these rights can establish that the subject matter is in fact worthy of protection, the same concepts are applicable in the trade secrets area.

2. Analysis of Contract Provision

Inclusion of a clause such as the form provision above serves several purposes for the employer. First, the specification of particular items which, by implication, are acknowledged by the employee as deserving of protection, increases the likelihood that such items will be given legal protection, whereas they might not be given such protection under general legal trade secrets principles. Therefore, it is important to the employer that, in addition to having the clause include broad language such as "trade secrets, inventions, knowledge, and processes," the clause specify other particular details of knowledge which are to be protected. The form provision above was drafted for a computer software business which creates specific computer programs for individual customers for a fee. Obviously the particular form of the provision will vary depending upon the nature of the business and the employment.

The inclusion of such a provision may also have an inhibiting effect on an employee who might otherwise not be fully aware that general legal principles prohibit appropriation of trade secrets learned during employment. This is the kind of area where the very presence of a well-drafted, comprehensive clause may deter the employee from undertaking some act which would interfere with the employer's rights with respect to trade secrets and may encourage a court to afford protection where it otherwise might not.

The above provision also seeks to protect information as to customers of the employer. While this kind of information is not within the basic definition of a trade secret, it has often been afforded legal protection by the courts in certain instances, and, in many businesses, it represents the principal information which the employer would seek to protect from competitors.

Restrictive Covenants (Non-Competition Agreements)

Form Provision The following are typical examples of clauses which are intended to bar an employee from competing with the employer:

EXAMPLE

Non-Competition Agreement Provisions Form 1

Employee covenants and agrees that Employee will not, during the term of the employment hereunder and for a period of two years after the termination or expiration of the employment hereunder, for any reason whatsoever, within the continental United States, directly or indirectly engage in any activities relating to evaluation and selection of computer equipment and software, conversion of computer programs and information files from one computer system to another, or in any other activities or operations carried on by Corporation at any time during the period of employment by Corporation, or planned or contemplated by Corporation at the time of termination of Employee's employment by Corporation. The term "engage in" shall include, but shall not be limited to, activities, whether direct or indirect, as proprietor, partner, stockholder, principal, agent, employee, or consultant.

EXAMPLE

Non-Competition Agreement Provisions Form 2

In order to insure to Company the effective enjoyment of the property, assets, and business of Fletcher Packaging, Employee agrees that Employee will not engage in any business other than that of Company during Employee's employment under this Agreement, and that for a period of three (3) years after the termination of employment hereunder, regardless of the reason for such termination, Employee will not, within the states of California, Illinois, New Jersey, New York, and Pennsylvania engage in the manufacture or sale of products the same as, similar to, or in general competition with, products manufactured or sold by Company. The term "engage in" shall include, but shall not be limited to, activities, whether direct or indirect, as proprietor, partner, stockholder, principal, agent, employee, consultant, or lender.

Discussion

1. Underlying Legal Principles

As stated previously, there are significant legal and practical limitations on the use of restrictive covenants in employment agreements. State laws vary substantially with regard to the circumstances under which a restrictive covenant in an employment agreement will be enforced by a court. Unlike the trade secrets area, a covenant against competition will never be implied—that is, an employee will never be presumed to have agreed not to compete upon termination of employment in the absence of a specific provision in the employment agreement. Furthermore, all courts have a strong presumption against enforcement of such provisions because of a fundamental resistance to impairing an individual's ability to earn a living in the type of employment to which that individual is accustomed. Therefore, these covenants must be carefully drawn, reasonable, and limited in order to be enforced. Regardless of how well drawn and how severely limited the restriction, enforcement by a court will be strictly construed.

2. Length of Time

A restrictive covenant would probably never be enforced by a court of law if the provision attempted to restrict the employee from engaging in a competitive activity forever. A restrictive covenant must be reasonable as to length of time. There is no clear permissible maximum period. One often-used rule of thumb is that the period after termination of employment during which the employee is restricted can never be longer than the initial term of the employment agreement. The acceptable length of a restriction is a factual inquiry and will vary depending upon various circumstances of each particular case. For example, a court would probably be more likely to find a two-year restriction on a salesperson to be too long even though the same court might enforce a three-year restriction against an employee who, through the employment, acquired a great deal of specialized technological information developed by the employer. What is reasonable as to time depends generally on the nature of the employment and the length of the employment agreement.

3. Territorial Limit of Restriction

Similarly, the more reasonable the geographical area in which the restriction is applicable, the more likely that the restriction will be enforced. A clause restricting a salesperson from selling products competitive with those of the former employer in geographic areas in which the employer did not sell, or outside of the scope of the employee's sales territory (even though within the employer's market area), would probably be unenforceable. On the other hand, with respect to an executive or technical employee, a national restriction might well be enforced if the employer's actual or potential market were nationwide, or if the nature of the business was such that competition would be equally injurious whether generated by a business across the street from the employer or across the country. What is reasonable depends on the scope of the employee's activities and the employer's business.

4. Correlation with Trade Secrets Protection

Restrictive covenants are more likely to be enforced in accordance with their terms when the nature of the employment is such that there is a high probability that competitive activity would be likely to carry with it the appropriation of the employer's trade secrets. In certain businesses it would be very difficult, if not impossible, for an employer to prove the appropriation of a trade secret. In the area of computer software, for example, where certain mechanical changes in systems design or programming could make it most difficult to identify the materials as being the same as those developed by the employer, a restrictive covenant becomes, as a practical matter, the only effective means of protecting the information from appropriation.

5. Circumstances Which Give Rise to Implementation of Restriction

Both of the form provisions above provide that the restriction shall become applicable upon termination of the employment regardless of the reason for such termination. This is desirable from the employer's point of view, except that it increases the risk of the provision's being deemed unenforceable by a court sympathetic to an employee whose job was terminated by the employer. From the employee's point of view, it is wise to provide that the restriction is applicable only if the employment is terminated by the employee or by reason of the employee's breach of the agreement.[29]

QUESTION Who would determine that the termination was a result of the employee's breach or employer's breach? ☛

6. The Meaning of Unenforceability

Some courts take the position that if any aspect of the restriction (whether time, area, or restricted activity) is deemed unduly broad, it will be held totally unenforceable so that the employee will not be subject to any restrictions. In other cases courts have decided that the provision will be enforced but for a lesser period in a more limited territory or for a less broad activity

29. See, for example, paragraph 8 of Form Agreement 2.

than that prescribed in the agreement. Some employment agreements contain a provision such as the following:

> If any of the provisions of subparagraphs (a) or (b) are held to be in any respect an unreasonable restriction upon Employee, then the court so holding may reduce the territory to which the provisions pertain, and/or the period of time in which they operate, or effect any other change, to the extent necessary to render the provisions enforceable by said court.

In certain states, however, this kind of provision has been treated as an invitation to the court to restrict the noncompetition clause or hold it entirely unenforceable.

QUESTION   Is a court required to follow such a provision?

7. Procedural Provisions

The following is a typical example of a provision which would be included as part of the section of an employment agreement which sets forth trade secrets and restrictive covenants:

> Employee acknowledges that the restrictions contained in this paragraph 9, in view of the nature of the business in which Corporation is engaged, are reasonable and necessary to protect the legitimate interests of Corporation. Employee understands and agrees that the remedies at law for a violation of any of the covenants or provisions of this paragraph 9 will be inadequate, that such violations will cause irreparable injury within a short period of time, and that Corporation shall be entitled to preliminary injunctive relief and other injunctive relief against any such violation. Such injunctive relief shall be in addition to, and in no way in limitation of, any and all other remedies Corporation shall have in law and equity for the enforcement of those covenants and provisions. In the event of any violations or breaches of subparagraph (b) of this paragraph 9, the covenants therein contained shall remain in force during a period of two years subsequent to the termination of the conduct constituting a breach or violation.

Usually it will be more important to an employer to stop an employee from breaching a restrictive covenant through the obtaining of a court injunction than it will be to obtain money damages from the employee for the breach. As courts are generally reluctant to provide injunctive relief to require an individual to act in a specific manner, the foregoing provision is included in order to help establish the right of the employer to obtain an injunction against the competitior's employment of the employee.

QUESTION

Could an employer obtain an injunction against an employee to require the employee to work for the employer as the employee agreed to do?

8. Restrictions When Agreement is Related to Acquisition of a Business

A restrictive covenant is more likely to be enforced when the employment agreement is part of the acquisition of a business. The usual circumstances of this are that the principal shareholder of a business who also acted as one of its principal operating executives, negotiates, in connection with the sale of the business to another person or corporation, for an employment agreement. Because the acquiring company which will become the employer or the parent company of the employer has made a significant investment which will be threatened if a key employee enters into competition, the court is more likely to enforce a restrictive covenant in such situation. (Restrictive covenants connected with an acquisition are enforceable, even if there is no employment agreement, as part of the agreement respecting the purchase of the business, although those convenants also must contain territorial and time limitations.) It is to the employer's advantage to make it clear in the agreement that the employment agreement was entered into in connection with an acquisition. This can be done by a recital at the beginning of the agreement and it is also done by including language, at the outset of the restrictive covenant provisions such as:

> In order to insure to employer the effective enjoyment of the property, assets, and business of the ABC Company of which employee was a principal stockholder and operating executive prior to its acquisition by employer, . . .[30]

9. Other Drafting Considerations

Form 1 on page __ demonstrates an attempt to describe specifically particular activities of the company in which the employee is to be prohibited from engaging. This is important in circumstances in which the nature of the employer's business activities are not well known or common. When the business of the employer is essentially the production and sale of easily definable products, language such as that in Form 2 on page __ is adequate. From the employer's point of view the catchall language such as "or in any other activities or operations . . ." in Form 1 is, of course, important. From the employee's point of view, it would be wise to resist the "planned or contemplated by corporation" language of that provision or require some more specific definition.

---

30. See, for example, Form 2 on page 240.

Notwithstanding that broad language in restrictive covenants threatens the enforceability of the entire covenant, employers will sometimes want broadly drafted provisions. The theory is that, as discussed above in connection with trade secret provisions, the presence of the clause will deter the employee from competing because the employee (and a prospective successor employer) cannot be any more certain that the clause will not be enforced than the employer can be certain that the clause will be enforced.

Patent and Copyright Provisions In employment situations in which the employee may be doing original research or experimentation, or otherwise has technical skills such as may lead to the creation or development of something which is protected by law, the employer will want to obtain the rights to any such creative product of the employee. The following is an elaborate clause respecting this subject matter:

> Employee covenants and agrees that any and all writings, inventions, improvements, processes, systems, procedures, techniques, and/or computer programs which Employee may make, conceive, discover, or develop, either solely or jointly with any other person or persons, at any time during the term of this agreement and any renewal hereof, whether during working hours or at any other time, whether at the request or upon the suggestion of Corporation or otherwise, which relate to or are useful in connection with the business now or hereafter carried on or contemplated by Corporation, including developments or expansions of its present fields of operations, shall be and hereby are the sole and exclusive property of Corporation. Employee shall make full disclosure to Corporation of all such writings, inventions, improvements, processes, systems, procedures, techniques, and computer programs, and shall do all such acts and execute, acknowledge, and deliver all such instruments in writing as may be necessary to vest in Corporation the absolute title thereto. Employee further covenants and agrees to write and prepare all specifications and procedures and to aid and assist Corporation in all other ways in order that Corporation properly can prepare and present all applications for copyright or Letters Patent thereof, can secure such copyright or Letters Patent wherever possible, as well as reissues, renewals, and extensions thereof, and can obtain the record title to such copyright or patents so that Corporation shall be the sole and absolute owner thereof in all countries in which it may desire to have copyright or patent protection. It is understood and agreed that Employee shall not be entitled to any additional or special compensation or reimbursement in regard to any and all such writings, inventions, improvements, processes, systems, procedures, techniques, and computer programs.

The above provision is, of course, quite broad and favorable to the employer. Depending upon the circumstances involved, it may be totally unacceptable to the employee or acceptable only with significant limitations.[31]

Inclusion or Exclusion of Restrictive Covenants and Related Provisions in Employment Agreements   Although restrictive covenants and the other types of provisions discussed in this section represent a significant element of the employment relationship, many employment agreements, even though involving high level employees and substantial amounts of compensation, do not include restrictive covenants, trade secrets, patent, or copyright provisions.[32] The principal reasons for the absence of a restrictive covenant are that the employer is not concerned about the risk of competition, the employer regards a restrictive covenant as basically unfair, or the employee has some bargaining power and is totally unwilling to accept such a restriction, or a combination of these factors is present. In connection with the preparation of any material employment agreement, the lawyer representing the employer must discuss fully with the client whether or not such a restriction is to be included and must communicate to the drafting paralegal the results of such discussion. The importance of the covenant will vary depending upon the nature of the employer's business and the job to be performed by the employee. Similarly, many high level employment situations do not involve trade secret exposure, nor the likelihood of production of materials which may be patented or become subject to copyright, so that provisions relating to those matters are unnecessary. Restrictive covenants are included in many agreements in which trade secrets clauses and patent and copyright provisions are not included.

THE CORPORATION AS A PARTY TO THE EMPLOYMENT AGREEMENT

In order for the corporation to become a party to the employment agreement or any other important agreement, the board of directors must authorize the entry into the agreement by the corporation and must authorize the officers to execute the agreement on its behalf.[33] A form of resolution authorizing such an agreement might be as follows:

> RESOLVED, that this Corporation enter into an employment agreement (the "Employment Agreement") between the Corporation and John Albert ("Albert") pursuant to which this Corporation shall employ Albert as Sales Manager on the terms and subject to the

31. See Paragraph 9 of Form Agreement 4 for an example of the structure and coverage of a full employment agreement section dealing with this area.
32. See, for example, Form Agreement 1.
33. See Chapter Five for a general discussion of the role of directors and meetings of directors.

conditions of the Employment Agreement attached hereto, made a part hereof and incorporated herein by reference; and

RESOLVED, that any officer or officers of this Corporation be and each of them is hereby authorized and directed to execute the Employment Agreement, expend any monies, and do any and all acts and things necessary or appropriate to effectuate the purposes of the foregoing resolution.

Note that these resolutions call for a copy of the employment agreement to be attached to the resolutions and placed in the minute book. The authorized officers may execute the agreement on the corporation's behalf.

Employment Agreement Examples

The following pages contain four forms of employment agreements which include some of the form provisions previously set forth in these materials or alternative provisions. These form agreements illustrate the overall form and structure of employment agreements and include those provisions which are standard in nearly all employment agreements and many other written agreements. The standard provisions, sometimes referred to as "boilerplate," are essentially self-explanatory. To assist the student, comments have been added to the end of Form Agreement 1.

Following the form agreements is a checklist for paralegals to consider the drafting employment agreements.

PROBLEM

Utilizing Form Agreement 1 as a format, prepare the following employment agreement:

1. Employer: XYZ Corp., a Nevada corporation
2. Employee: Hugh Horning
3. Duties: Sales manager for employer's magazine "Flirtation"
4. Term: One year commencing October 15, 19__; automatic renewal from year to year unless either party gives other 90 days written notice of termination.
5. Compensation: $52,000 per year plus 5% of gross revenues of "Flirtation" for year in question
6. Additional Benefits: Same as other supervisory personnel of employer
7. Reimbursement of Expenses: Employer will reimburse for necessary expenses of employee incurred on business of employer; employee must submit receipts for reimbursement
8. Automobile: Employer to provide new car for use of employee in carrying out of duties

NOTE Do not fail to add additional necessary provisions. If information provided is inadequate, describe what additional information is needed or your assumptions.

EXAMPLE

Employee Agreement Form Agreement 1

Special Features

A. Employee's duties are set forth in detail in a schedule attached to, and made part of, the agreement (paragraph 1—Schedule A).

B. The employer is a nontechnical business enterprise (clothing manufacturer), and the employee will perform nontechnical services (sales manager). There is no restrictive covenant or trade secret or patent or copyright protection clause. The employer has relied, by implication, on general trade secrets principles for protection of customer information.

C. There is a significant cash incentive compensation arrangement (paragraph 3).

EMPLOYMENT AGREEMENT

[1][34]

AGREEMENT made this 12th day of July, 1987, by and between XYZ, Inc., a Pennsylvania corporation ("Employer") and John Albert ("Employee").

[2]

WITNESSETH:

WHEREAS, Employer and Employee desire to enter into an employment agreement on the terms and conditions hereinafter set forth.

[3]

NOW, THEREFORE, in consideration of the premises and the mutual agreements hereinafter set forth, the parties hereto, intending to be legally bound, hereby agree as follows:

[4]

1. *Capacity and Duties.* Employer hereby employs Employee and Employee hereby accepts employment by Employer as Sales Manager of Employer. In his capacity as Sales Manager, Employee shall carry out all of the functions set forth on Schedule A hereto and such other sales and sales supervisory activities as may be reasonably requested from time to time during the term of this Agreement by the officers of Employer. Employee agrees that throughout the term of his employment hereunder he will devote his entire time, energy, skill, and best efforts to the promotion of sales of Employer's products, and to promote generally the business and affairs of Employer, to the exclusion of all other business interests, and that he will perform faithfully and to the fullest extent of his ability all of his duties hereunder.

[5]

2. *Term.* The initial term of this Agreement shall be one year, which shall be deemed to have commenced on March 1, 1987. Thereafter, this Agreement shall remain in full force and effect so long as Employee is employed as Employer's Sales Manager, until terminated by Employer or Employee, with either party having the right to terminate this Agreement

---

34. Numbers in brackets refer to paragraph numbers in the comments at the end of this Form.

after the initial one-year term by written notice to the other party given not less than sixty (60) days prior to the specified termination date.

3. *Compensation.* (a) *Compensation During Initial Period.* By reason of the fact that the fiscal year of Employer ends on November 30, the initial period of employment for purposes of this paragraph 3 shall be the period from July 12, 1987, through November 30, 1987 (the "Initial Period"). Employer shall pay to Employee as full compensation for all services rendered by Employee in any capacity during the Initial Period:

(i) A fixed salary at the rate of $30,000 per annum, payable in such weekly, biweekly, or monthly installments as may be agreed upon between Employer and Employee, said salary to aggregate $12,500 during the Initial Period of employment provided that this agreement remains in effect throughout said Initial Period; plus

[6]

(ii) Incentive compensation, to be paid within ninety (90) days after November 30, 1987, computed by multiplying the amount by which the Adjusted Net Sales (as hereinafter defined) of Employer for Employer's fiscal year ending November 30, 1987, exceed $7,700,000 [which amount represents the Net Sales (as hereinafter defined) of Employer during its fiscal year ended November 30, 1986], by the applicable percentage set forth in subparagraph (iii) below.

(iii) For the purposes of subparagraph (ii) above and subparagraph 3(b) hereof, the percentages applicable to the amount by which the Adjusted Net Sales of Employer during the fiscal year in question exceeds the Net Sales of Employer for the immediately preceding fiscal year (herein called "Excess Net Sales") are as follows:

Up to $250,000 of Excess Net Sales	½%
More than $250,000 up to $500,000 of Excess Net Sales	¾%
More than $500,000 of Excess Net Sales	1%

(iv) For the purpose of this Agreement, "Net Sales" shall mean the gross sales of Employer, less all returns, allowances, credits, and discounts, as set forth on the income statement prepared by Employer's independent accountants for the fiscal year in question. For the purpose of this Agreement, "Adjusted Net Sales" shall mean Net Sales, reduced by the portion of Net Sales revenues attributable to increases in average unit prices over the average unit prices of the previous year, it being the understanding of the parties that Employee's incentive compensation is to be based upon increases in the number of units sold rather than increases in Net Sales revenues arising from price increases.

(b) *Compensation After Initial Period.* After the Initial Period, Employer shall pay to Employee as full compensation for all services rendered by Employee in any capacity during the term of this Agreement:

(i) A fixed annual salary equal to one hundred five per cent (105%) of the fixed salary payable for the immediately preceding fiscal year, provided that Employer's Adjusted Net Sales for the immediately preceding fiscal year were equal to or greater than Employer's Net Sales for the fiscal year prior to the immediately preceding fiscal year. If the aforesaid proviso has not been satisfied, then Employee's fixed annual salary shall be at the same rate as Employee's fixed annual salary for the immediately preceding fiscal year. For the purposes of this provision, Employee shall be deemed to have been paid a fixed salary of $30,000 for Employer's fiscal year ending November 30, 1987.

(ii) Incentive compensation, to be paid within ninety (90) days after the end of the fiscal year in question, computed by multiplying the Excess Net Sales by the applicable percentage set forth in subparagraph 3(a)(iii) hereof.

(iii) If Employee ceases to be employed hereunder on a date other than the last day of the fiscal year of Employer, then Employee shall be entitled to a portion of the incentive compensation which would have been payable to him if he had been employed throughout said fiscal year, determined by computing the full amount of incentive compensation which would have been payable and multiplying said amount by a fraction, the numerator of which shall be the number of working days of said fiscal year during which Employee was employed, and the denominator of which shall be the total number of working days in that fiscal year.

[7]

4. *Additional Benefits*. Throughout the term of his employment hereunder, Employee shall be entitled to participate in Employer's Profit Sharing Plan, Pension Plan, Group Insurance Plan, and Long Term Disability Protection Insurance Plan, and such other employee benefit plans as may hereafter be instituted by Employer, in the same manner and to the same extent as may from time to time be provided for other employees of Employer who are department heads.

5. *Reimbursement of Expenses*. During Employee's employment hereunder, Employer will reimburse Employee for all ordinary and necessary business expenses incurred by Employee in connection with the business of Employer. Such payment shall be made by Employer upon submission by Employee of vouchers itemizing such expenses in a form satisfactory to Employer.

6. *Clothing Allowance*. Employee shall be entitled to select, free of charge, clothing manufactured by Employer to the extent of five hundred dollars ($500) per annum, said amount being based upon Employer's regular wholesale prices less ten per cent (10%) thereof.

[8]

7. *Miscellaneous Provisions*. (a) Any notices pursuant to this Agreement shall be validly given or served if in writing and delivered personally or sent by registered or certified mail, postage prepaid, to the following addresses:

If to Employer: XYZ, Inc.
255 Main Street
Wilmington, Delaware

If to Employee: John Albert
14 Blossom Court
Cherry Hill, N.J. 08003

[9]

(b) The waiver by either party of a breach or violation of any provision of this Agreement shall not operate or be construed as a waiver of any subsequent breach or violation thereof.

---

[10]

(c) This writing represents the entire Agreement and understanding of the parties with respect to the subject matter hereof; it may not be altered or amended except by an Agreement in writing, signed by both parties.

[11]

(d) This Agreement has been made in and its validity, performance, and effect shall be determined in accordance with the laws of the Commonwealth of Pennsylvania.

[12]

(e) The headings of paragraphs in this Agreement are for convenience only; they form no part of this Agreement and shall not affect its interpretation.

[13]

IN WITNESS WHEREOF, the parties have executed this Agreement under seal on the day and year first above written.

[14]

XYZ, Inc.

[Corporate Seal]   By: /s/George Hallan
_____
                          George Hallan, President

                          Attest: /s/ Mary Tolan
                          _____
                          Mary Tolan, Secretary

/s/ Jill Moyer   /s/ John Albert
_____   _____
Witness   John Albert

Comments on Form Agreement 1 (1) The first paragraph sets forth the parties, defines them with a proper noun in quotation marks, and recites the date of the Agreement. This is standard not only for employment agreements but virtually every type of agreement.

(2) The "Witnesseth" section gives the background of the Agreement. Note Form Agreement 3, which actually calls the paragraph "Background of Agreement." The background may be a simple sentence, an elaborate series of sentences commencing with the term "Whereas," or may simply be a narrative paragraph as in Form Agreement 3.

A background section is present in virtually every type of well-drafted agreement. It states the purposes of the agreement to aid a court in interpreting the agreement if that becomes necessary. Form Agreements 2 and 3 do not contain such a paragraph, but it is much better to include it to spell out the purposes of the agreement. Whether the paragraph utilizes "whereas" clauses and is called "Background of Agreement" or headed by "Witnesseth" (the much older form) is a matter of personal preference of the person drafting the agreement and practice, not a matter of legal significance. The paralegal should determine what is the preferred form of the lawyer for whom the agreement is being drafted.

(3) The "Now, therefore" clause is present in all agreements to recite the mutual consideration necessary to make the agreement binding. It, too, may vary slightly according to the preference of the person drafting the agreement.

(4) Note that paragraph 1 leaves the Employee no room for other business involvements. Contrast paragraph 2(c) of Form Agreement 2.

(5) Note the definition of Initial Period to specify clearly what term is being discussed. If no incentive compensation were paid to the Employee, the compensation section could end for the Initial Period with subparagraph (i).

(6) Note particularly in paragraph 3 the method of referring to terms such as "Net Sales" which are to be defined after having been earlier stated. The definition of such terms prevents the necessity of repeating the concept they define, possibly in a different or erroneous manner. It also shortens the agreement greatly. Other comments regarding this paragraph are contained under "Compensation" earlier in this chapter.

(7) Paragraphs 4, 5, and 6 have been discussed under "Compensation" also.

(8) It is critical that the agreement provide for notices to be in writing, by registered or certified mail, return receipt requested, so that all parties are certain notices have been delivered. Often the attorneys for each side are required to receive a copy of all notices to assure early information to such attorneys. See, for example, paragraph 9 of Form Agreement 2. Review the Agreement to determine what circumstances could require a notice under the Agreement. This is a standard boilerplate clause in every type of agreement.

(9) This is a standard clause in all types of agreements indicating that a waiver one time by a party of a breach does not act as a waiver of any later breach.

(10) Although many courts may not enforce this provision, it is useful to encourage the parties to reduce changes to writing. This clause is called an "integration" clause and is standard in every type of agreement.

(11) The parties can select the state law which will be applied to construe the agreement. Courts usually enforce the provision if the state has any logical relationship to the agreement of the parties, e.g., the place of incorporation of a party, residence of a party, place of business of a party, or place where the agreement is to be performed. It is a standard clause in all types of agreements. Here it is at least the state of incorporation of the Employer. Note that New Jersey (as the residence of the Employee) or Delaware (as the place of business of the Employer) might logically have been chosen as well. Ordinarily the person drafting the agreement picks the applicable state law with which that

person has the most familiarity. It may be a matter of negotiation between the parties.

(12) This provision is intended to aid in construction by a court to show that the paragraphs themselves are the critical factors, not the headings. It is a standard clause in most agreements.

(13) This is the standard closing phrase for agreements in general.

(14) Note the method of having a corporation execute an agreement. Contrast this with execution by the individual. The authorizing resolutions (see page 231) and execution by duly authorized officers bind the corporation. The witness similarly is not a necessity. While often included, the corporate seal is not a necessity to make the agreement binding on the Employer.

EXAMPLE

Employee Agreement Form Agreement 2

Special Features

A. Employee is to be chief executive officer. The issue of the employee's election as President and director is covered as it relates to *capacity and duties* [paragraph 2(a)], *term of agreement* [paragraph 7(b)], and applicability of *restrictive covenant* (paragraph 8).

B. The applicability of the restrictive covenant depends upon who terminates or breaches the agreement (paragraph 8).

C. Termination provisions for employee if employee is not elected president, chief executive officer, and a director, and for employer under certain other circumstances (paragraph 7).

EMPLOYMENT AGREEMENT

This Agreement made as of this _____ day of May, 1978, by and between ABC, Inc., a Delaware corporation (the "Company"), and Tami Zandra, of Deerfield, Illinois ("Employee").

WITNESSETH:

1. *Employment.* The Company hereby agrees to employ Employee and Employee hereby accepts employment by the Company for the period and upon the terms and conditions hereinafter set forth.

2. *Capacity and Duties.* (a) Employee shall be employed by the Company exclusively in an executive capacity and Employee shall have such authority and shall perform such key executive duties and responsibilities as may from time to time reasonably (in view of the expectation of the parties referred to in the next sentence) be specified by the Board of Directors of the Company with respect to the Company and its affiliates. It is the present expectation of the parties that Employee will be elected and reelected during the entire term of this Agreement to serve as President and chief executive officer of the Company and as director of the Company, and, if elected, Employee agrees to serve in such capacities without any compensation in addition to that herein provided. Employee acknowledges that neither the Company nor its Board of Directors is legally obligated to elect or reelect Employee as President or chief executive officer of the Company.

(b) During the terms of this Agreement, Employee shall devote her full business time and her best efforts to the performance of her duties hereunder, and shall not be employed by, participate or engage in, or be a part of, in any manner, the management or operation of any business enterprise other than the Company and its affiliates. Employee shall be entitled to at least four weeks vacation with pay during each calendar year during the term hereof.

(c) Notwithstanding the foregoing, Employee shall be entitled to have investments in other business enterprises provided, however, that she shall not have any investment or financial interest in any business enterprise which conducts business activities competitive with any business activities conducted by the Company now or at any time during the term of Employee's employment hereunder (other than an investment of no more than 5% of any class of equity securities of a company whose securities are traded on a national securities exchange).

3. *Compensation.* Employee's basic compensation shall be at the rate of not less than $36,000 per year, plus such bonuses and additional compensation as the Board of Directors of the Company may, in its discretion, determine. Such basic compensation shall be paid to Employee in equal installments not less frequently than monthly. Employee shall be entitled to participate fully in and to receive the benefit of (on a basis no less favorable to Employee than that available to any other executive employee of the Company) all plans and benefit programs made available to any executive employee of the Company.

4. *Expenses.* Employee is authorized to incur reasonable expenses for promoting the business of the Company and in carrying out her duties hereunder, including without limitation, expenses for entertainment, automobile, travel, and similar items. The Company shall reimburse Employee for all such ordinary and necessary expenses upon the presentation by Employee from time to time of an itemized account of such expenditures. Employee shall present such an itemized account not less frequently than monthly. In addition, Company agrees to reimburse Employee for the reasonable moving expenses incurred by her in moving her family's residence from Illinois to the Phoenix area.

5. *Additional Benefits.* Employee shall be entitled to the benefits of the Company's accident and sickness policy and disability income plan underwritten by Provident Life and Accident Insurance Company. Benefits payable are $1,100/month lifetime for accident and $1,100/month for sickness disability to age sixty-five (65).

6. *Insurance.* Employee shall be entitled to receive the following life insurance coverage with benefits payable to beneficiaries designated by Employee:

Group Life	—$40,000 upon death $80,000 upon accidental death
Key person life	—$75,000 upon death, provided that Employee is insurable at regular rates
Travel group policy	—$60,000 upon accidental death

7. *Term of Agreement; Termination.* (a) The term of this Agreement shall be two (2) years commencing on the date hereof, and thereafter shall continue from year to year unless and until either party shall give notice to the other at least 180 days prior to the end of the original or then

current renewal term of her or its intention to terminate at the end of said term.

(b) Notwithstanding the provisions of subparagraph (a) above, in the event that Employee shall not be elected President and chief executive officer and a director of the Company within thirty (30) days after the date of this Agreement, or if at any time during the initial two-year term of this Agreement Employee shall be removed as President or chief executive officer or director of the Company or shall not be reelected as President and chief executive officer and director of the Company, Employee shall have the right to terminate her employment hereunder at her convenience, and, provided that as of the date of such removal or failure to reelect, Employee shall not have breached or otherwise failed to perform in accordance with this Agreement, such termination shall be considered a termination by reason of a breach of this Agreement by the Company.

(c) Notwithstanding the provisions of subparagraph (a) above, the Company shall have the right to terminate the employment under this Agreement, without further liability or obligation hereunder in the event that Employee (i) is adjudicated a bankrupt, (ii) is convicted of a felony involving moral turpitude, (iii) dies (but in such event the applicable benefits set forth in paragraph 6 above shall be effective), or (iv) becomes disabled such that she has been unable to perform her duties hereunder for ninety (90) days during any year of this Agreement or for any period of ninety (90) consecutive days (but in such event the applicable benefits set forth in paragraph 5 hereof shall be effective).

8. *Restrictions on Competition.* Employee covenants and agrees that: (a) during the initial term and any renewal terms of her employment hereunder and, (b) if but only if this Agreement is terminated by Employee (as hereinafter defined) during the initial term or any renewal term hereof for a period of two (2) years after the termination of her employment hereunder, she shall not directly or indirectly engage in any business activities within the continental United States, the same as, similar to, or in competition with business activities carried on by Company during the period of Employee's employment by Company, or in the definitive planning stages at the time of termination of Employee's employment. The term "engage in" shall include, without being limited to, activities as proprietor, partner, stockholder, principal, agent, employee, or consultant. However, nothing contained in this paragraph 8 shall prevent Employee from having investments of the types permitted in subparagraph 2(c) hereof. For the purposes of this paragraph 8, a termination of employment by Employee shall be deemed to have occurred only if Employee shall cease to be employed by Company pursuant to notice of election by Employee to terminate at the end of the initial term or any renewal term hereof, or if Employee shall fail to perform in accordance with this Agreement, or if Company shall terminate employment by reason of a breach of this Agreement by Employee.

If the employment is not terminated by Employee as defined in this paragraph 8 during the initial or any renewal term hereof, or if the Agreement is breached by Company, the restrictions on competition imposed by this paragraph 8 shall not apply.

9. *Miscellaneous Provisions.* (a) Any notices pursuant to this Agreement shall be validly given or served if in writing and delivered personally or sent by registered or certified mail, postage prepaid, to the following addresses:

If to Company: ABC, INC.
2401 First Avenue
Phoenix, Arizona 85003
Attention: President
with a copy to Hiram Lawyer, Esq.
1801 First Avenue
Phoenix, Arizona 85003
If to Employee: Ms. Tami Zandra
101 Second Lane
Deerfield, Illinois 60619
with a copy to Jane Wilson, Esq.
1213 North Square
Deerfield, Illinois 60619

or to such other addresses as either party may hereafter designate to the other in writing.

(b) If any provision of this Agreement shall be or become illegal or unenforceable in whole or in part for any reason whatsoever, the remaining provisions shall nevertheless be deemed valid, binding and subsisting.[35]

(c) The waiver by either party of a breach or violation of any provision of this Agreement shall not operate or be construed as a waiver of any subsequent breach or violation thereof.

(d) This writing represents the entire agreement and understanding of the parties with respect to the subject matter hereof; it may not be altered or amended except by an agreement in writing.

(e) This Agreement has been made in and its validity, performance, and effect shall be determined in accordance with the laws of the State of Arizona.

(f) The headings of paragraphs in this Agreement are for convenience only; they form no part of this Agreement and shall not affect its interpretation.

IN WITNESS WHEREOF, and intending to be legally bound, the parties have executed this Agreement under seal on the day and year first above written.

[*Corporate Seal*]

ABC, Inc.
By: /s/Henry George
President
Attest: /s/ John Henry
Secretary
/s/ Tami Zandra   [*Seal*]
Tami Zandra

35. This type of provision is called a "severability clause" and is a boilerplate provision for many agreements. It tells a court that, notwithstanding the fact that a provision such as the restrictive covenant is unenforceable, the remainder of the agreement shall be effective. Consider what this provision might do if a fundamental element of the agreement is unenforceable.

EXAMPLE

*Employee
Agreement
Form Agreement 3*

Special Features

A. This agreement is a relatively sophisticated agreement designed to be used by employer as a form agreement for a class of sales personnel. The agreement provides blanks for variables such as territory (paragraph 1), special customers (house accounts) in particular territories (paragraph 8), and commission rates and draw rates (paragraphs 9 and 10).

B. Commissions do not necessarily go to the employee responsible for the sales territory (paragraphs 7 and 8).

EMPLOYMENT AGREEMENT

This AGREEMENT entered into this _____ day of , 19___, by and between _____, New York, New York, hereinafter referred to as EMPLOYER, and _____ hereinafter referred to as EMPLOYEE.

In consideration of the mutual covenants herein contained, the parties hereto agree as follows:

1. EMPLOYER agrees to employ EMPLOYEE, and EMPLOYEE accepts employment as traveling representative of EMPLOYER in the following Territory:

2. EMPLOYEE agrees to devote his entire time, energy, skill, and attention to the sale of products manufactured by or for EMPLOYER or sold by EMPLOYER (the "Products"), and in that connection to actively solicit orders for the sale of the Products to retail stores. EMPLOYEE agrees not to accept or engage in any other employment or undertaking during the term of this agreement.

3. EMPLOYEE is to travel throughout the Territory, and give it thorough coverage in accordance, and in compliance with instructions and directions from EMPLOYER, which shall include the time or times when EMPLOYEE shall travel in the aforesaid Territory and the duration of the trips. EMPLOYEE is to submit periodic itineraries and call reports, and other data, as required, in accordance with EMPLOYER'S sales control program.

4. EMPLOYEE'S authority to act for EMPLOYER is limited strictly to the solicitations of orders, and all orders received as a result of EMPLOYEE'S solicitations shall be subject to acceptance or rejection by EMPLOYER at its principal office in New York, New York. EMPLOYER may refuse or reject, either in whole or in part, any order received as a result of EMPLOYEE'S solicitation, and may cancel any such order, either in whole or in part, after acceptance. EMPLOYER further may consent to the cancellation of any order, either in whole or in part, either before or after shipment, or may accept returns and grant such credits or allowances as it deems proper. EMPLOYEE agrees in all respects to observe the rules and regulations of EMPLOYER as to price, terms, and other conditions of sale, and he shall have no power to authorize returns or offer special prices, terms, or conditions unless written instructions are given to him by EMPLOYER, in which event EMPLOYEE shall be so empowered only with respect to the particular circumstances covered by such instructions.

5. All samples delivered by EMPLOYER to EMPLOYEE shall at all times remain the property of EMPLOYER, and EMPLOYEE agrees that he will keep, maintain, and preserve them in good condition. EMPLOYER shall have the right at any time to direct the sale of any such samples, and all samples sold by EMPLOYEE pursuant to EMPLOYER'S instruc-

tions shall be credited to EMPLOYEE'S account in full satisfaction of any charge made upon delivery of such samples to EMPLOYEE. All samples not sold by EMPLOYEE shall be returned in good condition to EMPLOYER at any time upon EMPLOYER'S request or upon termination of this Agreement. Notwithstanding any provisions to the contrary contained herein, EMPLOYEE shall reimburse EMPLOYER for the then prevailing wholesale price of any samples lost, stolen, destroyed, damaged, or misplaced while in the possession or control of EMPLOYEE. At EMPLOYER'S request, EMPLOYEE shall use his best efforts to obtain, and shall pay the premiums for, casualty insurance covering samples while in EMPLOYEE'S possession or control.

6. Except as provided in paragraph 7 or 8 of this agreement, EMPLOYEE shall be credited with commission on all shipments made on orders received after the date of this Agreement to men's retail clothing stores in his Territory, as specified in paragraph 1, and likewise will be charged with commission on all returns by and allowances to such accounts, during the term of this Agreement. It is understood that sales to customers other than men's retail clothing stores shall not be considered part of this Agreement, and no commission shall be paid on such sales except where specifically agreed in writing.

7. In the event that EMPLOYEE obtains an initial order from a new customer who requires that merchandise be delivered into an area which is not part of the Territory of EMPLOYEE, EMPLOYEE shall nevertheless receive the commission on the initial order received from such customer. On any subsequent orders from such customer the commission on merchandise shipped into territories other than the Territory of EMPLOYEE shall be credited to the account of the employee into whose territory such merchandise is shipped; provided, however, that in any case, EMPLOYER shall have the right to apportion commissions among EMPLOYEE and other employees in the event shipments are made into more than one employee's territory as a result of a single order, or if for any other reason, in EMPLOYER'S sole determination, considerations of fairness require it to make the apportionment.

8. EMPLOYEE shall not be entitled to receive or be credited with commissions on account of shipments made to those customers in his Territory which are designated as house accounts on Exhibit "A" to this Agreement attached hereto and hereby made part hereof. EMPLOYER shall have the right from time to time to designate additional customers in EMPLOYEE'S Territory as house accounts by giving thirty (30) days' written notice to EMPLOYEE. With respect to customers which may hereafter be designated as house accounts, it is intended that EMPLOYER shall make such designation only as to customers or potential customers whose business is not actively being solicited by EMPLOYEE, or who have not placed any orders with EMPLOYEE for the Products during the immediately preceding two years, or whose orders are primarily the result of the sales effort of EMPLOYER or other employees, rather than EMPLOYEE.

9. As sole compensation for EMPLOYEE'S services, EMPLOYER shall (subject to the withholding provisions of all applicable federal, state, and local employment taxes) pay EMPLOYEE the commissions hereinafter set forth on all orders which shall be filled by EMPLOYER and for which full payment is received. In the event of returns by, or credits or

allowances to any customer, or in the event of nonpayment, EMPLOY-EE'S commission account will be charged for any commissions previously credited or paid pertaining to such merchandise or accounts.

The commission on merchandise sold at regular prices will be paid on the following basis (less returns, credits, and allowances):

The commission paid on merchandise sold below regular wholesale price (when such merchandise is available) or with special terms and/or conditions will be two per cent (2%) of net sales, except if otherwise specified by EMPLOYER prior to such offering of merchandise. Furthermore, no commission shall be paid with respect to merchandise sold $33\frac{1}{3}$% or more below regular wholesale price, except if otherwise specified by EMPLOYER prior to such offering of merchandise.

10. If EMPLOYER shall agree to make periodic advances to EMPLOYEE, such advances are to be on account of, or advances against, commission to be earned by EMPLOYEE, and said advances shall be charged and deducted from commission as and when such commission shall be payable to EMPLOYEE.

The EMPLOYER agrees to furnish EMPLOYEE with a copy of all invoices covering any goods shipped into the above described territory and to furnish EMPLOYEE with a statement on or before the 25th of each month covering the amount of sales represented by such shipments for the previous month and the amount of commission due EMPLOYEE, which shall be paid at the time the statement is rendered.

EMPLOYEE shall bear all of his traveling and other out-of-pocket expenses incurred in connection with the employment hereunder, and the same shall not be reimbursable to him by EMPLOYER.

11. EMPLOYEE shall maintain liability insurance on each automobile used by him in the course of his employment hereunder at least in the amount of $100,000 for injury to any one person and $300,000 for injuries to all persons in any one occurrence, and property damage insurance at least in the amount of $50,000. EMPLOYER shall be named as an insured on such policy or policies so long as this Agreement shall be in effect, and EMPLOYEE shall deliver to EMPLOYER a certificate of insurance naming EMPLOYER as an insured within ten (10) days from the date hereof, which certificate shall provide that the coverage to which such certificate relates shall be noncancellable for a period of ten (10) days after notice to EMPLOYER. EMPLOYEE agrees that he will use no vehicle in the course of his employment hereunder which is not covered by such insurance, and the use of any such uninsured vehicle shall be grounds for immediate termination of this agreement.

12. EMPLOYER will make every effort to fill orders solicited by EMPLOYEE and make shipment thereon. It is understood, however, that EMPLOYER'S performance of and deliveries on any order are subject to delays or failure due to fires, floods, storms, and abnormal weather conditions, wars, riots, civil commotions, strikes, lockouts, shortages of or delays in receiving materials, credit restrictions, governmental regulations, or other causes or conditions beyond the EMPLOYER'S reasonable control, and in the event any of the foregoing occur, EMPLOYER may cancel any order or extend the time for delivery of any undelivered portion.

13. This agreement may be terminated in any of the following circumstances:

(a) Upon the sixty-sixth birthday of EMPLOYEE, or upon his death, this agreement will automatically terminate unless other arrangements in writing have been made at least sixty (60) days prior to the date of such occurrence.

In the event of EMPLOYEE'S inability to perform his duties by reason of illness, incapacity, or any other cause which shall continue for a period in excess of six (6) weeks, or the discontinuance of operations by the EMPLOYER, EMPLOYER shall have the right to terminate this agreement by ten (10) days written notice to EMPLOYEE.

(b) Either party shall have the right to terminate this agreement at any time upon thirty (30) days prior written notice.[36]

In the event of termination of this agreement, EMPLOYER shall continue to pay EMPLOYEE the commission above provided on all shipments made into EMPLOYEE'S Territory pursuant to orders received prior to the date of termination, subject to any charges outstanding against EMPLOYEE'S commission, and provided that EMPLOYER has received full payment for the merchandise shipped.

14. All notices required or permitted to be given under this agreement shall be in writing sent by first class mail, addressed if directed to EMPLOYEE to:

and if directed to EMPLOYER, at _____ , New York, New York, Attention: _____ , or to such other address as each party may hereafter notify the other in writing.

15. This Agreement shall be governed by and construed in accordance with the laws of the State of New York and shall be binding upon and inure to the benefit of the parties hereto and their respective heirs, personal representatives, successors, and assigns.

IN WITNESS WHEREOF, EMPLOYEE has fixed his hand and seal and EMPLOYER has caused this Agreement to be executed by a duly authorized person the day and year first above written.

_____ [Seal][37]

Witness _____

By: _____

EXAMPLE

Employee Agreement Form Agreement 4

Special Features

This agreement is for an employer engaged in a technical business activity. The employee is performing technical and creative services. A rather elaborate set of provisions deals with restrictive covenants and the forms of employer protection (paragraph 9).

EMPLOYMENT AGREEMENT

AGREEMENT made this ___ day of _____ , 19___, by and between _____ ("Corporation") and ("Employee").

BACKGROUND OF AGREEMENT:

Employee has served Corporation as Vice President since the commencement of Corporation's business operations in December,

---

36. Note that this agreement is, in effect, a thirty-day agreement by this provision.

37. The term "Seal" is often added to a signature line to make the document a sealed instrument which, in many states, is enforceable even without consideration.

1987. Corporation and Employee now desire to enter into an Employment Agreement on the terms and conditions as hereinafter set forth.

NOW, THEREFORE, in consideration of the premises and the mutual covenants herein contained, the parties hereto, intending to be legally bound, hereby agree as follows:

1. *Employment Term.* Corporation hereby employs Employee and Employee hereby accepts said employment, subject to all the terms and conditions of this Agreement. This Agreement shall be for a term of three (3) years, commencing on the date hereof, and thereafter shall automatically be renewed from year to year unless either party shall give notice to the other no less than ninety (90) days prior to the end of the initial term or any renewal term of his or its intention to terminate the Agreement at the end of said term.

2. *Capacity.* Employee is employed as a technical director of Corporation, and to assist the chief executive officer of Corporation in the operation and management of the business and affairs of Corporation, subject to the supervision and direction of Corporation's Board of Directors, and to perform such other technical, managerial, and executive functions and services for Corporation as he may from time to time be requested to perform by the President or the Board of Directors.

3. *Duties.* During the period of his employment hereunder, Employee agrees to devote his time, energy, skill, and best efforts to promote the business and affairs of Corporation, and to perform faithfully to the fullest extent of his ability all the duties which relate to his position as an executive and a technical director of Corporation as may be requested of him by Corporation's Board of Directors or President. Employee agrees that during the original term of this Agreement and any renewal term he will not be employed by, participate or engage in, or be a part of in any manner, directly or indirectly, the affairs of any other business enterprise or occupation which would interfere with the performance of his full-time duties hereunder.

4. *Compensation.* Corporation shall pay to Employee, as compensation for all services rendered by Employee during his employment hereunder, a salary at the rate of $40,000 per annum, payable in biweekly installments, subject to such revisions as Corporation's Board of Directors and Employee may, from time to time, approve and agree upon.

5. *Reimbursement of Expenses.* During Employee's employment hereunder, Corporation will reimburse Employee for all ordinary and necessary business expenses incurred by him in connection with the business of Corporation. Such payments shall be made by Corporation upon submission by Employee of vouchers itemizing such expenses in a form satisfactory to Corporation.

6. *Automobile.* During Employee's employment hereunder, Corporation will provide Employee with a suitable automobile selected by Corporation for his use in connection with the performance of his duties hereunder.

7. *Other Benefits.* Corporation shall, during the period of Employee's employment hereunder, maintain in effect such hospitalization, medical, group life, and other insurance coverage and such other benefits as Corporation presently has in effect with respect to Employee or hereafter during the term of Employee's employment hereunder provides to its executive personnel.

8. *Disability.* If Employee should become unable to perform his duties hereunder, because of partial or total disability or incapacity due to illness, accident, or other cause, Corporation shall continue Employee's salary at the full rate set forth in this Agreement for a period of six (6) months. If Employee is still unable to perform his duties hereunder at the end of said six (6) month period, Corporation shall have the right at any time thereafter to terminate Employee's employment, in which event Corporation shall have no further liability or obligation under this Agreement.

9. *Trade Secrets, Noncompetition, etc.* (a) Employee covenants and agrees that he will not, during the term of his employment or thereafter, for any reason or purpose whatsoever, use for his personal benefit, or disclose, communicate or divulge to, or use for the benefit, direct or indirect, of any person, firm, association, or corporation other than Corporation, any information as to business methods, business policies, systems, procedures, techniques, computer programs, research or development projects or results thereof, trade secrets, inventions, knowledge and processes used or developed by Corporation, any forms, names, and addresses of customers or clients, data on or relating to past, present, or prospective customers or clients, or any other information relating to or dealing with the business operations or activities of Corporation, made known to Employee or learned or acquired by Employee while in the employ of Corporation.

(b) Employee covenants and agrees that he will not, during the term of his employment hereunder and for a period of two (2) years after the termination or expiration of his employment hereunder for any reason whatsoever, within the continental United States, directly or indirectly engage in any activities relating to evaluation and selection of computer equipment and software, conversion of computer programs and information files from one computer system to another, or in any other activities or operations carried on by Corporation at any time during the period of his employment by Corporation, or planned or contemplated by Corporation at the time of termination of his employment by Corporation. The term "engage in" shall include, but shall not be limited to, activities, whether direct or indirect, as proprietor, partner, stockholder, principal, agent, employee, or consultant.

(c) Employee covenants and agrees that any and all writings, inventions, improvements, processes, systems, procedures, techniques, and/or computer programs which he may make, conceive, discover, or develop, either solely or jointly with any other person or persons, at any time during the term of this Agreement and any renewal hereof, whether during working hours or at any other time, whether at the request or upon the suggestion of Corporation or otherwise, which relate to or are useful in connection with the business now or hereafter carried on or contemplated by Corporation, including developments or expansions of its present fields of operations, shall be and hereby are the sole and exclusive property of Corporation. Employee shall make full disclosure to Corporation of all such writings, inventions, improvements, processes, systems, procedures, techniques, and computer programs, and shall do all such acts and execute, acknowledge and deliver all such instruments in writing as may be necessary to vest in Corporation the absolute title thereto. Employee further covenants and agrees to write and prepare all specifications and procedures and to aid and assist Corporation in all other ways in order that Corporation properly can prepare and present all applications for copyright or Letters Patent thereof, can secure such copyright or Letters Patent wherever possible, as well as reissues, renewals, and extensions thereof, and can obtain the record title to such copyright or patents so that Corporation shall be the sole and absolute owner thereof in all countries in which it may desire to have copyright or patent protection. It is understood and agreed that Employee shall not be entitled to any additional or special compensation or reimbursement in regard to any and all such writings, inventions, improvements, processes, systems, procedures, techniques, and computer programs.

(d) Employee covenants and agrees that he will, upon termination of his employment with Corporation for any reason whatsoever, deliver to Corporation any and all records, forms, contracts, lists of names and other customer data, and any other articles or papers which have come into his possession by reason of his employment with Corporation or which he holds for Corporation, irrespective of whether or not any of said items were prepared by him, and he shall not retain memoranda or copies of any of said items.

(e) Employee acknowledges that the restrictions contained in this paragraph 9, in view of the nature of the business in which Corporation is engaged, are reasonable and necessary to protect the legitimate interests of Corporation. Employee understands and agrees that the remedies at law for his violation of any of the covenants or provisions of this paragraph 9 will be inadequate, that such violations will cause irreparable injury within a short period of time, and that Corporation shall be entitled to preliminary injunctive relief and other injunctive relief against any such violation. Such injunctive relief shall be in addition to, and in no way in limitation of, any and all other remedies Corporation shall have in law and equity for the enforcement of those covenants and provisions. In the event of any violations or breaches of subparagraph (b) of this paragraph 9, the covenants therein contained shall remain in force during a period of two years subsequent to the termination of the conduct constituting a breach or violation.

(f) Employee covenants and agrees that even though his employment by Corporation may be terminated, he will at any time, either before or after such termination, cooperate with Corporation in the prosecution or defense of any litigation relating to Corporation's activities during the course of his employment or in connection with any copyright or patent rights of Corporation, at Corporation's expense.

10. *Miscellaneous Provisions.* (a) Any notices pursuant to this Agreement shall be validly given or served if in writing and delivered personally or sent by registered or certified mail, postage prepaid, to the following addresses:

If to Corporation:

If to Employee:

or to such other addresses as either party may hereafter designate to the other in writing.

(b) If any provision of this Agreement shall be or become illegal or unenforceable in whole or in part for any reason whatsoever, the remaining provisions shall nevertheless be deemed valid, binding, and subsisting.

(c) The waiver by either party of a breach or violation of any provisions of this Agreement shall not operate or be construed as a waiver of any subsequent breach or violation thereof.

(d) This writing represents the entire agreement and understanding of the parties with respect to the subject matter hereof; it may not be altered or amended except by an agreement in writing.

(e) This Agreement has been made in and its validity, performance, and effect shall be determined in accordance with the laws of the Commonwealth of Pennsylvania.

(f) The headings of paragraphs in this Agreement are for convenience only; they form no part of this Agreement and shall not affect its interpretation.

IN WITNESS WHEREOF, the parties have executed this agreement under seal on the day and year first above written.

By: _____

[*Corporate Seal*]   Attest: _____

_____ [*Seal*]

_____
Witness

Checklist of Information Required for Drafting Employment Agreement

  I. Name and address (for notices) of employer

  II. Name and address (for notices) of employee

  III. Term of agreement and date of commencement of term

  IV. Capacity and duties of employee

    A. Nature of duties and functions

    B. Title

    C. Territory (if a sales representative)

    D. Full-time or part-time

    E. Limitations on outside activity

    F. Limitations on authority (sales representatives, particularly)

    G. Provision for vacation

    H. Persons to whom employee reports

  V. Compensation

    A. Straight salary, escalation provisions

    B. Commission (which sales is it based upon, any variations in rate, provisions for drawing account)

      C. Incentive compensation

      D. Stock options

      E. Stock bonus

      F. Fringe benefits

         1. Car

         2. Coverage under insurance or health and accident plans

         3. Pension or profit sharing plans

      G. Expense account

VI. Special provisions for termination

      A. Disability provisions

      B. Breach of agreement

VII. Restrictive covenants

      A. Length of time

      B. Geographical area

      C. Description of restricted activity

VIII. Need for trade secrets or patent protection clause

CHAPTER EIGHT

Shareholders' Agreements

Agreements among shareholders are very common for closely held corporations. Since these agreements fall into certain patterns, the preparation of the initial draft of this type of agreement can be delegated to a lawyer's assistant. Moreover, the basic drafting techniques applicable to such agreements are relevant to many other types of agreements as well.

The term "Shareholders' Agreement" has many meanings, but usually it refers to a written agreement entered into among two or more shareholders of a corporation that has a small number of shareholders (which corporation may or may not be a "close corporation" as that term is defined under state corporate laws[1]). A shareholders' agreement contains restrictions on the transferability of shares of stock in the corporation by the parties during their lifetimes and also restricts the transferability of a deceased party's shares upon death. Frequently all shareholders of the corporation are parties to such an agreement, and the corporation itself is generally a party as well. Such agreements are sometimes referred to as "Buy-Out Agreements," "Buy-Sell Agreements," "Stock Purchase Agreements," or "Shareholders' Restrictive Agreements."

Shareholders' agreements are most frequently executed upon or shortly following incorporation of a business, upon an issuance or transfer of stock to a shareholder or group of shareholders, when a shareholder is retiring from the business and the purchase of such shareholders' interest is being negotiated, or when there has been some disagreement among the shareholders which is resolved by, or avoided for the future by, a shareholders' agreement.

In the case of corporations whose stock is held by a few persons, the shareholders are often also the directors and officers of the corporation and work together intimately in the business; they frequently are members of the same family; their livelihoods often depend largely on the profits of the corporate business; and their shares are not readily saleable because of the absence of a public market for the shares and because the benefits of stock ownership are often realized indirectly, e. g., in the form of the salary received as an officer or employee of the corporation. To this

---

1. See Chapter Two for a discussion of statutory close corporations.

extent, a closely held business corporation is very much like a partnership.

It is often of utmost importance to a shareholder of a closely held corporation to have some control over who the other shareholders are, just as a partner in a partnership must have some say as to who the partners are. Moreover, the person becoming a part of a closely held corporation should not easily be able to terminate the "corporate marriage" which would cause great uncertainty for the remaining shareholders. If shareholders in a closely held corporation are looked upon as partners, it is not surprising to find the existence of agreements which severely limit the right of a shareholder to transfer shares during lifetime and thereby prevent the former coshareholders from being surprised by a new partner. Such agreements also govern the disposition of shares upon death and thereby protect the surviving coshareholders from having a widow or widower or personal representative as their new partner. The typical shareholders' agreement, therefore, provides that a shareholder may not dispose of shares during lifetime without first offering them to the corporation and/or the coshareholders, and provides that, upon the death of a shareholder, the corporation or the surviving shareholders can, or must, purchase the deceased shareholder's shares. Shareholders' agreements also frequently contain, as do partnership agreements, provisions respecting the manner in which certain aspects of the business are to be managed. The provisions normally found in shareholders' agreements are discussed in detail in the following sections of this chapter.

PROVISIONS RESTRICTING TRANSFER OF SHARES DURING LIFETIME

General Considerations

Whose Interests Are to Be Protected? Under the laws of most states, the holder or holders of a majority of the outstanding shares of voting stock of a corporation have virtually absolute control over corporate decisions. This is true as a practical matter even with respect to corporations which grant shareholders cumulative voting in the election of directors.[2] Consequently, a majority block of shares, carrying with it corporate control, is much more readily saleable than a minority block of shares. A minority shareholder who is suddenly confronted with a new incompatible majority shareholder is in a very poor position. The minority shareholder may be dismissed as an officer and employee of the corporation and may not receive any dividends on the shares of stock. The

2. See the discussion of cumulative voting in Chapter Two.

minority stock interest, for all practical purposes, may become virtually worthless. A minority shareholder, therefore, generally has much to gain by restrictions on the transfer of stock by all shareholders during lifetime. From the standpoint of majority shareholders, difficulties can be created by a troublesome minority shareholder who, with cumulative voting, may be able to be elected a director of the corporation, or who, even without being a director, may initiate lawsuits and otherwise harass existing directors and officers. For these reasons, majority shareholders frequently desire restrictions as much as do minority shareholders.

Should All Shareholders Be Party to the Agreement? There is no absolute answer to this question. The facts and circumstances of each situation determine the answer. Although in most cases all shareholders are party to a shareholders' agreement, this is not invariable. Sometimes one or more shareholders may simply refuse to sign the agreement. The remainder must then decide whether to have an agreement absent the refusing shareholder. Sometimes one or more shareholders are not invited to sign the agreement. For example, in instances where the shareholders fall into two or more ascertainable groups, such as different family groups, an agreement may be limited to those shareholders falling within a particular group.

Should the Corporation Be Party to the Agreement? When all of the shareholders are party to a shareholders' agreement, the corporation is almost always an additional party to the agreement. Where all shareholders are not a party, however, as a matter of preference the remaining shareholders may wish the corporation not to be a party.

In most cases, however, the agreement will contain provisions granting certain rights and imposing certain obligations on the corporation, thus requiring the corporation to be a party in order to bind the corporation to the obligations set forth in the agreement. For example, the entire effort to preserve the percentage stock interest of a minority shareholder could be completely thwarted if the corporation were free to issue new shares, whether to certain existing shareholders or to third parties. Absent the corporation's agreement not to do so, the corporation could issue such shares upon the authorization of a majority of the board of directors of the corporation. Moreover, the agreement of the corporation is required to prevent it from honoring transfers in violation of the agreement. Shareholders' agreements also frequently require the corporation to purchase shares under certain circumstances, and the corporation's written agreement to do so is therefore necessary.

Absolute Restrictions on Transferability

The considerations which suggest the use of a shareholders' agreement often, if carried to their logical extreme, lead to the conclusion that an absolute prohibition on any lifetime transfers of stock by shareholders of a corporation would be the most desirable alternative. If embodied in a shareholders' agreement, such a restriction would most likely be unenforceable by court action because of the well established legal principle that "unreasonable" restraints on transfers of property of a person are not permitted. The examples of restrictions on transferability which follow represent, under most, if not all state laws, reasonable restrictions on transferability and are used, in effect, to achieve a result which cannot be achieved directly by an absolute prohibition on transferability.

Right of First Refusal to Purchase Shares Upon a Proposed Transfer

Faced with the dilemma of desiring to restrict a shareholder's right to sell the shareholder's stock in a closely held corporation, but unable to impose an absolute restriction on such a transfer, a paralegal or lawyer drafting shareholders' agreements normally provides that any shareholder who wants to transfer stock and who has received a valid offer (often described as a "bona fide offer"[3]) for such stock must offer the stock first to the corporation or to all or some of the coshareholders upon the same terms and conditions as contained in the bona fide offer. This requirement is often referred to, from the perspective of the shareholders or corporation who may purchase the stock of a shareholder before it is sold to an outsider, as a "right of first refusal": the right to decide whether to buy or refuse to buy the stock before the stock can be sold to anyone else. This section of the chapter will analyze different varieties of the "right of first refusal."

Corporation's Right of First Refusal Shareholders' agreements may provide that if a shareholder receives a bona fide offer to purchase such shareholder's shares, the offer cannot be accepted until the shares are first offered to the corporation; if the corporation does not exercise its option to purchase such shares within a stipulated time, the shares may be sold to the bona fide offeror. Most agreements provide that the bona fide offer must cover all, and not less than all, of the offeree's shares. Some agreements also provide that a bona fide offeror, who actually purchases

---

3. A bona fide offer is often described as an offer in writing by a person who is ready, willing, and able to buy and who has no external constraint to buy. Such a person may be hard to find for the purchase of stock of a closely held corporation. Why?

such shares, must take the purchased shares subject to the restrictions contained in the shareholders' agreement as though the offeror were an original signatory to the agreement. Generally, the corporation is required to exercise its option in full or not at all since, as a practical matter, a prospective purchaser will not make a bona fide offer for shares without knowing how many shares will be available for purchase if the offer is accepted.[4]

Shareholders' Right of First Refusal A right of first refusal of the remaining shareholders to purchase the shares of a shareholder who desires to sell shares pursuant to a bona fide offer is sometimes found in lieu of, and sometimes found in addition to, the corporation's right of first refusal. In most instances the shareholders' right of first refusal is in addition and secondary to the corporation's right; that is, the agreement will provide that if the corporation fails to exercise its right of first refusal, the shares as to which the corporation has not exercised its option are then offered to the other shareholders, generally pro rata in accordance with their holdings. This type of provision is somewhat difficult to draft since it should cover the eventuality of the exercise by some shareholders and nonexercise by others. In such a case it is generally desirable to provide for a further right of first refusal to the exercising shareholders to purchase the shares not taken by the nonexercising group.[5] Again, as pointed out with respect to a corporation's right of first refusal, it is generally provided that if less than all of the offered shares are taken (whether by the corporation or the other shareholders or both), none of the options are deemed to have been exercised and the selling shareholder is free to sell the shares to the bona fide offeror.[6]

The most desirable format usually is to provide a right of first refusal to the corporation followed by a right of first refusal to the remaining shareholders.[7] From the viewpoint of the remaining shareholders, it is usually best to have the corporation purchase the shares of a selling shareholder. This is true because the remaining shareholders, if they are the purchasers, might have to obtain the funds to purchase the shares by borrowing, thus incurring interest expense, or by taking money out of the corporation as taxable dividends or taxable salary. However, there may be situations where the corporation is legally unable to purchase all

4. Sample provisions will appear shortly. The terms (e. g., the price, etc.) on which shares may be purchased by the corporation are discussed later in this chapter.
5. See, for example, paragraph A–5 of Form Agreement 2 in this chapter.
6. An example is contained in paragraph A–6 of Form Agreement 2.
7. This format is followed in paragraph 2 of Form Agreement 1 and paragraph A of Form Agreement 2.

or any of the shares, for example, when such a purchase would impair the corporation's ability to pay its debts in the ordinary course of its business. In that case the shareholders should have the right to purchase any shares the corporation does not purchase. A sample form of provision of this nature is set forth in paragraphs A–3 to A–6 of Form Agreement 2 of this chapter.[8]

Mandatory Sales and/or Purchases ("Puts" and "Calls")

Mandatory Purchases by the Corporation or Shareholders from a Selling Shareholder As noted above, the shares in a closely held corporation are not readily saleable, and this is particularly true of minority interests.[9] Shareholders' agreements sometimes provide, therefore, that if a shareholder desires to dispose of shares in the corporation, the shareholder may compel the corporation and/or the other shareholders to buy the shares at a stipulated price, so as not to be "locked in" forever into the investment. The right of one person to be able to compel another to purchase an asset at a specified price is referred to as "put." This sort of provision is most frequently given to certain shareholders, usually minority shareholders, and not to others. This right of a shareholder to put the stock to the corporation and/or the other shareholders is rarely exercisable at will by a shareholder, but rather is exercisable only upon the occurrence of a specified event or events, e. g., termination of employment with the corporation due to retirement, disability, or discharge. The right is sometimes given to a majority shareholder in cases where a majority shareholder uses control to have the corporation issue stock or sells some stock to new shareholders, in effect "junior partners." The understanding is that the new shareholders will be required to take over the entire business by purchasing the stock of the majority shareholder whenever the "senior partner" wants to retire.[10]

EXAMPLE *Shareholder's "Put" to Company or Other Shareholders*	Clark, at any time and from time to time after his 65th birthday, may notify the Company and other Stockholders in writing of his desire to sell some or all of his shares of Stock in the Company. Upon the Company's receipt of such a notice, the Company shall have the option, exercisable for a thirty (30) day period from the date of receipt of such a notice, to

8. Note that paragraph A–6 requires that a bona fide offeror who purchases must buy within a specified period of time after expiration of the options and will be subject to the restrictions in the Agreement.

9. Discussed earlier in this chapter.

10. For a discussion of an analogous problem, see the section in the chapter on mandatory purchases by the corporation and/or shareholders of a deceased shareholder's interest.

purchase from Clark all or any part of the stock offered for sale by his notice at the price and upon the terms set forth in Paragraph D–1. The option shall be exercised by the Company's giving written notice of its election to purchase to Clark and to the other Stockholders. If the Company shall decide not to purchase all of the shares of Stock set forth in Clark's notice, it shall give written notice of that fact to the other Stockholders within said thirty (30) day period. Should the Company fail to give any notice as provided in this paragraph, it shall be presumed conclusively that the Company has decided not to purchase any shares of Stock offered for sale by Clark. If the Company has not purchased all of the shares of Stock set forth in Clark's notice, the other Stockholders shall be obligated to purchase from Clark all of the Stock offered by him and not purchased by the Company. Each such Stockholder shall purchase such proportionate part of Clark's Stock which he has offered for sale but which has not been purchased by the Company as the number of shares of Stock in the Company owned by such Stockholder bears to the total number of shares of Stock owned by all Stockholders other than Clark. Purchases shall be at the price and upon the terms set forth in Paragraph D–1.

The sample provision above provides the corporation with an option to purchase the selling shareholder's stock, but requires the other shareholders to purchase the stock in the event that the corporation fails to exercise its option. The person drafting this provision probably realized that there might be circumstances when the corporation would be unable, as a matter of state law,[11] to purchase its own stock, and it would therefore be inappropriate to impose the obligation solely upon the corporation. The value of the mandatory put depends upon the ability of the other shareholders to purchase any stock offered for sale.

Mandatory Sales by a Shareholder to the Corporation or Other Shareholders Shareholders' agreements sometimes give the corporation or some of its shareholders the right to compel certain shareholders to sell their shares to the corporation or to the other shareholders. This right to "call" shares is almost always exercisable against particular shareholders who are parties to the agreement, not all shareholders. As with the case of puts discussed above, a call is rarely exercisable by the corporation or shareholders at will, but rather is exercisable only upon the occurrence of a specified event or events, most commonly termination of the employment relationship due to retirement, disability, or discharge of the employee shareholder. The provision is most often used to protect existing shareholders against the possibility that new shareholders who are also new employees may not "work

---

11. See § 6.40, MBCA.

out," and there is frequently a time limit upon its exercise. The theory underlying this device in such a case is that the new employee, if he or she proves to be capable, should have an equity interest in the business; therefore, the employee is allowed to purchase a stock interest at the inception of employment. If the employee does not work out, however, and is discharged or quits within a certain number of months or years, the employee can be compelled to sell back the shares, frequently at their original purchase price. The following provision is typical of such arrangements:

EXAMPLE

Optional "Call" by Company Upon Termination

In the event that Smith's employment with the Company is terminated on or prior to December 31, 19_____, due to her discharge by the Company with or without cause or by her voluntarily leaving the Company (but not due to her death or to serious illness which incapacitates her from performing her duties to the Company for a period of three consecutive months or longer), the Company shall have the option, exercisable by notice in writing to Smith given within 30 days of such termination of employment, to purchase from Smith all of her shares of Stock in the Company at a purchase price of $1.00 per share. Upon the receipt of said notice, Smith shall sell all of her shares of Stock to the Company in accordance with the following terms. Such purchase price shall be paid in full by the Company at settlement, in cash or by certified check, at the executive offices of the Company, on the date and at the hour fixed by the Company in its written notice to Smith, such time to be no later than on the 45th day following such termination of employment.

QUESTION

Why does the option not occur if Smith dies or is disabled? Could it be present in such situations?

Mandatory Purchase and Sale The two preceding sections described unilateral rights, or options, exercisable generally upon the occurrence of specified events. Specified events frequently trigger bilateral obligations, however. For example, there may be an obligation of the corporation to purchase and the concurrent obligation of the shareholder to sell such shareholder's shares upon retirement, disability, or discharge. Because of the similarity in the reason for puts, calls, and mandatory purchases and sales (particularly in the context of termination of employment) to the reason for the purchase of shares of a deceased shareholder upon death, agreements sometimes lump together retirement, disability, and discharge with death in a single section of the shareholders' agreement. More commonly, however, purchases on death are treated separately in light of the fact that the purchase price is frequently different (generally higher) with respect to such purchases and the payment terms are frequently different (generally payable sooner).[12] Moreover, purchase prices frequently differ, even where death is not involved, depending upon the event giving rise to the purchase. The purchase price to a disabled shareholder-employee, for example, generally will be higher than the purchase price to a discharged shareholder-employee.[13]

<table>
<tr><td>

EXAMPLE

Mandatory "Put" and "Call" by Company Upon Termination

</td><td>

Upon the termination of Green's employment with the Company for whatever reason other than death, the Company shall purchase from Green and Green shall sell to the Company all of his shares of Stock in the Company at a purchase price of $1.00 per share. Such purchase price shall be paid in full by the Company at settlement, in cash or by certified check, at the executive offices of the Company, on the date and at the hour fixed by the Company in a written notice to Green, such time to be no later than on the 45th day following such termination of employment.

</td></tr>
</table>

Special Restrictions for Two or More Groups of Shareholders

In some instances the shareholders of a corporation fall into two or more ascertainable groups, such as family groups. For example, where the shares of the corporation are owned in part by members of the Smith family and in part by members of the Jones family, particularly when the two families have equal or nearly equal interests, it is often necessary to preserve the balance of power and relative percentage ownership of the two families. If one of the Smiths wants to sell shares, the other Smiths will not want the corporation to have a right of first refusal, since a purchase by the corporation will result in a proportionately smaller ownership in the corporation by the Smith family in relation to the combined stock interest of the Jones family. Indeed, control of the corporation could shift from the Smith family to the Jones family in such a case. Nor would the Smith family want all of the shareholders to have the right of first refusal pro rata, since that also could lead to the same adverse result. This is illustrated in the following two examples:

12. This is true particularly when funded by life insurance to be discussed later. Consider the reasons for differences in price and terms of payment under different circumstances.

13. Why would such a disparity in price exist? Consider in your answer the main purpose of shareholders' agreements—discouraging transfers.

EXAMPLE 1

Corporation purchases John Smith's shares

Shareholder	Shares Outstanding Before Purchase	Shares Outstanding After Purchase
John Smith	200	None
Helen Smith	300	300
Bill Smith	50	50
Dan Jones	200	200
Pauline Jones	100	100
Dick Jones	150	150
	1,000	800

EXAMPLE 2

Remaining Shareholders purchase, pro rata, John Smith's shares

Shareholder	Shares Outstanding Before Purchase	Shares Outstanding After Purchase
John Smith	200	None
Helen Smith	300	375.0
Bill Smith	50	62.5
Dan Jones	200	250.0
Pauline Jones	100	125.0
Dick Jones	150	187.5
	1000	1,000.0

In each of the above examples, the Smith family controlled 55% of the outstanding shares of the corporation before the purchase, whereas in each case after the purchase it would control only 43.75% of the outstanding shares. Accordingly, shareholders' agreements in this situation generally define the groups involved and provide the members of each group the initial right of first refusal to purchase the shares of a group member who proposes to transfer shares or who had died. Where a group does not exercise its right of first refusal in full, the corporation and/or the other group will usually have a right of first refusal before shares can be sold to an outsider. See paragraphs A–5 to A–7 of Form Agreement 3 of this chapter.

DISPOSITION OF SHARES OF A DECEASED SHAREHOLDER UPON DEATH

General Considerations

Whose Interests are to Be Protected? As a general rule, the beneficiaries receiving the stock of a deceased shareholder upon the death of the shareholder are more likely to be favored than the surviving shareholders. (In the same way, the interests of the younger shareholders, and the interests of the minority shareholders are more likely to be protected than the interests of the majority shareholders.) The reason for protecting the beneficiaries of a deceased shareholder is that shares in a closely held corporation rarely pay dividends and rarely prove saleable. The stock can constitute a virtually worthless asset in an estate, although it was the deceased shareholders' principal asset during lifetime because the decedent was drawing a salary from the corporation. If the beneficiaries of the stock of a deceased shareholder are minority shareholders then, by virtue of their lack of control, they are not in a position to direct the flow of cash out of the corporation in the form of dividends or other distributions.

Option or Obligation to Purchase and to Sell

Shareholders' agreements frequently provide that upon the death of a shareholder, the corporation is obligated to purchase, and the personal representatives[14] of the deceased shareholder are obligated to sell, the shares of the deceased shareholder. A minority shareholder, particularly one more advanced in age, should generally insist that the corporation be obligated to purchase all shares owned by such shareholder upon death, so that the beneficiaries will have cash rather than noncash-producing shares of stock. In light of the obligation of the corporation to purchase, the majority shareholder will generally insist that the personal representatives of the deceased shareholder be obligated to sell the shares to the corporation, rather than have an option to do so.

EXAMPLE

Mandatory Reciprocal "Put" and "Call" by Company in Event of Death of Shareholder

Upon the death of a Stockholder, the Company shall purchase from the personal representatives of the deceased Stockholder, and the personal representatives of the deceased Stockholder shall sell to the Company, all of the shares of Stock in the Company owned by the deceased Stockholder, at the price and upon the terms set forth in Paragraph C–2, and the surviving Stockholders shall adopt such resolutions and take such action as may be required by law to authorize such purchase at such time.

If the purchase price to be paid to the personal representatives of the deceased Stockholder is in excess of the then legally allowable purchase price to the Company, each of the surviving Stockholders shall be obligated to make a contribution in cash to the Company, five (5) or more days prior to the settlement date set forth in Paragraph C–2, in an amount equal to that proportion of the amount by which the purchase price exceeds the legally allowable purchase price to the Company, as the number of shares of Stock in the Company owned by such surviving Stockholder bears to the number of shares of Stock in the Company owned by all of the surviving Stockholders.

14. The personal representative is the individual who administers the estate of a decedent or carries out the will of the decedent.

Shareholders' agreements frequently obligate the surviving shareholders to purchase the deceased shareholder's shares in the event that the corporation cannot, or does not, purchase the shares. In some cases the corporation has no obligation to purchase the shares, and the obligation falls directly on the surviving shareholders. There are situations, moreover, in which there is no mandatory purchase or sale but where the corporation and/or the surviving shareholders have the option to purchase the deceased shareholder's shares, or, conversely, agreements in which the personal representatives of the deceased shareholder have an option to compel the corporation and/or the surviving shareholders to purchase. An example of a corporation's option clause follows:

EXAMPLE

Optional "Call" by Company in the Event of Death of Shareholder

> Upon the death of Clark, and for a period of 30 days thereafter, the Company shall have the option, exercisable by notice in writing to Clark's personal representatives and to the Smith Group Stockholders, to purchase all or a part of the shares of Stock in the Company owned by Clark at the time of his death at the price and upon the terms set forth in Paragraph C–2 hereof.

Insurance Funding by Corporation and/or by Surviving Shareholders

A corporation or surviving shareholders obligated to purchase a deceased shareholder's shares may be obligated to make a substantial payment for such shares without any certainty that, at the time, they will be in a sufficiently liquid cash position to make the payment. Many corporations with millions of dollars of assets are, from time to time, very short of cash, for example, when their current assets are tied up primarily in inventory or receivables. As a safeguard against the difficulties occasioned by such a situation, a corporation may carry life insurance on the lives of its shareholders—most commonly on the lives of its principal shareholders—in order to provide the cash with which to purchase the deceased shareholder's interest in the corporation.[15] Similarly, shareholders may carry insurance on the lives of their coshareholders for the same purpose. Shareholders' agreements in such situations sometimes provide for an affirmative obligation of the corporation or shareholders to carry such insurance.

---

15. Consider the impact of the possibility of funding a purchase through life insurance on the question raised by footnote 13 of this chapter.

EXAMPLE

Maintenance by Company of Insurance Funding

> The Company shall promptly obtain and maintain in force for the duration of this Agreement, as owner and as beneficiary, a policy of life insurance insuring the life of each Stockholder for $50,000. The parties acknowledge that the principal purpose for such life insurance is to fund the purchase by the Company of the Stock of a deceased Stockholder; accordingly, the Company shall, as and when appropriate, increase the amount of life insurance on the life of each Stockholder so as to be reasonably certain of having sufficient net proceeds from such policies to redeem completely a deceased Stockholder's interest in accordance with the terms of this Agreement. Any proceeds from such life insurance policies received by the Company shall be held by the Company in trust for the purposes of this Agreement. The Company shall pay all premiums on such life insurance policies, and it shall be a provision of each of such policies that each Stockholder shall be notified by the insurance company, before the expiration of any grace period, of the failure of the Company to pay the necessary premiums.

QUESTIONS

What is the problem of insurance funding where there is an old shareholder and a young shareholder? Where one shareholder has high blood pressure?

THE PURCHASE PRICE

General Considerations

In the event that shares of stock of a shareholder (whether during lifetime or upon death) are to be purchased by the corporation and/or the other shareholders, the interest of the shareholder disposing of shares generally is to receive the highest possible purchase price immediately in cash, while the interest of the purchaser is to have a lower purchase price which is payable over a long period of time at the lowest interest rate that can be negotiated. The problem with an immediate cash payment in full is that it is often unrealistic to expect a substantial cash payment on short notice. This is particularly true in the case of lifetime purchases which cannot be funded by life insurance. On the other hand, there are several problems with providing for payment over time. First, circumstances may occur between the time the payments begin and the time they are scheduled to be completed which make payment in full impossible, such as the insolvency of the purchaser. Second, there is always a danger that the purchaser may refuse to pay, even though able to, for any number of reasons. Third, the interest rate provided in a shareholders' agreement, if fixed, may be fixed at a level bearing a relationship to prevailing interest rates at the time the agreement is executed. Yet many years, possibly decades, later, when payments are to be made, interest rates may be materially higher (or lower) than the rates prevailing at the time the agreement was executed. As a consequence, the recipient of the purchase price (who might be able to invest the cash proceeds at a 10% return if received immediately) may be locked into a mandatory investment which yields only 5%. The parties can ameliorate the problem caused by fluctuating interest rates by providing for a variable rate of interest, such as by tying the interest rate in the agreement to the prevailing "prime rate."[16]

Matching Offers

When the corporation or remaining shareholders have a right of first refusal with respect to a proposed transfer of stock by a shareholder to a bona fide offeror, it is common to provide that the corporation or remaining shareholders may purchase such shares at the price and upon the terms contained in the bona fide offer, thus involving no economic prejudice to the selling shareholder. Alternatively, the agreement might provide that the purchase price shall be the same as that contained in the bona fide offer, but that the terms of payment may be, at the option of the corporation or other shareholders, either the terms contained in the bona fide offer or alternative terms (generally payment over a long period of time at a low interest rate). Agreements frequently provide, however, that the corporation or shareholders have a right to buy at the lesser of two or more alternative prices, one of which is the bona fide offer price. What is finally agreed upon is a decision of the shareholder. However, in executing the agreement each shareholder must consider that any shareholder, including himself or herself, in the future may be either buyer or seller.

A formula price may be used, such as the lesser of the bona fide offer or book value. This kind of formula, particularly where the book value or other stipulated measure is materially less than the bona fide offer, obviously discourages proposed transfers.

EXAMPLE

Settlement Terms— Installment Payments

Settlement for the purchase by the Company or by a Stockholder of shares of Stock in the Company pursuant to the options granted in Paragraph A–6 shall be made within sixty (60) days from the date of exercise of the option. At the option of the purchaser, the purchase price per share and the terms of payment shall be either (a) the price per share contained in the bona fide offer referred to in Paragraph A–3, payable upon the terms contained in said bona fide offer, or (b) the Book Value per share, payable in twenty (20) equal quarterly installments of principal, the first of which is to be paid at settlement, with interest on the unpaid balance of the purchase price at the rate of 6% per annum, payable quarterly when payments of principal are due.

16. "Prime rate" was defined in Chapter Six under "Types of Debt Securities."

Agreed Values

An occasional, though generally undesirable, provision with respect to price, applicable with respect to both lifetime transfers and dispositions upon death, is to fix a specified dollar purchase price, such as $10.00 per share. This is not usually selected as a pricing method as an economic matter since such a price, while perhaps realistic at the time the agreement is entered into, could lead to a undesirable result when applied many years later to an actual transfer.

EXAMPLE

Settlement Terms—Cash

> Settlement for the purchase by the Company or by a Stockholder of shares of Stock in the Company pursuant to the options granted in Paragraph A–6 shall be made within sixty (60) days from the date of exercise of the option. The purchase price shall be $10.00 per share, payable in full, by cash or certified check, at settlement.

Adjustable Agreed Values

In order to eliminate the inequity of a fixed agreed value as discussed in the preceding paragraph, an agreed value can be designated at the time of execution of the agreement with a provision that the shareholders and corporation must redetermine the agreed value on an annual or other periodic basis in order to maintain the agreed value, as adjusted, at a realistic level. Such provisions generally require complete unanimity in order to modify the agreed value, although, of course, it is possible to provide for some percentage vote, majority or greater, to control. As the value of the shares increases, the motivation of the younger shareholders generally is to keep the price low, while the motivation of the older shareholders generally is to set the agreed value high. Why? As a result of this conflict, or any other conflict, shareholders under such a procedure frequently are unable to reach agreement with respect to adjusting the agreed value. For that reason it is desirable in using such a format to provide for the eventuality of failure, whether by neglect or by disagreement, of the parties to adjust the agreed value periodically.[17] The common manner of doing this is to provide that, if an agreed value is not readjusted for a period of some established number of consecutive years, the agreed value shall be deemed to be the last established agreed value plus or minus some formula value. As is always true, the following sample is only one variation, the parties may create many other alternatives.

17. A form of agreement for periodically adjusting agreed values is attached as Schedule A to Form Agreement 3.

Agreed Value of Stock

> The Agreed Value per share of the Stock of the Company is hereby determined to be as set forth on Schedule A hereto. On January 31 and on July 31 of each year the Stockholders shall redetermine in writing the Agreed Value of the Stock for purposes of this Agreement and shall record such agreed redetermination of Agreed Value on a Schedule substantially in the form of Schedule A hereto. A redetermination of Agreed Value shall be effective only if agreed to unanimously in writing by all the Stockholders. Should the parties fail to redetermine the Agreed Value for a period of 12 consecutive months, then the Agreed Value per share shall, subsequent to the expiration of such 12-month period and until a redetermination of Agreed Value by the Stockholders, be the last determined Agreed Value per share, plus or minus the aggregate of the net income or loss (on a consolidated basis with subsidiaries, if any), after federal and other income and other taxes, less the aggregate of dividends paid on the Company's capital stock, from the beginning of the Company's last fiscal year in which there occurred a determination of Agreed Value until the close of the fiscal year last preceding the time in question, divided by the total number of shares of common stock of the Company then outstanding. The aggregate of the net income or loss shall be as computed by the Company's regularly engaged public accountants in accordance with generally accepted accounting principles and practices applied on a basis consistent with that of preceding years, whose determination shall be binding and conclusive upon the parties.

QUESTION

If it is possible to get regular redetermination of agreed values, do you believe it to be a good basis for determining the purchase price?

Formula Prices

Book Value or Appraisal Value   Shareholders' agreements often provide that the purchase price applicable to lifetime and/or death transfers is the book value of the shares purchased. Although the definition of "book value" in these agreements can become quite complicated, book value per share is essentially determined by dividing the net assets (gross assets less liabilities) of the corporation by the number of outstanding shares of stock of the corporation. Under this formula, the purchase price will increase as the corporation's net assets increase and will correspondingly decrease upon a decrease in net assets.

A book value formula frequently is not a realistic measure of the worth of shares of stock and must be used carefully. It is a mechanistic approach to valuation depending on accounting principles. For example, in a highly profitable service business, such as

266

a law firm or an accounting firm which is incorporated, a corporation may have negligible assets (i. e., desks, chairs, typewriters, and telephones) and yet produce several hundred thousand dollars or more of income each year, all of which is withdrawn from the corporation in the form of salaries. In such a situation the book value of a 40% interest in the corporation may be measured in hundreds of dollars, while the actual worth of a 40% interest may as an economic matter be properly measured in tens or even hundreds of thousands of dollars because of the earnings potential of the business. However, book value is an objective measure and may have a real relation to value where the corporation is a manufacturing company with much inventory and assets in machinery, equipment, and accounts receivable. Many times book value will be used because of its ease of application even where it may not be the best pricing method.

As with much else discussed herein, the best pricing method will depend upon the unique facts presented in the relevant circumstance.

EXAMPLE

Book Value of Stock

> The "Book Value" per share of the Company's Stock shall be equal to the net assets of the Company (on a consolidated basis with subsidiaries, if any[18]) on the date in question divided by the number of shares of Common Stock of the Company outstanding on such date, as determined by the Company's regularly engaged independent public accountants in accordance with generally accepted accounting principles and practices applied on a basis consistent with prior years. For purposes of Paragraph C–1 hereof, the Book Value shall be determined as of the close of the fiscal year preceding exercise of the option pursuant to Paragraph A–4 or A–5 hereof, unless such option is exercised more than 100 days following the close of such fiscal year, in which case the Book Value shall be determined as of the end of the month preceding the month in which the option was exercised.

In certain circumstances, particularly where a corporation's assets are for the most part real estate holdings, fair market value—as distinguished from book value—is a satisfactory measure of the corporation's value. Book value is not a satisfactory measure of asset value due to depreciation of buildings and other improvements on the financial books of the corporation. Depreciation decreases the book value of the real estate even though, as an economic fact, the fair market value of the real estate may be appreciating in value. In such circumstances a shareholders' agreement might provide for the purchase price to be based on fair

---

18. A "consolidated basis" means combination of the financial statements of the company and its subsidiaries in computing Book Value.

market value, with the asset value to be determined by a disinterested appraiser. In such event the appraiser should be named, preferably with an alternate if the first choice is unavailable. If naming an appraiser in the agreement is impractical, the agreement may nevertheless provide that, at the appropriate time, the parties shall select a mutually satisfactory appraiser.

QUESTIONS

What are the advantages of an appraiser? What are its disadvantages?

EXAMPLE

Alternative Values of Stock

The Book Value per share of the Company's Stock shall be equal to the net assets of the Company (on a consolidated basis with subsidiaries, if any) on the date in question divided by the number of shares of Common Stock of the Company outstanding on such date, as determined by the Company's regularly engaged independent public accountants in accordance with generally accepted accounting principles and practices applied on a basis consistent with prior years, except with respect to the valuation of the Company's consolidated real estate assets and improvements thereon. With respect to such real estate assets and improvements, they shall be valued at fair market value in lieu of the value, net of depreciation, at which they are reflected on the books of the Company or the subsidiary. The fair market value shall be determined by unanimous agreement among the purchasers and sellers involved; in the event they are not able to unanimously agree upon a valuation within thirty (30) days of the event giving rise to the exercise of the options, the valuation shall be made by an appraiser acceptable to all of the purchasers and sellers, whose appraisal shall be conclusive and binding upon the purchasers and sellers; in the event that the purchasers and sellers are not able to unanimously agree upon an appraiser within thirty (30) days of the event giving rise to the exercise of the options, the valuation shall be made by a disinterested appraiser designated by the American Arbitration Association in New York, New York, whose determination shall be conclusive and binding upon the purchasers and sellers.[19]

Earnings Multiples A formula that is often used to fix the purchase price for both lifetime and death transfers is the so-called "earnings multiple" formula, which provides in effect that the value of the corporation for purposes of determining the purchase

19. The American Arbitration Association is a group of lawyers and other private persons who stand willing to serve as arbitrators of disputes between parties in order to avoid the necessity of litigation in court with its attendant delay and expense. Many types of agreements will call for arbitration of disputes for this purpose. See paragraph 12 of Form Agreement 1 as an example. If an arbitration clause is provided, the party drafting the agreement should be careful to designate a location for the arbitration which is convenient to its side. After all, there will be travel costs, legal fees, and other expenses with an arbitration, just as there are with litigation, although the expenses are usually less in an arbitration. Sometimes different types of arbitration provisions are utilized, for example, as in paragraph I of Form Agreement 3. Are there any circumstances under which an agreement should not contain an arbitration clause?

price for a number of shares is determined by multiplying the net income of the corporation by a fixed number, such as three times earnings or ten times earnings. The multiple is a number that must be selected by shareholders and provided for in the agreement because the number is totally subjective. The net income may be the net income in the preceding fiscal year or the average of several preceding fiscal years. The following is one form of such a provision.

QUESTION

What difficulties can you perceive in utilizing an earnings multiple?

_____

EXAMPLE

Earnings Multiple Formula

> The aggregate "fair market value" of the Company's Stock for purposes of Paragraph C–1 is hereby stipulated and agreed to be five (5) times the aggregate net income, if any (on a consolidated basis with subsidiaries, if any), for the two (2) full fiscal years of the Company last preceding the time in question, but without reducing such income or increasing such loss in either year by virtue of any dividends paid in such years on the Company's Stock; provided, however, that in no event shall the fair market value of the Company's Stock for purposes of Paragraph C–1 be less than $1.00 per share. The aggregate net income or loss for the two (2) fiscal years in question shall be determined by the Company's regularly engaged independent public accountants in accordance with generally accepted accounting principles and practices applied on a basis consistent with prior years.

Other Special situations frequently make the more traditional purchase price fixing methods inapplicable. For example, in a closely held corporation where one particular shareholder is the person primarily responsible for the success of the corporation and is a person without whom the corporation will have difficulty remaining in business, it may be appropriate to provide for different purchase prices for different shareholders.

Another special situation can exist where the success of the business is determined primarily by the existence of an important contract which produces the major share of the corporation's income. In such a situation it is judicious to provide one method for determining the purchase price with respect to a transaction taking place while that contract is still in force and a different method of determining the price if that contract has been terminated and no equivalent contract or contracts obtained. These examples are only samples of many possible alternatives for pricing the shares.

269

Terms of Payment

Cash and/or Notes As mentioned earlier, it is frequently impractical, particularly in the case of lifetime transfers, to provide for a prompt lump sum cash payment for the purchase of shares. It is therefore common to provide for an extended payment over a period of years, with either a fixed interest rate or a variable interest rate. Frequently cash and notes are used in combination; that is, the agreement provides for an initial cash payment and payment of the balance over a period of time. Where the entire purchase price is not to be paid immediately, it is not always necessary to provide for separate promissory notes. The agreement itself may contain the obligation of the purchaser to pay the purchase price over time, and the obligation is as binding as it would be if the obligation were represented by notes.

EXAMPLE

Settlement Terms—Term Payment

> At settlement, the stock certificate or stock certificates representing the shares being sold shall be delivered by the seller to the purchaser or purchasers, duly endorsed for transfer, with the necessary documentary and transfer tax stamps, if any, affixed by the seller. The unpaid balance of the purchase price payable by each purchaser shall be represented by such purchaser's promissory note in negotiable form, payable to the order of the seller, dated the date of settlement and providing for an interest rate of 10% per annum. It is hereby agreed that upon any default in payment under the note, whether of an installment of principal or of interest, the full amount due under the note shall accelerate and become immediately due and payable, and the note shall contain a provision providing as aforesaid.

QUESTION

What does the provision for acceleration of the unpaid balance of a note do for the holder of a note?

Where payments over time are contemplated, it is advisable, if possible, whether or not notes are used, to have the spouse of the obligor join in the agreement and in any notes delivered at a closing, so that upon a default in payment of the obligation, joint property owned by both husband and wife can be reached by an execution on their property.

QUESTION

What property may be reached by a creditor if the debtor, but not the spouse, signs the note?

270

Security Devices Where payments over a period of time are contemplated, it is customary to provide for some sort of collateral security to protect the selling shareholder. If there is no security a default in one of the installment payments leaves the selling shareholder with only the option of filing a lawsuit, which might take several years, in order to obtain payment.

One security device used to protect the selling shareholders is a "confession of judgment" note which will in some cases substantially expedite litigation. Confession of judgment authorizes any attorney, even the attorney for the holder of the note, to enter judgment against the obligor. The use of the "confession of judgment" is limited to those states where the procedure is permitted. This device has become severely limited by the courts in recent years, even in those states where it is permitted.

QUESTION

Is it permitted in your state?

_____

Another type of security device is to require the obligor to give to the obligee a mortgage on real property or to deposit marketable securities or other property.

Still another means of securing the debt is to provide that the actual shares of the corporation being purchased are to be pledged as collateral security pending payment in full of the purchase price, and that upon default in such payment, the shares are to be returned to the seller. A sample provision follows, but, as is always the case, it is advisable to ascertain whether the lawyer for whom the paralegal is working has a model to use rather than the sample. These provisions can be quite complex and are seldom completely satisfactory since they may prove unfair to one shareholder or another if a default should occur. For example, in the sample provision below the selling shareholder may receive all of the stock back in the event of a default even though a great portion of the purchase price has been paid. This could be corrected, perhaps, by providing a sliding scale of stock that could be retained by the selling shareholder on default based upon the percentage of payments that have been made.

QUESTION

What problem arises from such a sliding scale?

_____

EXAMPLE

Security Interest in Purchased Stock

Whenever a Shareholder or the Company purchases shares of Stock pursuant to the rights or obligations contained in this agreement, such purchaser (unless the purchaser shall have paid the entire purchase price in cash) shall, following the delivery of said Stock, endorse the new certificates of Stock issued and deliver the same in pledge to Selling Shareholder or the Selling Shareholder's designated agent (herein called the "Holder") as collateral security for payment of the unpaid purchase price. The Holder shall hold the collateral only as security for the sole benefit of the Selling Shareholder until the entire purchase price has been paid. If the balance of the purchase price is paid while the Stock is held in pledge, the Holder shall deliver the Stock to the purchaser. While the Stock is held in pledge as collateral security, the purchaser shall be entitled to all voting rights and all dividends with respect thereto so long as the purchaser is not in default in its obligations to the Selling Shareholder. If the purchaser is in default then the Holder shall deliver the Stock to the Selling Shareholder who shall have the option of retaining the Stock in full payment of the debt or of selling the Stock in a commercially reasonable manner (without first offering the Stock to the Shareholders or the Company pursuant to the terms of this Agreement) and applying the proceeds towards the unpaid balance of the purchase price. Any proceeds in excess of the unpaid balance shall be sent forthwith to the purchaser. The Selling Shareholder shall exercise this option by notifying the purchaser in writing within fifteen (15) days after receipt of the Stock. A failure to notify the purchaser within this time period shall be deemed to be an election by the Selling Shareholder to retain the Stock in full payment of the balance of the debt.

The Holder shall release the Stock only upon receipt of a written notice from the Selling Shareholder, with a copy to the other party or parties, that an event has occurred which warrants the release of the Stock. In the event of a dispute concerning the Stock, the Holder may request an arbitration of the dispute in accordance with the provisions of paragraph 15 of this Agreement. The Holder shall be liable only for willful misconduct or bad faith in the performance of its duties.

PROVISIONS RESPECTING MANAGEMENT

General Considerations

Whose Interests Are to Be Protected?   An interest in a closely held corporation is frequently the principal asset of the shareholder as well as the principal source of income through salary or dividends. Whether the holder of a majority or minority interest, the shareholder is vitally interested in the management and growth of the business operated by the corporation and can be entirely dependent upon distributions from the corporation for a livelihood. Particularly in a corporation with a small number of shareholders, all of whom actively participate in the business, it is common to find salaries fixed in the same or a similar proportion to the respective stock interests of the shareholders. The motivation to take cash out of the business by way of salary rather than by way of dividends is obvious: salaries are deductible by the corporation for tax purposes, while dividends are not.[20]

The majority shareholders control the business of the corporation, including hiring, firing, and the fixing of salaries (subject to employment contracts). The majority shareholders are thus in a position, should disagreements arise between them and the minority shareholders, to revise the salary structure to the detriment of the minority shareholders. The minority shareholders may realize partial protection against this abuse through the device of long-term employment contracts. Employment contracts, however, generally provide for a stipulated dollar amount of salary and do not protect against majority shareholder-employees taking considerable increases in their salaries which are disproportionately greater than the other shareholders' salaries. It is difficult to structure employment contracts to protect against this possibility. Moreover, corporations may become involved in certain material transactions in which a minority shareholder is vitally interested but is powerless to control; these transactions might include liquidation and dissolution of the corporation, merger of the corporation, change in the nature of the business of the corporation, sale of substantially all of the assets of the corporation, composition of the board of directors of the corporation, and other matters. Although a 49% stockholder, as a practical matter, has virtually the same economic stake in a corporation as a 51% shareholder, the former is virtually powerless while the latter is virtually in complete control.[21]

Concentration of Voting Power: Voting Trusts

In order to give minority shareholders a voice in the management of the corporation, shareholders' agreements sometimes provide for greater than majority vote—in some cases unanimity—of the shareholders in order for the corporation to take certain action. Matters requiring this greater percentage or unanimity might include a liquidation and dissolution, merger, etc., as listed above. Such a device, however, is not always a complete solution. For example, a corporation with several shareholders, no one of whom is in control when acting alone, can experience intershareholder "deals" whereby a group of shareholders may make alliances with certain other shareholders to the detriment of excluded shareholders. In order to avoid intershareholder politics, some or all share-

20. See Chapter Nine for a discussion of "double taxation."
21. For sample provisions with respect to management, see generally Section F of Form Agreement 2.

holders may select one or more shareholders, or even nonshareholders, to give them sole voting authority with respect to the shares of the corporation. The legal device used to accomplish this is the voting trust, which is generally provided for by statute and which generally has a legally limited term.[22] During the term of the voting trust, the shares of stock deposited in trust are actually registered in the names of the voting trustees. As a result only the designated voting trustees have a right to vote the shares of the corporation which are deposited with them in trust. The statutory prescription for a particular state must be carefully reviewed for implementation of a voting trust.[23]

Dilution of Stock Interests

As a matter of corporate law, shares of stock of a corporation are generally issuable at the times, in the amounts, and at the prices (so long as the prices equal or exceed any par value where appropriate) determined from time to time by the board of directors acting by majority vote, and may be issued for money, property, or services rendered.[24] It is of utmost importance to a minority shareholder, in order to preserve his or her percentage interest in the corporation, to have limits imposed on the board with respect to the issuance of additional shares of capital stock. Most frequently, shareholders' agreements prohibit the issuance of any additional shares of capital stock without the agreement of all the shareholders. Where this restriction is unacceptable to the majority shareholders, a common substitute is a provision, sometimes effectuated by an actual amendment to the corporation's articles of incorporation, granting "preemptive rights" to the shareholders.[25]

Covenants Not to Compete

Although generally and more appropriately covered in employment contracts,[26] shareholders' agreements sometimes contain provisions prohibiting shareholders from engaging in business competitive with that of the corporation. Such restrictions invari-

22. Section 7.30 of the MBCA limits a voting trust to ten years; § 218 of the Delaware General Corporation Law similarly limits the period to ten years. Why do you believe time limits are placed on the life of voting trusts? Section 1768 of the Pennsylvania Business Corporation Law limits voting trusts by the law of contracts and the Rule Against Perpetuities.
23. § 7.30, MBCA.
24. See "Concept of 'Fully Paid and Nonassessable'" under "Equity Securities" in Chapter Six of this text.
25. See Chapter Two for a discussion of preemptive rights near the end of the section on "Incorporation."
26. See Chapter Seven generally for a discussion of covenants not to compete.

ably embrace the period of time the shareholder is employed by the corporation, the period of time the shareholder remains as a shareholder even if not employed by the corporation, and also some period of time following the termination of the shareholder's stock interests and/or employment. The importance and scope of a covenant not to compete depends generally on the collective estimate by the shareholders of the threat to the corporation which a particular shareholder would pose as a competitor; thus, covenants not to compete are not always uniform in their applicability to all shareholders.

EXAMPLE

Noncompetition Clause

Each Stockholder hereby agrees that he or she will not, for so long as he or she owns, directly or indirectly, any shares of the Stock of the Company and for a period of two (2) years after having disposed of the last remaining interest in any of the Stock of the Company, engage in, be financially interested in, or be employed by any business in the states of New York, Pennsylvania, and New Jersey which is competitive with the Company or any of its subsidiaries. The term "engage in" as used in the preceding sentence shall include, but shall not be limited to, activities, whether direct or indirect, as proprietor, partner, stockholder, principal, agent, employee, or consultant. Each Stockholder acknowledges that the restrictions contained in this paragraph, in light of the nature of Company's industry, are reasonable and necessary to protect the Company's legitimate interests, and that a violation thereof would result in irreparable injury to the Company and thus to its Stockholders. Each Stockholder acknowledges that, in the event of a violation of any such restrictions the Company and/or the remaining Stockholders shall be entitled to preliminary and permanent injunctive relief as well as an equitable accounting of all of such defaulting Stockholder's income, gain, or benefits arising out of such violation (which rights shall be cumulative and in addition to any other rights or remedies to which the Company and/or the Stockholders may be entitled). In the event of a violation, the two-year period referred to above shall be extended by an amount of time equal to the time during which such violations took place.[27]

MISCELLANEOUS

Multiple Class of Shares

The simplest form of capital structure for a corporation is to have a single class of common stock. However, many corporations have more complicated capital structures in which several classes of stock might exist, some of which are preferred and some of which

---

27. See also paragraph 8 of Form Agreement 1.

are common, some of which are voting and some of which are nonvoting, and some of which are convertible and some of which are not.[28] In such cases the shareholders' agreement must be drafted with particular care to achieve the intended result. For example, the shareholders' agreement might only apply to dispositions of voting common stock, since the transfer by a shareholder of nonvoting preferred stock is likely to have less impact on the corporation or its shareholders.

Interfamily Transfers

Notwithstanding the general purpose of shareholders' agreements to avoid the disposition of shares, it is common to find in shareholders' agreements the right of a shareholder to transfer during lifetime a portion of the shares to members of the immediate family or to trusts for the benefit of members of the immediate family. This right is frequently granted in order to facilitate estate planning by shareholders who wish to make gifts during their lifetime of property which is less likely to appreciate in the future, in order to avoid having those assets included in their estate upon their death. The shareholders' agreement will generally provide, in such cases, that the transferees must take such shares subject to all of the restrictions contained in the shareholders' agreement.

Shareholders' agreements also frequently provide that when shares of a shareholder are divided among family members, the family members must act as a unit with respect to any proposed sales. For example, if a shareholder transfers some shares to a spouse, some to a son, and some to a daughter, the shares owned by the entire family group must be the subject of a bona fide offer to purchase before the shares can be transferred or offered to the corporation pursuant to a right of first refusal.

With respect to death, shareholders' agreements frequently discriminate between the death of one of the transferees and the death of the initial shareholder. If the initial shareholder dies, the transferees, as well as the personal representatives of the decedent, must comply with the death provisions with regard to the decedent's shares; in the event of the death of one of the transferees while the initial shareholder is still living, the personal representatives of that transferee are obligated to resell the shares to the initial shareholder.[29]

---

28. See the discussion generally in Chapter Six relative to different classes of securities of a corporation.

29. For sample provisions see paragraphs A–7, B–1, B–2, B–3, and of Form Agreement 2.

Term of Agreement

A shareholders' agreement usually remains in effect until all but the last surviving shareholder has died, unless lifetime transfers or various other intervening circumstances, such as a public offering of the corporation's stock, lead the shareholders to terminate the agreement prematurely. Some agreements however, do expire by their terms after a fixed period of time or upon the occurrence of a specified event such as the death of a certain shareholder or a public offering of securities of the corporation:

EXAMPLE

Term of Agreement

> G–1. Unless terminated sooner by unanimous agreement in writing of the Company and the Stockholders then living, this Agreement shall terminate on the earlier of the following dates: (1) ten (10) years from the date hereof or (2) upon the repurchase of the shares of Stock of the next to the last of the Stockholders upon his death pursuant to Section K of this Agreement.
>
> G–2. Notwithstanding anything to the contrary contained in this Agreement, in the event that all of the Stockholders die within sixty (60) days of each other, then the provisions of this Agreement shall be of no further legal force and effect, and this Agreement shall terminate in all respects. Any and all transfers, payments, or other action made or taken with respect to the sale of Stock of the Company during said sixty (60) day period, except transfers to family transferees, shall be rescinded by the parties or their respective personal representatives.[30]

Authorization of Agreement

Where a corporation is a party to a shareholders' agreement, the agreement should be formally approved by the board of directors and the shareholders of the corporation. Where a corporation is a party to the agreement as a shareholder of the subject corporation (rather than the subject corporation itself), approval by the board of directors alone is sufficient. The precise language of the authorizing resolution should be determined in light of the applicable state law, but a form of resolution might be as follows:

EXAMPLE

Authorized Agreement

> RESOLVED, that this Board of Directors hereby authorizes, empowers, and directs the proper officers of this corporation to execute and deliver, and thereafter to perform, on behalf of this corporation, a certain agreement among this corporation and John Smith, John Brown, and Jean Jones, providing, *inter alia*, for the purchase of shares of stock of this corporation by this corporation under certain circumstances, a copy of which agreement is attached hereto and incorporated herein by reference.

---

30. What is the purpose of sample provision G–2?

It is also generally considered prudent, because one does not know when courts will hold otherwise, to insert language along the following lines at the very end of a shareholders' agreement following the signatures of the shareholders and the corporation. It is a waiver of any rights of a nonshareholder spouse to object to the agreement and its provisions.

EXAMPLE

Binding Effect

> Each of the undersigned hereby acknowledges that he or she has read and approves the foregoing Agreement dated January 12, 19 ___ , by and among Thomas Brown, Alice Brown, Joseph Brown, and Brown Company, Inc., and each of the undersigned, intending to be legally bound hereby, covenants and agrees to be bound by its restrictions, terms, and conditions in the event he or she should acquire, by virtue of death or otherwise, any interest in any shares of stock of Brown Company, Inc., now owned by his or her spouse or hereafter acquired by such spouse.
>
> _____ [*Seal*]
> Mary Brown
>
> _____ [*Seal*]
> Harold Brown
>
> _____ [*Seal*]
> Ruth Brown

"Boilerplate" Clauses

"Boilerplate" clauses for a certain type of agreement are generally found in substantially identical language in all agreements of that type. Many of the boilerplate clauses in shareholders' agreements are found in many other agreements as well. The subject matter of the various boilerplate clauses in shareholders' agreements follows:

1. As required by the Uniform Commercial Code,[31] the face of the stock certificates representing the shares within the scope of the agreement must be prominently marked with a legend indicating the restrictions on transfer to place prospective transferees on notice of the existence of restrictions;[32]

2. Neither the shareholders nor the company may assign, transfer, pledge, or otherwise encumber or dispose of any of their rights or obligations under the agreement;[33]

31. See Chapter Six for a description of the Uniform Commercial Code.

32. See, for example, paragraph 11 of Form Agreement 1 and paragraph H of Form Agreements 2 and 3.

33. See paragraph I of Form Agreements 2 and 3.

3. Specific enforcement is an available remedy for breach of the agreement;[34]

4. The agreement may not be modified or amended other than by an agreement of all parties in writing;[35]

5. The agreement is binding upon the parties and their respective personal representatives, successors, and assigns;[36]

6. All notices must be in writing and sent to the addresses specified in the agreement;[37]

7. Paragraph headings are for convenience only and do not form a part of the agreement;[38]

8. The law of a particular jurisdiction controls the interpretation and enforceability of the agreement.[39]

Samples of these provisions may be found in the Form Agreements which follow. In order to understand more general rules of drafting agreements, see the comments to Form Agreement 1 of Chapter Seven. Many of the considerations discussed therein are equally applicable to shareholders' agreements.

A checklist of considerations in drafting shareholders' agreements is included at the end of this chapter. It should be reviewed and retained for future reference.

PROBLEMS

Smitty Corp. has an authorized capital of 100 shares of common stock, par value $1.00 per share. John Smith owns 70 shares and Harry Smith, his younger brother, owns 30 shares. In discussing a shareholders' agreement, John Smith, the dominant brother, rejects the concept of a right of first refusal based upon a bona fide written offer. John says that it is impossible to negotiate for a bona fide written offer when the offeror knows that, after expending the time and expense, including legal fees, of investigating the corporation, and of preparing an offer, the shares will be bought out by the other shareholder at a stipulated low value. It is John's view, therefore, that if either shareholder desires to sell his interest, he should first offer all of his shares at book value to the other shareholder; if the other

---

34. See paragraph I of Form Agreements 2 and 3.

35. For example, see paragraph J of Form Agreements 2 and 3. However, some courts may not enforce this provision in view of statutes such as the Statute of Frauds, which has been enacted in many states. The Statute of Frauds defines what agreements must be in writing in order to be enforceable. In view of this, why would we put this provision in the agreement? What benefit does it have if it is enforceable?

36. See paragraph K of Form Agreements 2 and 3. Would the agreement be binding upon such persons without such a provision?

37. See paragraph L of Form Agreements 2 and 3. What purpose does the paragraph serve? Is a notice effective if it is oral and not in writing?

38. See paragraph M of Form Agreements 2 and 3. For whose benefit is this provision included? Why is it important to include such a provision?

39. See paragraph O of Form Agreements 2 and 3. See also the comments to Form Agreement 1 in Chapter Seven relating to Employment Agreements.

shareholder does not purchase them, the offering shareholder is then free to find a buyer at the same or a higher price at any time during the ensuing year. Harry agrees with this approach. John also feels that, insofar as it was he who built up the business, he should have the right to buy out Harry at book value at any time he pleases. Harry agrees with this proposition but points out a problem. Suppose John learns of a buyer who is willing to pay a considerable amount of money for all of the stock of the company. John might be tempted to exercise his right to purchase Harry's shares at book value, and then turn around and sell all of the stock to the prospective purchaser at a much higher price. John agrees that he should not have that right and that, if he should reach any agreement to sell substantially all of the stock of the Company within a year following the exercise of his call on Harry's shares, then Harry should have the option to return the price paid to him by John in exchange for 30% (i.e., his former interest) of the consideration received by John upon the subsequent sale. Both brothers are satisfied with the foregoing, and you are asked to prepare the section relating to restrictions on transfer of stock during lifetime in accordance with the foregoing. In drafting the section, you can refer to book value without defining it, on the assumption that it is defined elsewhere in the agreement. Any problems that you anticipate in drafting should be pointed out in your answer.

EXAMPLE

*Shareholders'
Agreement
Form Agreement 1*

Special Features:

A. Straightforward agreement for Company with only two shareholders. Spouses join as parties. Transfers to spouses permitted.

B. Price to be determined yearly and then adjusted based upon changes in book value.

C. Short form of a covenant not to compete, specific performance provision, and arbitration provision.

SHAREHOLDERS RESTRICTIVE AGREEMENT

AGREEMENT made this 1st day of January, 19 ___ , by and between Albert Able and Benjamin Baker (hereinafter referred to individually as "Shareholder" and jointly as "Shareholders"), Alice A. Able, and Betty B. Baker (the respective spouses of the Shareholders and hereinafter referred to individually as "Spouse" and jointly as "Spouses"), and AB corporation (hereinafter referred to as the "Company").

WITNESSETH:

The Company is a Pennsylvania corporation having an authorized capitalization of 100,000 shares of Common Stock, par value $10.00 per share (the "Stock"), 40,000 shares of which are issued and outstanding. Each Shareholder now owns 20,000 shares of the Stock.

Shareholders desire to impose certain restrictions on their right to transfer Stock and otherwise to establish certain rights between themselves.

NOW, THEREFORE, in consideration of the mutual covenants contained herein, the parties hereto, each intending to be legally bound hereby, agrees as follows:

1. *Restriction on Transfer.*
   a. Shareholders shall not sell, assign, transfer, give, donate, pledge, deposit, alien, or otherwise encumber or dispose of any Stock now or hereafter held by them, except as permitted by this Agreement and in accordance with its terms.
   b. The Company shall not cause or permit the transfer of any shares of the Stock to be made on its books unless the transfer is permitted by this Agreement and has been made in accordance with its terms.

2. *Inter Vivos Sale.*[40]
   a. If either Shareholder shall receive a bona fide written offer for the purchase of all, but not less than all, of the Stock owned by him which such Shareholder desires to accept (hereinafter referred to as the "Selling Shareholder"), the Company and the other Shareholder shall have options, as hereinafter described, to purchase all of the stock of the Selling Shareholder.
   b. The option price for all Stock owned by Selling Shareholder shall be the higher of (1) the price contained in such bona fide written offer, or (2) $10.00 per share, as adjusted pursuant to Paragraph 5.
   c. The Selling Shareholder shall give the Company and the other Shareholder written notice of the receipt by him of the above-mentioned offer, together with a copy of said offer and a statement as to the identity of the real party in interest making the offer. The Company shall have a period of twenty (20) days from the receipt of such written notice to exercise in writing its option to purchase all of the Stock owned by the Selling Shareholder.
   d. If the Company does not exercise its option in full, the other Shareholder shall have a period of ten (10) additional days beyond the twenty-day period mentioned in Paragraph 2(c) to exercise in writing his option to purchase any of the Stock owned by the Selling Shareholder not theretofore purchased by the Company.
   e. If the Company and the other Shareholder fail to exercise the options herein granted in full, the Selling Shareholder may accept the offer referred to in Paragraph 2(a) and, pursuant thereto, may dispose of all of his Stock free and clear of all the restrictions, terms and conditions of this Agreement.[41] However, if such offer made to Selling Shareholder is not accepted by him within thirty (30) days after the expiration of the options

---

40. "Inter vivos" means between the living.

41. Contrast this provision with paragraph A–6 of Form Agreement 2. What considerations go into the selection of one of these approaches?

herein granted to the Company and to the other Shareholder, and the closing of said sale is not held within thirty (30) days thereafter or in accordance with the terms of the offer, whichever is the earlier, the Selling Shareholder may not thereafter transfer any of his Stock in the Company without again complying with the provisions of this Paragraph 2.

3. *Sale Associated with Legal Proceedings Against Any Shareholder.*
   a. In the event that (1) voluntary proceedings by, or involuntary proceedings against, any Shareholder are commenced under any provision of any federal or state act relating to bankruptcy or insolvency,[42] or (2) the Stock of any Shareholder is attached or garnished, or (3) any judgment is obtained in any legal or equitable proceeding against any Shareholder and the sale of his Stock is contemplated or threatened under legal process as a result of such judgment, or (4) any execution process is issued against any Shareholder or against his Stock, or (5) any other form of legal proceedings or process is threatened or commenced, by which the Stock of any Shareholder may be sold either voluntarily or involuntarily, then the Company, and, alternatively, the other Shareholder, are hereby granted options, as hereinafter described, to purchase from such Shareholder, or his successor in interest, as the case may be, all, but not less than all, of the Stock owned by such Shareholder prior to such event. The price to be paid shall be $10.00 per share, as adjusted pursuant to Paragraph 5, for each share of such Shareholder's Stock.
   b. The Company shall have a period of forty (40) days from the date on which it receives actual notice of the event which gives rise to such option to exercise in writing its option.
   c. In the event the Company does not exercise its option in full, the other Shareholder shall have a period of twenty (20) additional days beyond the forty-day period mentioned in Paragraph 3(b) to exercise in writing his option.

4. *Death of a Shareholder.* Upon the death of either Shareholder (hereinafter called the "Deceased Shareholder"),[43] the other Shareholder shall purchase, and the Deceased Shareholder's estate shall sell all, but not less than all, of the Stock which had been owned by the Deceased Shareholder at the time of his death at a price of $10.00 per share, as adjusted pursuant to Paragraph 5, for all of the Deceased Shareholder's Stock.

5. *Adjustment of Purchase Price.* After October 31st and on or before December 15th of each year following execution of this Agreement, the Shareholders shall redetermine the prices to be paid pursuant

---

42. Insolvency default clauses generally are not enforceable in the event of federal bankruptcy. This clause is reprinted here as an example of a broad insolvency default clause and may not be wholly enforceable.

43. Notice how creating the defined term "Deceased Shareholder" simplifies and shortens the agreement where the concept is needed later on.

to Paragraphs 2, 3, and 4 in a writing signed by the Shareholders. Each such determination of the purchase price shall prevail until a new purchase price shall have been determined, except that it shall be adjusted to the extent of the increase or decrease in the "Book Value" (as hereinafter defined) of the shares of Stock from October 31st of the year in which a determination was last made to the end of the month in which a Shareholder receives an offer to purchase his Stock, an event specified in Paragraph 3 occurs, or a Shareholder dies, as the case may be. Shareholders shall cause the most current written determination to be attached to the copy of this Agreement kept on file at the Company's registered office. Until the first redetermination hereunder is made, the prices specified in Paragraphs 2, 3, and 4 of this Agreement shall, for purposes of this paragraph, be deemed to have been determined as October 31, 19 ___ .

6. *Terms and Conditions of Sale.*

   a. In the event of a sale of Stock to the Company or either Shareholder pursuant to Paragraph 2 hereof, twenty-five percent (25%) of the total purchase price shall be paid in cash or by certified check at closing, and the balance by the delivery of a negotiable note providing for payment of the balance in twenty-four (24) equal, successive monthly installments, with the first such installment due one (1) month after the date of the closing. The note shall bear interest at the rate of ten percent (10%) per annum, shall provide for acceleration of the remaining balance in the event of default, and shall give the maker the right to prepay all or any part of the remaining balance without penalty, any such prepayment of less than all of the remaining balance to be applied to the payments last becoming due.

   b. In the event of a sale of stock to the Company or either Shareholder pursuant to Paragraph 3 hereof, the total purchase price shall be paid by the delivery of a negotiable note, containing the provisions set forth in Paragraph 6(a) hereof, except that the note shall be payable in sixty (60) equal, successive monthly installments.[44]

   c. In the event of a sale of Stock pursuant to Paragraph 4 hereof, the purchase price shall be paid in cash or by certified check at closing.

   d. Closing shall be held at such time and place as may be mutually agreed by the parties to the transaction, but, in default of such agreement, closing shall take place at the offices of the Company at 2:00 p.m. on the 60th day after the date of exercise of the option if the sale is pursuant to Paragraph 2 or 3, or on the 10th day after the receipt of the life insurance proceeds or the 90th day after the death of Deceased Shareholder, whichever is later, if the sale is pursuant to Paragraph 4; provided however, that if such day is a Saturday,

---

44. What is the basis for the different payment terms for a purchase under paragraph 3 as contrasted with paragraph 2? Under paragraph 4 as contrasted with paragraphs 2 and 3?

Sunday, or legal holiday in the Commonwealth of Pennsylvania the closing shall take place at such time and place on the next business day.

e. At closing, the Stock being sold shall be delivered to the purchaser properly endorsed for transfer and with all necessary transfer tax stamps affixed, if any, and if the sale is pursuant to Paragraph 4, with all necessary evidence of the authority of the persons completing the sale on behalf of the Deceased Shareholder's estate.

7. *Determination of Book Value.* "Book Value" per share shall be determined by the Company's regularly employed certified public accountant in accordance with generally accepted accounting principles, applied on a basis consistent with that of the preceeding year, as of the applicable date for which such determination is to be made, and such determination shall be conclusive and binding upon all of the parties affected by it. No value for goodwill, firm name, or any other intangible shall be included in Book Value, nor shall any independent appraisal or valuation of the Company's assets be made.

8. *Covenant Not to Compete.* No Shareholder, so long as he holds any Stock and for a period of three (3) years thereafter, shall engage, as principal, partner, agent, employee, shareholder, director, officer, or in any other manner or capacity, or have any financial interest, in any business which is competitive to that of the Company.

9. *Specific Performance.* The parties agree that any violation of this Agreement (other than a default in the payment of money) cannot be compensated for by damages, and any aggrieved party shall have the right, and is hereby granted the privilege, of obtaining specific performance of this Agreement in any court of competent jurisdiction in the event of any breach hereunder.

10. *Transfers Between Shareholders and to Spouses.* Notwithstanding anything else in this Agreement to the contrary, each Shareholder may transfer all or any part of his Stock to the other Shareholder or to his Spouse or the Spouse of the Shareholder. If any Stock is transferred to a Spouse, such Stock shall, for all purposes of this Agreement, be deemed to be owned by the Shareholder and shall be subject to purchase by the Company or other Shareholder pursuant to Paragraphs 2, 3, and 4 as if owned by the Shareholder.

11. *Stock Certificates to be Marked with Legend.* The face of all certificates of stock now or hereafter issued by the Company shall be marked with the following legend:
"This certificate of stock and the shares represented thereby are held subject to the terms, covenants, and conditions of a certain agreement among this company and its then shareholders, dated

January 1, 19 ___ , and all amendments thereto, and may not be transferred except in accordance with the terms and provisions thereof."

12. *Arbitration.* In the event of any dispute whatsoever arising as to the interpretation of any provision of this Agreement or arising as to the rights, duties, or obligations of any of the parties hereto in connection with any provision of this Agreement, such dispute shall be submitted to arbitration in accordance with the rules then obtaining of the American Arbitration Association in Philadelphia, Pennsylvania, and any decision made in accordance with such rules shall be binding on all parties in interest.

13. *Notices.*

    a. All notices required or permitted to be given to any of the Shareholders pursuant to any of the terms hereof shall be sent by registered or certified mail, return receipt requested, postage prepaid, addressed to the following addresses of the Shareholders:

Albert Able		Harold Lawyer, Esq.
1 Main Street	with a copy to	3 Bay Street
Philadelphia, PA		Philadelphia, PA
Benjamin Baker		Joan Barrister, Esq.
2 Second Street	with a copy to	14 Sage Place
Philadelphia, PA		Philadelphia, PA

    b. All notices required or permitted to be given to the Company pursuant to any of the terms hereof shall be sent by registered or certified mail, return receipt requested, postage prepaid, addressed to the Company at 2600 Market Street, Philadelphia, Pennsylvania.

    c. All notices required or permitted to be given to the personal representative or heirs of a Deceased Shareholder pursuant to any of the terms hereof shall be given by registered or certified mail, return receipt requested, addressed to the last address of the Deceased Shareholder appearing on the records of the Company, or to such address as may have been supplied in writing and received by the Company from the personal representative of said Deceased Shareholder.

    d. Either of the Shareholders or the Company may change his or its address for notice purposes by notice given to the other parties hereto in accordance with the provisions of this paragraph.

14. *Joinder of Spouses.* The Spouses of the Shareholders have joined in this Agreement for the purpose of acknowledging that they have full knowledge of its contents and that they approve the prices which are agreed upon herein, and approve specifically the provisions of Paragraph 5, providing for redetermination of the prices by future action of the Shareholders, and the provisions of

Paragraph 10, providing for the treatment of any Stock transferred to a Spouse as if it were still owned by the Shareholder, including purchase by the Company or other Shareholder pursuant to Paragraphs 2, 3, and 4.

15. *General.*

   a. The masculine pronoun, wherever used herein, shall be construed to include the feminine and the neuter where appropriate. The singular form, wherever used herein, shall be construed to include the plural, where appropriate.

   b. All rights, obligations, duties, restrictions, and qualifications herein provided for shall inure to and be binding upon the parties hereto, and each of their heirs, personal representatives, successors, and assigns, and upon all Shareholders of the Company whether they become such by the exercise or any rights or options hereunder or by transfer pursuant to or contrary to the terms of this Agreement.

   c. In computing a number of days for any purpose of this Agreement, all days shall be counted including Saturdays, Sundays, and holidays.

   d. The headings of paragraphs in this Agreement are for convenience only; they form no part of this Agreement and shall not affect its interpretation.

   e. This writing represents the entire agreement and understanding of the parties with respect to the subject matter hereof; it may not be altered or amended except by an agreement in writing.

   f. In the event that any provision hereof shall be unenforceable, the agreement shall continue in full force and effect and construed as if such unenforceable provision had never been contained herein.

   g. This agreement shall be governed by and construed in accordance with the laws of the Commonwealth of Pennsylvania.

IN WITNESS WHEREOF, Company has caused this Agreement to be executed by its President and its corporate seal affixed, duly attested by its Secretary, and Shareholders and Spouses have hereunto set their hands and seals, the date and year first above written.

AB CORPORATION

Attest:

_____   By:_____

Secretary   President

SHAREHOLDERS AND SPOUSES

_____ [*Seal*]

Albert Able

_____ [*Seal*]

Alice A. Able

_____ [*Seal*]

Benjamin Baker

_____ [*Seal*]

Betty B. Baker

EXAMPLE

*Shareholders'
Agreement
Form Agreement 2*

Special Features:

A. Three equal shareholders. Transfers permitted to spouse, adult children, and trusts for their benefit, who must agree in writing to be bound by agreement and to grant irrevocable proxy to transferor shareholder.

B. Mandatory purchase upon death.

C. Purchase price to be price in offer, the agreed value or book value.

D. Life insurance provision.

E. Management provisions.

F. Agreement terminates upon the occurrence of one of several specified events.

G. If all shareholders die within short time of each other, all transfers are rescinded.

AGREEMENT made this 31st day of July, 19 ___ , by and among THOMAS BROWN, ALAN BROWN, and JOSEPH BROWN (hereinafter referred to collectively as "Stockholders" and individually as "Stockholder") and BROWN COMPANY, INC., a Delaware corporation (hereinafter referred to as the "Company").

WITNESSETH:

The Company is a Delaware corporation having an authorized capitalization of 500,000 shares of Common Stock, par value $.10 per share; and

WHEREAS, there are presently outstanding 75,000 shares of Common Stock, of which each Stockholder owns 25,000 shares; and

WHEREAS, the Stockholders and the Company wish to enter into an agreement respecting limitations on the transfer of shares of stock in the Company, respecting disposition of such shares upon the death of a Stockholder, and certain other matters;

NOW, THEREFORE, in consideration of the premises and the mutual covenants, conditions, and agreements herein contained, the parties hereto, each intending to be legally bound hereby, agree as follows:

A. Restrictions on Transfer of Stock

A–1. No Stockholder will sell, assign, transfer, give, donate, pledge, or otherwise encumber or dispose of any of the shares of common stock (the "Stock") in the Company now owned or hereafter acquired by him, except as permitted by this Agreement and in accordance with its terms.

A–2. The Company, by its execution of this Agreement, agrees that it will not cause or permit the transfer of any common stock to be made on its books except in accordance with the terms of this Agreement. The Company further agrees not to issue any common stock, whether by original issue or in connection with the sale of common stock now or hereafter held in the Company's treasury.

A–3. If any Stockholder receives a bona fide written offer to purchase all of his shares of Stock in the Company which offer he desires to accept (said offeree hereinafter sometimes referred to as "Selling Stockholder"), he may transfer such Stock to the bona fide offeror as hereinafter provided only if he complies with the provisions of Paragraphs A–4 and A–5.

A–4. Within five (5) days after receiving such a bona fide offer, which he desires to accept, the Selling Stockholder shall notify the Company and each of the other Stockholders in writing of the receipt thereof, together with a copy of such offer, and of his desire to accept the offer. The Company shall have the option, exercisable within thirty (30) days of receipt of such notice, to purchase from the Selling Stockholder all or any part of the shares of Stock in the Company owned by him at the price and upon the terms set forth in Paragraph C–1 hereof; provided, however, that the option to purchase less than all of the shares of Stock owned by the Selling Stockholder shall not be effective unless the other Stockholders purchase the shares of stock of the Selling Stockholder not purchased by the Company. The Company shall exercise its option by giving written notice of its election to the Selling Stockholder and to each of the other Stockholders, specifying the number of shares of Stock, if less than all, the Company has elected to purchase from the Selling Stockholder. If the Company does not notify the Selling Stockholder or the other Stockholders of its election to purchase shares of stock of the Selling Stockholder within said 30-day period, it shall be deemed to have not exercised its purchase option.

A–5. If the Company has elected to purchase none or less than all of the shares of Stock of the Selling Stockholder, the other Stockholders shall have the option to purchase the shares of Stock of the Selling Stockholder not purchased by the Company (the "Remaining Stock") in such proportions as may be agreed upon between them. The exercise of such option shall be reflected in a written notice signed by all of the other Stockholders and delivered to the Selling Stockholder and the Company within ten (10) days after the end of the above-mentioned 30-day period. If an agreement among the other Stockholders cannot be reached, then each Stockholder shall have the right, by giving written notice thereof to the Company and all other Stockholders, including the Selling Stockholder, during the next 10-day period, to purchase all or any part of that proportion of the Remaining Stock as the number of shares of Stock owned by him bears to the total number of shares of Stock owned by all of the Stockholders other than the Selling Stockholder. If the other Stockholders elect to purchase less than all of the Remaining Stock, then the Stockholder who elected to purchase the maximum number permissible pursuant to the preceding sentence shall have the further right, by giving written notice thereof to the Company and all other Stockholders, including the Selling Stockholder, during the next 10-day period to purchase the shares of Stock of the Selling Stockholder not theretofore purchased. Shares purchased pursuant to this Paragraph A–5 will be at the price and on the terms set forth in Paragraph C–1.

A–6. If the Company and the other Stockholders do not elect to purchase all of the Stock of the Selling Stockholder pursuant to Paragraphs A–4 and A–5, above, no elections to purchase a portion of such Stock shall be effective and the Selling Stockholder shall have the right to sell all, but not less than all, of the shares of Stock covered by the bona fide offer on the terms set forth in such bona fide offer, provided that such sale shall be consummated and the shares of Stock transferred to the offeror within thirty (30) days after expiration of the options granted in Paragraph A–5, and provided further that such purchaser shall agree in writing, prior to such transfer, with the Company and the other then living Stockholders, to be bound by all of the terms and provisions of this Agreement as though such purchaser were an original signatory hereto.

A–7. Notwithstanding anything foregoing in this Section A, each Stockholder shall have the right to sell or make gifts of up to forty percent (40%) of his Stock in the aggregate to his wife, his adult children, or trusts for the sole benefit of his wife, his children, and their issue (said wife, children, and trusts hereinafter collectively referred to as "Family Transferees"); provided, however, that shares of Stock owned by a Family Transferee shall, during the lifetime of the Stockholder transferor, be deemed to be shares of stock owned by such Stockholder transferor for purposes of Paragraphs A–3 through A–6; and provided further, that a Family Transferee may not, during the lifetime of the Stockholder transferor, sell, assign, transfer, give, donate, pledge, or otherwise encumber or dispose of any shares of Stock in the Company owned by such Family Transferee except (a) to the Stockholder transferor or (b) together with all Stock owned by the Stockholder transferor and by all other of such Stockholder's Family Transferees, pursuant to Paragraphs A–3 through A–6. Prior to any transfer of shares of Stock to a Family Transferee, said Family Transferee shall (a) agree in writing with the Company and the then living Stockholders to be bound by all of the terms and provisions of this Agreement relating to Family Transferees, and (b) grant to the Stockholder transferor an irrevocable proxy for the lifetime of the Stockholder transferor, satisfactory in form and substance to the Company's counsel as constituting a "proxy coupled with an interest," which irrevocable proxy such Stockholder transferor hereby agrees in advance he will not surrender or release during his lifetime.[45]

B. Dispositions Upon Death

B–1. Upon the death of a Stockholder, the Company shall purchase from the personal representatives of the deceased Stockholder and from all Family Transferees of such deceased Stockholder, and the personal representatives of the deceased Stockholder and all Family Transferees of such deceased Stockholder shall sell to the Company, all of the shares of Stock in the Company owned by the deceased Stockholder and his Family Transferees, at the price and upon the terms set forth in Paragraph C–2, and the surviving Stockholders and their Family Transferees shall adopt such resolutions and take such action as may be required by law to authorize such purchase at such time.

B–2. If the purchase price to be paid to the personal representatives of the deceased Stockholder and the Family Transferees of the deceased Stockholder is in excess of the then existing aggregate of capital surplus and earned surplus of the Company, each of the surviving Stockholders and their Family Transferees shall be obligated to make a contribution in cash to the capital of the Company, five (5) or more days prior to the settlement date set forth in Paragraph C–2, in an amount equal to that proportion of the amount by which the purchase price

---

45. For a description generally of proxies, see Chapter Five. A "proxy coupled with an interest" is, contrary to the general rule, not revocable. An "interest" is a relationship between the granter and recipient of the proxy, such as debtor-creditor or donor-donee, which may render the proxy irrevocable. Is such a proxy irrevocable forever?

exceeds the aggregate of capital surplus and earned surplus which the number of shares of Stock in the Company owned by such surviving Stockholder or Family Transferee bears to the number of shares of Stock in the Company owned by all of the surviving Stockholders and their Family Transferees. Should any Family Transferee of a surviving Stockholder fail to make the required capital contribution as aforesaid, such Stockholder shall forthwith make such contribution on behalf of the defaulting Family Transferee.

B–3. Upon the death of a Family Transferee, the Stockholder transferor shall, unless the shares of Stock owned by such deceased Family Transferee are bequeathed outright or pass by intestacy to such Stockholder or to one or more of his existing Family Transferees, purchase from the personal representatives of the deceased Family Transferee, and the personal representatives of the deceased Family Transferee shall sell to such Stockholder, all of the shares of Stock in the Company owned by such deceased Family Transferee. Such purchase shall be made within thirty (30) days of the death of the Family Transferee and shall be at a price of $1.00 per share, payable in cash or by certified check at settlement, unless some other price and/or terms have been previously agreed to between such Stockholder and the deceased Family Transferee or some other price is agreed to between such Stockholder and the personal representatives of the deceased Family Transferee within the aforesaid thirty-day period.

C. Purchase Price and Terms

C–1. Settlement for the purchase by the Company or by a Stockholder of shares of Stock in the Company pursuant to the options granted in Paragraphs A–4 and A–5, respectively, shall be made within sixty (60) days from the date of exercise of the option. At the option of the purchaser, the purchase price per share and the terms of payment shall be either (a) the price per share contained in the bona fide offer referred to in Paragraph A–3, payable upon the terms contained in said bona fide offer, or (b) the "Agreed Value" (as hereinafter defined) per share, payable in cash or by certified check at settlement, or (c) the "Book Value" (as hereinafter defined) per share payable in cash or by certified check at settlement.

C–2. Settlement for the purchase by the Company of shares of Stock in the Company pursuant to the obligations set forth in Section B hereof shall be within sixty (60) days from the date of death of the deceased Stockholder. The purchase price per share shall be the higher of the Agreed Value per share or the Book Value per share payable in cash or by certified check at settlement.

C–3. At settlement, the stock certificate or stock certificates representing the shares being sold shall be delivered by the seller to the purchaser or purchasers, duly endorsed for transfer, with the necessary documentary and transfer tax stamps, if any, affixed by the seller.

C–4. All settlements for the purchases and sales of shares of Stock shall, unless otherwise agreed to by all of the purchasers and sellers, be held at the principal executive offices of the Company during regular business hours. The precise date and hour of settlement shall be fixed by the purchaser or purchasers (within the time limits allowed by the provisions of this Agreement) by notice in writing to the seller or sellers given at least five (5) days in advance of the date specified. In the event that more than one purchaser is involved in a settlement and the purchasers cannot agree on a precise time of settlement, the precise time of settlement shall be fixed by the President of the Company by five (5) days' written notice to the purchasers and sellers.

D. Agreed Value and Book Value

D–1. The "Agreed Value" of the Stock of the Company is hereby determined to be $1.00 per share, which determination shall remain in effect for a period of six (6) months from the date hereof. The parties may, from time to time, unanimously redetermine in writing the Agreed Value per share of the Stock, and each such written redetermination shall remain in effect for a period of six (6) months from the date of such written redetermination. There shall be no Agreed Value for the Stock at times more than twelve (12) months remote from a written determination of Agreed Value. No Family Transferee shall participate in the determinations of Agreed Value, but all Family Transferees shall be bound by such determinations thereof.

D–2. The "Book Value" per share of the Company's Stock shall be equal to the net assets of the Company (on a consolidated basis with subsidiaries, if any) on the date in question divided by the number of shares of Common Stock of the Company outstanding on such date, as determined by the Company's regularly engaged independent public accountants in accordance with generally accepted accounting principles and practices applied on a basis consistent with prior years. For purposes of Paragraph C–1 hereof, the Book Value shall be determined as of the close of the fiscal year preceding exercise of the option pursuant to Paragraph A–4 or A–5 hereof, unless such option is exercised more than 100 days following the close of such fiscal year, in which case the Book Value shall be determined as of the end of the month preceding the month in which the option was exercised. For purposes of Paragraph C–2 hereof the Book Value shall be determined as of the close of the fiscal year preceding the date of death (with respect to Section B) unless such date of death or exercise of option is more than 100 days following the close of such fiscal year, in which case the Book Value shall be determined as of the end of the month preceding the date of death (with respect to Section B).

E. Insurance

The Company shall promptly obtain and maintain in force for the duration of this Agreement, as owner and as beneficiary, a policy of life insurance insuring the life of each Stockholder for $50,000. The parties acknowledge that the principal purpose for such life insurance is to fund the purchase by the Company of the Stock of a deceased Stockholder; accordingly, the company shall, as and when appropriate, increase the amount of life insurance on the life of each Stockholder so as to be reasonably certain of having sufficient net proceeds from such policies to redeem completely a deceased Stockholder's interest in accordance with the terms of this Agreement. Any proceeds from such life insurance policies received by the Company shall be held by Company in trust for the purposes of this Agreement. The Company shall pay all premiums on such life insurance policies, and it shall be a provision of each of such policies that each Stockholder shall be notified by the insurance company, before the expiration of any grace period, of the failure of the Company to pay the necessary premiums.

F. Certain Provisions with Regard to Management of the Company

F–1. The Stockholders agree that promptly following execution of this Agreement they shall:

a. Elect Thomas Brown, Alan Brown, and Joseph Brown to the Board of Directors of the Company; a transferee of shares pursuant to Paragraph A–6 shall not, by virtue of acquiring the stock interest of a Stockholder, be entitled to election to the Board of Directors of the Company.

b. Use their best efforts to cause the following persons to be elected, so long as they are Stockholders, as the only officers of the Company:

President	—Thomas Brown
Sales Vice President	—Alan Brown
Manufacturing Vice President	—Joseph Brown
Treasurer	—Thomas Brown
Secretary	—Joseph Brown

c. Use their best efforts[46] to cause the following officers to receive the following annual compensation:

President	—$30,000
Sales Vice President	—$22,500
Manufacturing Vice President	—$20,000
Treasurer	—None
Secretary	—None

d. Adopt bylaws containing provisions to effect the provisions of Paragraph F–2 hereof, and a provision fixing the size of the Board of Directors at three (3) members.

F–2. The Stockholders agree that throughout the term of this Agreement, except with the unanimous consent in writing of the then living Stockholders who are not disqualified from voting pursuant to Paragraph F–3:

a. The Company shall not merge, consolidate, liquidate, dissolve, sell all or substantially all of its assets out of the ordinary course of business, amend its Articles of Incorporation, incur any debt on which payment is due beyond one (1) year, incur any debt in excess of $50,000, or declare or pay dividends.

b. Neither Thomas Brown, Alan Brown, nor Joseph Brown will be removed from the Board of Directors while a Stockholder.

c. The Company shall not remove from office the officers of the Company set forth in Paragraph F–1(b) hereof.

---

46. Note the difference in terminology between subparagraphs (a), (b), and (c). The stockholders cannot agree to vote on matters within the province of the directors. Directors are fiduciaries and have obligations not to fetter their ability to act. See "Proxies" under "Directors' Meetings" in Chapter Five.

d. The compensation of the officers of the Company shall not be changed, unless the ratios established in Paragraph F–1(c) are maintained, in which latter case such compensation may be changed by vote of a majority of the Board of Directors.

e. The bylaws of the Company will not be amended.

f. The Company will not exercise any of its options pursuant to Section A of this Agreement.

F–3. A Selling Stockholder pursuant to Section A, and his Family Transferees, shall not be entitled to vote, as stockholders or directors of the Company, on the question whether the Company should exercise its option pursuant to Paragraph A–4.

G. Term of Agreement

G-1. Unless terminated sooner by unanimous agreement in writing of the Company and the Stockholders then living, this Agreement shall terminate on the earlier of the following dates: (1) ten (10) years from the date hereof, (2) upon the death of the next to the last of the Stockholders, or (3) upon the receipt by the Company of the proceeds from a public distribution of securities of the Company.

G–2. Notwithstanding anything to the contrary contained in this Agreement, in the event that all of the Stockholders die within sixty (60) days of each other, then the provisions of this Agreement shall be of no further force and effect, and this Agreement shall terminate in all respects. Any and all transfers, payments, or other action made or taken with respect to the sale of Stock of the Company during said sixty-day period, except transfers to Family Transferees, shall be rescinded by the parties or their respective personal representatives.[47]

H. Stock Certificates to be Marked with Legend

All certificates of Stock now or hereafter issued by the Company shall be marked with the following legend:

"This certificate of stock and the shares represented hereby may not be transferred except in accordance with the provisions of a certain agreement dated July 31, 19 ___ , and all amendments thereto, a copy of which Agreement and any amendment thereto is on file at the principal office of the Company."

I. Rights, Obligations, and Remedies

Neither any Stockholder nor the Company may assign, transfer, pledge, or otherwise encumber or dispose of any of his or its rights or obligations or both under this Agreement. The rights and obligations under this Agreement and the remedies to enforce them are joint and several as to each of the parties hereto, with each party being completely free to enforce any or all rights of obligations under this Agreement against any other party with or without the concurrence or joinder of any other party hereto. The shares of capital stock of the Company are unique, and the damages which might result to any of the parties by breach of this Agreement by a party or parties or their personal representatives,

---

47. This provision is to prevent the undue burden of requiring payments for two purchases within a very short period of time.

successors, or assigns are difficult to determine, and therefore, in addition to all of the other remedies which may be available under applicable law, any party hereto shall have the right to equitable relief, including without limitation, the right to enforce specifically the terms of this Agreement by obtaining injunctive relief against any violation hereof, or otherwise.

J. Amendment, Modification, Termination

This Agreement may be amended, modified, or terminated at any time or times by mutual agreement in writing executed by the Company and signed by all the Stockholders then living. No such amendment, modification, or termination, however, shall effect the right of any person to receive, or the obligation of any person to pay, on the terms and conditions of this Agreement, the purchase price for Stock sold pursuant to this Agreement prior to such amendment, modification, or termination, or the right or obligation of any person to sell or purchase stock on the terms and conditions of this Agreement, if such purchase or sale is to occur hereunder immediately upon the death of a Stockholder and that Stockholder has in fact died prior to such amendment, modification, or termination.

K. Representatives, Successors, and Assigns

This Agreement shall be binding upon and inure to the benefit of the respective parties hereto, and their personal representatives, successors, and assigns, including a Family Transferee of Stock of the Company pursuant to Paragraph A–6.

L. Notices

Notices, requests, demands, and other communications relating to this Agreement and the transactions contemplated herein shall be in writing and shall be deemed to have been duly given or made if mailed by United States registered or certified mail, postage prepaid, return receipt requested, addressed as follows:

    a. If to Brown Company, Inc.:
       Attention: Thomas Brown, President

       [NOTE: If Thomas Brown is the person directing the communication to the Company, then the communication shall be addressed to the Company to the attention of "Alan Brown, Vice President."]

    b. If to Thomas Brown:

    c. If to Alan Brown:

    d. If to Joseph Brown:

    e. Any addressee may designate a different address to which communications are to be sent by giving notice of such change of address in conformity with the provisions of this paragraph for giving of notice. All communications shall be deemed to have been given as of the date mailed in accordance herewith.

M. Headings and Miscellaneous

The paragraph headings in this Agreement are for convenience only; they form no part of this Agreement and shall not affect its interpretation.

Words used herein, regardless of the number and gender specifically used, shall be deemed and construed to include any other number, singular or plural, and any other gender, masculine, feminine, or neuter, as the context requires. No indulgences extended by any party hereto to any other party shall be construed as a waiver of any breach on the part of such other party, nor shall any waiver of one breach be construed as a waiver of any rights or remedies with respect to any subsequent breach. This Agreement may be executed in any number of counterparts, each of which when so executed and delivered shall be deemed an original, and it shall not be necessary, in making proof of this Agreement, to produce or account for more than one counterpart.

N. Controlling Law
This Agreement shall be governed by and construed in accordance with the laws of the Commonwealth of Pennsylvania.

O. Severability
In the event that any provision hereof shall be unenforceable, the Agreement shall continue in full force and effect and be construed as if such unenforceable provision had never been contained herein.

IN WITNESS WHEREOF, the parties hereto have executed this Agreement the day and year first above written.

BROWN COMPANY, INC.

Attest:

_____ [Seal]   By: _____ [Seal]
Secretary   President

_____ [Seal]
Thomas Brown

_____ [Seal]
Alan Brown

_____ [Seal]
Joseph Brown

[Corporate Seal]

Each of the undersigned hereby acknowledges that she has read and approves the foregoing Agreement dated July 31, 19 ___ , by and among Thomas Brown, Alan Brown, Joseph Brown, and Brown Company, Inc., and each of the undersigned, intending to be legally bound hereby, hereby covenants and agrees to be bound by its restrictions, terms, and conditions in the event she should acquire, by virtue of the death of her husband or otherwise, any interest in any shares of stock of Brown Company, Inc., now owned by her husband or hereafter acquired by him.

_____ [Seal]
Mary Brown

_____ [Seal]
Alice Brown

_____ [Seal]
Ruth Brown

EXAMPLE

Shareholders'
Agreement
Form Agreement 3

Special Features:

A. One individual and a "group" of related shareholders. Individual has a "put" to the group. Each group member has an option as to any shares being offered by another group member.

B. Purchase price will depend upon who is the selling shareholder.

C. Prepayment permitted. Payments to individual are guaranteed pro rata by group members.

D. Noncompetition provision.

E. Insurance provision. Insurance can be purchased if selling shareholder is covered and sells all stock owned by such shareholder.

F. Long arbitration provision with arbitrators selected by each of parties to dispute.

G. Voting restricted on certain matters such as the Company's exercise of an option.

AGREEMENT made this 21st day of July, 19 ___ , by and among JOHN SMITH, HELEN SMITH, and BILL SMITH (hereinafter sometimes referred to collectively as the "Smith Group"), and DAN JONES (hereinafter sometimes referred to as "Jones") (Jones and the members of the Smith Group are hereinafter sometimes referred to collectively as "Stockholders" and individually as "Stockholder"), and SMIJO CORP., a New York corporation (hereinafter referred to as the "Company").

BACKGROUND OF AGREEMENT

The Company is a New York corporation having an authorized capitalization of 5,000 shares of common stock, par value $10 per share, of which 1,000 shares are issued and outstanding and owned as follows:

Stockholder	No. of Shares
John Smith	200
Helen Smith	300
Bill Smith	50
Dan Jones	450
	1,000

The Stockholders and the Company wish to enter into an agreement respecting limitations on the transfer of shares of stock in the Company, respecting disposition of such shares upon the death of a Stockholder, and certain other matters;

NOW, THEREFORE, in consideration of the premises and the mutual covenants, conditions, and agreements herein contained, the parties hereto, each intending to be legally bound hereby, agree as follows:

A. Restrictions on Transfer of Stock

A–1. No Stockholder will sell, assign, transfer, give, donate, pledge, or otherwise encumber or dispose of any shares of common stock in the Company now owned or hereafter acquired (the "Stock"), except as permitted by this Agreement and in accordance with its terms.

A–2. The Company, by its execution of this Agreement, agrees that it will not cause or permit the transfer of any common stock to be made on its books except in accordance with the terms of this Agreement. The Company further agrees not to issue any common stock, whether by original issue, or in connection with the sale of common stock now or hereafter held in the Company's treasury, or in connection with any transfer, except in accordance with the terms of this Agreement.

A–3. If Jones desires to dispose of any of his Stock during his lifetime, he shall make an offer in writing to the Company to sell such shares of his Stock to the Company, and shall at the same time deliver a copy of such written offer to each of the then living Smith Group Stockholders. Upon the Company's receipt of such notice, the Company shall have the option, exercisable for a 30-day period, to purchase from Jones all or, at the Company's option, a part of the Stock owned by Jones which is being offered for sale, at the price and upon the terms set forth in Paragraph C–1. The option shall be exercised by the Company's giving written notice of its election to do so to Jones and to the then living Smith Group Stockholders.

A–4. If the Company shall decide not to exercise in full its option to purchase, it shall give written notice of that fact to Jones and to the then living Smith Group Stockholders within the said 30-day period. Should the Company fail to give notice within the said 30-day period of its election to exercise the option as provided in Paragraph A–3, it shall be presumed conclusively that the Company has decided not to exercise the option. If, within the said 30-day period, the Company has not exercised in full the option or has decided not to exercise in full its option, as herein provided, the then living Smith Group Stockholders shall be obligated to purchase from Jones all of the Stock in the Company offered by him and not purchased by the Company pursuant to its option. Each then living Smith Group Stockholder shall purchase such proportionate part of Jones' Stock not purchased by the Company pursuant to its option which the number of shares of Stock in the Company owned by such Smith Group Stockholder bears to the total number of shares of Stock owned by all Smith Group Stockholders. Purchases shall be at the price and upon the terms set forth in Paragraph C–1.

A–5. If any Smith Group Stockholder receives a bona fide written offer to purchase all shares of Stock in the Company, which offer such Smith Group Stockholder desires to accept (said offeree hereinafter sometimes referred to as "Selling Stockholder"), the Selling Stockholder may transfer such Stock to the bona fide offeror as hereinafter provided only after compliance with the following provisions of this Section A.

A–6. Within five (5) days after receiving such a bona fide written offer, the Selling Stockholder shall notify each of the other then living Smith Group Stockholders and Jones, if then living, of the desire to accept the offer, and shall deliver to each of such Stockholders together with such notice, a copy of such offer. Upon receipt by the other Smith Group Stockholders of such notice, the other Smith Group Stockholders shall have the option to purchase from the Selling Stockholder, in such proportions as may be agreed upon between them, all of the shares of Stock in the Company owned by the Selling Stockholder at the price and upon the terms set forth in Paragraph C–1 hereof. The exercise of such option shall be reflected in a written notice signed by all of the other Smith Group Stockholders and delivered to the Selling Stockholder and to Jones within twenty (20) days after receipt of the above-mentioned notice. If an agreement among the other Smith Group Stockholders cannot be reached, then each of the other Smith Group Stockholders shall have the option, exercisable by written notice to the Selling Stockholder and to Jones within twenty (20) days after the end of the above-mentioned 20-day period, to purchase such proportionate part of the Selling Stockholder's Stock which the number of shares of Stock in the Company owned by such purchasing Stockholder bears to the total number of shares of such Stock owned by all Smith Group Stockholders entitled to exercise the option.

In the event that one or more Smith Group Stockholders entitled to exercise an option pursuant to this Paragraph A–6 does not exercise his option, the Selling Stockholder shall immediately notify the purchasing Stockholder or Stockholders of such fact, and each purchasing Stockholder shall thereupon have a further 10-day period in which to agree to purchase that proportion of the Selling Stockholder's Stock not taken up by the exercise of the option mentioned in this Paragraph A—6 which the number of shares owned by such purchasing Stockholder bears to the total number of shares owned by all Stockholders who exercised in the first instance their option first mentioned in this Paragraph A–6.

In the event the balance of Selling Stockholder's Stock is not sold as aforesaid, the Selling Stockholder shall immediately notify Jones, if then living, of such fact and of the number of shares not covered by the options exercised to such time by the Smith Group Stockholders, and such notice shall constitute an option to Jones, exercisable by Jones within ten (10) days of receipt of such notice, to elect to purchase the balance of the shares not covered by the options exercised to such time, at the price and upon the terms set forth in Paragraph C–1 hereof. In the event the balance of Selling Stockholder's Stock is not sold as aforesaid, all of the options exercised pursuant to this Paragraph A–6 shall be deemed not to have been exercised.

A–7. If the options contained in Paragraph A–6 are not exercised for purchase of all of the Selling Stockholder's Stock offered for sale, then none of such options shall be deemed to have been exercised, and the Selling Stockholder shall have the right to sell all, but not less than all , of the shares of Stock, free of restrictions, covered by the bona fide offer on the terms set forth in such bona fide offer, provided that such sale shall be consummated and the shares of Stock transferred to the offeror within thirty (30) days after expiration of the option granted to Jones in Paragraph A–6.

A–8. Notwithstanding the provisions of Paragraphs A–3 and A–4 hereof, the Smith Group Stockholders shall not be obligated to purchase Jones' Stock pursuant to Paragraph A–4 if, within twenty (20) days from the expiration of the 30-day period referred to in Paragraphs A–3 and A–4 hereof, (1) the Board of Directors and stockholders of the Company adopt and do not thereafter rescind a resolution providing for the prompt liquidation and dissolution of the Company, and (2) Jones and his nominees are offered and are allowed to retain at least fifty percent (50%) representation on the Board of Directors of the Company until completion of dissolution.

B. Dispositions Upon Death

B–1. Upon the death of Jones, and for a period of thirty (30) days thereafter, the Company shall have the option, exercisable by notice in writing to Jones' personal representatives and to the then living Smith Group Stockholders, to purchase all or a part of the shares of Stock in the Company owned by Jones at the time of his death, at the price and upon the terms set forth in Paragraph C–2 hereof.

B–2. If the Company shall not exercise in full its option to purchase or shall decide not to do so, it shall notify the then living Smith Group Stockholders and Jones' personal representatives of that fact, and of the amount of the Stock as to which the Company has not exercised its option, within the said 30-day period. Should the Company fail to give any notice as aforesaid within the said 30-day period, it shall be presumed conclusively that the Company has decided not to exercise its option. Upon receipt of such notice or upon failure of the Company to give such notice, the then living Smith Group Stockholders shall be obligated to purchase, and Jones' personal representatives shall be obliged to sell, all of the Stock in the Company owned by Jones at the time of his death which is not purchased by the Company pursuant to its option under Paragraph B–1 hereof.

B–3. Each of the then living Smith Group Stockholders shall be obligated to purchase and shall purchase such proportionate part of Jones' Stock which the number of shares of Stock in the Company owned by such purchasing Stockholder bears to the total number of shares of such Stock owned by all then living Smith Group Stockholders. The purchase shall be at the price and upon the terms set forth in Paragraph C–2.

B–4. Upon the death of a Smith Group Stockholder, the surviving Smith Group Stockholders shall be obligated to purchase, and the personal representatives of the deceased Stockholder shall be obliged to sell, all of the Stock in the Company owned by the deceased Smith Group Stockholder at the time of death.

B–5. Each of the surviving Smith Group Stockholders shall be obligated to purchase such proportionate part of the deceased Stockholder's Stock which the number of shares of Stock in the Company owned by such purchasing stockholder bears to the total number of shares of such Stock owned by all surviving Smith Group Stockholders. The purchase shall be at the price and upon the terms set forth in Paragraph C–2.

B–6. Notwithstanding the provisions of Paragraphs B–2 and B–3 hereof, the surviving Stockholders upon the death of Jones shall not be obligated to purchase the Stock owned by Jones at the time of his death if, within sixty (60) days following the death of Jones, (1) the Board of Directors and stockholders of the Company adopt and do not thereafter rescind a resolution providing for the prompt liquidation and dissolution of the Company, (2) the Company, within thirty (30) days of the adoption of such resolution, makes a distribution of $100,000 to Jones' personal representatives in partial liquidation, and (3) the personal representatives of Jones are offered and are allowed to retain at least fifty percent (50%) representation on the Board of Directors of the Company until completion of dissolution.

C. Purchase Price and Terms

C–1. Settlement for the purchase by the Company or by a Stockholder of shares of Stock in the Company pursuant to Paragraph A–3 and/or A–4 hereof shall be made within sixty (60) days from the date of exercise of the option (if all of Jones' Stock being offered for sale is purchased pursuant to Paragraph A–3) or from the date of the partial exercise of the option or the expiration of the option, as the case may be (if all or a part of Jones' Stock being offered for sale is purchased pursuant to Paragraph A–4). The purchase price per share shall be the "Agreed Value" (as hereinafter defined) per share, payable in twenty (20) equal quarterly installments of principal, the first of which is to be paid at settlement. The unpaid balance of the purchase price shall bear interest at the rate of ten percent (10%) per annum, payable quarterly when payments of principal are due.

Settlement for the purchase by the Company or by a Stockholder of shares of Stock in the Company pursuant to the options granted in Paragraph A–6 shall be made within sixty (60) days from the date of exercise of the option. At the option of the purchaser, the purchase price per share and the terms of payment shall be either (a) the price per share contained in the bona fide offer referred to in Paragraph A–5, payable upon the terms contained in said bona fide offer, or (b) the "Agreed Value" per share, payable in twenty (20) equal quarterly installments of principal, the first of which is to be paid at settlement, with interest on the unpaid balance of the purchase price at the rate of six percent (6%) per annum, payable quarterly when payments of principal are due.

C–2. Settlement for the purchase by the Company or by a Stockholder of shares of Stock in the Company pursuant to the obligations set forth in Section B hereof shall be within sixty (60) days from the date of death of the deceased Stockholder. The purchase price per share shall be the Agreed Value per share. With regard to Section B, the purchase price shall be paid as follows: (a) If the Company is purchasing shares of Stock upon the death of Jones, the Company shall pay at settlement the full purchase price or $100,000, whichever is less; the unpaid balance of principal, if any, shall be payable in twenty (20) equal quarterly installments of principal, the first of which is to be paid three (3) months from the date of settlement; (b) If the surviving Stockholders are purchasing shares of Stock upon the death of Jones, they shall, on a pro rata basis, pay at settlement an amount equal to $100,000 reduced by the amount, if any, of the payment to be made at settlement by the Company pursuant to subparagraph (a) immediately above; the unpaid balance of principal, if any, shall be payable in twenty (20) equal quarterly installments of principal, the first of which is to be paid three (3) months from the date of settlement; (c) if the surviving Smith Group Stockholders are purchasing shares of Stock upon the death of a Smith Group Stockholder, the purchase price shall be paid in twenty (20) equal quarterly installments of principal, the first of which is to be paid at settlement. The unpaid balance of the purchase price pursuant to this Paragraph C–2 shall bear interest at the rate of ten percent (10%) per annum, payable quarterly when payments of principal are due.

C–3. At settlement, the stock certificate or stock certificates representing the shares being sold shall be delivered by the seller to the purchaser or purchasers, duly endorsed for transfer, with the necessary documentary and transfer tax stamps, if any, affixed by the seller.

C–4. All settlements for the purchases and sales of shares of Stock shall, unless otherwise agreed to by all of the purchasers and sellers, be held at the principal executive offices of the Company during regular business hours. The precise date and hour of settlement shall be fixed by the purchaser or purchasers (within the time limits allowed by the provisions of this Agreement) by notice in writing to the seller or sellers given at least five (5) days in advance of the date specified. In the event that more than one purchaser is involved in a settlement, the precise time of settlement shall be fixed by the President of the Company by five (5) days' written notice to the purchasers and sellers.

D. Agreed Value

The "Agreed Value" per share of the Stock of the Company is hereby determined to be set forth on Schedule A hereto. On January 31 and July 31 of each year, the then living Stockholders shall redetermine in writing the Agreed Value of the Stock for purposes of this Agreement and shall record such agreed redetermination of Agreed Value on a Schedule substantially in the form of Schedule A hereto. A redetermination of Agreed Value shall be effective only if agreed to unanimously in writing by the then living Stockholders. Should the parties fail to redetermine the Agreed Value for a period of twelve (12) consecutive months, then the Agreed Value per share shall, subsequent to the expiration of such 12-month period and until a redetermination of Agreed Value by the Stockholders, be the last determined Agreed Value per share, plus or minus the aggregate of the net income or loss (on a consolidated basis with subsidiaries, if any), after federal and other income and other taxes, less the aggregate of dividends paid on the Company's capital stock, from the beginning of the Company's last fiscal year in which there occurred a determination of Agreed Value until the close of the fiscal year last preceding the time in question, divided by the total number of shares of common stock of the Company then outstanding; provided, however, that in no event shall the Agreed Value be less than $1.00 per share. The aggregate of the net income or loss shall be as computed by the Company's regularly engaged public accountants in accordance with generally accepted accounting principles and practices applied on a basis consistent with that of preceding years, whose determination shall be binding and conclusive upon the parties.

E. Prepayment, Guarantee, Noncompetition, Allocation, Insurance

E–1. Any amounts payable pursuant to Section C hereof may be prepaid at any time, in whole or in part, without premium or penalty.

E–2. The Smith Group Stockholders hereby guarantee to Jones, severally but not jointly, payment by the Company to Jones of any amounts which might become payable to Jones pursuant to Section C hereof, to the following extent: John Smith—$36\frac{4}{11}$%; Helen Smith—$54\frac{6}{11}$%; Bill Smith—$9\frac{1}{11}$%. The foregoing guarantees shall survive the deaths of the respective guarantors.[48]

E–3. Each Stockholder hereby agrees that such Stockholder will not, for so long as such Stockholder owns directly or indirectly any shares of the Stock of the Company and for a period of two (2) years after

---

48. Note that the Smith Group stockholders are only guaranteeing a payment by the company to a limited extent—the relative percentage in the company owned by such stockholder.

having disposed of the last remaining interest in any of the Stock of the Company, engage in, be financially interested in, or be employed by any business in the United States which is competitive with the Company or any of its subsidiaries. The term "engage in" as used in the preceding sentence shall include, but shall not be limited to, activities, whether direct or indirect, as proprietor, partner, stockholder, principal, agent, employee, or consultant. Each Stockholder acknowledges that the restrictions contained in this paragraph, in light of the nature of Company's industry, are reasonable and necessary to protect the Company's legitimate interests, and that a violation thereof would result in irreparable injury to the Company and thus to its Stockholders. Each Stockholder acknowledges that, in the event of a violation of any such restrictions, the Company and/or the remaining Stockholders shall be entitled to preliminary and permanent injunctive relief as well as an equitable accounting of all of such defaulting Stockholder's income, gain, or benefits arising out of such violation (which rights shall be cumulative and in addition to any other rights or remedies to which the Company and/or Stockholders may be entitled). In the event of a violation, the two-year period referred to above shall be extended by an amount of time equal to the time during which such violations took place.

E–4. So long as Jones is a Stockholder, the Company will maintain a policy or policies of life insurance on his life in a face amount of not less than $100,000, and shall not borrow against such policies. Upon the death of Jones, to the extent that the Company rather than the Smith Group Stockholders is purchasing Jones' Stock pursuant to Section B, the net proceeds of such insurance shall be used to make the initial payment by the Company at settlement pursuant to Paragraph C–2 hereof, and any excess shall be used to prepay, in whole or in part, any remaining obligation of the Company pursuant to Paragraph C–2. In the event that Jones sells all of his Stock during his lifetime, he may purchase from the Company the policies of insurance on his life for the cash surrender values of such policies on the date of transfer. Jones' right to purchase such policies shall terminate absolutely if not exercised by Jones within sixty (60) days following the sale of his Stock, and thereafter the Company will cease to be obligated to maintain such insurance.

F. Voting

F–1. Neither Jones (if offering to sell his Stock pursuant to Section A) nor a Selling Stockholder pursuant to Section A hereof shall be entitled to vote as a director of the Company on the question whether the Company should exercise any option pursuant to Section A, nor may Jones vote as a director of the Company on the question whether the Company should liquidate and dissolve pursuant to Paragraph A–8. Neither the personal representatives of a deceased Stockholder nor their nominees may vote as directors of the Company on the question whether the Company should exercise any option, or liquidate and dissolve, pursuant to Section B.

F–2. In a vote, if any, of Stockholders of the Company on the question whether the Company should exercise an option or liquidate and dissolve pursuant to Section A, or exercise an option or liquidate and dissolve pursuant to Section B, the shares of the Selling Stockholder (or Jones, if Jones proposes to sell) with respect to Section A, or of the deceased Stockholder with respect to Section B, as the case may be, shall be voted in the same manner as the majority of all other votes cast have been voted, and this Agreement shall constitute a proxy coupled with an interest for so long as this Agreement is in effect, by each Stockholder to the other Stockholders to implement the foregoing.

G. Term of Agreement

G–1. Unless terminated sooner by unanimous agreement in writing of the Company and the Stockholders then living, this Agreement shall terminate upon the repurchase of the shares of Stock of the next to the last of the Stockholders.

G–2. Notwithstanding anything to the contrary contained in this Agreement, in the event that all of the Stockholders die within one hundred twenty (120) days of each other, then the provisions of this Agreement shall be of no further force and effect, and this Agreement shall terminate in all respects. Any and all transfers, payments, or other action made or taken with respect to the sale of Stock of the Company during said 120-day period shall be rescinded by the parties or their respective personal representatives.

H. Stock Certificates to Be Marked with Legend

All certificates of Stock now or hereafter issued by the Company shall be marked with the following legend:

"This certificate of stock and the shares represented hereby may not be transferred except in accordance with the provisions of a certain agreement dated July 31, 19 ___ , and all amendments thereto, a copy of which agreement and any amendment thereto is on file at the principal office of the Company."

I. Rights, Obligations, and Remedies

Neither any Stockholder nor the Company may assign, transfer, pledge, or otherwise encumber or dispose of any rights or obligations or both under this Agreement. The rights and obligations under this Agreement and the remedies to enforce them are joint and several as to each of the parties hereto, with each party being completely free to enforce any or all rights or obligations under this Agreement against any other party with or without the concurrence or joinder of any other party hereto.

Any and all disputes and controversies arising under or in connection with the terms or provisions of this Agreement, or in connection with or relating to the application or interpretation of any of the terms or provisions hereof, or in respect to anything not herein expressly provided, but germane to the subject matter of this Agreement, which the Smith Group and Jones have been unable to adjust, shall be submitted to arbitration at the request of either Jones or a member of the Smith Group, said arbitration to be conducted in the following manner: Jones and the Smith Group shall each choose one arbitrator, and all matters in dispute shall be referred for decision to said two (2) arbitrators, whose decision shall be final, binding, and conclusive upon the parties. If the said two arbitrators shall be unable to agree upon the decision of the disputed matters so referred to them within ten (10) days after referral, then they shall, within the following ten (10) days, jointly select a third arbitrator. The decision of any two (2) of the said three (3) arbitrators shall be final, binding, and conclusive upon the parties. If either party shall refuse or neglect to appoint an arbitrator within five (5) days after the other party shall have appointed an arbitrator, and such other party shall have served a written notice upon the first-mentioned party requiring such party to make such appointment, then the arbitrator appointed as aforesaid shall, at the request of the appointing party, proceed to hear and determine the matters in contest as if such arbitrator were an arbitrator appointed by both parties for such purpose, and the decision of such arbitrator shall be final, binding, and conclusive upon the parties. If the two (2) arbitrators appointed by the parties hereto shall be unable to agree upon a third arbitrator within the time limit above provided, the matter shall be referred to the American Arbitration Association in New York, New York, for decision by a panel of three (3) arbitrators under such Association's then current rules and procedures relating to commercial arbitration, and the decision of such Association's panel of arbitrators shall be final, binding, and conclusive upon the parties hereto. With respect to expenses incurred in connection with any arbitration hereunder, Jones shall bear the expenses relating to any arbitrator appointed by him, the Smith Group shall bear the expenses of any arbitrator appointed by it, and any expenses in connection with a third arbitrator or in connection with an arbitration referred to the American Arbitration Association shall be borne one-half by Jones and one-half by the Smith Group.

The parties acknowledge that the shares of capital stock of the Company are unique, and the damages which might result to any of the parties by breach of this Agreement by a party or parties or their personal representatives, successors, or assigns are difficult to determine, and therefore, in addition to all of the other remedies which may be accorded by the arbitrators, the arbitrators shall have the right to afford equitable relief, including, without limitation, the right to enforce specifically the terms of this Agreement, by enjoining any violation hereof, or otherwise.

J. Amendment, Modification, Termination

This Agreement may be amended, modified, or terminated at any time or times by mutual agreement in writing executed by the Company and signed by all Stockholders then living. No such amendment, modification, or termination, however, shall affect the right of any person to receive, or the obligation of any person to pay, on the terms and conditions of this Agreement, the purchase price for Stock sold pursuant to this Agreement prior to such amendment, modification, or termination, or the right or obligation of any person to sell or purchase Stock, on the terms and conditions of this Agreement, if such purchase or sale is to occur hereunder immediately upon the death of a Stockholder and that Stockholder has in fact died prior to such amendment, modification, or termination.

K. Representatives, Successors, and Assigns

This Agreement shall be binding upon and inure to the benefit of the respective parties hereto, and their personal representatives, successors, and assigns, except that a transferee of Stock of the Company pursuant to Paragraph A–7 hereof shall not be subject to the terms and provisions of this Agreement and shall not succeed to any of the rights granted to Stockholders pursuant to this Agreement.

L. Notices

Notices, requests, demands, and other communications relating to this Agreement and the transactions contemplated herein shall be in writing and shall be deemed to have been duly given or made when wired or when deposited in the United States mail, postage prepaid, registered or certified with return receipt requested, addressed as follows:

a. If to the Company:
   Smijo Corp.
   12 E. 3rd Street
   New York, New York 10016
   Attention: Dan Jones, President

   [NOTE: If Dan Jones is the person directing the communication to the Company, then the communication shall be addressed to the Company to the attention of John Smith.]

b. If to Dan Jones:
   [Address]

c. If to John Smith:
   [Address]

d. If to Helen Smith:
   [Address]

e. If to Bill Smith:
   [Address]

f. Any addressee may designate a different address to which communications are to be sent, by giving notice of such change of address in conformity with the provisions of this paragraph for giving notice.

M. Headings and Miscellaneous

The paragraph headings in this Agreement are for convenience only; they form no part of this Agreement and shall not affect its interpretation. Words used herein, regardless of the number and gender specifically used, shall be deemed and construed to include any other number, singular or plural, and any other gender, masculine, feminine, or neuter, as the context requires. No indulgences extended by any party hereto to any other party shall be construed as a waiver of any breach on the part of such other party, nor shall any waiver of one breach be construed as a waiver of any rights or remedies with respect to any subsequent breach. This Agreement may be executed in any number of counterparts, each of which when so executed and delivered shall be deemed an original, and such counterparts shall, together, constitute and be one and the same instrument. In the event that any provision hereof shall be unenforceable, the Agreement shall continue in force and effect and construed as if such unenforceable provision had never been contained herein.

N. Controlling Law

This Agreement shall be governed by and construed in accordance with the laws of the State of New York.

IN WITNESS WHEREOF, the parties hereto have executed this Agreement the day and year first above written.

SMIJO CORP.

Attest:

_____   By: _____
Secretary   President
[*Corporate Seal*]

_____ [*Seal*]
Dan Jones

_____ [*Seal*]
John Smith

_____ [*Seal*]
Helen Smith

_____ [*Seal*]
Bill Smith

SCHEDULE A

AGREED VALUE OF STOCK

The undersigned shareholders hereby agree that the Agreed Value (as defined in a certain Agreement dated _____ , 19 __ , to which they are all parties) of the common stock of Smijo Corp. is $ _____ per share.

_____ [*Seal*]
Dan Jones

_____ [*Seal*]
John Smith

_____ [*Seal*]
Helen Smith

_____ [*Seal*]
Bill Smith

Dated: _____ , 19 __

EXAMPLE

*Shareholders'
Agreement
Checklist*

1. Exact name and address of corporation.

2. Is corporation a party to the agreement?

3. Shareholders who are party to the agreement:
   Name   **Address**   **No. of Shares**

4. Do the above constitute all of the shareholders of the corporation?

5. Authorized capital of the corporation.

6. Lifetime transfers:
   a. Are all shareholders treated alike?
   b. What are conditions to transfers during lifetime?

   1. Must there first be a bona fide written offer? If not, what conditions?
   2. Can a shareholder dispose only of all, and not less than all, of the shares owned by such shareholder pursuant to offer or other conditions?

   c. Does corporation have right of first refusal? At what price and upon what terms?

   d. Do other shareholders have right of first refusal? If so, do all shareholders have right pro rata or does a particular group of shareholders have the right? If so, do all shareholders have right pro rata or does a particular group of shareholders have the right? At what price and upon what terms?

   e. Does a third-party transferee take shares free of restrictions? If not, does the transferee get the benefits as well as the restrictions which were applicable to the transferor?

   f. Do any shareholders have the right to "put" their shares to the corporation? To the other shareholders? If so, upon what conditions? At what price and upon what terms?

   g. Does the corporation or do any shareholders have the right to "call" the shares of any shareholder? If so, upon what conditions? At what price and upon what terms?

   h. Are interfamily transfers permitted?

   i. Are intershareholder transfers permitted?

   j. Is there an option to purchase shares of a shareholder in financial jeopardy?

7. Dispositions upon death:

   a. Are all shareholders treated alike?

   b. Does corporation have obligation to purchase shares upon death? Option to purchase? Must estate sell? If so, at what price and upon what terms?

   c. Do surviving shareholders have obligation to purchase shares upon death? Option to purchase? Must estate sell? Do all surviving shareholders participate pro rata, or does a particular group of shareholders participate differently? What price and upon what terms?

   d. Will there be any insurance funding?

8. Terms of payment:

   a. All cash at settlement?

   b. If installment payments:
      1. Amounts and payment dates.
      2. Any notes? Wives to sign? Confession of judgment? Negotiable?
      3. Any collateral security for payment?
      4. Interest rate? Interest payable when?
      5. Is prepayment allowed in year of settlement?

9. Provisions respecting management:
   a. Composition of board of directors.
   b. Designation of officers.
   c. Regulation of salaries.
   d. Limitations on mergers and consolidations? On liquidation and dissolution? On sale of assets out of the ordinary course of business? On amendment of articles or certificate of incorporation? On amendment of bylaws? On payment of dividends? On incurring large or long-term debt? Other?
   e. Noncompetition agreement?
   f. Right of corporation to issue additional shares? Preemptive rights?

10. Term of agreement.

11. Provision for Subchapter S election.

CHAPTER NINE

Corporate Distributions

Chapter Nine is designed to expand the ability of a lawyer's assistant to draft resolutions dealing with certain corporate activities and to acquaint the student with a variety of tax considerations and reporting requirements relating to corporate distributions. The chapter is also designed to familiarize the student with state law restrictions on a corporation's ability to pay dividends or purchase its own shares. Finally, Chapter Nine is intended to provide a simple introduction to accounting for the student.

Stock ownership yields economic benefit to the owner of the stock. This benefit may be achieved in many ways: (a) a shareholder who owns a majority of the voting shares of the corporation may control election of directors who may, in turn, elect the shareholder as an officer of the corporation and pay a salary;[1] (b) if the corporation is profitable, and its net assets increase, a shareholder may be able to sell the shares at a higher price than the amount paid for them and realize a profit on the difference; and (c) a shareholder may benefit if the corporation distributes its cash or property. It is this latter category, corporate distributions, which is the subject of this chapter.

QUESTIONS

Can the majority shareholder require the directors to elect the shareholder as an officer as a condition of the shareholder's voting for him or her as a director? Why or why not? If not, what can the majority shareholder do?

A corporate distribution may be in the form of cash, tangible property, stock of the distributing corporation, stock of another corporation which is owned by the distributing corporation, or other intangible property. The distribution may be of all or a portion of the corporation's property and may, or may not, be distributed in exchange for stock owned by the corporation's shareholders. These different types of corporate distributions have

---

1. See Chapter Five for a discussion of election of shareholders and directors and actions taken by directors.

various economic effects on the shareholders and the corporation may be treated differently under corporate laws and federal and state tax laws. Each principal type of corporate distribution will be discussed in this chapter.

THE CORPORATE BALANCE SHEET

Before examining the different types of corporate distributions, it is important to see how the assets and liabilities of a corporation are described by the use of a balance sheet. In the course of analyzing a balance sheet, certain terms which are used in state corporate laws will be defined. These terms are important because their function is to establish limits on the amount of assets which a corporation may distribute. State law imposes these limits on corporate distributions in order to protect creditors who, because of the concept of "limited liability," are limited to the assets of the corporation and cannot recover corporate debts from the personal assets of the shareholders.[2]

For purposes of this chapter our model will be the X Corporation. X Corporation is engaged in the business of the manufacture and sale, through retail stores, of house paint and has certain assets. For example, it owns a plant and equipment for manufacturing paint. X Corporation also owns raw materials to make paint, paint in the process of being manufactured and packaged, and paint which it had manufactured (raw materials, work in process, and finished goods are referred to collectively as "inventory"). In addition, the corporation owns the retail stores in which the paint is sold. In order to pay its bills, the X Corporation must have cash, either on hand or deposited in bank accounts. Moreover, if X Corporation sold paint to customers and had to wait for payment, it would have as an asset the amounts owing from these customers ("accounts receivable").

X Corporation also has some liabilities. For example, it has not paid all of the bills it received from suppliers of raw materials or electric and telephone bills ("accounts payable"). Moreover, it owes money for goods and services for which it has not yet been billed.

A balance sheet is used to describe, in dollar terms, the assets and liabilities of a corporation at a given point in time. It is sometimes referred to as a "snapshot," at a specific moment, of the financial condition of the corporation. The dollar amounts assigned to various assets are referred to as the "book value" of these assets. The book value of an asset is determined by accounting

---

2. Chapter One discusses generally the concept of limited liability of shareholders and contrasts it with the personal liability of a proprietor and partners.

rules and may or may not bear any relation to the current fair market value of the asset.[3]

A balance sheet will also show the corporation's "net worth" (alternatively called "net assets," "shareholder's equity," or "capital") which may generally be defined as the difference between its assets and liabilities. If the assets exceed the liabilities, then net worth is a positive number; if the liabilities exceed the assets, net worth is a negative number. A balance sheet must always "balance" because the assets of a corporation must always equal its liabilities and net worth.

Before proceeding further, it would be helpful to set forth a hypothetical balance sheet of X Corporation:

EXAMPLE

Balance Sheet

X CORPORATION
Balance Sheet as of June 30, 1989

Assets		Liabilities	
Cash	$30,000	Accounts Payable	$50,000
Accounts Receivable	50,000		
Inventory	20,000	**Net Worth**	
Equipment	21,000		
Real Estate	25,000	Common Stock	
Investment in Y Corporation (100 shares at $40 per share)	4,000	(1,000 shares, $10 par value, authorized, 100 shares issued and outstanding)	1,000
Total Assets	$150,000	Capital surplus	9,000
		7% Preferred Stock (100 shares, $100 par value, authorized and outstanding)	10,000
		Earned Surplus	80,000
		Total Liabilities and Net Worth	$150,000

Note the reference on the balance sheet under the heading "Net Worth" to outstanding shares of common stock, preferred stock, capital surplus, and earned surplus. These terms are defined in the state corporate laws. Different state laws have somewhat different definitions. The MBCA has done away with certain definitions, including stated capital and par value, among others.

---

3. Generally speaking, the "book value" is the historical cost to a corporation of an asset. Inflation, obsolescence, scarcity, depreciation, wear and tear, and many other factors can make the historical book value substantially different from the current fair market value. For example, a building built fifty years ago may be worth more now than when it was built, yet is may be fully depreciated to zero on the balance sheet.

On the balance sheet of X Corporation, the stated capital is $11,000, representing the aggregate par value of all shares of common stock and preferred stock outstanding.

If X Corporation had stock with no par value, what would have been the stated capital under the MBCA definition if $20,000 had been received in payment therefor?[4]

The balance sheet also shows earned surplus of $80,000. When the term is used, earned surplus means the cumulation of profits and losses of the corporation (less distributions to shareholders) since its inception.

If X Corporation was incorporated on July 1, 1988, and had never made a distribution to shareholders or made a transfer from earned surplus to stated capital and capital surplus, the $80,000 of earned surplus would mean that X Corporation had net profits of $80,000 during the period from July 1, 1988, to June 30, 1989.

If the $9,000 of capital surplus represented a transfer from earned surplus to capital surplus (as a stock dividend or otherwise) prior to June 30, 1989, how much money did X Corporation earn during the fiscal year?

Where used, "par value" means the minimum acceptable consideration to be paid for shares.

On the balance sheet of X Corporation, the surplus is $89,000, consisting of $80,000 of earned surplus and $9,000 of capital surplus. The capital surplus may have arisen because X Corporation sold 100 shares of common stock, with a par value of $10 per share, for $100 per share.

What would have been the capital surplus under the MBCA definition if X Corporation sold 1000 shares of common stock, par value $10 per share, for $85 per share?

What is the "book value per share of common stock" for a corporation with the following shareholders' equity:

---

4. See Chapter Four in this text for a discussion of par and no par value stock.

Stated Capital	$1,200,000
(1,000,000 shares of Common Stock, par value $1 per share, outstanding and 200,000 shares of Preferred Stock, par value $1 per share, outstanding)	
Capital Surplus	2,800,000
Earned Surplus	4,000,000
	$8,000,000

The liquidation price for the Preferred Stock is $10 per share.

CASH AND PROPERTY DIVIDENDS

Definition

A dividend may generally be defined as a distribution by a corporation to shareholders with respect to its stock. A dividend is paid to shareholders in direct proportion to their shareholdings. Although dividends may be paid on one or more separate classes or series of stock, all holders of any series or class of stock must be treated equally and receive dividends in direct proportion to the number of shares of the class or series owned by them.

Right to Dividends

Chapter Six contains a description of the rights that holders of common stock and preferred stock have to receive dividends.

QUESTION Does any shareholder have an absolute right to receive dividends?

Payment of Dividends

Restrictions Because the common shareholders are the residual owners of the corporation and are entitled to anything left after all creditors and preferred stockholders have been fully paid, corporate statutes ordinarily place a limit on the amount that can be distributed to shareholders. The idea is to require some permanent commitment by shareholders to the corporation as some assurance that creditors will be paid. Section 6.40 of the MBCA is typical of a restriction that permits the payment of dividends in cash or property only to the extent that such distribution does not render the corporation equitably insolvent or insolvent in the "balance sheet" sense.

Some statutes permit distributions only if the corporation has adequate earned surplus. Remember, earned surplus is not a fund of money or an asset of any kind.

The balance sheet of X Corporation would appear to indicate that a maximum dividend of $80,000 could be declared and paid, since this is the amount of earned surplus. While legally this may be so, as a practical matter there are two reasons why an $80,000 dividend is unlikely:

1. X Corporation has only $30,000 in cash, some of which is obviously needed to continue the ordinary business operations.[5] Therefore, it does not have sufficient cash to pay an $80,000 dividend. If the dividend were paid in the form of inventory, equipment, or real property, the business would need still more cash to replenish these items.

2. The board of directors must leave X Corporation with sufficient "liquid assets" (i.e., cash and other assets which may be quickly reduced to cash, such as accounts receivable) to pay the liabilities of $50,000 when payment is due and to allow for future growth and/or future losses. Otherwise the corporation may be insolvent and unable to meet its debts as they become due in the usual course of business.

Procedure for payment

Board of Directors' Action   Dividends can only be declared by action of the board of directors. The shareholders cannot declare dividends.

QUESTION

Why should shareholders not be entitled to be the body to declare dividends?

Sample resolutions for the payment of dividends by X Corporation on the outstanding Common and Preferred Stock, including the establishment of both a record date and a payment date, are as follows:

EXAMPLE

Common Stock

> RESOLVED, that there shall be distributed on August 31, 19 ___ , to holders of Common Stock of the Corporation of record on August 15, 19 ___ , a cash dividend of $500 on the basis of $5.00 per share for each issued and outstanding share of Common Stock.

---

5. Funds required for ordinary business operations are often referred to as "working capital."

RESOLVED, that any officer of the Corporation be and each of them hereby is authorized and directed to take such action as any one of them may deem necessary or proper to effect the foregoing dividend.

RESOLVED, that the Treasurer of the Corporation be and hereby is authorized and directed to charge the earned surplus account with $500 and to make such other entries in the books of account of the Corporation as are necessary or proper to reflect the foregoing distribution.

EXAMPLE

Preferred Stock

RESOLVED, that there shall be distributed on August 31, 19 ___ , to holders of 7% Preferred Stock of the Corporation of record on August 15, 19 ___ , the regular quarterly cash dividend of $175, on the basis of $1.75 per share for each issued and outstanding share of 7% Preferred Stock.

RESOLVED, that any officer of the Corporation be and each of them hereby is authorized and directed to take such action as any one of them may deem necessary or proper to effect the foregoing dividend.

RESOLVED, that the Treasurer of the Corporation be and hereby is authorized and directed to charge the earned surplus account with $175 and to make such other entries in the books of account of the Corporation as are necessary or proper to reflect the foregoing distribution.

Note that the resolutions effect the declaration of a dividend which differs from the actual payment of the dividend. The paralegal will ordinarily have the duty of drafting resolutions declaring the dividend.

Payment of Dividends Pursuant to the authorization in the above resolutions, the shareholders of record of X Corporation on August 15, 19 ___ , would receive on August 31, 19 ___ , an aggregate of $500 in cash, as the dividend on the Common Stock, and an aggregate of $175 in cash, as the dividend on the Preferred Stock.

Adjustment of Capital Accounts On August 31, 19 ___ , the balance sheet of X Corporation would reflect the payment of the cash dividend by a reduction in cash of $675 (the total amount of the dividends) and a reduction in earned surplus of $675.

QUESTION

If X Corporation had paid a dividend aggregating $1000 on the common stock and $175 on the preferred stock, how would the entries on the balance sheet be reflected?

Tax Treatment of Dividends

Introduction State corporate law and federal income tax law define "dividend" differently. For federal income tax purposes, in order to be taxable, a dividend must be paid out of the corporation's "earnings and profits." The term earnings and profits for tax purposes is not synonymous with the term earned surplus for corporate purposes. For example, a transfer from earned surplus to stated capital in connection with an increase in the par value of outstanding stock serves to reduce earned surplus for purposes of state law but does not reduce earnings and profits for purposes of the federal tax law. A very simplistic definition of earnings and profits would be the cumulation of all profits of the corporation during its existence reduced by distribution to shareholders. Dividends (as defined under federal income tax law) constitute ordinary income to the recipient shareholders and are subject to tax at the shareholders' normal federal income tax rates.

Double Taxation All of a corporation's income is taxed at the corporate level. Dividends cannot be deducted from a corporation's profits in computing federal income taxes. When the shareholders receive a dividend they, too, pay a personal income tax on such distributions. For example, the X Corporation must earn $758 of pretax income, assuming the pretax income is taxed at the 1990 maximum 34% corporate rate, in order to have enough income to pay a dividend of $500 to common stockholders. The distribution of $500 by X Corporation to A and B is taxed to them at their normal individual rates. If A and B are each in the 28% marginal tax bracket, they will each net $180 after payment of federal income taxes.

Many small corporations do not look upon dividends with favor. The payment of dividends is not a deductible expense to the corporation and results in taxable income to the recipient shareholder. If the shareholders are also employees of the corporation, an increase in salary or a bonus may possibly be given rather than a declaration of dividends. Additional salaries or bonuses will qualify as deductible expense to the corporation, if they are reasonable, and will satisfy the shareholder-employee's desire for additional income.

Consider that combined corporate and shareholder taxes on the $758 of pretax income of X Corporation were $398. X Corporation paid taxes of $258 and distributed the remainder as a dividend to A and B, who collectively paid taxes of $140. If A and B were to each receive a salary increase of $379, in lieu of dividends of $250 each, the combined taxes to X Corporation and to A and B would be $212 (28% of the aggregate salary increase of $758). The salary would be a deductible expense to X Corporation and thus no taxes would be paid by it with respect to the $758 amount. By increasing salaries instead of paying dividends, A and B would each net, after taxes, $272.88 instead of the $180 from dividend payments, and the cash flowing out of the corporation would remain the same as if the dividend had been paid.

Many large corporations will issue debt securities rather than preferred stock because the interest on the debt is deductible while the preferred stock dividend is not. However, against this advantage must be weighed the disadvantage that interest is a legal obligation that must be paid while dividends are paid if and only if the board of directors determines, in its discretion, to declare them.[6]

Property Dividends

State Corporate Law   As can be seen in § 1.40 (6) and § 6.40 of the MBCA, state laws typically treat property dividends as they do cash dividends.[7] When property of the corporation is distributed as a dividend, the value of the property, as shown on the corporation's balance sheet (the "book value"), will be removed from the asset side of the balance sheet, and earned surplus will be reduced by the same amount.

Federal Tax Laws   For federal income tax purposes, when property is distributed as a dividend, the earnings and profits of the corporation are reduced by the book value of the property so distributed. On the other hand, the shareholders of the corporation who receive property as a dividend must report as income the fair market value of the property received.

QUESTION

Can the book value be greatly different from the fair market value?

If X Corporation distributes a dividend of 10 shares of Y stock which it owns, having a fair market value of $100 per share, but which originally cost X only $40 per share, X charges $400 to earned surplus and reduces its tax earnings and profits by the same $400. A and B, however, each recognize ordinary income of $500.

PROBLEM

Using the format of resolutions contained earlier in this chapter, draft resolutions declaring a dividend of X Corporation of $100 book value in inventory on each share of common stock outstanding.

---

6. See Chapter Six for a discussion of dividends on preferred stock.

7. QUESTIONS: What kinds of property can a corporation distribute to its shareholders? As a practical matter, are all types of property distributable?

STOCK DIVIDENDS, STOCK SPLITS, AND REVERSE STOCK SPLITS

General

This section covers certain corporate actions which result in reducing or increasing the number of shares of outstanding stock of a particular class without the receipt by the corporation of any assets. In each of these corporate actions the relative stock ownership of the shareholders of a corporation never changes. Each shareholder ends up with the same percentage ownership in the corporation as that held prior to the action. Only the number of shares held by the shareholder changes, and each shareholder's holdings will change in the same proportion.

Stock Dividends

Definition   A stock dividend is a distribution by a corporation of shares of one or more of its classes of stock to the holders of that class or of a different class of stock. No change in the par value or stated capital of any class of stock occurs in a stock dividend. Unlike a cash dividend, a stock dividend in shares similar to those already held is really not a distribution at all. A stock dividend merely serves to dilute each previously outstanding share and increase the number of units into which the evidence of a shareholders' ownership is divided. Example: If a corporation with 1000 outstanding shares declares a 10% stock dividend, there will be 1100 shares outstanding after the dividend. The assets of the corporation are unchanged, and each share is reduced in value by 10%.

QUESTIONS   If the above corporation declared a 25% stock dividend after the 10% dividend, how many shares would then be outstanding? Would the shareholders or corporation have experienced any change in real assets by the dividend?

The corporation often issues a stock dividend rather than a cash or property dividend because it does not desire a distribution of assets. However, the stock dividend increases the number of shares in the market. The corporation may desire to do this. Why? Furthermore, even though nothing has really been given to the shareholders, a small stock dividend, such as 5%—five shares for each 100 owned—may tend to benefit the shareholders. Investors in the stock market are accustomed to seeing a stock at a certain level, and the stock may tend to return to that level. For example, a stock that sells at $100 per share would decline to $95 when a 5%

stock dividend is declared if all other factors remain equal. However, the stock may tend to return to its customary level of $100 after the dividend. In such cases, the shareholders have benefited by holding 5% more stock with no offsetting decline in price.

QUESTIONS How much should the market price of a $100 stock decline if a 10% stock dividend is declared? A 200% stock dividend?

Restrictions   Section 6.40 of the MBCA is a modern provision that excludes stock dividends from most distribution restriction since they do not remove assets from the corporation.

Title 15, Pennsylvania Business Corporation Law, § 1524 (b), provides for a pro-rata distribution to shareholders so long as no payment of consideration is involved and no shareholder is thereby treated adversely. Of course, the corporation's articles and bylaws must first be consulted to determine requisite authority.

If the amount of authorized but unissued stock is insufficient to pay the dividend, it follows that the corporation's articles of incorporation must be amended to increase the authorized number of shares of stock.[8]

Tax Treatment of Stock Dividends   The general rule is that dividends of common stock to holders of common stock are not taxable as income to the recipient shareholders. Early in the history of the federal income tax law, the Supreme Court of the United States held that it was unconstitutional to tax as income to the shareholders a distribution of common stock on common stock because a stock dividend takes nothing from the property of the corporation and adds nothing to that of its shareholders.

Payment of Stock Dividends

Board Authorization   The first step in the payment of a stock dividend is for the board of directors to adopt resolutions specifying the amount of the dividend and the record and payment dates:

> RESOLVED, that a dividend payable in Common Stock of the Corporation shall be paid on August 31, 19 __ , to holders of Common Stock of record on August 15, 19 __ , at the rate of one-tenth of a share for each share of outstanding Common Stock.
>
> RESOLVED, that the Treasurer of the Corporation be and hereby is authorized and directed to charge the earned surplus account of the Corporation with the aggregate par value of the

---

8. See Chapter Four for a discussion of the amendment of a corporation's articles of incorporation.

shares to be issued in the foregoing stock dividend and to credit the stated capital of the Corporation with such amount.

RESOLVED, that no fractional shares of Common Stock shall be issuable pursuant to the foregoing stock dividend and that this Corporation shall pay in lieu of any fractional share an amount in cash which bears the same proportion to the closing price of the Common Stock on the American Stock Exchange on the date of the dividend as the fractional share bears to a whole share.

RESOLVED, that any officer of the Corporation be and each of them hereby is authorized and directed to take all steps and prepare and sign all such documents as any one of them may deem necessary or proper to carry out the foregoing resolutions.

Fractional shares may be avoided by paying cash or rounding off the fraction.

QUESTION

Why would a corporation desire to avoid issuing fractional shares?

PROBLEM

Draft resolutions authorizing a 200% stock dividend in common stock payable on November 15 to holders of record on November 1. Include a resolution authorizing rounding off of a fractional share to the nearest whole share.

Issuance of Shares On the payment date for the stock dividend, the officers of the corporation must execute certificates representing the shares of common stock of the corporation being issued in the stock dividend and deliver them to the shareholders of record as of the record date in accordance with the terms of the stock dividend resolution.

Accounting for Stock Dividends The accounting adjustments to reflect the issuance of a stock dividend take place solely in the capital and surplus accounts, inasmuch as no cash or other property is being distributed. The par value of the shares issued in the stock dividend may have to be added to the corporation's stated capital and the same amount removed from the corporation's earned surplus. Using the foregoing resolutions of X Corporation as an example, the capital account of X Corporation on the payment date of the stock dividend would be revised as follows:

The common stock account would be increased by $100:

Common Stock (1,000 shares, $10 par value, authorized, 110 shares issued and outstanding) $1,100

The earned surplus account would be reduced by $100:

Earned Surplus $79,900

Stock Splits

Definition A stock split is a division of the issued shares of any class of a corporation into a greater number of shares. Typically, where appropriate, the par value or stated value per share will be reduced by an amendment to the articles of incorporation in a stock split so that the aggregate stated capital of the corporation will be unaffected by the stock split.

QUESTIONS How does this procedure differ from a stock dividend? Does a stock dividend require an amendment to the articles?

The aggregate stated capital of a corporation does not have to remain constant in a stock split, however, and it may increase or decrease depending upon the terms of the stock split and (in the case of an increase) the availability of capital surplus or earned surplus to increase the stated capital of the corporation.

Mechanics of a Stock Split Depending upon state law, a stock split of a class of stock (whether with or without par value) will be accomplished by board action, shareholder approval, or amendment of the articles of incorporation. Pennsylvania law provides in PBCL Title 15, § 1524 (b) and § 1914 (c) (3), that, absent provisions in the articles or bylaws to the contrary, the board itself may authorize a stock split.

If the corporation has an insufficient number of authorized shares to accomplish the stock split, the articles of incorporation must be amended to increase the authorized number of shares. If, in the case of par value stock, the par value per share is to be reduced in connection with the stock split, the articles of incorporation must also be amended to reflect the lower par value per share in effect after the stock split. If, in the case of no par value stock, the stated capital per share is to be reduced, it is appropriate to reflect such adjustment in the articles of amendment.[9]

Once the appropriate action has been taken by the shareholders or directors of a corporation, the stock split is effected by the filing of articles of amendment. Typically, the corporation will deliver certificates to existing shareholders to represent only the additional shares of stock which are outstanding as a result of the stock split to avoid the difficulty of calling back the outstanding certificates.

Tax Treatment Stock splits are not taxable income to the recipient shareholders since no distribution of the assets of the corporation has occurred.

9. Chapter Four specifies the procedures for an amendment to the Articles of Incorporation.

Accounting for Stock Splits   Typically, there will be no changes in the dollar amounts of stated capital or any other capital account of the corporation as a result of a stock split. The only change will be in the number of shares issued. For example, if a corporation with 100 shares of Common Stock, par value $1.00 per share, authorized and outstanding, had a 2-for-1 stock split, the changes would be reflected as follows:

Before Stock Split
   Common Stock (100 shares, $1.00 par value, authorized,
      100 shares issued and outstanding) $100

After Stock Split
   Common Stock (200 shares, $.50 par value, authorized,
      200 shares issued and outstanding) $100

QUESTION   How does this contrast to the accounting for a stock dividend?[10]

Reverse Stock Split

A reverse stock split is a combination of the issued shares of any class of a corporation so that there are a fewer number of shares issued after the reserve stock split than before it. As with a stock split, the relative interests of shareholders in a corporation does not change as a result of a reverse stock split. It is a very unusual occurrence, as shareholders do not like having the number of shares held reduced even if their proportionate interest in the corporation is unchanged.

A reverse stock split can only be effected under Chapter 10 of the MBCA through an amendment of the articles of incorporation which reduces the authorized stock. In addition to proposing an amendment of the articles, the board of directors must provide a procedure by which holders of certificates representing the issued shares prior to the reverse stock split turn in their old certificates. This procedure can be difficult, if not impossible, to carry out in practice where there are many shareholders, some of whom may be difficult to locate or reluctant to send in their shares.

A reverse stock split may or may not increase the par value or stated capital of the shares of issued stock. For example, if a corporation had 100,000 shares of Common Stock, par value $1.00 per share, outstanding prior to a reverse stock split, and a 1-for-5 reverse stock split occurred, the corporation would have 20,000 shares of Common Stock outstanding after the split. The par value per share, however, could be $1.00 per share or $5.00 per share. The

10. Accounting for stock dividends was discussed earlier in this chapter.

amendment to the articles would indicate the change, if any, in the par value.

Reduction of Stated Capital

A corporation may decide, independently of any stock split, to reduce the stated capital per share of its outstanding stock. The purpose of such an action would be to eliminate a negative earned surplus account or to increase capital surplus. Why would a corporation do this?[11] In either case, the objective would be to permit the corporation to be free to make distributions (or larger distributions) to shareholders.

In the case of par value stock, a reduction in stated capital means a reduction in the par value of outstanding shares. In the case of no par value stock, most corporate laws have a specific procedure for reducing stated capital.

Resolutions of both the directors and shareholders are required to reduce stated capital. A statement of reduction of stated capital would also be filed with the state. No tax consequences occur upon a reduction in stated capital, and no other reports are required to be filed.

PURCHASE BY CORPORATION OF ITS OWN SHARES

Authorization by Board of Directors

State corporate statutes generally permit the board of directors of a corporation to authorize the corporation to purchase its own shares,[12] but only to the extent (a) of the corporation's unreserved and unrestricted earned surplus,[13] or limits of solvency and (b) the articles of incorporation permit *or* with the affirmative vote of the holders of a majority of all shares entitled to vote on the question, to the extent of unreserved and unrestricted capital surplus or limits of solvency.

Reference to the balance sheet of X Corporation illustrates that the corporation could purchase its own shares up to a maximum consideration of $80,000 or, under a statute with an MBCA-type approach, if shareholder approval is obtained, up to a maximum of $89,000.

11. See "Payment of Dividends" under "Cash and Property Dividends" earlier in this chapter.
12. Why do the shareholders not vote on the question of a corporation's repurchase of its own stock?
13. Note that the purchase of treasury shares is restricted in a manner similar to that of cash and property dividends. This is because a purchase of treasury shares is another way of distributing property to shareholders.

Sample Resolution

A sample resolution authorizing the officers of a corporation to purchase its own shares follows:

> RESOLVED, that the President, any Vice President, the Secretary, or the Treasurer of this Corporation be and each of them hereby is authorized and empowered to purchase on behalf of the Corporation 25 shares of its Common Stock for cash in the amount of $25,000.

Purchased Shares Held as Treasury Shares

If the common stock of X Corporation is not redeemable, the purchase of shares will not constitute a cancellation of those shares. Instead, the shares will remain "issued" but not "outstanding," and will be referred to as "treasury shares." Remember that the MBCA omits this definition and instead calls such shares "authorized but unissued."[14]

Cancellation of Purchased Shares

If the articles of incorporation provide that purchased shares may not be reissued, then the number of authorized shares must be reduced and the corporation's articles of incorporation amended to reflect that reduction. In Pennsylvania, for example, the foregoing may be accomplished by action of the board of directors alone.[15]

Tax Treatment of Purchase of Shares

A corporation does not realize a gain or loss for tax purposes upon the purchase of its stock. On the other hand, the selling shareholder generally will realize a gain or loss when selling stock to the issuing corporation. If A paid $2,500 for 25 shares of X stock which was later sold back to X for $25,000, A would recognize a gain of $22,500.

Reporting of Stock Purchased to Internal Revenue Service

Within 30 days after the adoption of the resolution to purchase shares of its stock, a corporation should file Form 966 with the Internal Revenue Service because such a purchase constitutes a partial liquidation for tax purposes. A sample Form 966 follows:

14. § 6.31, MBCA.
15. Title 15, § 1914 (c) (2), PBCL.

EXAMPLE *Corporate Dissolution or Liquidation—Form 966.*

Form **966** (Rev. April 1990) Department of the Treasury Internal Revenue Service	**Corporate Dissolution or Liquidation** (Required under Section 6043(a) of the Internal Revenue Code)	OMB No. 1545-0041 Expires 4-30-93

Please type or print

Name of corporation	Employer identification number

Number and street (or P.O. box number if mail is not delivered to street address)	Check type of return
City or town, state, and ZIP code	☐ 1120 ☐ 1120L ☐ 1120-IC-DISC ☐ 1120S ☐ Other ▶

1 Date incorporated	2 Place incorporated	3 Type of liquidation ☐ Complete ☐ Partial

4 Internal Revenue Service Center where last income tax return was filed and tax year covered }	Service Center	Tax year ending Month Year

5 Date of adoption of resolution or plan of dissolution, or complete or partial liquidation

6 Tax year of final return . . . .

Was final return filed with a parent corporation (consolidated return)? . . ☐ Yes   ☐ No

If "Yes," enter:

Name of parent corporation ▶ ------------------------------

Employer identification number ▶ ------------------------------

IRS Center where consolidated return was filed ▶

	Common	Preferred
7 Total number of shares outstanding at time of adoption of plan or liquidation		

8 Dates of any amendments to plan of dissolution . . . .

9 Section of the Code under which the corporation is to be dissolved or liquidated. . . . .

10 If this return concerns an amendment or supplement to a resolution or plan for which a return was filed, give the date filed. . . . .

Attach a certified copy of the resolution or plan, together with all amendments or supplements not previously filed.

Under penalties of perjury, I declare that I have examined this return, including accompanying schedules and statements, and to the best of my knowledge and belief it is true, correct, and complete.

▶

Signature of officer	Title	Date

Instructions

Paperwork Reduction Act Notice.—We ask for this information to carry out the Internal Revenue laws of the United States. We need it to ensure that taxpayers are complying with these laws and to allow us to figure and collect the right amount of tax. You are required to give us this information.

The time needed to complete and file this form will vary depending on individual circumstances. The estimated average time is:

Recordkeeping	5 hrs., 1 min.
Learning about the law or the form	6 min.
Preparing and sending the form to IRS	11 min.

If you have comments concerning the accuracy of these time estimates or suggestions for making the form more simple, we would be happy to hear from you. You can write to both the **Internal Revenue Service,** Washington, DC 20224, Attention: IRS Reports Clearance Officer, T:FP; and the **Office of Management and Budget,** Paperwork Reduction Project (1545-0041), Washington, DC 20503.

Who Must File.—A corporation files Form 966 if it is to be dissolved or if any of its stock is to be liquidated. Exempt organizations are not required to file Form 966. These organizations should see the instructions for Form 990 or 990-PF.

When To File.—File Form 966 within 30 days after the resolution or plan is adopted to dissolve the corporation or liquidate any of its stock. If the resolution or plan is amended or supplemented after Form 966 is filed, file an additional Form 966 within 30 days after the amendment or supplement is adopted. The additional form will be sufficient if you show the date the earlier form was filed and attach a certified copy of the amendment or supplement and all other information required by Form 966 and not given in the earlier form.

Where To File.—File Form 966 with the Internal Revenue Service Center where the corporation is required to file its income tax return.

Distribution of Property.—A corporation must recognize gain or loss on the distribution of its assets in the complete liquidation of its stock. For purposes of determining gain or loss, the distributed assets are valued at fair market value. Exceptions to this rule apply to liquidation of a subsidiary and to a distribution that is made pursuant to a plan of reorganization.

Signature.—The return must be signed and dated by the president, vice president, treasurer, assistant treasurer, chief accounting officer, or any other corporate officer (such as tax officer) authorized to sign. A receiver, trustee, or assignee must sign and date any return required to be filed on behalf of a corporation.

Form **966** (Rev. 4-90)

LIQUIDATIONS AND DISSOLUTIONS

Prior to Commencement of Business

Most state laws permit the incorporators, prior to the commencement of business and the issuance of shares, to elect to dissolve voluntarily, such as the MBCA provision at § 14.01. The form of Articles of Dissolution of Incorporators to be filed with the state of incorporation in such a case, as recommended by the MBCA, follows:

EXAMPLE

Articles of Dissolution by Incorporators (MBCA)

Filing fee: $ _____

ARTICLES OF DISSOLUTION
BY INCORPORATORS
OF _____

Pursuant to the provisions of Section _____ of the _____ Business Corporation Act, the undersigned of the corporation hereinafter named, adopt the following Articles of Dissolution:

FIRST: The name of the corporation is _____ .

SECOND: The date of incorporation was _____ .

THIRD: None of its shares has been issued.

FOURTH: The corporation has not commenced business.

FIFTH: No debts of the corporation remain unpaid.

SIXTH: The sole incorporator or a majority of the incorporators elects that the corporation be dissolved.

Dated _____ , 19 ___ .

_____
_____
_____
Incorporators (Note 1)

(Add Verification Form B)

NOTE: 1. The sole incorporator or, if more than one, a majority, must execute and verify these Articles.

Dissolution After Commencement of Business

State law establishes very specific procedures in order for an active corporation to terminate its existence. Each state's law has a different procedure which must be carefully carried out. The step-by-step requirements of the MBCA follow.

Initial Action by Shareholders and Directors A state adopting a procedure such as the MBCA law requires that either (a) the shareholders express their intention to dissolve or (b) the board of directors adopt resolutions recommending dissolution and directing the matter to shareholders who, at a meeting of shareholders, approve the dissolution by majority vote.[16]

Could the shareholders vote by a unanimous consent in writing in lieu of a meeting under a § 14.02 dissolution?

Many times a dissolution will be structured so as to take advantage of certain provisions of the Internal Revenue Code. In such a case, a Plan of Complete Liquidation complying with the specific statutory provision must be adopted by the board of directors and shareholders and filed with the Internal Revenue Service with Form 966.

One type of Plan of Complete Liquidation is included below:

EXAMPLE

*Board of Directors'
Resolutions
Adopting a Plan of
Complete
Liquidation*

WHEREAS, in the judgment of the Board of Directors of this Company, it is deemed advisable and for the benefit of this Company and its shareholders that it should be dissolved, it is:

RESOLVED, that, subject to the approval of the shareholders of this Company and effective with the date of such approval, a plan of complete liquidation be, and it hereby is, adopted to effect such liquidation and dissolution of this Company in accordance with the resolutions set forth below:

RESOLVED, that the directors, officers and counsel for the Company are authorized and directed to take the following steps to effect the complete liquidation and dissolution of the Company prior to August 1, 19 ___ , which shall be liquidated under the provisions of the Internal Revenue Code of 1954, as amended.

1. Promptly after the date of the meeting at which the shareholders adopt the plan of liquidation, any officer of this Company be and each of them hereby is authorized and directed to file Articles of Dissolution in accordance with the laws of the state of incorporation.

2. Within thirty (30) days after the date of the meeting at which the shareholders adopt the plan of liquidation, counsel for this Company shall file Form 966 with the District Director of Internal Revenue, together with a certified copy of this resolution.

3. Promptly after adoption of the plan of liquidation, the President of this Company be and hereby is authorized and directed to sell all of the assets of this Company, subject to all of its liabilities, for cash in an amount not less than $400,000.

4. The officers of this Company be and each of them hereby is authorized and directed to satisfy such advertising and notice requirements as may be required by applicable law in connection with this Plan of Complete Liquidation.

16. § 14.02, MBCA.

5. After the necessary notice has been given and advertising has appeared and after the sale of assets has occurred, the duly authorized officers and directors shall distribute the net proceeds of said sale, after the payment of all liabilities and obligations of this Company, first to the holders of Preferred Stock of this Company in the amount of $110 per share, being the liquidation price for said shares, plus any accrued and unpaid dividends thereon to the date of distribution, and no more, and the remaining assets of the corporation shall be distributed to the holders of the Common Stock of this Company in proportion to the number of shares of Common Stock held by each of them.

6. The complete liquidation of this Company shall be effected within 12 months from the time of the adoption by the shareholders of this Company of this plan of liquidation.

7. The proper officers and Company counsel shall file all other forms and documents required by the state and the federal government, including tax returns in connection with the liquidation and dissolution of this Company.

8. Specific authorization is given to counsel for this Company to prepare, sign, and forward to the Commissioner of Internal Revenue, after the final tax return has been filed for this Company, a request for prompt assessment of all federal taxes due from this Company.

9. The officers and directors of this Company are empowered, authorized, and directed to carry out the provisions of this resolution, and to adopt any further resolutions that may be necessary in liquidating and dissolving this Company in accordance with the expressed intent of the shareholders under the plan adopted.

RESOLVED, that a special meeting of the shareholders of this Company be called for August 25, 19 ___ , for the purpose of voting upon the resolution to liquidate and dissolve this Company, and for discussion and voting upon any other matters that may properly come before the meeting with respect to the means of carrying out the plan of liquidation and dissolution of this Company.

Articles of Dissolution At any time after dissolution is authorized, the corporation may file Articles of Dissolution with the state. The effect of the filing of these Articles is to prohibit the corporation from carrying on any business and to direct it to wind up its affairs.[17] A sample form of Articles of Dissolution suggested by the MBCA is included below:

---

17. § 14.93 and 14.05, MBCA.

EXAMPLE

Articles of Dissolution (MBCA)

Filing fee: $ _____

ARTICLES OF DISSOLUTION
PURSUANT TO SECTION _____ OF THE
_____ BUSINESS CORPORATION ACT
OF

Pursuant to the provisions of Section _____ of the _____ Business Corporation Act, the undersigned corporation adopts the following Articles of Dissolution for the purpose of dissolving the corporation:

FIRST: The name of the corporation is _____ .

SECOND: Dissolution of the corporation was authorized on . This Dissolution was approved by the shareholders in accordance with Section 14.03 of the MBCA.

THIRD: All debts, obligations, and liabilities of the corporation have been paid and discharged, or adequate provision has been made therefor.

Dated _____ , 19 __

_____ (Note 1)

By _____

Its President

(Note 2)

and _____

Its _____ Secretary

(Add Verification Form A)

NOTES: 1. Exact corporate name of corporation making the statement.
2. Signatures and titles of officers signing for the corporation.

CHAPTER TEN

Regulation of Securities and the Securities Markets in the United States

In the aftermath of the stock market debacle of 1929 which preceded the Great Depression of the 1930s, the United States Congress undertook the exhaustive task of establishing a legislative framework for regulating the nation's securities[1] industry. The Securities Act of 1933 (the "'33 Act") regulates the distribution of securities from issuing companies into public hands, and the Securities Exchange Act of 1934 (the "Exchange Act") regulates the markets for continuous trading of outstanding securities.

Clause 4 in § 2 of the Exchange Act shows the significance Congress placed upon this historic legislation:

> National emergencies, which produce wide-spread unemployment and dislocation of trade, transportation and industry, and which burden interstate commerce and adversely affect the general welfare, are precipitated, intensified and prolonged by manipulation and sudden and unreasonable fluctuations of securities prices and by excessive speculation on such exchanges and markets, and to meet such emergencies, the Federal government is put to great expense as to burden the national credit.

Notwithstanding the market crises of the 1980s, the insider trading scandals, economic depressions, recessions, and the like, the '33 Act and the Exchange Act have withstood the test of time and continue to provide consistency and structure to the securities markets.

THE SECURITIES ACT OF 1933

The Securities Act of 1933 is the cornerstone of all federal regulation of the public offering and sale of securities. The '33 Act was enacted with two principal objectives in mind: (1) to provide potential investors with material financial, business, and industry-specific information concerning "issuers" and their securities in an attempt to enable the investor to make an intelligent and informed investment decision; and (2) to prohibit misrepresentation, deceit, and other fraudulent acts and practices in connection with the sale of securities. To achieve this goal, the '33 Act requires that a

---

1. A "security" will be defined shortly.

company which desires to raise capital through the public issuance of securities file a registration statement with the Securities and Exchange Commission (SEC), an independent, bipartisan, quasi-judicial agency of the United States. The registration statement contains material information about the issuer and the securities, the risks and consequences to the investor of owning the securities, and complete financial information. The '33 Act also requires that a prospectus,[2] which forms a part of the registration statement, be delivered to potential investors in connection with offers to sell and sales of securities.

Created by Congress, the SEC is composed of five members appointed by the President with the advice and consent of the Senate. The division of Corporation Finance, one of several divisions of the Commission, is responsible for examining registration statements and other reports filed by issuers under the Exchange Act in order to evaluate the sufficiency of the disclosure to ensure that the public can make an informed and intelligent decision. The SEC does not, nor is it legislatively empowered to, assess the merits of an offering of securities; assuming proper disclosure and compliance with the '33 Act, the offering of securities cannot be barred.

What is a Security?

The first step in developing an understanding of the '33 Act and whether or not it applies to a particular transaction is to determine whether you have a "security." The term security is defined as follows:

§ 2 (1), Securities Act of 1933.

(1) The term "security" means any note, stock, treasury stock, bond, debenture, evidence of indebtedness, certificate of interest or participation in any profit-sharing agreement, collateral-trust certificate, preorganization certificate or subscription, transferable share, investment contract, voting-trust certificate, certificate of deposit for a security, fractional undivided interest in oil, gas, or other mineral rights, any put, call, straddle, option, or privilege on any security, certificate of deposit, or group or index of securities (including any interest therein or based on the value thereof), or any put, call, straddle, option, or privilege entered into on a national securities exchange relating to foreign currency, or, in general, any interest or instrument commonly known as a "security," or any certificate of interest or participation in, temporary or interim certificate for, receipt for, guarantee of, or warrant or right to subscribe to or purchase any of the foregoing.

---

2. A "prospectus" is a document by which a company actually offers the securities for sale to the public.

The foregoing definition, as are all definitions contained in the '33 Act, is preceded by the clause "unless the context otherwise requires." This prefatory clause has led many commentators to suggest that the definition of a security is elusive and that substance, rather than form, governs. Accordingly, the term security is not limited to a share of stock but has very broad implications. In 1946 the United States Supreme Court in *SEC vs. W. J. Howey Co.*, 328 U.S. 293 (1946), stated that the judicial test to determine whether a transaction is a security is whether the scheme involves an "investment of money" in a "common enterprise" with profits to come solely from the "efforts of others." This analysis has led courts to consider the following as perhaps involving the purchase or sale of a security: assignments of oil leases; pyramid sales plans; franchises; limited partnerships; charter memberships in country clubs; investments in real estate; and condominium units coupled with rental pool agreements.

PROBLEM

What arguments exist in support of or against the status of each as a security?

Section 5 of the '33 Registration Act:

The linchpin of the '33 Act is § 5. Section 5 compels full disclosure and prescribes those actions which may and may not be taken during three time periods: (1) prior to the filing of a registration statement; (2) during which the registration statement has been filed but has not been declared effective by the SEC; and (3) after effectiveness of the registration statement.

Section 5 (a) makes unlawful the use of the mails or any other instrument of interstate commerce (e.g., television or telephone) to sell a security through the use of a prospectus or otherwise, or to carry through the mails or in interstate commerce any such security for the purpose of sale or for delivery after sale unless a registration statement has been declared effective by the Securities and Exchange Commission.[3]

The significance of § 5 (a)—prohibiting sales prior to effectiveness of the registration statement—is evident in the overall process of the issuer's attempt to raise capital. Typically in a public offering, an issuer engages one or more investment banking firms to underwrite, or sell, the securities on behalf of the issuer through their network of institutional and retail buyers. In many cases this underwriting takes the form of a "firm commitment," which means that the underwriter agrees to purchase the securities of the

---

3. The '33 Act does contain certain exemptions from registration. Regulations of the SEC implement these exemptions.

issuer for its own account and assumes the risk of reselling the securities to its institutional and retail buyers. If no secondary buyers are available, the issuer still receives the entire proceeds of the offering, although from the underwriter's own account rather than from the public. A firm-commitment underwriting is different from a "best-efforts" underwriting in which the underwriter merely agrees to use its best efforts to sell the securities. In a best-efforts underwriting, if no secondary buyers are available the underwriters are not obligated to purchase the securities for their own accounts, and the issuer realizes only those proceeds from the sale of its securities into the secondary market.

The relationship between the underwriter and the issuer is reflected in the underwriting agreement. The agreement is a contractual document which, when executed in a firm-commitment underwriting, obligates the issuer to sell the securities to the underwriter and obligates the underwriter to purchase the securities from the issuer. Section 5 (a) of the '33 Act makes it unlawful to execute an underwriting agreement prior to the effectiveness of the registration statement (thereby creating an obligation for a purchase and sale of the securities). Accordingly, the underwriting agreement is never executed until the registration statement is declared effective by the SEC; and, in most cases, the agreement is executed on the same day the SEC declares the registration statement effective.

Section 5 (b) (1) governs the period between filing the registration statement and the declaration by the SEC of its effectiveness. Section 5 (b) (1) makes unlawful the use of any prospectus after the registration statement has been filed, unless the prospectus meets the disclosure requirements of § 10 of the '33 Act. Section 5 (b) (1) does permit, however, the use of a preliminary or "red-herring" prospectus (so called because of the required red-printed legend on its cover) after the registration statement has been filed but prior to its effectiveness, and the use of certain "tombstone" advertisements (because of their similarity in shape to a tombstone) which meet the requirements of the '33 Act. Section 5 (b) (2) requires that a prospectus which meets the requirements of § 10 of the '33 Act accompany or precede the sale or delivery of any security.

Although § 5 (b) (1) limits the use of written solicitation materials to the statutory prospectus and the tombstone advertisements, it does permit oral solicitations, whether by telephone or face-to-face, so long as no contractual obligation arises relating to the sale or purchase of a security.

Section 5 (c) makes it unlawful for any person to make use of interstate facilities or mails to offer to sell or offer to buy any security before a registration statement with respect to that security has been filed with the Securities and Exchange Commission. These restrictions are encompassing and apply to telephone calls, face-to-face discussions, and even prospectuses, even if they meet the requirements of § 10. Section 5 (c) governs the prefiling period and addresses the problem of early advertising. The dissemination to the public of information relating to an offering of securities or relating to the issuer before a registration statement covering the securities is filed with the SEC may serve to "condition" the investor's mind or arouse public interest before the selling effort is legally permitted to begin. This period is often called the "gun jumping" period. Section 5 (c) severely restricts the type of activities in which an issuer and other people involved in the registration process may engage during this time. Section 5 (c) imposes on underwriters and dealers (who help underwriters to sell the securities into the secondary market) the same restrictions on disclosure it imposes upon an issuer of securities. However, preliminary negotiations are permitted between issuers and underwriters in connection with negotiating the underwriting agreement and structuring the public offering.

Although § 5 (c) is designed to prevent arousing public interest about an issuer before the selling effort is legally permitted to begin, case law recognizes a distinction between normal corporate communications (including a company's obligation to file periodic reports under the Exchange Act) and those types of communications which are more forward looking or forecast oriented. Generally, a company is permitted to engage in the following activities without violating § 5 (c): advertising products; filing periodic reports under the Exchange Act; disclosing factual business and financial developments, including contract signings, strike settlements, and openings of manufacturing plants and other facilities; and answering unsolicited telephone inquiries from shareholders, the press, and analysts regarding historic financial information.

Activities which are deemed "gun jumping" activities and which violate § 5 (c) include issuing forecasts, projections, and predictions, and publishing opinions relating to the value of the company's stock.

The registration statement and other required forms As previously noted, once the determination is made that a security is subject to the registration requirements of the '33 Act, a registration statement must be filed with the Securities and Exchange Commission. The registration statement is divided into two parts—the prospectus, which is the only part normally delivered to the public, and Part II, which contains supplemental information filed with the SEC and which is available for public inspection at the SEC's public reference facilities.

The '33 Act prescribes several forms for use in registering a security. The determination of which form is required depends upon a number of items. For example, if the securities are being issued in connection with an employee benefit plan or a stock option plan, a Form S–8 is used to register the securities. If the securities are being issued in connection with an exchange of securities for other securities or in a merger or other transaction in which a vote of security holders is required, a Form S–4 is required. Additionally, "short-form" registration statements, such as a Form S–3, which require less company-specific disclosure, may be employed if the issuer already is a "reporting company" under the Exchange Act, since most of the information already would be available to the public.

Each of the registration statement forms employed for purposes of registering securities contains a series of detailed items and instructions in response to which disclosure is made. The registration statement, although presented as a "form" in the securities regulations, is not intended to be filled out as an income tax form. The prospectus is generally in narrative form and is a stylized document. In fact, the prospectus often is considered to be a "schizophrenic" document; on one hand, it is a selling document to be used by the underwriters; on the other hand, it is deemed an "insurance policy" against liability from the company's point of view, since the company's goal is to disclose all of the blemishes and other risks associated with an investment so that an investor cannot later sue the issuer, claiming that he or she was unaware of the risks involved in purchasing the securities.

Unlike the prospectus, Part II of the registration statement is generally prepared in an item-and-answer format and contains supplemental financial statement schedules and exhibits.

Regulation S–K contains the disclosure which is required to be included in the registration statement. These integrated disclosure regulations promulgated by the Securities and Exchange Commission set forth instructions and forms for use in answering the questions in the registration statement. Regulation S–K also provides the integrated disclosure guidelines for reports filed by issuers under the Exchange Act. Generally, the SEC will refer to Regulation S–K to determine whether the disclosure contained in the registration statement complies with law. Assuming proper disclosure, the registration statement will be declared effective.

Section 6 of the '33 Act: Procedural Requirements for Filing the Registration Statement

Section 6 of the '33 Act establishes certain procedural requirements relating to the execution and filing of a registration statement, the filing fee, and the availability to the public of the information contained in the registration statement. A registration statement must be signed by an officer on behalf of the corporation and by each of the following persons: the chief executive officer of the corporation; the principal financial and accounting officers of the corporation; and a majority of the directors on the corporation's board of directors then in office.

At the time the registration statement is filed, the issuer is required to pay to the Securities and Exchange Commission a fee of ¼₀th of 1% of the maximum aggregate offering price of the securities proposed to be offered.

QUESTION

What function is served by statutorily mandating specific signatures, as detailed above?

Sections 11 and 12—Antifraud Provisions Under the Securities Act of 1933

Section 11: Standards of conduct and liability The '33 Act imposes a high standard of conduct on specific persons, including directors and officers, associated with a registered public offering of securities. This standard of conduct is given enforcement effect by § 11 of the '33 Act, which makes the signers of the registration statement, the issuer's directors, and certain other persons civilly liable for any untrue statement of a material fact contained in an effective registration statement and for the omission of any further material fact required to be stated or needed to make the other statements not misleading. Section 11 allows purchasers of a registered security to sue the issuer, its directors, underwriters, accountants who are named as having prepared or certified the registration statement, and company officers who have signed the statement.

The statute was designed to assure compliance with disclosure provisions of the '33 Act by imposing a stringent standard of liability on the parties who play a direct role in the registered offering. It mandates a form of strict, or absolute, liability upon certain persons for material misstatements or omissions in the registration statement.

Directors may be liable under § 11 whether they did or did not sign the registration statement. In contrast, generally only officers who sign the registration statement are potentially liable under the statute.

Section 11 places a relatively minimal burden on a purchaser seeking to utilize its remedies. If a plaintiff purchased a security pursuant to a registration statement, he or she need only show a material misstatement or omission to establish a prima facie case. A claim does not require proof of reliance, of causation, or even of an intent to defraud. Liability under § 11 is "joint and several," meaning that all or any one or more of the persons listed in the statute can be held liable.

Liability under the statute, however, is subject to several important provisos. First, the misstatements and omissions must be material. Second, while a purchaser does not have to show a causal connection between a decline in the stock's price and the statement, the defendant may escape liability in whole or in part by proving that a decline in the market value is unrelated to the misstatement. Furthermore, each of those persons (other than the issuer) who may be subject to a lawsuit under § 11 may escape liability if he or she can prove any one of the following circumstances: (a) that he or she resigned from his or her position with the issuer before the effective date of the registration statement and had sent notice to the Securities and Exchange Commission of that resignation; (b) that he or she had no knowledge of the effectiveness of the registration statement and gave notice to the SEC and to the public of that lack of knowledge upon becoming aware of the registration statement's existence; (c) that he or she had reasonable grounds to believe, and did in fact believe, the truthfulness of the misleading or false statement after having made a reasonable investigation (normally called the "due-diligence defense"); or (d) that he or she had relied on the authority of an expert for expertised material which proved to have a misstatement and that there was an absence of reasonable grounds on which to question the truthfulness of the statement.

What constitutes a "reasonable investigation" and "reasonable grounds to believe" will, of course, vary with the degree of the individual's involvement, expertise, and access to pertinent data. What is reasonable for one director may not be reasonable for another, by virtue of their differing positions. For example, inside directors (those who also are officers or employees of the issuer) with intimate knowledge of corporate affairs and of the particular transactions involved are usually expected to make a more complete investigation than outside directors. Similarly, accountants and underwriters are expected to investigate to degrees commensurate with their respective positions. The law generally holds that each such person must undertake an investigation that a "reasonably prudent person in that position" would conduct.

Section 11 (e) provides an explicit measure of damages for investors who are entitled to recover under the law's liability provisions. That measure of damages equals the difference between what was paid for the security and its value at the time the suit was brought. However, a determination of the amount paid for the security does not always entirely resolve the damages question. Section 11 (e) also provides what is essentially a causation defense, allowing a defendant to show that some identifiable portion of the damages suffered is attributable to a source other than the registration statement's falsity. Under the standard, courts are not likely to consider any damages caused by forces independent of the defendants' misstatements or omissions. For example, in certain cases the damages figure has been adjusted to take into account a drastic decline in the stock market.

QUESTION

How, if at all, would you expect a "reasonable" investigation to differ if undertaken by an inside director, accountant, and underwriter?

Section 12: "Seller" liability Section 12 of the '33 Act is another liability statute relating to the registration statement. Section 12 (1) states that anyone who sells an unregistered security "shall be liable to the person purchasing such security from him" and § 12 (2) imposes liability on one who offers or sells a security by means of a prospectus or other communication containing material misstatements or failing to state material facts. As in § 11, the test of whether something is "material" has been established by the United States Supreme Court, which has stated that a fact is material if there is a "substantial likelihood" that a reasonable investor would consider it important in making an investment decision.

By its terms, § 12 (1) is essentially a strict, or absolute, liability statute that conditions an investor's recovery on the jurisdictional use of the mails or interstate commerce, the lack of the required registration, and the sale of a security by the defendant without regard to the seller's awareness of the violation. On the other hand, § 12 (2) requires a plaintiff to show, in addition to the use of the mails or other instruments of interstate commerce, that there were materially misleading statements or omissions. Section 12 (2), unlike § 12 (1), would not impose liability on a seller of securities who did not know, and in the exercise of reasonable care could not have known, of the violation.

Unlike § 11 of the '33 Act, § 12 is specifically limited to sellers of securities and to directors and officers. It is true that the statute's express language does appear to confine liability to only immediate "sellers" of the stock in question, a term whose definition is not found in the '33 Act. Nonetheless, since the 1960s the federal courts have been expanding the definition of the seller beyond persons who have actually sold the security to the purchaser.

Labeling a person a seller under § 12 (2) does not in and of itself result in automatic liability. Rather, liability may be avoided by showing exercise of ordinary care. The defendants are entitled to show that they "in the exercise of reasonable care could not have known" of the claimed untruth. Similar to the "reasonable investigation" defense of § 11, the "reasonable-care" defense of § 12 (2) depends on the facts of each case.

The appropriate remedy provided by § 12 depends on whether the purchaser still owns the stock. On tendering the security, the purchaser may recover the consideration paid for it, plus interest, and minus any amount of income received on the stock; this remedy is known as "recission." A purchaser who no longer owns the security may recover damages. The purchaser cannot choose between remedies. If the purchaser owns the stock, he or she is entitled to recission, but not damages. If the purchaser no longer owns the stock, he or she is entitled to damages, but not recission.

THE SECURITIES EXCHANGE ACT OF 1934

The objectives of the Securities Exchange Act of 1934 (the "Exchange Act"), like the objectives of the '33 Act, are to provide full and fair disclosure to the public regarding companies whose stock is publicly traded and to prohibit manipulative and deceptive devices in connection with securities trading. Unlike the '33 Act, which regulates the disclosure of information in one document (the registration statement) at one point in time (the offering of securities to the public by the issuer), the Exchange Act regulates the continuous disclosure required in connection with securities trading in the secondary markets after the registration statement has been declared effective. The Exchange Act also regulates the national securities exchanges, the conduct of brokers and dealers in connection with their securities trading activities, and "margin" requirements, which pertain to the use of securities as collateral for the purchase of additional securities.

The Exchange Act generally applies to issuers most directly through compliance with the periodic reporting requirements of § 13 (a), the proxy rules governed by § 14 (a), the "short-swing" profit recovery trading rules and reporting requirements found in § 16 (a) and § 16 (b), and the antifraud prohibitions of § 10 (b). Additional regulations promulgated by the Securities and Exchange Commission under the Exchange Act pertain to tender offers, accumulations of stock in one company by individuals, and purchases by companies of their own securities on the public markets.

How Issuers Become Subject to the Exchange Act

An issuer becomes subject to the reporting requirements under the Exchange Act in three basic ways. Pursuant to § 15 (d), any issuer whose registration statement under the '33 Act is declared effective must file "such supplementary and periodic information, documents and reports as may be required pursuant to Section 13 of the Exchange Act" with respect to the securities for which the registration statement has been declared effective. Additionally under § 15 (d) the duty to file these public reports under § 15 (d) is suspended automatically (by filing a Form 15) if the issuer registers its securities under § 12 of the Exchange Act (which otherwise requires compliance with the reporting requirements under § 13) or if the issuer has a fiscal year in which, at the beginning of such fiscal year, fewer than 300 persons are record holders of the class of securities registered under the '33 Act.

In addition to § 15 (d), § 12 (g) provides an issuer with a class of equity securities held of record by 500 or more persons and more than $3 million in total (consolidated) assets must register that class of equity securities under the Exchange Act, even if the class of securities was not subject to a registration statement filed under the '33 Act. Section 12 (g) does not apply, however, to securities which are listed and registered on a national securities exchange (e.g., the New York Stock Exchange and the American Stock Exchange), to securities which are issued either by an investment company, a savings and loan, or similar association, or by a charity, or to securities issued by other entities which meet certain criteria established under the Exchange Act. Additionally, although not required by the statute to register under the Exchange Act under § 12 (g), those companies which desire to have their securities traded in the over-the-counter markets under the National Association of Securities Dealers Automated Quotation (NASDAQ) system are required by NASDAQ to register under the Exchange Act under § 12 (g).

In addition to § 12 (g), § 12 (a) prohibits the trading of securities on a national securities exchange unless the security is registered with the SEC pursuant to § 12 (b) of the Exchange Act.

If an issuer is subject to the Exchange Act pursuant to § 15 (d), the duty to file periodic reports under § 15 (d) is automatic; no additional filing is required to be made under the Exchange Act to activate the issuer's obligation. If, however, the same issuer becomes subject to the Exchange Act by virtue of § 12 (b) or § 12 (g), it is required to register its class of securities under the Exchange Act by using a registration statement. The type of registration statement typically employed in this instance is a Form 8–A. Form 8–A only requires information about the securities being registered (which often may be incorporated by reference to the original prospectus used by the issuer to register its securities under the '33 Act). Form 8–A does not require any additional information about the company itself, since most of the information would otherwise be included or provided in one or more of the periodic reports which previously were filed by virtue of complying with § 15 (d).

If the issuer has not been subject to the reporting requirements under § 15 (d) but is otherwise required to register under the Exchange Act under § 12 (b) or § 12 (g), it must register its securities using a Registration Statement on Form 10. The Form 10 Registration Statement requires the type of disclosure normally required in a registration statement filed under the '33 Act; because no prior '33 Act registration statement has been filed, the Form 10 Registration Statement would be the first time that such information becomes publicly available.

One major distinction between a company that is subject to the periodic reporting requirements under § 13 of the Exchange Act pursuant to § 15 (d), but is not subject to the Exchange Act by virtue of § 12 (b) or § 12 (g), is that a § 15 (d) company, unlike a § 12 (b) or § 12 (g) company, is not subject to the proxy[4] rules or to the short-swing profit recovery rules under § 16 (a) and § 16 (b) and other Exchange Act regulations. It is important to note, therefore, that a company which is subject to the periodic reporting requirements of the Exchange Act by virtue of having registered a security under the '33 Act is not deemed an "Exchange Act" company as it has not been "registered" under the Exchange Act. A company only becomes registered under the Exchange Act if it is required to file a Form 8–A or a Form 10 by virtue of complying with § 12 (b) or § 12 (g).

Periodic Reporting Under the Exchange Act

A corporation required to file reports pursuant to § 13 or § 15 (d) of the Exchange Act must file an Annual Report on Form 10–K, a Quarterly Report on Form 10–Q for the first three fiscal quarters of each fiscal year, and a Current Report on Form 8–K upon the occurrence of certain specified events as set forth in the regulations. Much of the disclosure required in these periodic reports and, additionally, the information required in proxy statements has been standardized in Regulation S–K, as previously discussed.

The Annual Report on Form 10–K must be filed within 90 days after the end of the issuer's fiscal year. Certain of the information otherwise required to be included in the Form 10–K may be included in the issuer's proxy statement pertaining to its annual meeting of shareholders, provided that the proxy statement in its definitive form has been filed with the SEC within 120 days from the end of the issuer's fiscal year. If the information is not

---

4. The term proxy will be defined shortly.

filed within this 120-day period, the issuer may file the information under cover of a Form 8 (the Exchange Act form which is employed to amend other Exchange Act reports). The Form 10–K is divided into four parts and generally requires disclosure of the company's business, operations, and other matters during its most recently completed fiscal year and in comparison to prior fiscal years.

The Quarterly Report on Form 10–Q is required to be filed with the Securities and Exchange Commission within 45 days after the end of each of the first three fiscal quarters of the issuer's fiscal year. No Form 10–Q is required to be filed for the fourth quarter since the information otherwise required in a fourth-quarter Form 10–Q is included in the Annual Report on Form 10–K.

The Current Report on Form 8–K must be filed with the SEC within 15 days of the occurrence of any event required to be reported under items 1–4 or 6 of the Form 8–K. These items include changes in control of the registrant, an acquisition or disposition of assets of the registrant, the occurrence of a bankruptcy or receivership, changes in the registrant's certifying accountant, and the resignation of a director of the registrant. Additionally, a Current Report on Form 8–K may be filed for other events under item 5, although there is no mandatory filing date.

Three complete copies of the Annual Report on Form 10–K, including financial statements and exhibits, and five additional copies without exhibits must be filed with the SEC. One of the three complete copies must be manually executed by an officer on behalf of the registrant, by the registrant's principal executive, accounting, and financial officers, and by a majority of the registrant's board of directors. A filing fee of $250 is required with the filing. The Form 10–Q must be signed by an officer on behalf of the registrant, and no filing fee is required. Additionally, the Form 8–K need only be signed by an officer on behalf of the registrant, and, again, no filing fee is required.

As previously mentioned, an amendment to any report filed under the Exchange Act may be filed under cover of a Form 8. Additionally, under certain circumstances an extension of the filing date required for a Form 10–K, 10–Q, or 8–K may be requested by the issuer by filing a Form 12b–25 which requires the registrant to disclose the circumstances under which the filing extension is being requested.

QUESTIONS

Why should a Current Report on Form 8–K be required to be filed? Under what circumstances would you expect the SEC to grant an extension of time to file reports?

The Proxy Rules

Section 14 (a) of the Exchange Act imposes rules on the solicitation and dissemination of proxies by issuers with a class of securities registered under § 12 of the Exchange Act. As previously mentioned, issuers who are required to file reports under § 15 (d) are not registered under the Exchange Act and, therefore, are not required to comply with the proxy rules. The purpose of § 14 (a) and the regulations promulgated thereunder is to assure that shareholders receive adequate information about those matters to be voted upon at an issuer's annual or special meeting of shareholders.

The term "proxy" refers to the assignment by a shareholder to a third party of such shareholder's right to vote his or her shares. In the context of an annual or special meeting of shareholders, typically the board of directors asks a shareholder to appoint one or more members of the board or management as such shareholder's proxy so that the proxy may vote in accordance with the instructions of the shareholder without the shareholder having to attend the meeting in person.

Generally speaking, the proxy rules apply to any solicitation of a proxy with respect to securities registered under § 12 of the Exchange Act, except with respect to certain circumstances which pertain generally to solicitations made by persons other than the issuer or the issuer's board of directors. The actual proxy rules are contained in Regulation 14A and Rules 14a–1 to 14a–12 promulgated thereunder. Additionally, the disclosure required in the proxy statement is found in Schedule 14A. The disclosure requirements vary depending upon whether the meeting is: an annual meeting of shareholders at which directors will be elected; or a shareholders' meeting relating to approval of amendments to the company's articles or certificate of incorporation, shareholder votes on certain acquisitions, mergers, and consolidations, and shareholder action with respect to the establishment or amendment of stock option plans or the issuance of options to purchase stock of the issuer.

Rule 14a–3 provides that no solicitation subject to Regulation 14A may be made unless each person who is solicited is concurrently furnished or has previously been furnished with a written proxy statement containing the information specified in Schedule 14A. Additionally, Rule 14a–3 (b) provides that if the solicitation is made on behalf of the issuer and relates to an annual meeting at which directors are to be elected, each proxy statement which is provided to security holders must be accompanied or preceded by an annual report. Rule 14a—3 provides the information which is required to be included in an annual report. In lieu of preparing a separate "glossy" annual report to security holders, registrants often will provide to its security holders the Annual Report on Form 10–K filed with the SEC with respect to the fiscal year immediately preceding the year in which the annual meeting is to be held. Seven copies of the annual report must be sent to the SEC, and no filing fee is required.

Rule 14a–6 requires that five preliminary copies of the proxy statement and form of proxy be furnished to the Securities and Exchange Commission at least ten calendar days prior to the date that definitive copies are sent to security holders. A registrant is not required to file a preliminary proxy statement if the only matters to be acted upon at the annual or special meeting are the election of directors, the election, approval, or ratification of the company's certified public accountants, a proposal by a security holder (rather than a proposal by the board of directors of the company), and certain proposals relating to investment companies.

During this ten-day period, the Securities and Exchange Commission has the opportunity to review and comment upon the proxy statement and may require an amendment or other change to the proxy statement before it is "cleared" for mailing to shareholders. Upon clearance of the preliminary proxy statement (or in the event that no preliminary proxy statement is required to be filed), eight definitive copies of the proxy statement and form of proxy must be filed with the commission no later than the date that the material is first sent or given to the security holders. Rule 14a–6 (j) provides for a filing fee to accompany a preliminary proxy statement (or, if no preliminary proxy statement is required, for a definitive proxy statement) of at least $125; however, a higher fee may be required depending upon the nature of the proposal being submitted to shareholders for their action. Rule 14a–8 provides information regarding the inclusion in a registrant's proxy statement of proposals submitted by security holders and the conditions upon which a security holder's proposal may be included in management's proxy statement. Rule 14a–9 is the antifraud portion of Regulation 14A and provides that no proxy statement or other materials sent in connection with a proxy solicitation may contain false or misleading statements.

As previously mentioned, the disclosure requirements for proxy statements are set forth in Schedule 14A which contains a number of items requiring disclosure depending upon the nature of the proposal to be submitted to the security holders. In many instances, the items set forth in Schedule 14A are cross-referenced to Regulation S–K.

Section 14 (a) and the regulations promulgated thereunder address the preparation and submission to security holders of the proxy statement, the form of proxy, and the annual report. It is important to note that the procedures governing the actual meeting of shareholders, whether an annual or special meeting—including, but not limited to determining the shareholders who are entitled to vote, the number of days' notice shareholders are required to have in advance of a meeting, and the number of votes required for approval of a proposal—are governed by the laws of the state in which the issuer is incorporated.[5] This distinction reiterates the notion that the federal securities laws are "disclosure-oriented" and are not intended to supplant or preempt the general corporate laws of the state. Accordingly, in the course of preparing for a meeting of a registrant's security holders, it is necessary to review not only the federal securities laws but the laws of the state in which the issuer is incorporated.

QUESTION

Many individuals purchase one share of a public company for the purpose of soliciting proxies for votes on certain issues. Over what types of issues would you expect that individuals instigate proxy contests?

Section 16—Beneficial Ownership Reporting Requirements and the Short-Swing Profits Recovery Rules

In general, directors and officers of issuers that have a class of securities registered under § 12 of the Exchange Act are subject to the reporting and liability provisions of § 16. Unlike those Exchange Act provisions which primarily are concerned with obligations of the company issuing the securities and with the disclosure of information regarding the company and its securities on the secondary markets, § 16 of the Exchange Act focuses on directors and officers of the issuer together with persons who beneficially own 10% of a class of equity securities registered under the Exchange Act. These persons are commonly called "insiders," and the beneficial ownership statements which they are required to file are often called "insider reports."

Section 16 deals chiefly in three areas: Section 16 (a) establishes disclosure requirements for officers, directors, and 10% beneficial shareholders; Section 16 (b) establishes liability for short-swing trading profits; Section 16 (c) relates to short-sales, making certain conduct of insiders unlawful.

Not every company's directors and officers are subject to the beneficial reporting requirements of § 16. A company must have a class of equity securities registered under § 12 of the Exchange Act in order for the obligation to apply.

Under § 16 (a), officers, directors, and beneficial owners of 10% or more of a class of equity securities registered under the

---

5. See Chapter Five on shareholders' meetings.

Exchange Act are required to make continuing disclosure as to their beneficial ownership of and transactions in those securities. A Form 3, the initial statement of beneficial ownership, must be filed within ten days after the occurrence of any event which requires the filing. These events would include, for example, the appointment of an individual as a director or officer of the company or the registration of a class of equity securities under the Exchange Act. A Form 4, which relates to statements of changes in beneficial ownership of securities, must be filed on or before the tenth day after the end of each month in which any change of beneficial ownership has occurred. Disclosure of information is mandatory, and the filed statements become a matter of public record.

Officers and directors generally are subject to the requirement of filing Form 3s and Form 4s during the period in which they maintain the status as a director or officer. Upon obtaining beneficial ownership of 10% of the equity securities of an issuer which is registered under the Exchange Act, such beneficial owner must file a Form 3 and then must continue to file Form 4s until such time that the beneficial ownership falls below 10%.

The term "beneficial ownership" is not specifically defined in either the '33 Act or the Exchange Act. Generally, however, the term has been defined by the SEC to include a person's ability to vote or to control the voting of the securities, the ability to transfer the securities or control the transfer of the securities, the right to receive income from the securities, or the right to control the disposition of the proceeds. Additionally, beneficial ownership does not necessarily require that the holder directly own the securities. In certain circumstances, the executor of an estate or the trustee of a trust which owns equity securities may be deemed to be the beneficial owner of those securities. Furthermore, the Exchange Act contains "attribution rules" which generally provide that equity securities owned by immediate family members may be attributed to any other immediate family member for purposes of the reporting requirements under § 16 (a) of the Act.

Section 16 (b) is often called "the insider short-swing profits liability provision." The term short-swing refers to the period of less than six months that is examined on a continuing basis to determine whether an officer, a director, or a 10% beneficial owner has engaged in trading activities during such period. The concept of profit liability refers to the fact that any person subject to § 16 (b) who obtains a profit from trading securities in that six-month period must disgorge the profit to the issuer. Section 16 (b) is designed to prevent the unfair use of insider information by insiders when trading in the equity securities of their company. It is not necessary that the trade be based on inside information; rather, the rule is prophylactic (preventive) in nature in that a trade occurring within the six-month period is subject to § 16 (b) whether or not inside information is used in connection with the trade.

Section 16 (b) generally provides that any profit arising from a purchase and sale or a sale and purchase of securities which may be matched within a six-month period must be disgorged by that person to the issuer. The profit disgorgement provisions focus on an insider's purchase/sale or sale/purchase transaction within the six-month period. Although an insider entering into a transaction may have had an intention to hold the security purchased, or not to repurchase the security sold, for a period of more than six months, that intention is irrelevant if there is in fact a profit on the matching purchase and sale within the six-month period.

Under § 16 (b), any short-swing profits which arise within the context of § 16 (b) are payable to the issuer, and the issuer is afforded the right to bring suit against the insider. Additionally, another security holder of the company may bring suit on behalf of the corporation (a "derivative action") to recover the profits.

The calculation of profit is designed to require the insider to disgorge the highest profit which is recoverable within the six-month period. Accordingly, the lowest purchase price and the highest sales price will be matched within the six-month period irrespective of intervening purchases and sales of securities. Additionally, it is not necessary that the exact securities purchased be sold within a six-month period. On the contrary, equity securities of the issuer are considered fungible (or interchangeable) and, accordingly, any transactions within the six-month period with respect to securities of an issuer subject to § 16 (b) which result in a profit are subject to disgorgement.

A number of rules promulgated under § 16 (b) exempt certain short-swing transactions from the profit recovery provisions of § 16 (b). These include: transactions relating to certain mergers and consolidations;[6] transactions relating to the exercise of stock options and the purchase of options under an employee benefit plan or stock option plan which meets certain conditions imposed by the rules; certain exemptions relating to transactions involving the conversion of equity securities; and exemptions with respect to certain transactions by registered investment companies, public utility holding companies and railroads.

The rules enacted under § 16 (b) are very complex and in some cases are considered to be inconsistent. Recent changes to the rules which are designed to address these inconsistencies have been approved by the Securities Exchange Commission, and in most instances are effective as of May 1, 1991.

6. See Chapter 11.

Section 10—Antifraud Provisions Under the Securities Exchange Act of 1934

The general antifraud provisions of the Exchange Act are contained in Section 10 and Rule 10b–5 promulgated thereunder. Rule 10b–5 prohibits: the employment of any device, scheme, or artifice to defraud; the making of any untrue statement of a material fact or the omission of material facts which are necessary to make a statement not misleading; or the engaging in any act, practice, or course of conduct which operates as a fraud or deceit upon any person. The rule is designed to prohibit manipulative and deceptive devices in connection with the purchase and sale of securities through interstate commerce. The antifraud provisions of the Exchange Act, unlike the '33 Act antifraud provisions, are applicable to securities transactions generally, whether conducted face to face, over the counter, or on national securities exchanges. They include transactions which are private as well as public and sales and purchases of securities involving corporations and corporate leaders.

A substantial amount of federal case law addresses the issues of whether private rights of action are permitted in connection with Rule 10b–5 and the duty of insiders who have access to inside information to disclose such information to prospective purchasers of securities. The general rule is that a person who fails to disclose material nonpublic information commits fraud only if he or she is under a duty to disclose such information. Such duty may arise from the existence of a fiduciary relationship between the parties or due to the status of the purchaser as a director or officer of a corporation.

PROBLEM

Corporate employees often receive corporate stock and options to purchase corporate stock as part of their compensation packages. How, if at all, can these employees trade the stock or options granted by the company?

CONCLUSION

The rules and regulations promulgated under the Securities Act of 1933 and the Securities Exchange Act of 1934 are complex and many faceted. They attempt to address the dynamic pace of the securities industry in the United States. The regulations imposed by this legislation on the original issuance of securities and the trading of those securities in the secondary markets facilitates confidence on the part of investors and provides consistency in an industry which has an important bearing on the state of the nation's economy. Changes to the rules and regulations are enacted each year to better protect investors and to assure the continuity of the securities markets which result in the flow of capital into private enterprise.

CHAPTER ELEVEN
Mergers and Acquisitions

"Mergers and acquisitions" commonly refers to the combination of two or more business enterprises or to the acquiring of one business enterprise by another. Businesses acquire other businesses for a variety of reasons: to enter new markets or acquire additional, established distribution networks, to acquire new product lines, to diversify, to eliminate a competitor, and to acquire product technology, among others. Businesses are also sold for various purposes, including the discontinuation of a specific line of business and the deployment of corporate assets in other lines of businesses, for estate planning purposes, and others. When two or more enterprises determine that a combination of ownership is in their best interests, they can accomplish this by using any one or a combination of three basic methods: asset acquisition, stock acquisition, and statutory merger or consolidation. The chosen method is called the structure of the transaction.

ASSET TRANSACTION

In an asset acquisition the acquiring company, or buyer, and the target company, or seller, agree to transfer all or substantially all of the target company's property to the acquiring company in exchange for various forms of consideration, discussed later. The parties agree upon the specific assets that will be transferred and the specific assets, if any, that will be retained by the target company. These assets include balance-sheet property—such as accounts receivable, inventory, real estate, and machinery and equipment—and nonbalance-sheet items such as contracts, leases, and employee benefit plans.

Upon agreement between the parties, a written contract specifying assets subject to sale is executed. The actual transfer of ownership is accomplished by the target company executing individual documents of transfer for each specific type of property. For example, accounts receivable and other intangible personal property are transferred by assignment; inventory, machinery and equipment, and other tangible property are transferred by bill of sale; and real estate is transferred by deed.

In addition, the acquiring company and the target company may agree that the acquiring company will assume all or some of the liabilities of the target company. These liabilities may include accounts payable (obligations to suppliers), accrued liabilities (obligation of a more general nature such as employees' wages, rent, utilities, and supplies), and bank debt. The written contract contains the agreement to assume these liabilities, and the actual transfer is by an "assumption of liabilities agreement." This document is delivered by the acquiring company at the closing when the transfer of ownership of the assets takes place. Any liabilities that are assumed will be paid off and discharged by the acquiring company after the closing in accordance with their terms. The acquiring company is solely responsible for those liabilities that it expressly agrees to assume and is unaffected by those it does not specifically agree to assume, except in certain areas such as product liability and union contract obligations.

The effect of the asset acquisition is that the acquiring company will have title to the assets acquired and liability for those obligations that it agreed to assume. Any assets not acquired by the acquiring company and any liabilities not assumed by the acquiring company will remain with the target company. If all assets are sold, the target company can take various courses of action. For example, it may use the consideration that has been received from the acquiring company to acquire another unrelated business, or it may distribute the consideration received to its shareholders and dissolve the corporate entity, in accordance with the dissolution procedures set forth in the general business corporation law enacted by the state of its incorporation.

STOCK TRANSACTION

In a stock acquisition, the shareholders (or sole shareholder) of the target company agree to transfer their shares to the acquiring company in exchange for consideration. The shareholders may sell all or less than all of the company's issued and outstanding shares to the acquiring company. The transfer is effectuated by the execution of an assignment of share certificates representing the shares to be transferred.

The effect of the stock acquisition is that the acquiring company becomes the majority shareholder of the target corporation. The selling shareholders hold a proportionately smaller interest in the target corporation. No change occurs at the corporate level. The target corporation retains the same characteristics after the closing as prior to the closing (except in the case of mergers, as discussed later). It retains the same assets and liabilities as well as governing documents—for example, its articles of incorporation and bylaws. This type of transaction applies to a privately held corporation where there are relatively few shareholders to negotiate the terms and conditions of the sale of their stock directly with the acquiring company.

The acquisition of stock from shareholders of a public corporation takes the form of a "tender offer" whereby the acquiring company unilaterally sets the terms and conditions of the transaction without direct negotiation with the shareholders. However, the transfer of ownership in the public corporation may also be effectuated by the assignment of share certificates which results in the tender offer, or with the acquiring company becoming a shareholder of the target corporation.

MERGERS AND CONSOLIDATIONS

Merger

A statutory merger occurs when one or more corporations are absorbed by another corporation by operation of law in accordance with a statutory procedure prescribed by the laws of the state or states of incorporation of the corporations involved in the transactions. Corporations may merge whether or not they are incorporated under the laws of the same state. The corporation that disappears ceases to exist upon the consummation of the merger and is referred to as the "merging" corporation. All of its assets and liabilities automatically become the assets and liabilities of the corporation that remains in existence. That corporation is referred to as the "surviving" corporation. It is not necessary to execute or deliver any transfer documents such as assignments, bills of sale, or deeds, but the statutory procedure of the state of incorporation of each corporation involved in the transaction must be followed. The state laws generally require that the corporation execute a written agreement, called an agreement or plan of merger, that specifies certain types of terms and conditions. This is followed by the filing of articles of merger with the Secretary of State of the states in which the merging and surviving corporations are incorporated.

Consolidation

A consolidation is the combination of two or more existing corporations to create a newly formed corporation. Both of the existing corporations disappear, and all of their assets and liabilities are subsumed by the newly formed corporation. The consolidation is accomplished by following a statutory procedure that is similar to the merger procedure. Each corporation that disappears is referred to as a "consolidating" corporation, and the newly formed corporation is called the "consolidated corporation."

In both the merger and consolidation, the merging and consolidating corporations' shareholders receive cash or securities or a combination thereof in exchange for their shares. If they receive cash only, they are no longer involved with the surviving or consolidated corporation. However, if they receive securities in the form of stock in the acquiring corporation, they become shareholders of the surviving or consolidated corporation.

Model Business Corporation Act Merger

The MBCA requires the boards of directors of the merging and surviving corporations to adopt a plan of merger and to submit it to a shareholder vote, with or without the recommendation of the boards of directors. A majority of each voting group or class of shareholders, voting separately, must vote affirmatively unless a greater vote is required by the MBCA, the company's articles of incorporation, or its board of directors. Under certain circumstances, no action of the surviving corporation's shareholders is necessary.

The plan of merger contains mandatory and optional provisions. The mandatory provisions are:

1. the name of each corporation planning to merge and the name of the surviving corporation into which each other corporation plans to merge;
2. the terms and conditions of the merger; and
3. the manner and basis of converting the shares of each corporation into shares, obligations, or other securities of the surviving or any other corporation or into cash or other property in whole or part.

The optional provisions are:

1. amendments to the articles of incorporation of the surviving corporation; and
2. other provisions relating to the merger.

After approval of the plan of merger by the shareholders, the surviving or acquiring corporation delivers "articles of merger" to the Secretary of State. The articles of merger contain the following:

1. the plan of merger;
2. if shareholder approval was not required, a statement to that effect; and

3. if approval of the shareholders of one or more corporations party to the merger was required:

   a. the designation, number of outstanding shares, and number of votes entitled to be cast by each voting group entitled to vote separately on the plan as to each corporation; and

   b. either (i) the total number of votes cast for and against the plan by each voting group entitled to vote separately on the plan or (ii) the total number of undisputed votes cast for the plan separately by each voting group and a statement that the number cast for the plan by each voting group was sufficient for approval by that voting group.

The merger takes effect on the date of filing the articles of merger with the Secretary of State or on a later date if specified in the articles of merger.

A parent subsidiary merger, in which the parent owns at least 90% of the issued and outstanding shares of each class of stock of the subsidiary, requires the approval of the parent's board of directors; however, no approval of the subsidiary's board of directors or the parent or subsidiary's shareholders is necessary. Each shareholder of the subsidiary is entitled to receive a copy or summary of the plan of merger, adopted by the parent's board of directors, unless the shareholder has waived the right. A waiting period of 30 days from the date of mailing must be observed before articles of merger may be delivered to the Secretary of State.

The effect of filing articles of merger is as follows:

1. Every other corporation party to the merger merges into the surviving corporation, and the separate existence of every corporation except the surviving corporation ceases.

2. The title to all real estate and other property owned by each corporation party to the merger is vested in the surviving corporation without reversion or impairment.

3. The surviving corporation assumes all liabilities of each corporation party to the merger.

4. A proceeding pending against any corporation party to the merger may be continued as if the merger did not occur, or the surviving corporation may be substituted in the proceeding for the corporation whose existence ceased.

5. The articles of incorporation of the surviving corporation are amended to the extent provided in the plan of merger.

6. The shares of each corporation party to the merger that are to be converted into shares, obligations, or other securities of the surviving or any other corporation or into cash or other property are converted, and the former holders of the shares are entitled only to the rights provided in the articles of merger or in the MBCA.

Triangular Mergers

The merger transaction can take a variety of forms including the triangular merger and the reverse triangular merger.

A triangular merger occurs when the acquiring corporation forms a subsidiary and merges the target corporation into the subsidiary. The target is the merging corporation, and the acquiring company's subsidiary is the surviving corporation. A reverse triangular merger takes place when the acquiring corporation forms a subsidiary and merges the subsidiary into the target corporation. The acquiring corporation's subsidiary is the merging corporation, and the target corporation is the surviving corporation.

The result in either case is that the assets and liabilities of the target corporation are now owned directly by a wholly-owned subsidiary of the acquiring corporation. The same statutory merger procedure that was described above is applicable. The triangular merger makes unnecessary the approval of the parent corporation's shareholders, which can be expensive and time-consuming if the parent corporation is a public corporation.

COMPARISON OF THE STRUCTURES

The following is a comparison of the three basic structures:

Parties to the Transaction

In an asset acquisition, the two parties to the transaction are the acquiring company and the target corporation. The target corporation sells its assets and liabilities directly to the acquiring corporation.

In the stock acquisition, the parties are the acquiring corporation and the target company's shareholders. The target corporation is usually not a party unless special circumstances exist, such as a shareholders' agreement whereby the corporation has the right of first refusal to acquire the selling shareholders' stock.

In a merger or consolidation, the transaction takes place between two or more corporations, and the shareholders are not parties to the transaction.

Basic Documentation

In an asset acquisition, the acquiring corporation and the target corporation enter into an asset purchase or asset acquisition agreement. The basic documentation of the stock transaction is the stock purchase or stock acquisition agreement. No statutory requirements exist with respect to the structure and contents of these documents but the documents usually contain traditional provisions. The parties to a merger or consolidation execute an agreement or plan of merger or consolidation which is required by the corporate law statutes of the states of incorporation of the parties. The statutes require the parties to consider and negotiate certain types of terms and conditions and to include these in the agreement or plan of merger or consolidation. The document is executed either in advance of the closing—called a deferred closing, which allows for a period of time for due diligence to take place—or contemporaneously with the closing, called a simultaneous closing.

BASIC CORPORATE REQUIREMENTS

The law of the state of incorporation and the governing corporate documents must be reviewed during the due-diligence process to determine what corporate approvals must be produced at the closing.

Board of Directors' Approval, Target Corporation Perspective

The board of directors determines corporate policy and authorizes officers to implement that policy. The sale of a business is a policy decision, and the corporate laws of the company's state of incorporation as well as the corporate governing documents must be reviewed to determine whether board approval is required to effectuate a specific transaction.

Generally, approval of the board of directors is required when all or substantially all of the corporate assets are to be sold. In most states a majority of the members of the board of directors must vote in favor of the transaction. In some states, the law may require a greater number of votes.

In the sale of stock, the target corporation's board of directors does not vote on the proposed transaction, because the corporation is not a party to the transaction unless a shareholders' agreement exists requiring shareholders to offer their shares to the corporation prior to a sale to an unrelated party.

In a merger, the target corporation's board of directors must approve the transaction.

Model Business Corporation Act Asset Transaction

The Model Business Corporation Act permits the sale of all or substantially all of a corporation's property other than in the usual and ordinary course of business on the terms and conditions determined by the board of directors. The board of directors submits the proposed transaction to the shareholders for approval and recommends the proposed transaction, unless it is determined that no recommendation should be made due to a conflict of interest or in other special circumstances. Shareholders who are entitled to vote must approve the transaction by a majority of all votes entitled to be cast unless the articles of incorporation or the board of directors requires a greater vote or a vote by groups entitled to vote.

Board of Directors' Approval, Acquiring Corporation Perspective

The acquiring corporation must also consider the necessity of obtaining the approval of its board of directors. In both the acquisition of assets and acquisition of stock, there is no statutory requirement for approval; corporate tradition, however, indicates that it is common for the board to authorize and direct the corporate officers to negotiate and execute the transaction documentation.

With respect to the merger transaction, the acquiring corporation's board of directors' approval is required by statute. Generally, a majority of the members must vote affirmatively. The MBCA applies in the same manner as described above.

Shareholders' Approval, Target Corporation Perspective

In an asset transaction, the state business corporation laws require the board of directors to submit the proposed transaction to the target corporation's shareholders for their approval. Under most state laws, the transaction must be approved by affirmative vote of a majority of the shares of issued and outstanding voting stock.

In a stock transaction, a shareholder vote is not required by statute, nor is it common. A shareholder in the target corporation who agrees to sell shares will signify consent by executing the stock purchase agreement. If the shareholder is a parent corporation selling shares of a subsidiary, the board of directors of the parent corporation will authorize its officers to execute and deliver the stock purchase agreement and the assignment of share certificates.

In a merger transaction, an affirmative shareholders' vote is required—in most states, a majority. The target corporation's governing corporate documents must be reviewed to determine whether a greater percentage is mandated.

Shareholders' Approval, Acquiring Corporation Perspective

Statutes do not require the acquiring corporation's shareholders to approve a proposed asset or stock acquisition. However, in a merger transaction, statutes and governing corporate documents require a certain percentage of shareholders to vote in favor of the proposed merger in order for it to take place.

Approvals Required by Contract

The approvals of entities that are parties to existing contracts with the target corporation and other entities may need to be obtained prior to consummation of the transaction. Many commercial contracts and leases contain prohibitions against these transactions without prior written consent of the outside party. During the due-diligence period, the target company's legal team must review contracts to determine the necessity for obtaining these consents. These provisions apply in an asset transaction because the acquiring corporation is acquiring rights and assuming liabilities of the target corporation under these contracts. The outside party now looks for performance from the acquiring company with whom it did not negotiate the contract. In this situation, the target corporation tries to obtain a release from the outside party so that the outside party must look solely to the acquiring corporation for performance.

Outside-party consent is becoming a more frequent requirement in the stock transaction. Although the target company with whom the outside party negotiated remains a party to the contract, a change of control necessitates the outside party's consent. A merger transaction may also necessitate consent, especially where the target corporation is the merging rather than the surviving corporation. The easiest way to obtain consent is to present the outside party with a three-party document; this document consists of an assignment to be executed by the target corporation and acquiring corporation and the consent of the outside party to be held in escrow pending the closing.

Other Approvals

Another typical outside-party consent is that of the federal government, for example where government defense contracts are involved or where regulatory bodies govern the target corporation's business activities. Formal applications describing the proposed transaction may have to be submitted a specific number of days in advance of the proposed closing. An additional approval, the premerger notification requirement under the Hart-Scott-Rodino act, is discussed later.

Frequently, the target corporation's lending institution must consent to the transaction, since the acquiring corporation may wish to assume the target corporation's existing debt. Failure to obtain consent prior to the closing may necessitate full payment of the debt from the proceeds of the sale.

CONSIDERATION

The consideration used by the acquiring corporation may consist of cash or securities, in the form of a promissory note or stock, or a combination of the foregoing. Other types of consideration, called payment in kind or barter transactions, exist but are not discussed here.

Cash

Payment in cash is the easiest type of consideration that can be used to pay for the acquisition. Because the entire purchase price is paid in full at the closing, many representations and warranties are eliminated from the contract. One advantage to the target corporation and the selling shareholders is that the risk of not receiving the entire purchase price is eliminated. In exchange for the elimination of this risk, the target corporation and selling shareholders may receive a lower price than if the risk of future payments were assumed. A disadvantage to the target corporation and selling shareholders is that the tax due on any gain from the sale of the business must be paid for the tax year in which the cash is received.

A cash payment requires that the target corporation use its own funds or borrow, or both, so the acquiring company may be occupied with obtaining financing during a great deal of the preclosing period. The acquiring company must also have a financing closing on the same date as the closing of the acquisition. A disadvantage to the acquiring company of an all-cash payment is the inability to offset any damages for the seller's misrepresentations against future payments of the purchase price.

Promissory Notes

Payment by promissory note involves the promise to make a deferred cash payment. The promissory note is delivered to the target corporation or selling shareholders at the closing. Payment deferral usually results in a higher price for the business than if the price were paid in whole at the closing. Part of the negotiation of the sale of the business is negotiation of the terms of the promissory note. The final version of the promissory note is attached to the acquisition agreement as an exhibit.

Stock

When the acquiring company decides to issue its own stock in exchange for the target corporation's stock or assets, federal and state securities laws must be consulted. (Federal securities laws are discussed in Chapter Ten.)

TAX ASPECTS

Taxable Transactions

Asset, stock, and merger transactions are generally taxable to the target corporation and selling shareholders when the consideration received is cash and when the amount exceeds the tax basis of the assets or stock that are given in exchange for cash. However, a stockholder of a target corporation can postpone the recognition of any gain or loss realized in the transaction by adopting a structure that meets the guidelines of § 368 of the Internal Revenue Code.

Common Law Principles

In addition to the statutory requirements, certain principles fashioned by the courts apply to this area. The first is the "business-purpose requirement" which forces the business combination to have a business purpose; the purpose of the reorganization cannot merely be to distribute stock to existing shareholders. The second is the "step-transaction" prohibition. The Internal Revenue Service may disallow the tax-free treatment of a multi-step transaction by deeming the separate steps to be one. The third principle is "continuity of interest" whereby the selling shareholders are required to retain an equity interest in the acquiring corporation following the consummation of the transaction.

ANTITRUST MATTERS

Federal and state antitrust laws also apply to business acquisitions. The primary federal antitrust laws are the Sherman act (which generally prohibits monopolies), the Federal Trade Commission act (which generally prohibits unfair or deceptive trade practices), and the Clayton act (which prohibits certain business combinations with anticompetitive effects). Section 7 of the Clayton act prohibits acquisition by a person engaged in interstate commerce where the effect may be to substantially lessen competition or may tend to create a monopoly in any line of commerce in any section of the country. These substantive antitrust laws must be considered in any business acquisition, particularly those involving an acquisition by a large entity which may result in an anticompetitive concentration of economic power.

The Department of Justice and the Federal Trade Commission have responsibility to enforce the Clayton act. To aid enforcement, parties to certain large business acquisitions must notify both agencies prior to the closing of the transaction for agency review of any anticompetitive effect and, if violative of the Clayton act, for injunction through judicial proceedings. This reporting requirement was enacted as § 7A of the Clayton act by the Hart-Scott-Rodino Antitrust Improvements Act of 1976. The Federal Trade Commission has also adopted regulations implementing this requirement, which contain extensive definitions of terms which must be consulted when analyzing the applicability of and compliance with Hart-Scott-Rodino.

Only those business acquisitions and parties must be reported which meet all of the size and interstate commerce tests described in the following paragraphs.

Size of Parties

If the acquiring person has annual net sales or total assets of $100 million or more, and the acquired person has annual net sales or total assets of $10 million or more, or vice versa, the size-of-parties test is met. The "acquiring person" includes all corporations within the group controlling, controlled by, or under control with, the purchaser; all of the annual net sales and total assets of those entities must be added together to determine if this test is met. The definition of "acquired person" is narrower and generally includes only the specific entity whose stock or assets will be acquired in the transaction.

Size of Transaction

This test may be met in any one of several ways. For example, if the acquiring person will own 15% or more of the acquired person's voting stock or assets, or $15 million or more of its voting stock or assets, this test is met. A *de minimus* threshold excludes any transaction involving a purchase price of less than $15 million. However, even that threshold does not apply if the acquiring person buys sufficient voting stock to control an acquired person with annual net sales of at least $25 million.

These formulas are also complicated by the fact that when the acquiring person acquires additional voting securities or assets of the acquired person so as to hold at least 25% and then 50% of either, at each step the parties must report those acquisitions to the Department of Justice and the Federal Trade Commission.

Commerce

In order to satisfy the constitutional requirements applicable to the regulation of interstate commerce by Congress, either the acquiring person or the acquired person must be engaged in commerce or an activity affecting commerce.

If all of these tests—the size of parties, the size of transaction, and interstate commerce—are met in a particular business acquisition, then all of the parties must file a "Notification and Report Form" with the Department of Justice and the Federal Trade Commission. In a tender offer, only the acquiring person must file the form. The format required for the information submitted, as well as other requirements applicable to the filing, are set forth in the regulations adopted by the Federal Trade Commission. Copies of the form currently acceptable for filing are available from the commission. A party may use its own form as long as the information required by both Hart-Scott-Rodino and the regulations is provided.

The Hart-Scott-Rodino reporting requirements are designed to allow the federal agencies time to review the proposed business acquisition and determine if any possible antitrust violation will result. Accordingly, when all parties have filed their forms they must wait 30 days before closing; in the case of a cash tender offer, the waiting period is 15 days after filing. In many situations, the parties will ask for early termination of the waiting period; if the agencies determine that there is no anticompetitive effect or no violation of the antitrust laws, the request will be granted. However, either agency may request additional information from the parties in order to complete the review of the acquisition, in which case the waiting period will be extended. The parties may close after the waiting period expires if no action has been taken by either agency to enjoin it or after either agency grants early termination.

If either the Department of Justice or the Federal Trade Commission has reason to believe that the business acquisition will violate the antitrust laws, the agency will seek an injunction from a federal court to stop the closing. After a full hearing on the merits of the case, the court will decide whether § 7 of the Clayton act will be violated by the acquisition. The parties may also enter into a consent order with the agency addressing the objectionable portion of the acquisition, such as by agreeing to resell immediately those portions of the acquired person which are directly competitive with the existing business of the acquiring person.

Hart-Scott-Rodino is a procedural statute requiring only that prior notice of certain acquisitions be given to the Federal Trade Commission and the Department of Justice. However, failure to comply can result in a civil penalty to any person, officer, director, or partner of a noncomplying party, up to $10,000 for each day of violation. In addition, criminal penalties under federal law may also be imposed in an appropriate case.

Hart-Scott-Rodino also may affect acquisitions by or of foreign businesses. Acquisitions by a United States person of the voting securities or assets of a foreign person will require compliance with Hart-Scott-Rodino if the three tests described above are met and if the foreign person has made sales into the United States during the fiscal year preceding the acquisition by a foreign person.

DISSENTERS' RIGHTS

Dissenters' rights gives shareholders the right to dissent from certain corporate actions and to obtain payment of the fair value of their shares in cash in the event that the action takes place. These actions include a merger, a de facto merger, and the acquisition of substantially all assets and the assumption of all liabilities of a target corporation in exchange for stock in the acquiring corporation. Dissenters' rights allow shareholders who would be forced to participate in a transaction against their will a way out other than having to resort to injunctive relief.

Model Business Corporation Act

The MBCA includes the following procedures in its Chapter 13, "Dissenters' Rights."

§ 13.02, MBCA. Right to Dissent.

(a) A shareholder is entitled to dissent from, and obtain payment of the fair value of his shares in the event of, any of the following corporate actions:

    (1) consummation of a plan of merger to which the corporation is a party
       (i) if shareholder approval is required for the merger by section 11.03 or the articles of incorporation and the shareholder is entitled to vote

on the merger or (ii) if the corporation is a subsidiary that is merged with its parent under section 11.04;

(2) consummation of a plan of share exchange to which the corporation is a party as the corporation whose shares will be acquired, if the shareholder is entitled to vote on the plan;

(3) consummation of a sale or exchange of all, or substantially all, of the property of the corporation other than in the usual and regular course of business, if the shareholder is entitled to vote on the sale or exchange, . . .

The MBCA makes clear, however, that shareholders may not dissent simply because they do not approve of the pending corporate action:

§ 13.02 (b), MBCA.

A shareholder entitled to dissent and obtain payment for his shares under this chapter may not challenge the corporate action creating his entitlement unless the action is unlawful or fraudulent with respect to the shareholder of the corporation.

Section 13.22 describes the procedure for delivering a written dissenters' notice to shareholders. Once the notice has been sent, the shareholder who wishes to dissent must:

§ 13.23 (a), MBCA.

. . . demand payment, certify whether he acquired beneficial ownership of the shares before the date required to be set forth in the dissenters' notice pursuant to section 13.22 (b) (3), and deposit his certificates in accordance with the terms of the notice.

(b) The shareholder who demands payment and deposits his shares under section (a) retains all other rights of a shareholder until these rights are cancelled or modified by the taking of the proposed corporate action.

Within 60 days after the date set for demanding payment and depositing share certificates, the dissenting shareholder is entitled to payment of an amount that the corporation estimates to be the fair value of the shares, plus accrued interest. Within 30 days after the corporation made or offered payment for shares, the dissenting shareholder may notify the corporation in writing of the shareholder's own estimate of the fair value of shares and amount of interest due, and demand payment of that estimate.

If the dissenting shareholders' demand for payment remains unsettled, MBCA's Subchapter C provides that ". . . the corporation shall commence a proceeding within 60 days after receiving the shareholder's payment demand and petition the court to determine the fair value of the shares and accrued interest."[1] Furthermore, "... The court may appoint one or more persons as appraisers to receive evidence and recommend decision on the question of fair value."[2]

BULK SALES ACT

The Bulk Sales Act, embodied in Article 6 of the Uniform Commercial Code, is an attempt to ensure that creditors of the target corporation are protected upon the sale of the target corporation's assets. The act applies to bulk sales of inventory outside the ordinary course of business. Prior to a sale, the target corporation must prepare a list of creditors and a description of the assets subject to sale. Ten days prior to the proposed closing date, a notice is sent to the creditors advising them of the details of the impending sale, thereby giving the creditors the opportunity to seek payment of obligations from the debtor, the target corporation. After completion of the transaction and assuming notice, the creditors will have no rights against the assets in the possession of the acquiring corporation. Failure to comply with the act may result in creditors reaching the assets in the acquiring company's possession.

Of course, compliance with the Bulk Sales act is not required where the acquiring corporation assumes all of the liabilities of the target corporation. If the acquiring corporation fails to make payment, creditors have rights against the acquiring corporation and its assets. In situations where the act applies there may be a waiver of compliance by the acquiring corporation, sometimes accompanied by the placement of a portion of the purchase price to cover possible claims of creditors.

TENDER OFFER

A "tender offer" is a method used to acquire shares of a target corporation from its public shareholders. Often a target corporation's stock is held by thousands of shareholders and it is impractical for an acquiring corporation to negotiate directly with each one for the purchase of shares. Therefore, the acquiring corporation initiates a tender offer whereby the target corporation's shareholders are invited through newspaper advertisements and direct communication to "tender" their shares to the acquiring corporation in accordance with the terms and conditions of sale established by the acquiring corporation. In exchange for their

1. § 13.30 (a), MBCA.
2. § 13.30 (d), MBCA.

shares, the shareholders receive cash or stock in the acquiring corporation, or a combination thereof. The offering of cash is called a "cash tender offer" whereas offering of shares is called a "registered exchange offer."

The tender offer is regulated by federal and state laws. The federal law is known as the Williams Act. It was enacted into law in 1968 as § 14 (d) and § 14 (e) of the Securities Exchange Act of 1934. Its thrust is to ensure full disclosure so that the shareholders can make an informed decision whether to accept or reject the tender offer. The Williams Act applies to friendly and hostile tender offers alike, and to tender offers made by an acquirer, whether or not related to the target corporation, or by the target corporation itself in a so-called self-tender. Regulations of the Securities and Exchange Commission apply to tender offers.

The most salient feature of the Williams Act is that it requires the acquiring corporation to file an information statement prior to the commencement of the tender offer. This information statement, Schedule 14D–1, must be filed with the Securities and Exchange Commission, the target corporation, and the appropriate stock exchange or National Association of Securities Dealers, when the acquiring corporation makes an offer for more than 5% of a class of registered stock.

Additional provisions in the Williams Act govern procedural aspects of the tender offer. One provision requires that tender offers be open for a minimum of 20 business days in order to give the target corporation's shareholders adequate time to evaluate their decision. Any increase in the offering price necessitates an additional 10-day period following notice of the price increase. Shareholders who have tendered their shares are permitted to withdraw these shares at times provided in the Act.

If fewer than all outstanding shares are sought by the acquiring corporation and if the target corporation's shareholders tender a greater number than sought within the first 10 days of the first publication date, the acquiring corporation must accept the deposited shares on a pro-rata basis. Regulations have extended the 10-day period to the entire tender offer period.

Any price increase must be offered to each and every shareholder who tendered shares before the increase in price was announced.

Upon the announcement of a tender offer, the target corporation's board of directors has a fiduciary duty to assess the merits of the tender offer and to make a response within the first 10 days of the publication date. There are four possible responses: acceptance, rejection, neutrality, or no position. Acceptance or rejection requires the filing of Schedule 14D–9 with the Securities and Exchange Commission and submission of the filing to the acquir-

Chapter Eleven

ing corporation. Rejection of the tender offer characterizes it as hostile; acceptance characterizes it as friendly.

Target corporations can take defensive measures against tender offers either in advance of any actual tender offer or during the time that the tender offer is proceeding. Prior measures include "poison pills," charter amendments (so-called shark-repellant provisions), and "golden parachutes," to name a few. During the tender offer, the target corporation may resort to litigation challenging the acquiring corporation's compliance with the Williams Act, may seek a "White Knight," sell the "crown jewels," or offer "greenmail," among others.

Poison-pill plans can be created in advance of an actual tender offer or in response to a specific tender offer. They exist in many varieties. In one form, the target corporation issues to its common shareholders a dividend of stock or rights to acquire stock in the target corporation, or in any acquiring corporation, under certain circumstances. The poison pill is exercisable upon the occurrence of certain events, including merger or other types of business combinations between the target corporation and acquiring corporation. As such, the pill is poison to the acquiring company, which will be left with target shareholders. Charter amendments may include staggering the terms of the board of directors and requiring a super majority vote of the shareholders for a merger or sale of assets of the target corporation. Golden parachutes are agreements with certain members of target management to pay to them significant sums of money in the event of a change in control of the target corporation.

A White Knight is a company that is friendly to the target corporation's management and agrees to make a competing bid that results in the acquisition of the target corporation's shares. A target corporation may sell a valuable piece of its business (the so-called crown jewels) to another party thereby depriving the acquiring corporation of an attractive asset. Greenmail is the purchase by the target corporation of a block of its stock, usually at a premium over market price, from the acquiring corporation; the inference is that the target is forced to do so or risk takeover.

TYPICAL SEQUENCE OF EVENTS

While each transaction is factually unique, there is a common method for accomplishing a privately negotiated business combination. Listed here are the usual steps—from the initial phases to the consummation—of a typical transaction.

1. The target corporation and the acquiring corporation determine their corporate development objectives in either a formal or informal strategic planning process.

2. The services of an investment banker are engaged to find a suitable party with which to combine, and the investment banker acts as a financial advisor throughout the process.

3. The purchase price structure and other significant terms and conditions of the transaction are negotiated and an agreement in principle is reached.

4. The agreement in principle is embodied in a letter of intent from the acquiring corporation to the target corporation, and the letter of intent may be either binding or nonbinding on the parties.

5. The due-diligence process, which is an investigation of the legal, financial, and business aspects of the target corporation, is conducted by the lawyer and paralegal, the accountant, and the management of the acquiring corporation.

6. Concurrently with the due-diligence process, the negotiation of the definitive acquisition agreement takes place along with the preparation of ancillary documentation to be delivered at the closing.

7. Certain conditions to closing are handled, such as the filing of the Hart-Scott-Rodino Pre-Merger Notification and Report Form, the registration of the acquiring corporation's stock, where appropriate, and the obtaining of consents of lessors, other parties to contracts, and governmental agencies, where the target corporation is regulated.

8. A preclosing, which takes place prior to the actual closing, gives the parties the opportunity to resolve any outstanding issues and to finalize the closing documents.

9. The closing is the mechanical exchange of documents and consideration. At the closing the documents that transfer ownership to the stock or assets of the target corporation are executed and delivered, and the consideration is usually wire transferred from the acquiring corporation to the target corporation or its shareholders.

10. Following the closing, certain matters are handled, such as the filing of articles of merger with the appropriate secretaries of state; the recording of deeds and mortgages; and the assembling of the closing binders which contain all of the documents delivered at the closing.

SIGNIFICANCE OF THE CONTRACT

The stock or asset purchase agreement, the acquisition agreement, and the merger agreement set forth the specific terms of a transaction between the parties. Each transaction is privately negotiated between the parties. The structure of the document is dictated by tradition and the document contains types of provisions that are commonly used, except that, in the case of the merger, certain provisions are required by statute.

PARALEGAL'S ROLE

Paralegals on both sides of the transaction play a very significant role in the combination process, including the performance of due diligence, preparation of closing documents, attendance at closings, and handling postclosing matters.

The target corporation's paralegal performs due diligence by investigating and ensuring the veracity of the client's representations and warranties and by providing the acquiring corporation with contracts and other corporate and legal documents that pertain to the target corporation. The preparation of closing documents includes deeds, bills of sale, assignments of contracts and corporate resolutions in an asset sale, assignments of share certificates in a stock transaction, articles of merger and corporate resolutions in a merger transaction, and, in all transactions, legal opinions and various certificates.

The acquiring corporation's paralegal due diligence consists of investigating the client's representations and warranties to be set forth in the agreement and certificates, and reviewing documents provided by the target corporation. In addition, the paralegal assists in the preparation of stock registration documents and financing documents, where appropriate.

One party's paralegal prepares and the other party's paralegal reviews a "Closing Memorandum," which is a list of all documents to be delivered at the closing by all parties, together with a notation of the name of the person who is responsible for preparation. Each party's paralegal reviews the other party's closing documents and indicates final approval. Where required, each paralegal prepares a Hart-Scott-Rodino Pre-Merger Notification and Report Form.

At the closing, each paralegal is in charge of the client's documents. The documents may already have been signed or the paralegal may obtain the signatures in person at the closing. An appropriate number of copies of each document should be placed in a folder clearly marked to indicate the title of the document. The acquiring company's documents are lined up on one side of the table, and the target company's documents are lined up on the other, all in order of appearance in the Closing Memorandum. When all documents have been executed, the acquiring corporation telephones its bank and directs the consideration to be transferred to the target company's bank account and, in some instances, to an escrow agent's account. Upon confirmation of receipt from the target corporation's bank, the transaction is consummated and each party receives a complete set of executed documents.

After the closing, each paralegal prepares closing binders. Paralegals will also be responsible for any necessary filing of documents with government officials.

CHAPTER TWELVE

Computers and C
Paralegals

Use of computers by attorneys
Paralegals in law firms or corporate lega.
access to different types of computers, so it is use..
understanding of the capabilities of some computer syst.

COMPUTER HARDWARE

Computers are classified into three general categories—mainframe computers, minicomputers, and microcomputers.

Mainframe Computers

Large computers that process data at millions of instructions per second are called mainframe computers. A large corporation or law firm often uses a mainframe computer to keep track of internal financial affairs. Multiple users access data on the mainframe via terminals.

Operating a mainframe computer requires the purchase of custom designed software. Designing software for an individual company is an expensive and time-consuming process. Unless the corporation has an in-house staff of programmers responsible for designing legal systems, the expense of hiring computer consultants may make it difficult to utilize the mainframe for legal practice.

Large law firms and corporations often need the storage capacity, speed, and multi-user capability of a mainframe computer. In order to avoid the high cost of developing legal software for the mainframe, many firms use specially configured microcomputers designed to communicate with the mainframe computer. This configuration gives a legal professional access to the centralized general information stored on the mainframe computer and lets him or her select programs from the large number of business and legal software programs available for microcomputers.

Minicomputers

Minicomputers process data at a slower rate and are generally less powerful than mainframes. Multiple users access data via dedicated minicomputer terminals. For many years, law firms have used minicomputers for their financial management, and many software vendors have designed programs geared to the needs of law firm accounting systems.

If a law firm decides to use the minicomputer for substantive legal practice, the customized software may be designed in-house or by an outside consultant or software vendor. Despite the high cost of software development, a large law firm might select a minicomputer in order to take advantage of its multi-user capability. The law firm may use a terminal dedicated to a particular minicomputer or may opt to configure microcomputers to emulate minicomputer terminals.

Microcomputers

Microcomputers, although generally less powerful than either the mainframe or minicomputer, are attractive to corporate legal departments and law firms for many reasons. These include:

Ready access to a large market of predesigned, relatively inexpensive software. Due to the large number of installed microcomputers in business, it is cost-effective for software manufacturers to develop programs for the general public. Microcomputer programs are generally less expensive and more "user friendly" than the customized programs designed for mainframe or minicomputers.

Law firms can select from a wide variety of general business programs as well as from a growing number of programs designed especially for the legal market. If a law firm cannot find a software program suited to its unique needs, it is fairly easy to customize a general business program. A law firm may customize the program in-house or may hire outside consultants to do the job. Regardless of the approach, the cost in terms of hardware and software is much less for a microcomputer than for a mainframe or minicomputer.

Connectivity of personal computers. Initially, the microcomputer was designed as a standalone computer, hence the nickname personal computer or PC. Corporations and law firms (as well as other businesses) have recognized the need to share information among various individuals. Local Area Networks (LANs) of computers enable individuals who are physically located in the same general area of the firm to share computerized data. Wide Area Networks (WANs) of computers enable individuals in different cities or states to share computerized information between many different types of computers.

Multi-purpose machines. The dedicated terminals attached to mainframe or minicomputers are usually called "dumb terminals," meaning they cannot do anything without instructions from the main computer. Microcomputers are very flexible; they can run many different types of software designed specifically for personal computers, and they can also be configured to communicate and share data with mainframe or minicomputers. Many firms that need to manage large amounts of data utilize the power and speed of a mini or mainframe computer but use microcomputers rather than dumb terminals to access the data. Remote computers not operated by the law firm are also accessible via telecommunications and/or electronic bulletin boards. Some examples of remote information sources accessible by a properly configured microcomputer include Lexis, Nexis, Westlaw, Dow Jones News/Retrieval, and Dialog. Many of these services are particularly valuable to corporate legal professionals.

Cost. While the cost of hardware and software for microcomputer may seem initially expensive, it is relatively inexpensive compared with that of a mini or mainframe system.

MICROCOMPUTER SOFTWARE

Word Processing

Word processing is the most commonly used type of microcomputer software. Many lawyers and paralegals have or soon will have computers on their desks. It is much more efficient to manage and create words directly on a computer than on a yellow legal pad. It soon will be common practice for the attorney or paralegal to draft a document on a microcomputer and have the secretary perform final document formatting on his or her computer.

If the firm uses a local or wide area network, word processing systems enable legal professionals to access a centralized storehouse of documents. The addition of a program designed to search and retrieve prior work products greatly reduces redundant drafting of documents by different personnel.

An added advantage of a word processing system is the ability to set up a document assembly system for frequently used forms, paragraphs, or clauses. Document assembly systems can be purchased as supplementary packages for word processors, or they can be designed using a word processor built in macro language.

Spreadsheets

A spreadsheet is a computerized version of a ledger book. Once the data and calculation instructions are entered, the program automatically performs the calculations and produces the results. If one number changes, all numbers linked to that value automatically change. Spreadsheets can also be designed to plot out various scenarios, often referred to as "what if" scenarios. In finance and investment industries, spreadsheets are often used to analyze investment portfolios by keeping track of dividends and of increases or decreases in the value of investment. The spreadsheet program gives users the tools to quickly analyze masses of complex data quickly and accurately.

Data Bases

Data bases have been a major factor in the computerization of our society. The data base program enables businesses to manage quantities of data unmanageable by manual methods.

A data base is a collection of information organized in a manner that makes the data accessible. There are two broad categories of data base—structured and unstructured. A computerized telephone book is an example of a structured data base; everything is organized into categories—last name, address, phone number. Westlaw, while allowing the user access to a structured system of searching through the key number system, is one example of an unstructured data base. To obtain a list of citations for a particular legal issue, you do not search categories; rather, you search the entire text of case decisions for particular words or concepts. Since unstructured data bases store full text and not abstracts of data (the full case decision, the full text of an SEC filing, etc.), large unstructured data bases such as Westlaw require the power and processing capacity of a mainframe computer. Using telecommunications, a paralegal with a properly configured microcomputer or terminal has access to a large number of mainframe data bases.

A structured data base usually (depending upon the volume of information) requires less processing power and less storage capacity than an unstructured data base. In some firms, paralegals use structured data bases on a microcomputer in order to track prior work, outside counsel, fee payments for different cases, conflict of interest, incorporation process, foreign corporations, and bankruptcy filings.

Structured data bases are either flat file or relational. A flat file data base consists of a single table or chart. A flat file is very easy to set up and operate, and many firms allow a paralegal to set up his or her own simple data bases in a flat file system. A flat file data base has two major disadvantages—data redundancy and wasted disk space. Since the entire file consists of one charge, any category that requires multiple entries in a field creates a problem. Either the user has to design the chart with a category for every possible entry, or the user must reenter basic information over and over again.

For example, assume a paralegal has designed a flat file data base to track locations where a corporation is registered to do business as a foreign corporation. The paralegal has the option of designing categories such as FOREIGN STATE 1, FOREIGN STATE 2, FOREIGN STATE 3, but this presents two major problems. (1) If many corporations only register in two foreign states and the paralegal has set up five such categories, disk space is wasted for the unused categories. (2) If the paralegal encounters a corporation that is registered in six foreign states, there is no place to record the sixth foreign state unless the paralegal creates a whole new entry, including the redundant data entry of corporation name, address, etc.

Whenever a field requires a variable number of multiple entries, it is recommended that the paralegal use a relational data base rather than a flat file. In a relational data base system, data is stored in multiple charts. Data for one entity (a corporation, an individual, an outside counsel) is linked together or "related" by a unique identifier assigned to the entity. A corporate identification number, a tax identification number, or an individual's Social Security number are good examples of a unique value that keeps track of all data relevant to that entity. A corporation name or an individual's name could not serve as a unique identifier since there is a possibility either may be duplicated.

Relational data bases are more complicated than flat file systems. Often the paralegal does not have the expertise nor the time to develop a complex relational data base. When a complex relational data base is required, the actual design and management is often handled by consultants. A paralegal may be appointed project manager to assure that the design suits the needs of the law practice.

Whatever the application, data bases enable a legal professional to quickly and easily access information that would be extremely difficult to locate manually. A data base also allows the user to organize the information by any category stored in the data base. A request such as SHOW ALL CORPORATIONS INCORPORATED BETWEEN 1980 AND 1985 SORTED BY DATE OF INCORPORATION is a commonplace request to a data base system.

Graphics

Often a corporate legal professional needs to keep track of corporations and subsidiaries. Graphics packages enable a user to create charts and diagrams that illustrate complex corporate relationships more clearly than do verbal descriptions. Once a chart or diagram is created, it can be inserted into a document stored in a word processor.

Communications

Communications programs enable the microcomputer user to communicate with a wide variety of other computers. An inexpensive microcomputer properly equipped for communications can access a whole world of information. A large corporation with many different offices can effectively coordinate remote personnel through electronic mail systems. Electronic mail enables users to send and receive information from another computer instantaneously, thus eliminating the need for repeated attempts to reach people by telephone (telephone tag) and for paper-based memos.

All corporate legal departments and corporate law firms will soon be forced to utilize communications systems. The SEC has set 1992 as the date for mandatory electronic filing of corporate filings via EDGAR: Electronic Data Gathering, Analysis and Retrieval System. The SEC has been running the pilot program since September 1984. Since then, more than 5,000 entities have completed more than 80,000 electronic filings. In 1989 the SEC began to increase the capability of EDGAR to enable the system to receive, analyze, and disseminate the approximately twelve million pages of disclosure documents the SEC receives annually. In 1991 certain corporations, investment management companies, and public utilities will be required to file on EDGAR. By 1995, EDGAR will be mandatory for all filings.[1] Understanding and interacting with EDGAR will become part of a corporate legal professional's job description.

A corporate legal professional will have to be more than just "computer literate" once EDGAR is mandatory. The legal professional will have to know how to convert standard word processing documents into the American Standard Code for the Interchange of Information (ASCH) so EDGAR can read the documents. The SEC requires that certain portions of the document be "tagged" or highlighted to facilitate SEC review of the filing documents.

EDGAR will also revolutionize corporate research. EDGAR filings will create a centralized storehouse of computerized information, available to anyone with the proper equipment and skills. The legal professional will be able to search the data base of

---

1. D. M. Osborne. "Getting to know EDGAR," *American Lawyer Media, L.P.* (November 1989):5.

corporate filings for models of corporate documents, shareholder rights plans, stock swaps, bond offerings, and similar items.

ROLE OF THE PARALEGAL

Even the most conservative firms are beginning to realize the value of computers in practicing law. In some firms computers have practically replaced the traditional yellow legal pad. The legal professional can no longer afford to be computer illiterate.

Basic Knowledge

Paralegals should be comfortable with the fundamental features of word processing such as correct paragraph structure, centering, underlining, boldfacing, line spacing, margin setting, and block manipulations. Many law firms and corporate legal departments use WordPerfect, but there are many competitive products on the market. A paralegal should be comfortable with at least one major product but should know enough about word processing in general that learning another program is fairly easy. Also, paralegals should understand the basic structure of a spreadsheet, how to interpret, edit, and update, and how to set up basic formulas and functions. Lotus 1-2-3 and Excel are popular spreadsheet programs used in law firms. Last, paralegals should understand the basic concepts of structured data bases, how to edit data, retrieve and sort specific information, and generate reports sorted by various criteria. Exposure to remote data bases, such as Westlaw, is a plus.

Beyond the Basics

This is an exciting time for a paralegal with computer skills who is interested in legal computer management. Law firms planning to automate the practice of law need a person they can trust who is knowledgeable about computers and about law. The paralegal with computer skills is the person in the law firm most suited to act as the liaison between programmers, consultants, systems analysts, and the attorneys.

A paralegal interested in the position of electronic information manager should have a basic understanding of the capabilities of different software programs, computer hardware, computer operating systems, systems analysis, data base design, networks, and communications. The paralegal does not have to know all the technical details about computers but should know enough to ascertain that the firm is selecting the proper computer tools for the practice of law. Future developments in expert systems and artificial intelligence programs assure that law firms will require the services of computer literate legal professionals for many years to come.

For further reading suggestions, see Appendix III in this text.

Revised Model Business Corporation Act of 1984

In 1984 the Revised Model Business Corporation Act was finally adopted by the Committee on Corporate Laws of the Section of Corporation, Banking and Business Law of the American Bar Association. The revised act completely reorganized and renumbered all of the sections of the Model Act. Many of the amendments to the Model Business Corporation Act passed during the twenty years preceding the adoption of the revised act are a basis for many of the provisions in the revised act. At the same time there are some important differences between the Revised Model Business Corporation Act and its predecessor.

CHAPTER 3. PURPOSES AND POWERS

CHAPTER 4. NAME

CHAPTER 5. OFFICE AND AGENT

CHAPTER 6. SHARES AND DISTRIBUTIONS

CHAPTER 7. SHAREHOLDERS

CHAPTER 1. GENERAL PROVISIONS

Subchapter A. Short Title and Reservation of Power

§1.01. Short Title.—This Act shall be known and may be cited as the "[name of state] Business Corporation Act."

§1.02. Reservation of Power To Amend or Repeal.—The [name of state legislature] has power to amend or repeal all or part of this Act at any time and all domestic and foreign corporations subject to this Act are governed by the amendment or repeal.

Subchapter B. Filing Documents

§1.20. Filing Requirements.—
(a) A document must satisfy the requirements of this section, and of any other section that adds to or varies these requirements, to be entitled to filing by the secretary of state.
(b) This Act must require or permit filing the document in the office of the secretary of state.
(c) The document must contain the information required by this Act. It may contain other information as well.
(d) The document must be typewritten or printed.
(e) The document must be in the English language. A corporation name need not be in English if written in English letters or Arabic or Roman numerals, and the

certificate of existence required of foreign corporations need not be in English if accompanied by a reasonably authenticated English translation.

(f) The document must be executed:

(1) by the chairman of the board of directors of a domestic or foreign corporation, by its president, or by another of its officers;

(2) if directors have not been selected or the corporation has not been formed, by an incorporator; or

(3) if the corporation is in the hands of a receiver, trustee, or other court-appointed fiduciary, by that fiduciary.

(g) The person executing the document shall sign it and state beneath or opposite his signature his name and the capacity in which he signs. The document may but need not contain: (1) the corporate seal, (2) an attestation by the secretary or an assistant secretary, (3) an acknowledgment, verification, or proof.

(h) If the secretary of state has prescribed a mandatory form for the document under section 1.21, the document must be in or on the prescribed form.

(i) The document must be delivered to the office of the secretary of state for filing and must be accompanied by one exact or conformed copy (except as provided in sections 5.03 and 15.09), the correct filing fee, and any franchise tax, license fee, or penalty required by this Act or other law.

§1.21. Forms.—

(a) The secretary of state may prescribe and furnish on request forms for: (1) an application for a certificate of existence, (2) a foreign corporation's application for a certificate of authority to transact business in this state, (3) a foreign corporation's application for a certificate of withdrawal, and (4) the annual report. If the secretary of state so requires, use of these forms is mandatory.

(b) The secretary of state may prescribe and furnish on request forms for other documents required or permitted to be filed by this Act but their use is not mandatory.

§1.22. Filing, Service, and Copying Fees.—

(a) The secretary of state shall collect the following fees when the documents described in this subsection are delivered to him for filing:

Document	Fee
(1) Articles of incorporation	$ _____
(2) Application for use of indistinguishable name	$ _____
(3) Application for reserved name	$ _____
(4) Notice of transfer of reserved name	$ _____
(5) Application for registered name	$ _____
(6) Application for renewal of registered name	$ _____
(7) Corporation's statement of change of registered agent or registered office or both	$ _____
(8) Agent's statement of change of registered office for each affected corporation	$ _____
not to exceed a total of	$ _____
(9) Agent's statement of resignation	No fee
(10) Amendment of articles of incorporation	$ _____
(11) Restatement of articles of incorporation with amendment of articles	$ _____
(12) Articles of merger or share exchange	$ _____
(13) Articles of dissolution	$ _____
(14) Articles of revocation of dissolution	$ _____
(15) Certificate of administrative dissolution	No fee
(16) Application for reinstatement following administrative dissolution	$ _____

(17) Certificate of reinstatement	No fee
(18) Certificate of judicial dissolution	No fee
(19) Application for certificate of authority	$ _____
(20) Application for amended certificate of authority	$ _____
(21) Application for certificate of withdrawal	$ _____
(22) Certificate of revocation of authority to transact business	No fee
(23) Annual report	$ _____
(24) Articles of correction	$ _____
(25) Application for certificate of existence or authorization	$ _____
(26) Any other document required or permitted to be filed by this Act.	$ _____

(b) The secretary of state shall collect a fee of $ _____ each time process is served on him under this Act. The party to a proceeding causing service of process is entitled to recover this fee as costs if he prevails in the proceeding.

(c) The secretary of state shall collect the following fees for copying and certifying the copy of any filed document relating to a domestic or foreign corporation:

(1) $ _____ a page for copying; and
(2) $ _____ for the certificate.

§1.23. Effective Time and Date of Document.—

(a) Except as provided in subsection (b) and section 1.24.(c), a document accepted for filing is effective:

(1) at the time of filing on the date it is filed, as evidenced by the secretary of state's date and time endorsement on the original document; or
(2) at the time specified in the document as its effective time on the date it is filed.

(b) A document may specify a delayed effective time and date, and if it does so the document becomes effective at the time and date specified. If a delayed effective date but no time is specified, the document is effective at the close of business on that date. A delayed effective date for a document may not be later than the 90th day after the date it is filed.

§1.24. Correcting Filed Document.—

(a) A domestic or foreign corporation may correct a document filed by the secretary of state if the document (1) contains an incorrect statement or (2) was defectively executed, attested, sealed, verified, or acknowledged.

(b) A document is corrected:

(1) by preparing articles of correction that (i) describe the document (including its filing date) or attach a copy of it to the articles, (ii) specify the incorrect statement and the reason it is incorrect or the manner in which the execution was defective, and (iii) correct the incorrect statement or defective execution; and
(2) by delivering the articles to the secretary of state for filing.

(c) Articles of correction are effective on the effective date of the document they correct except as to persons relying on the uncorrected document and adversely affected by the correction. As to those persons, articles of correction are effective when filed.

§1.25. Filing Duty of Secretary of State.—
(a) If a document delivered to the office of the secretary of state for filing satisfies the requirements of section 1.20, the secretary of state shall file it.
(b) The secretary of state files a document by stamping or otherwise endorsing "Filed," together with his name and official title and the date and time of receipt, on both the original and the document copy and on the receipt for the filing fee. After filing a document, except as provided in sections 5.03 and 15.10, the secretary of state shall deliver the document copy, with the filing fee receipt (or acknowledgment of receipt if no fee is required) attached, to the domestic or foreign corporation or its representative.
(c) If the secretary of state refuses to file a document, he shall return it to the domestic or foreign corporation or its representative within five days after the document was delivered, together with a brief, written explanation of the reason for his refusal.
(d) The secretary of state's duty to file documents under this section is ministerial. His filing or refusing to file a document does not:

   (1) affect the validity or invalidity of the document in whole or part;
   (2) relate to the correctness or incorrectness of information contained in the document;
   (3) create a presumption that the document is valid or invalid or that information contained in the document is correct or incorrect.

§1.26. Appeal from Secretary of State's Refusal To File Document.—
(a) If the secretary of state refuses to file a document delivered to his office for filing, the domestic or foreign corporation may appeal the refusal within 30 days after the return of the document to the [name or describe] court [of the country where the corporation's principal office (or, if none in this state, its registered office) is or will be located] [of _____county]. The appeal is commenced by petitioning the court to compel filing the document and by attaching to the petition the document and the secretary of state's explanation of his refusal to file.
(b) The court may summarily order the secretary of state to file the document or take other action the court considers appropriate.
(c) The court's final decision may be appealed as in other civil proceedings.

§1.27. Evidentiary Effect of Copy of Filed Document.—A certificate attached to a copy of a document filed by the secretary of state, bearing his signature (which may be in facsimile) and the seal of this state, is conclusive evidence that the original document is on file with the secretary of state.

§1.28. Certificate of Existence.—
(a) Anyone may apply to the secretary of state to furnish a certificate of existence for a domestic corporation or a certificate of authorization for a foreign corporation.
(b) A certificate of existence or authorization sets forth:

   (1) The domestic corporation's corporate name or the foreign corporation's corporate name used in this state;
   (2) that (i) the domestic corporation is duly incorporated under the law of this state, the date of its incorporation, and the period of its duration if less than perpetual; or (ii) that the foreign corporation is authorized to transact business in this state;
   (3) that all fees, taxes, and penalties owed to this state have been paid, if (i) payment is reflected in the records of the secretary of state and (ii) non-payment affects the existence or authorization of the domestic or foreign corporation;
   (4) that its most recent annual report required by section 16.22 has been delivered to the secretary of state;
   (5) that articles of dissolution have not been filed; and

(6) other facts of record in the office of the secretary of state that may be requested by the applicant.

(c) Subject to any qualification stated in the certificate, a certificate of existence or authorization issued by the secretary of state may be relied upon as conclusive evidence that the domestic or foreign corporation is in existence or is authorized to transact business in this state.

§1.29. Penalty for Signing False Document.—

(a) A person commits an offense if he signs a document he knows is false in any material respect with intent that the document be delivered to the secretary of state for filing.

(b) An offense under this section is a [_____] misdemeanor [punishable by a fine of not to exceed $ _____].

Subchapter C. Secretary of State

§1.30. Powers.—The secretary of state has the power reasonably necessary to perform the duties required of him by this Act.

Subchapter D. Definitions

§1.40. Act Definitions.—In this Act:

(1) "Articles of incorporation" include amended and restated articles of incorporation and articles of merger.

(2) "Authorized shares" means the shares of all classes a domestic or foreign corporation is authorized to issue.

(3) "Conspicuous" means so written that a reasonable person against whom the writing is to operate should have noticed it. For example, printing in italics or boldface or contrasting color, or typing in capitals or underlined, is conspicuous.

(4) "Corporation" or "domestic corporation" means a corporation for profit, which is not a foreign corporation, incorporated under or subject to the provisions of this Act.

(5) "Deliver" includes mail.

(6) "Distribution" means a direct or indirect transfer of money or other property (except its own shares) or incurrence of indebtedness by a corporation to or for the benefit of its shareholders in respect of any of its shares. A distribution may be in the form of a declaration or payment of a dividend; a purchase, redemption, or other acquisition of shares; a distribution of indebtedness; or otherwise.

(7) "Effective date of notice" is defined in section 1.41.

(8) "Employee" includes an officer but not a director. A director may accept duties that make him also an employee.

(9) "Entity" includes corporation and foreign corporation; not-for-profit corporation; profit and not-for-profit unincorporated association; business trust, estate, partnership, trust, and two or more persons having a joint or common economic interest; and state, United States, and foreign government.

(10) "Foreign corporation" means a corporation for profit incorporated under a law other than the law of this state.

(11) "Governmental subdivision" includes authority, county, district, and municipality.

(12) "Includes" denotes a partial definition.

(13) "Individual" includes the estate of an incompetent or deceased individual.

(14) "Means" denotes an exhaustive definition.

(15) "Notice" is defined in section 1.41.

(16) "Person" includes individual and entity.

(17) "Principal office" means the office (in or out of this state) so designated in the annual report where the principal executive offices of a domestic or foreign corporation are located.

(18) "Proceeding" includes civil suit and criminal, administrative, and investigatory action.

(19) "Record date" means the date established under chapter 6 or 7 on which a corporation determines the identity of its shareholders for purposes of this Act.

(20) "Secretary" means the corporate officer to whom the board of directors has delegated responsibility under section 8.40(c) for custody of the minutes of the meetings of the board of directors and of the shareholders and for authenticating records of the corporation.

(21) "Share" means the unit into which the proprietary interests in a corporation are divided.

(22) "Shareholder" means the person in whose name shares are registered in the records of a corporation or the beneficial owner of shares to the extent of the rights granted by a nominee certificate on file with a corporation.

(23) "State," when referring to a part of the United States, includes a state and commonwealth (and their agencies and governmental subdivisions) and a territory and insular possession (and their agencies and governmental subdivisions) of the United States.

(24) "Subscriber" means a person who subscribes for shares in a corporation, whether before or after incorporation.

(25) "United States" includes district, authority, bureau, commission, department, and any other agency of the United States.

(26) "Voting group" means all shares of one or more classes or series that under the articles of incorporation or this Act are entitled to vote and be counted together collectively on a matter at a meeting of shareholders. All shares entitled by the articles of incorporation or this Act to vote generally on the matter are for that purpose a single voting group.

§1.41. Notice.—

(a) Notice under this Act must be in writing unless oral notice is reasonable under the circumstances.

(b) Notice may be communicated in person; by telephone, telegraph, teletype, or other form of wire or wireless communication; or by mail or private carrier. If these forms of personal notice are impracticable, notice may be communicated by a newspaper of general circulation in the area where published; or by radio, television, or other form of public broadcast communication.

(c) Written notice by a domestic or foreign corporation to its shareholder, if in a comprehensible form, is effective when mailed, if mailed postpaid and correctly addressed to the shareholder's address shown in the corporation's current record of shareholders.

(d) Written notice to a domestic or foreign corporation (authorized to transact business in this state) may be addressed to its registered agent at its registered office or to the corporation or its secretary at its principal office shown in its most recent annual report or, in the case of a foreign corporation that has not yet delivered an annual report, in its application for a certificate of authority.

(e) Except as provided in subsections (c) and (d), written notice, if in a comprehensible form, is effective at the earliest of the following:

    (1) when received;
    (2) five days after its deposit in the United States Mail, as evidenced by the postmark, if mailed postpaid and correctly addressed;
    (3) on the date shown on the return receipt, if sent by registered or certified mail, return receipt requested, and the receipt is signed by or on behalf of the addressee.

(f) Oral notice is effective when communicated if communicated in a comprehensible manner.

(g) If this Act prescribes notice requirements for particular circumstances, those requirements govern. If articles of incorporation or bylaws prescribe notice requirements, not inconsistent with this section or other provisions of this Act, those requirements govern.

§1.42. Number of Shareholders.—
(a) For purpose of this Act, the following identified as a shareholder in a corporation's current record of shareholders constitutes one shareholder:

(1) three or fewer coowners;
(2) a corporation, partnership, trust, estate, or other entity;
(3) the trustees, guardians, custodians, or other fiduciaries of a single trust, estate, or account.

(b) For purposes of this Act, shareholdings registered in substantially similar names constitute one shareholder if it is reasonable to believe that the names represent the same person.

CHAPTER 2. INCORPORATION

§2.01. Incorporators.—One or more persons may act as the incorporator or incorporators of a corporation by delivering articles of incorporation to the secretary of state for filing.

§2.02. Articles of Incorporation.—
(a) The articles of incorporation must set forth:

(1) a corporate name for the corporation that satisfies the requirements of section 4.01;
(2) the number of shares the corporation is authorized to issue;
(3) the street address of the corporation's initial registered office and the name of its initial registered agent at that office; and
(4) the name and address of each incorporator.

(b) The articles of incorporation may set forth:

(1) the names and addresses of the individuals who are to serve as the initial directors;
(2) provisions not inconsistent with law regarding:
(i) the purpose or purposes for which the corporation is organized;
(ii) managing the business and regulating the affairs of the corporation;
(iii) defining, limiting, and regulating the powers of the corporation, its board of directors, and shareholders;
(iv) a par value for authorized shares or classes of shares;
(v) the imposition of personal liability on shareholders for the debts of the corporation to a specified extent and upon specified conditions; and
(3) any provision that under this Act is required or permitted to be set forth in the bylaws.

(c) The articles of incorporation need not set forth any of the corporate powers enumerated in this Act.

§2.03. Incorporation.—
(a) Unless a delayed effective date is specified, the corporate existence begins when the articles of incorporation are filed.
(b) The secretary of state's filing of the articles of incorporation is conclusive proof that the incorporators satisfied all conditions precedent to incorporation except in a proceeding by the state to cancel or revoke the incorporation or involuntarily dissolve the corporation.

§2.04. Liability for Preincorporation Transactions.—All persons purporting to act as or on behalf of a corporation, knowing there was no incorporation under this Act, are jointly and severally liable for all liabilities created while so acting.

§2.05. Organization of Corporation.—

(a) After incorporation:

(1) if initial directors are named in the articles of incorporation, the initial directors shall hold an organizational meeting, at the call of a majority of the directors, to complete the organization of the corporation by appointing officers, adopting bylaws, and carrying on any other business brought before the meeting;

(2) if initial directors are not named in the articles, the incorporator or incorporators shall hold an organizational meeting at the call of a majority of the incorporators:

(i) to elect directors and complete the organization of the corporation; or

(ii) to elect a board of directors who shall complete the organization of the corporation.

(b) Action required or permitted by this Act to be taken by incorporators at an organizational meeting may be taken without a meeting if the action taken is evidenced by one or more written consents describing the action taken and signed by each incorporator.

(c) An organizational meeting may be held in or out of this state.

§2.06. Bylaws.—

(a) The incorporators or board of directors of a corporation shall adopt initial bylaws for the corporation.

(b) The bylaws of a corporation may contain any provision for managing the business and regulating the affairs of the corporation that is not inconsistent with law or the articles of incorporation.

§2.07. Emergency Bylaws.—

(a) Unless the articles of incorporation provide otherwise, the board of directors of a corporation may adopt bylaws to be effective only in an emergency defined in subsection (d). The emergency bylaws, which are subject to amendment or repeal by the shareholders, may make all provisions necessary for managing the corporation during the emergency, including:

(1) procedures for calling a meeting of the board of directors;

(2) quorum requirements for the meeting; and

(3) designation of additional or substitute directors.

(b) All provisions of the regular bylaws consistent with the emergency bylaws remain effective during the emergency. The emergency bylaws are not effective after the emergency ends.

(c) Corporate action taken in good faith in accordance with the emergency bylaws:

(1) binds the corporation; and

(2) may not be used to impose liability on a corporate director, officer, employee, or agent.

(d) An emergency exists for purposes of this section of a quorum of the corporation's directors cannot readily be assembled because of some catastrophic event.

CHAPTER 3. PURPOSES AND POWERS

§3.01. Purposes.—
(a) Every corporation incorporated under this Act has the purpose of engaging in any lawful business unless a more limited purpose is set forth in the articles of incorporation.
(b) A corporation engaging in a business that is subject to regulation under another statute of this state may incorporate under this Act only if permitted by, and subject to all limitations of, the other statute.

§3.02. General Powers.—Unless its articles of incorporation provide otherwise, every corporation has perpetual duration and succession in its corporate name and has the same powers as an individual to do all things necessary or convenient to carry out its business and affairs, including without limitation power:

(1) to sue and be sued, complain and defend in its corporate name;
(2) to have a corporate seal, which may be altered at will, and to use it, or a facsimile of it, by impressing or affixing it or in any other manner reproducing it;
(3) to make and amend bylaws, not inconsistent with its articles of incorporation or with the laws of this state, for managing the business and regulating the affairs of the corporation;
(4) to purchase, receive, lease, or otherwise acquire, and own, hold, improve, use, and otherwise deal with, real or personal property, or any legal or equitable interest in property, wherever located;
(5) to sell, convey, mortgage, pledge, lease, exchange, and otherwise dispose of all or any part of its property;
(6) to purchase, receive, subscribe for, or otherwise acquire; own, hold, vote, use, sell, mortgage, lend, pledge, or otherwise dispose of; and deal in and with shares or other interests in, or obligations of, any other entity;
(7) to make contracts and guarantees incur liabilities, borrow money, issue its notes, bonds, and other obligations (which may be convertible into or include the option to purchase other securities of the corporation), and secure any of its obligations by mortgage or pledge of any of its property, franchises, or income;
(8) to lend money, invest and reinvest its funds, and receive and hold real and personal property as security for repayment;
(9) to be a promoter, partner, member, associate, or manager of any partnership, joint venture, trust, or other entity;
(10) to conduct its business, locate offices, and exercise the powers granted by this Act within or without this state;
(11) to elect directors and appoint officers, employees, and agents of the corporation, define their duties, fix their compensation, and lend them money and credit;
(12) to pay pensions and establish pension plans, pension trusts, profit sharing plans, share bonus plans, share option plans, and benefit or incentive plans for any or all of its current or former directors, officers, employees, and agents;
(13) to make donations for the public welfare or for charitable, scientific, or educational purposes;
(14) to transact any lawful business that will aid governmental policy;
(15) to make payments or donations, or do any other act, not inconsistent with law, that furthers the business and affairs of the corporation.

§3.03. Emergency Powers.—
(a) In anticipation of or during an emergency defined in subsection (d), the board of directors of a corporation may:

(1) modify lines of succession to accommodate the incapacity of any director, officer, employee, or agent; and

(2) relocate the principal office, designate alternative principal offices or regional offices, or authorize the officers to do so.

(b) During an emergency defined in subsection (d), unless emergency bylaws provide otherwise:

(1) notice of a meeting of the board of directors need be given only to those directors whom it is practicable to reach and may be given in any practicable manner, including by publication and radio; and
(2) one or more officers of the corporation present at a meeting of the board of directors may be deemed to be directors for the meeting, in order of rank and within the same rank in order of seniority, as necessary to achieve a quorum.

(c) Corporate action taken in good faith during an emergency under this section to further the ordinary business affairs of the corporation:

(1) binds the corporation; and
(2) may not be used to impose liability on a corporate director, officer, employee, or agent.

(d) An emergency exists for purposes of this section if a quorum of the corporation's directors cannot readily be assembled because of some catastrophic event.

§3.04. Ultra Vires.—
(a) Except as provided in subsection (b), the validity of corporate action may not be challenged on the ground that the corporation lacks or lacked power to act.
(b) A corporation's power to act may be challenged:

(1) in a proceeding by a shareholder against the corporation to enjoin the act;
(2) in a proceeding by the corporation, directly, derivatively, or through a receiver, trustee, or other legal representative, against an incumbent or former director, officer, employee, or agent of the corporation; or
(3) in a proceeding by the Attorney General under section 14.30.

(c) In a shareholder's proceeding under subsection (b)(1) to enjoin an unauthorized corporate act, the court may enjoin or set aside the act, if equitable and if all affected persons are parties to the proceeding, and may award damages for loss (other than anticipated profits) suffered by the corporation or another party because of enjoining the unauthorized act.

CHAPTER 4. NAME

§4.01. Corporate Name.—
(a) A corporate name:

(1) must contain the word "corporation," "incorporated," "company," or "limited," or the abbreviation "corp.," "inc.," "co.," or "ltd.," or words or abbreviations of like import in another language; and
(2) may not contain language stating or implying that the corporation is organized for a purpose other than that permitted by section 3.01 and its articles of incorporation.

(b) Except as authorized by subsections (c) and (d), a corporate name must be distinguishable upon the records of the secretary of state from:

(1) the corporate name of a corporation incorporated or authorized to transact business in this state;

(2) a corporate name reserved or registered under section 4.02 or 4.03;
(3) the fictitious name adopted by a foreign corporation authorized to transact business in this state because its real name is unavailable; and
(4) the corporate name of a not-for-profit corporation incorporated or authorized to transact business in this state.

(c) A corporation may apply to the secretary of state for authorization to use a name that is not distinguishable upon his records from one or more of the names described in subsection (b). The secretary of state shall authorize use of the name applied for if:

(1) the other corporation consents to the use in writing and submits an undertaking in form satisfactory to the secretary of state to change its name to a name that is distinguishable upon the records of the secretary of state from the name of the applying corporation; or
(2) the applicant delivers to the secretary of state a certified copy of the final judgment of a court of competent jurisdiction establishing the applicant's right to use the name applied for in this state.

(d) A corporation may use the name (including the fictitious name) of another domestic or foreign corporation that is used in this state if the other corporation is incorporated or authorized to transact business in this state and the proposed user corporation:

(1) has merged with the other corporation;
(2) has been formed by reorganization of the other corporation; or
(3) has acquired all or substantially all of the assets, including the corporate name, of the other corporation.

(e) This Act does not control the use of fictitious names.

§4.02. Reserved Name.—
(a) A person may reserve the exclusive use of a corporate name, including a fictitious name for a foreign corporation whose corporate name is not available, by delivering an application to the secretary of state for filing. The application must set forth the name and address of the applicant and the name proposed to be reserved. If the secretary of state finds that the corporate name applied for is available, he shall reserve the name for the applicant's exclusive use for a nonrenewable 120-day period.
(b) The owner of a reserved corporate name may transfer the reservation to another person by delivering to the secretary of state a signed notice of the transfer that states the name and address of the transferee.

§4.03. Registered Name.—
(a) A foreign corporation may register its corporate name, or its corporate name with any addition required by section 15.06, if the name is distinguishable upon the records of the secretary of state from the corporate names that are not available under section 4.01(b)(3).
(b) A foreign corporation registers its corporate name, or its corporate name with any addition required by section 15.06, by delivering to the secretary of state for filing an application:

(1) setting forth its corporate name, or its corporate name with any addition required by section 15.06, the state or country and date of its incorporation, and a brief description of the nature of the business in which it is engaged; and
(2) accompanied by a certificate of existence (or a document of similar import) from the state or country of incorporation.

(c) The name is registered for the applicant's exclusive use upon the effective date of the application.

(d) A foreign corporation whose registration is effective may renew it for successive years by delivering to the secretary of state for filing a renewal application, which complies with the requirements of subsection (b), between October 1 and December 31 of the preceding year. The renewal application renews the registration for the following calendar year.

(e) A foreign corporation whose registration is effective may thereafter qualify as a foreign corporation under that name or consent in writing to the use of that name by a corporation thereafter incorporated under this Act or by another foreign corporation thereafter authorized to transact business in this state. The registration terminates when the domestic corporation is incorporated or the foreign corporation qualifies or consents to the qualification of another foreign corporation under the registered name.

CHAPTER 5. OFFICE AND AGENT

§5.01. Registered Office and Registered Agent.— Each corporation must continuously maintain in this state:

(1) a registered office that may be the same as any of its places of business; and
(2) a registered agent, who may be:
(i) an individual who resides in this state and whose business office is identical with the registered office;
(ii) a domestic corporation or not-for-profit domestic corporation whose business office is identical with the registered office; or
(iii) a foreign corporation or not-for-profit foreign corporation authorized to transact business in this state whose business office is identical with the registered office.

§5.02. Change of Registered Office or Registered Agent.—
(a) A corporation may change its registered office or registered agent by delivering to the secretary of state for filing a statement of change that sets forth:

(1) the name of the corporation,
(2) the street address of its current registered office;
(3) if the current registered office is to be changed, the street address of the new registered office;
(4) the name of its current registered agent;
(5) if the current registered agent is to be changed, the name of the new registered agent and the new agent's written consent (either on the statement or attached to it) to the appointment; and
(6) that after the change or changes are made, the street addresses of its registered office and the business office of its registered agent will be identical.

(b) If a registered agent changes the street address of his business office, he may change the street address of the registered office of any corporation for which he is the registered agent by notifying the corporation in writing of the change and signing (either manually or in facsimile) and delivering to the secretary of state for filing a statement that complies with the requirements of subsection (a) and recites that the corporation has been notified of the change.

§5.03. Resignation of Registered Agent.—
(a) A registered agent may resign his agency appointment by signing and delivering to the secretary of state for filing the signed original and two exact or conformed copies of a statement of resignation. The statement may include a statement that the registered office is also discontinued.

(b) After filing the statement the secretary of state shall mail one copy to the registered office (if not discontinued) and the other copy to the corporation at its principal office.

(c) The agency appointment is terminated, and the registered office discontinued if so provided, on the 31st day after the date on which the statement was filed.

§5.04. Service on Corporation.—

(a) A corporation's registered agent is the corporation's agent for service of process, notice, or demand required or permitted by law to be served on the corporation.

(b) If a corporation has no registered agent, or the agent cannot with reasonable diligence be served, the corporation may be served by registered or certified mail, return receipt requested, addressed to the secretary of the corporation at its principal office. Service is perfected under this subsection at the earliest of:

> (1) the date the corporation receives the mail;
> (2) the date shown on the return receipt, if signed on behalf of the corporation; or
> (3) five days after its deposit in the United States Mail, if mailed postpaid and correctly addressed.

(c) This section does not prescribe the only means, or necessarily the required means, of serving a corporation.

CHAPTER 6. SHARES AND DISTRIBUTIONS

Subchapter A. Shares

§6.01. Authorized Shares.—

(a) The articles of incorporation must prescribe the classes of shares and the number of shares of each class that the corporation is authorized to issue. If more than one class of shares is authorized, the articles of incorporation must prescribe a distinguishing designation for each class, and prior to the issuance of shares of a class the preferences, limitations, and relative rights of that class must be described in the articles of incorporation. All shares of a class must have preferences, limitations, and relative rights identical with those of other shares of the same class except to the extent otherwise permitted by section 6.02.

(b) the articles of incorporation must authorize (1) one or more classes of shares that together have unlimited voting rights, and (2) one or more classes of shares (which may be the same class or classes as those with voting rights) that together are entitled to receive the net assets of the corporation upon dissolution.

(c) The articles of incorporation may authorize one or more classes of shares that:

> (1) have special, conditional, or limited voting rights, or no right to vote, except to the extent prohibited by this Act;
> (2) are redeemable or convertible as specified in the articles of incorporation
>> (i) at the option of the corporation, the shareholder, or another person or upon the occurrence of a designated event;
>> (ii) for cash, indebtedness, securities, or other property;
>> (iii) in a designated amount or in an amount determined in accordance with a designated formula or by reference to extrinsic data or events;
> (3) entitle the holders to distributions calculated in any manner, including dividends that may be cumulative, noncumulative, or partially cumulative;
> (4) have preference over any other class of shares with respect to distributions, including dividends and distributions upon the dissolution of the corporation.

(d) The description of the designations, preferences, limitations, and relative rights of share classes in subsection (c) is not exhaustive.

§6.02. Terms of Class or Series Determined by Board of Directors.—
(a) If the articles of incorporation so provide, the board of directors may determine, in whole or in part, the preferences, limitations, and relative rights (within the limits set forth in section 6.01) of (1) any class of shares before the issuance of any shares of that class or (2) one or more series within a class before the issuance of any shares of that series.
(b) Each series of a class must be given a distinguishing designation.
(c) All shares of a series must have preferences, limitations, and relative rights identical with those of other shares of the same series and, except to the extent otherwise provided in the description of the series, with those of other series of the same class.
(d) Before issuing any shares of a class or series created under this section, the corporation must deliver to the secretary of state for filing articles of amendment, which are effective without shareholder action, that set forth:

(1) the name of the corporation;
(2) the text of the amendment determining the terms of the class or series of shares;
(3) the date it was adopted; and
(4) a statement that the amendment was duly adopted by the board of directors.

§6.03. Issued and Outstanding Shares.—
(a) A corporation may issue the number of shares of each class or series authorized by the articles of incorporation. Shares that are issued are outstanding shares until they are reacquired, redeemed, converted, or cancelled.
(b) The reacquisition, redemption, or conversion of outstanding shares is subject to the limitations of subsection (c) of this section and to section 6.40.
(c) At all times that shares of the corporation are outstanding, one or more shares that together have unlimited voting rights and one or more shares that together are entitled to receive the net assets of the corporation upon dissolution must be outstanding.

§6.04. Fractional Shares.—
(a) A corporation may:

(1) issue fractions of a share or pay in money the value of fractions of a share;
(2) arrange for disposition of fractional shares by the shareholders;
(3) issue scrip in registered or bearer form entitling the holder to receive a full share upon surrendering enough scrip to equal a full share.

(b) Each certificate representing scrip must be conspicuously labeled "scrip" and must contain the information required by section 6.25(b).
(c) The holder of a fractional share is entitled to exercise the rights of a shareholder, including the right to vote, to receive dividends, and to participate in the assets of the corporation upon liquidation. The holder of scrip is not entitled to any of these rights unless the scrip provides for them.
(d) The board of directors may authorize the issuance of scrip subject to any condition considered desirable, including:

(1) that the scrip will become void if not exchanged for full shares before a specified date; and
(2) that the shares for which the scrip is exchangeable may be sold and the proceeds paid to the scripholders.

Subchapter B. Issuance of Shares

§6.20. Subscription for Shares Before Incorporation.—

(a) A subscription for shares entered into before incorporation is irrevocable for six months unless the subscription agreement provides a longer or shorter period or all the subscribers agree to revocation.

(b) The board of directors may determine the payment terms of subscriptions for shares that were entered into before incorporation, unless the subscription agreement specifies them. A call for payment by the board of directors must be uniform so far as practicable as to all shares of the same class or series, unless the subscription agreement specifies otherwise.

(c) Shares issued pursuant to subscriptions entered into before incorporation are fully paid and nonassessable when the corporation receives the consideration specified in the subscription agreement.

(d) If a subscriber defaults in payment of money or property under a subscription agreement entered into before incorporation, the corporation may collect the amount owed as any other debt. Alternatively, unless the subscription agreement provides otherwise, the corporation may rescind the agreement and may sell the shares if the debt remains unpaid more than 20 days after the corporation sends written demand for payment to the subscriber.

(e) A subscription agreement entered into after incorporation is a contract between the subscriber and the corporation subject to section 6.21.

§6.21. Issuance of Shares.—

(a) The powers granted in this section to the board of directors may be reserved to the shareholders by the articles of incorporation.

(b) The board of directors may authorize shares to be issued for consideration consisting of any tangible or intangible property or benefit to the corporation, including cash, promissory notes, services performed, contracts for services to be performed, or other securities of the corporation.

(c) Before the corporation issues shares, the board of directors must determine that the consideration received or to be received for shares to be issued is adequate. That determination by the board of directors is conclusive insofar as the adequacy of consideration for the issuance of shares relates to whether the shares are validly issued, fully paid, and nonassessable.

(d) When the corporation receives the consideration for which the board of directors authorized the issuance of shares, the shares issued therefor are fully paid and nonassessable.

(e) The corporation may place in escrow shares issued for a contract for future services or benefits or a promissory note, or make other arrangements to restrict the transfer of the shares, and may credit distributions in respect of the shares against their purchase price, until the services are performed, the note is paid, or the benefits received. If the services are not performed, the note is not paid, or the benefits are not received, the shares escrowed or restricted and the distributions credited may be cancelled in whole or part.

§6.22. Liability of Shareholders.—

(a) A purchaser from a corporation of its own shares is not liable to the corporation or its creditors with respect to the shares except to pay the consideration for which the shares were authorized to be issued (section 6.21) or specified in the subscription agreement (section 6.20).

(b) Unless otherwise provided in the articles of incorporation, a shareholder of a corporation is not personally liable for the acts or debts of the corporation except that he may become personally liable by reason of his own acts or conduct.

§6.23. Share Dividends.—

(a) Unless the articles of incorporation provide otherwise, shares may be issued pro rata and without consideration to the corporation's shareholders or to the shareholders of one or more classes or series. An issuance of shares under this subsection is a share dividend.

(b) Shares of one class or series may not be issued as a share dividend in respect of shares of another class or series unless (1) the articles of incorporation so authorize, (2) a majority of the votes entitled to be cast by the class or series to be issued approve the issue, or (3) there are no outstanding shares of the class or series to be issued.

(c) If the board of directors does not fix the record date for determining shareholders entitled to a share dividend, it is the date the board of directors authorizes the share dividend.

§6.24. Share Options.—A corporation may issue rights, options, or warrants for the purchase of shares of the corporation. The board of directors shall determine the terms upon which the rights, options, or warrants are issued, their form and content, and the consideration for which the shares are to be issued.

§6.25. Form and Content of Certificates.—

(a) Shares may but need not be represented by certificates. Unless this Act or another statute expressly provides otherwise, the rights and obligations of shareholders are identical whether or not their shares are represented by certificates.

(b) At a minimum each share certificate must state on its face:

(1) the name of the issuing corporation and that it is organized under the law of this state;
(2) the name of the person to whom issued; and
(3) the number and class of shares and the designation of the series, if any, the certificate represents.

(c) If the issuing corporation is authorized to issue different classes of shares or different series within a class, the designations, relative rights, preferences, and limitations applicable to each class and the variations in rights, preferences, and limitations determined for each series (and the authority of the board of directors to determine variations for future series) must be summarized on the front or back of each certificate. Alternatively, each certificate may state conspicuously on its front or back that the corporation will furnish the shareholder this information on request in writing and without charge.

(d) Each share certificate (1) must be signed (either manually or in facsimile) by two officers designated in the bylaws or by the board of directors and (2) may bear the corporate seal or its facsimile.

(e) If the person who signed (either manually or in facsimile) a share certificate no longer holds office when the certificate is issued, the certificate is nevertheless valid.

§6.26. Shares Without Certificates.—

(a) Unless the articles of incorporation or bylaws provide otherwise, the board of directors of a corporation may authorize the issue of some or all of the shares of any or all of its classes or series without certificates. The authorization does not affect shares already represented by certificates until they are surrendered to the corporation.

(b) Within a reasonable time after the issue or transfer of shares without certificates, the corporation shall send the shareholder a written statement of the information required on certificates by section 6.25(b) and (c), and, if applicable, section 6.27.

§6.27. Restriction on Transfer of Shares and Other Securities.—

(a) The articles of incorporation, bylaws, an agreement among shareholders, or an agreement between shareholders and the corporation may impose restrictions on the transfer or registration of transfer of shares of the corporation. A restriction does not affect shares issued before the restriction was adopted unless the holders of the shares are parties to the restriction agreement or voted in favor of the restriction.

(b) A restriction on the transfer or registration of transfer of shares is valid and enforceable against the holder or a transferee of the holder if the restriction is authorized by this section and its existence is noted conspicuously on the front or back of the certificate or is contained in the information statement required by section 6.26(b). Unless so noted, a restriction is not enforceable against a person without knowledge of the restriction.

(c) A restriction on the transfer or registration of transfer of shares is authorized:

(1) to maintain the corporation's status when it is dependent on the number or identity of its shareholders;
(2) to preserve exemptions under federal or state securities law;
(3) for any other reasonable purpose.

(d) A restriction on the transfer or registration of transfer of shares may:

(1) obligate the shareholder first to offer the corporation or other persons (separately, consecutively, or simultaneously) an opportunity to acquire the restricted shares;
(2) obligate the corporation or other persons (separately, consecutively, or simultaneously) to acquire the restricted shares;
(3) require the corporation, the holders of any class of its shares, or another person to approve the transfer of the restricted shares, if the requirement is not manifestly unreasonable;
(4) prohibit the transfer of the restricted shares to designated persons or classes of persons, if the prohibition is not manifestly unreasonable.

(e) For purposes of this section, "shares" includes a security convertible into or carrying a right to subscribe for or acquire shares.

§6.28. Expense of Issue.—A corporation may pay the expenses of selling or underwriting its shares, and of organizing or reorganizing the corporation, from the consideration received for shares.

Subchapter C. Subsequent Acquisition of Shares by Shareholders and Corporation

§6.30. Shareholders' Preemptive Rights.—
(a) The shareholders of a corporation do not have a preemptive right to acquire the corporation's unissued shares except to the extent the articles of incorporation so provide.
(b) A statement included in the articles of incorporation that "the corporation elects to have preemptive rights" (or words of similar import) means that the following principles apply except to the extent the articles of incorporation expressly provide otherwise:

(1) The shareholders of the corporation have a preemptive right, granted on uniform terms and conditions prescribed by the board of directors, to provide a fair and reasonable opportunity to exercise the right, to acquire proportional amounts of the corporation's unissued shares upon the decision of the board of directors to issue them.
(2) A shareholder may waive his preemptive right. A waiver evidenced by a writing is irrevocable even though it is not supported by consideration.
(3) There is no preemptive right with respect to:
(i) shares issued as compensation to directors, officers, agents, or employees of the corporation, its subsidiaries or affiliates;

(ii) shares issued to satisfy conversion or option rights created to provide compensation to directors, officers, agents, or employees of the corporation, its subsidiaries or affiliates;

(iii) shares authorized in articles of incorporation that are issued within six months from the effective date of incorporation;

(iv) shares sold otherwise than for money.

(4) Holders of shares of any class without general voting rights but with preferential rights to distributions or assets have no preemptive rights with respect to shares of any class.

(5) Holders of shares of any class with general voting rights but without preferential rights to distributions or assets have no preemptive rights with respect to shares of any class with preferential rights to distributions or assets unless the shares with preferential rights are convertible into or carry a right to subscribe for or acquire shares without preferential rights.

(6) Shares subject to preemptive rights that are not acquired by shareholders may be issued to any person for a period of one year after being offered to shareholders at a consideration set by the board of directors that is not lower than the consideration set for the exercise of preemptive rights. An offer at a lower consideration or after the expiration of one year is subject to the shareholders' preemptive rights.

(c) For purposes of this section, "shares" includes a security convertible into or carrying a right to subscribe for or acquire shares.

§6.31. Corporation's Acquisition of its Own Shares.—

(a) A corporation may acquire its own shares and shares so acquired constitute authorized but unissued shares.

(b) If the articles of incorporation prohibit the reissue of acquired shares, the number of authorized shares is reduced by the number of shares acquired, effective upon amendment of the articles of incorporation.

(c) The board of directors may adopt articles of amendment under this section without shareholder action, and deliver them to the secretary of state for filing. The articles must set forth:

(1) the name of the corporation;

(2) the reduction in the number of authorized shares, itemized by class and series; and

(3) the total number of authorized shares, itemized by class and series, remaining after reduction of the shares.

Subchapter D. Distributions

§6.40. Distributions to Shareholders.—

(a) A board of directors may authorize and the corporation may make distributions to its shareholders subject to restriction by the articles of incorporation and the limitation in subsection (c).

(b) If the board of directors does not fix the record date for determining shareholders entitled to a distribution (other than one involving a repurchase or reacquisition of shares), it is the date the board of directors authorizes the distribution.

(c) No distribution may be made if, after giving it effect:

(1) the corporation would not be able to pay its debts as they become due in the usual course of business; or

(2) the corporation's total assets would be less than the sum of its total liabilities plus (unless the articles of incorporation permit otherwise) the amount that would be needed, if the corporation were to be dissolved at the time of the distribution, to satisfy the preferential rights upon dissolution of shareholders whose preferential rights are superior to those receiving the distribution.

(d) The board of directors may base a determination that a distribution is not prohibited under subsection (c) either on financial statements prepared on the basis of accounting practices and principles that are reasonable in the circumstances or on a fair valuation or other method that is reasonable in the circumstances.

(e) The effect of a distribution under subsection (c) is measured:

(1) in the case of distribution by purchase, redemption, or other acquisition of the corporation's shares, as of the earlier of (i) the date money or other property is transferred or debt incurred by the corporation or (ii) the date the shareholder ceases to be a shareholder with respect to the acquired shares;

(2) in the case of any other distribution of indebtedness, as of the date the indebtedness is distributed;

(3) in all other cases, as of (i) the date the distribution is authorized if the payment occurs within 120 days after the date of authorization or (ii) the date the payment is made if it occurs more than 120 days after the date of authorization.

(f) A corporation's indebtedness to a shareholder incurred by reason of a distribution made in accordance with this section is at parity with the corporation's indebtedness to its general, unsecured creditors except to the extent subordinated by agreement.

CHAPTER 7. SHAREHOLDERS

Subchapter A. Meetings

§7.01. Annual Meeting.—
(a) A corporation shall hold annually at a time stated in or fixed in accordance with the bylaws a meeting of shareholders.
(b) Annual shareholders' meetings may be held in or out of this state at the place stated in or fixed in accordance with the bylaws. If no place is stated in or fixed in accordance with the bylaws, annual meetings shall be held at the corporation's principal office.
(c) The failure to hold an annual meeting at the time stated in or fixed in accordance with a corporation's bylaws does not affect the validity of any corporate action.

§7.02. Special Meeting.—
(a) A corporation shall hold a special meeting of shareholders:

(1) on call of its board of directors or the person or persons authorized to do so by the articles of incorporation or bylaws; or
(2) if the holders of at least 10 percent of all the votes entitled to be cast on any issue proposed to be considered at the proposed special meeting sign, date, and deliver to the corporation's secretary one or more written demands for the meeting describing the purpose or purposes for which it is to be held.

(b) If not otherwise fixed under sections 7.03 or 7.07, the record date for determining shareholders entitled to demand a special meeting is the date the first shareholder signs the demand.
(c) Special shareholders' meetings may be held in or out of this state at the place stated in or fixed in accordance with the bylaws. If no place is stated or fixed in accordance with the bylaws, special meetings shall be held at the corporation's principal office.
(d) Only business within the purpose or purposes described in the meeting notice required by section 7.05(c) may be conducted at a special shareholders' meeting.

§7.03. Court-Ordered Meeting.—

(a) The [name or describe] court of the county where a corporation's principal office (or, if none in this state, its registered office) is located may summarily order a meeting to be held:

> (1) on application of any shareholder of the corporation entitled to participate in an annual meeting if an annual meeting was not held within the earlier of 6 months after the end of the corporation's fiscal year or 15 months after its last annual meeting; or
>
> (2) on application of a shareholder who signed a demand for a special meeting valid under section 7.02 if:
>> (i) notice of the special meeting was not given within 30 days after the date the demand was delivered to the corporation's secretary; or
>> (ii) the special meeting was not held in accordance with the notice.

(b) The court may fix the time and place of the meeting, determine the shares entitled to participate in the meeting, specify a record date for determining shareholders entitled to notice of and to vote at the meeting, prescribe the form and content of the meeting notice, fix the quorum required for specific matters to be considered at the meeting (or direct that the votes represented at the meeting constitute a quorum for action on those matters), and enter other orders necessary to accomplish the purpose or purposes of the meeting.

§7.04. Action Without Meeting.—

(a) Action required or permitted by this Act to be taken at a shareholders' meeting may be taken without a meeting if the action is taken by all the shareholders entitled to vote on the action. The action must be evidenced by one or more written consents describing the action taken, signed by all the shareholders entitled to vote on the action, and delivered to the corporation for inclusion in the minutes or filing with the corporate records.

(b) If not otherwise determined under sections 7.03 or 7.07, the record date for determining shareholders entitled to take action without a meeting is the date the first shareholder signs the consent under subsection (a).

(c) A consent signed under this section has the effect of a meeting vote and may be described as such in any document.

(d) If this Act requires that notice of proposed action be given to nonvoting shareholders and the action is to be taken by unanimous consent of the voting shareholders, the corporation must give its nonvoting shareholders written notice of the proposed action at least 10 days before the action is taken. The notice must contain or be accompanied by the same material that, under this Act, would have been required to be sent to nonvoting shareholders in a notice of meeting at which the proposed action would have been submitted to the shareholders for action.

§7.05. Notice of Meeting.—

(a) A corporation shall notify shareholders of the date, time, and place of each annual and special shareholders' meeting no fewer than 10 nor more than 60 days before the meeting date. Unless this Act or the articles of incorporation require otherwise, the corporation is required to give notice only to shareholders entitled to vote at the meeting.

(b) Unless this Act or the articles of incorporation require otherwise, notice of an annual meeting need not include a description of the purpose or purposes for which the meeting is called.

(c) Notice of a special meeting must include a description of the purpose or purposes for which the meeting is called.

(d) If not otherwise fixed under section 7.03 or 7.07, the record date for determining shareholders entitled to notice of and to vote at an annual or special shareholders' meeting is the close of business on the day before the first notice is delivered to shareholders.

(e) Unless the bylaws require otherwise, if an annual or special shareholders' meeting is adjourned to a different date, time, or place, notice need not be given of the new date, time, or place if the new date, time, or place is announced at the meeting before adjournment. If a new record date for the adjourned meeting is or must be fixed under section 7.07, however, notice of the adjourned meeting must be given under this section to persons who are shareholders as of the new record date.

§7.06. Waiver of Notice.—

(a) A shareholder may waive any notice required by this Act, the articles of incorporation, or bylaws before or after the date and time stated in the notice. The waiver must be in writing, be signed by the shareholder entitled to the notice, and be delivered to the corporation for inclusion in the minutes or filing with the corporate records.

(b) A shareholder's attendance at a meeting:

(1) waives objection to lack of notice or defective notice of the meeting, unless the shareholder at the beginning of the meeting objects to holding the meeting or transacting business at the meeting;

(2) waives objection to consideration of a particular matter at the meeting that is not within the purpose or purposes described in the meeting notice, unless the shareholder objects to considering the matter when it is presented.

§7.07. Record Date.—

(a) The bylaws may fix or provide the manner of fixing the record date for one or more voting groups in order to determine the shareholders entitled to notice of a shareholders' meeting, to demand a special meeting, to vote, or to take any other action. If the bylaws do not fix or provide for fixing a record date, the board of directors of the corporation may fix a future date as the record date.

(b) A record date fixed under this section may not be more than 70 days before the meeting or action requiring a determination of shareholders.

(c) A determination of shareholders entitled to notice of or to vote at a shareholders' meeting is effective for any adjournment of the meeting unless the board of directors fixes a new record date, which it must do if the meeting is adjourned to a date more than 120 days after the date fixed for the original meeting.

(d) If a court orders a meeting adjourned to a date more than 120 days after the date fixed for the original meeting, it may provide that the original record date continues in effect or it may fix a new record date.

Subchapter B. Voting

§7.20. Shareholders' List for Meeting.—

(a) After fixing a record date for a meeting, a corporation shall prepare an alphabetical list of the names of all its shareholders who are entitled to notice of a shareholders' meeting. The list must be arranged by voting group (and within each voting group by class or series of shares) and show the address of and number of shares held by each shareholder.

(b) The shareholders' list must be available for inspection by any shareholder, beginning two business days after notice of the meeting is given for which the list was prepared and continuing through the meeting, at the corporation's principal office or at a place identified in the meeting notice in the city where the meeting will be held. A shareholder, his agent, or attorney is entitled on written demand to inspect and, subject to the requirements of section 16.02(c), to copy the list, during regular business hours and at his expense, during the period it is available for inspection.

(c) The corporation shall make the shareholders' list available at the meeting, and any shareholder, his agent, or attorney is entitled to inspect the list at any time during the meeting or any adjournment.

(d) If the corporation refuses to allow a shareholder, his agent, or attorney to inspect the shareholders' list before or at the meeting (or copy the list as permitted by subsection (b)), the [name or describe] court of the county where a corporation's principal office (or, if none in this state, its registered office) is located, on application of the shareholder, may summarily order the inspection or copying at the corporation's expense and may postpone the meeting for which the list was prepared until the inspection or copying is complete.

(e) Refusal or failure to prepare or make available the shareholders' list does not affect the validity of action taken at the meeting.

§7.21. Voting Entitlement of Shares.—

(a) Except as provided in subsections (b) and (c) or unless the articles of incorporation provide otherwise, each outstanding share, regardless of class, is entitled to one vote on each matter voted on at a shareholders' meeting. Only shares are entitled to vote.

(b) Absent special circumstances, the shares of a corporation are not entitled to vote if they are owned, directly or indirectly, by a second corporation, domestic or foreign, and the first corporation owns, directly or indirectly, a majority of the shares entitled to vote for directors of the second corporation.

(c) Subsection (b) does not limit the power of a corporation to vote any shares, including its own shares, held by it in a fiduciary capacity.

(d) Redeemable shares are not entitled to vote after notice of redemption is mailed to the holders and a sum sufficient to redeem the shares has been deposited with a bank, trust company, or other financial institution under an irrevocable obligation to pay the holders the redemption price on surrender of the shares.

§7.22. Proxies.—

(a) A shareholder may vote his shares in person or by proxy.

(b) A shareholder may appoint a proxy to vote or otherwise act for him by signing an appointment form, either personally or by his attorney-in-fact.

(c) An appointment of a proxy is effective when received by the secretary or other officer or agent authorized to tabulate votes. An appointment is valid for 11 months unless a longer period is expressly provided in the appointment form.

(d) An appointment of a proxy is revocable by the shareholder unless the appointment form conspicuously states that it is irrevocable and the appointment is coupled with an interest. Appointments coupled with an interest include the appointment of:

(1) a pledgee;
(2) a person who purchased or agreed to purchase the shares;
(3) a creditor of the corporation who extended it credit under terms requiring the appointment;
(4) an employee of the corporation whose employment contract requires the appointment; or
(5) a party to a voting agreement created under section 7.31.

(e) The death or incapacity of the shareholder appointing a proxy does not affect the right of the corporation to accept the proxy's authority unless notice of the death or incapacity is received by the secretary or other officer or agent authorized to tabulate votes before the proxy exercises his authority under the appointment.

(f) An appointment made irrevocable under subsection (d) is revoked when the interest with which it is coupled is extinguished.

(g) A transferee for value of shares subject to an irrevocable appointment may revoke the appointment if he did not know of its existence when he acquired the shares and the existence of the irrevocable appointment was not noted conspicuously on the certificate representing the shares or on the information statement for shares without certificates.

(h) Subject to section 7.24 and to any express limitation on the proxy's authority appearing on the face of the appointment form, a corporation is entitled to accept the proxy's vote or other action as that of the shareholder making the appointment.

§7.23. Shares Held by Nominees.—

(a) A corporation may establish a procedure by which the beneficial owner of shares that are registered in the name of a nominee is recognized by the corporation as the shareholder. The extent of this recognition may be determined in the procedure.
(b) The procedure may set forth:

    (1) the types of nominees to which it applies;
    (2) the rights or privileges that the corporation recognizes in a beneficial owner;
    (3) the manner in which the procedure is selected by the nominee;
    (4) the information that must be provided when the procedure is selected;
    (5) the period for which selection of the procedure is effective; and
    (6) other aspects of the rights and duties created.

§7.24. Corporation's Acceptance of Votes.—

(a) If the name signed on a vote, consent, waiver, or proxy appointment corresponds to the name of a shareholder, the corporation if acting in good faith is entitled to accept the vote, consent, waiver, or proxy appointment and give it effect as the act of the shareholder.
(b) If the name signed on a vote, consent, waiver, or proxy appointment does not correspond to the name of its shareholder, the corporation if acting in good faith is nevertheless entitled to accept the vote, consent, waiver, or proxy appointment and give it effect as the act of the shareholder if:

    (1) the shareholder is an entity and the name signed purports to be that of an officer or agent of the entity;
    (2) the name signed purports to be that of an administrator, executor, guardian, or conservator representing the shareholder and, if the corporation requests, evidence of fiduciary status acceptable to the corporation has been presented with respect to the vote, consent, waiver, or proxy appointment;
    (3) the name signed purports to be that of a receiver or trustee in bankruptcy of the shareholder and, if the corporation requests, evidence of this status acceptable to the corporation has been presented with respect to the vote, consent, waiver, or proxy appointment;
    (4) the name signed purports to be that of a pledgee, beneficial owner, or attorney-in-fact of the shareholder and, if the corporation requests, evidence acceptable to the corporation of the signatory's authority to sign for the shareholder has been presented with respect to the vote, consent, waiver, or proxy appointment;
    (5) two or more persons are the shareholder as cotenants or fiduciaries and the name signed purports to be the name of at least one of the coowners and the person signing appears to be acting on behalf of all the coowners.

(c) The corporation is entitled to reject a vote, consent, waiver, or proxy appointment if the secretary or other officer or agent authorized to tabulate votes, acting in good faith, has reasonable basis for doubt about the validity of the signature on it or about the signatory's authority to sign for the shareholder.
(d) The corporation and its officer or agent who accepts or rejects a vote, consent, waiver, or proxy appointment in good faith and in accordance with the standards of this section are not liable in damages to the shareholder for the consequences of the acceptance or rejection.
(e) Corporate action based on the acceptance or rejection of a vote, consent, waiver, or proxy appointment under this section is valid unless a court of competent jurisdiction determines otherwise.

§7.25. Quorum and Voting Requirements for Voting Groups.—
(a) Shares entitled to vote as a separate voting group may take action on a matter at a meeting only if a quorum of those shares exists with respect to that matter. Unless the articles of incorporation or this Act provide otherwise, a majority of the votes entitled to be cast on the matter by the voting group constitutes a quorum of that voting group for action on that matter.
(b) Once a share is represented for any purpose at a meeting, it is deemed present for quorum purposes for the remainder of the meeting and for any adjournment of that meeting unless a new record date is or must be set for that adjourned meeting.
(c) If a quorum exists, action on a matter (other than the election of directors) by a voting group is approved if the votes cast within the voting group favoring the action exceed the votes cast opposing the action, unless the articles of incorporation or this Act require a greater number of affirmative votes.
(d) An amendment of articles of incorporation adding, changing, or deleting a quorum or voting requirement for a voting group greater than specified in subsection (b) or (c) is governed by section 7.27.
(e) The election of directors is governed by section 7.28.

§7.26. Action by Single and Multiple Voting Groups.—
(a) If the articles of incorporation or this Act provide for voting by a single voting group on a matter, action on that matter is taken when voted upon by that voting group as provided in section 7.25.
(b) If the articles of incorporation or this Act provide for voting by two or more voting groups on a matter, action on that matter is taken only when voted upon by each of those voting groups counted separately as provided in section 7.25. Action may be taken by one voting group on a matter even though no action is taken by another voting group entitled to vote on the matter.

§7.27. Greater Quorum or Voting Requirements.—
(a) The articles of incorporation may provide for a greater quorum or voting requirement for shareholders (or voting groups of shareholders) than is provided for by this Act.
(b) An amendment to the articles of incorporation that adds, changes, or deletes a greater quorum or voting requirement must meet the same quorum requirement and be adopted by the same vote and voting groups required to take action under the quorum and voting requirements then in effect or proposed to be adopted, whichever is greater.

§7.28. Voting for Directors; Cumulative Voting.—
(a) Unless otherwise provided in the articles of incorporation, directors are elected by a plurality of the votes cast by the shares entitled to vote in the election at a meeting at which a quorum is present.
(b) Shareholders do not have a right to cumulate their votes for directors unless the articles of incorporation so provide.
(c) A statement included in the articles of incorporation that "[all] [a designated voting group of] shareholders are entitled to cumulate their votes for directors" (or words of similar import) means that the shareholders designated are entitled to multiply the number of votes they are entitled to cast by the number of directors for whom they are entitled to vote and cast the product for a single candidate or distribute the product among two or more candidates.
(d) Shares otherwise entitled to vote cumulatively may not be voted cumulatively at a particular meeting unless:

(1) the meeting notice or proxy statement accompanying the notice states conspicuously that accumulative voting is authorized; or
(2) a shareholder who has the right to cumulate his votes gives notice to the corporation no fewer than 48 hours before the time set for the meeting of his intent to cumulate his votes during the meeting, and if one shareholder gives

this notice all other shareholders in the same voting group participating in the election are entitled to cumulate their votes without giving further notice.

Subchapter C. Voting Trusts and Agreements

§7.30. Voting Trusts.—

(a) One or more shareholders may create a voting trust, conferring on a trustee the right to vote or otherwise act for them, by signing an agreement setting out the provisions of the trust (which may include anything consistent with its purpose) and transferring their shares to the trustee. When a voting trust agreement is signed, the trustee shall prepare a list of the names and addresses of all owners of beneficial interests in the trust, together with the number and class of shares each transferred to the trust, and deliver copies of the list and agreement to the corporation's principal office.

(b) A voting trust becomes effective on the date the first shares subject to the trust are registered in the trustee's name. A voting trust is valid for not more than 10 years after its effective date unless extended under subsection (c).

(c) All or some of the parties to a voting trust may extend it for additional terms of not more than 10 years each by signing an extension agreement and obtaining the voting trustee's written consent to the extension. An extension is valid for 10 years from the date the first shareholder signs the extension agreement. The voting trustee must deliver copies of the extension agreement and list of beneficial owners to the corporation's principal office. An extension agreement binds only those parties signing it.

§7.31. Voting Agreements.—

(a) Two or more shareholders may provide for the manner in which they will vote their shares by signing an agreement for that purpose. A voting agreement created under this section is not subject to the provisions of section 7.30.

(b) A voting agreement created under this section is specifically enforceable.

Subchapter D. Derivative Proceedings

§7.40. Procedure in Derivative Proceedings.—

(a) A person may not commence a proceeding in the right of a domestic or foreign corporation unless he was a shareholder of the corporation when the transaction complained of occurred or unless he became a shareholder through transfer by operation of law from one who was a shareholder at that time.

(b) A complaint in a proceeding brought in the right of a corporation must be verified and allege with particularity the demand made, if any, to obtain action by the board of directors and either that the demand was refused or ignored or why he did not make the demand. Whether or not a demand for action was made, if the corporation commences an investigation of the changes made in the demand or complaint, the court may stay any proceeding until the investigation is completed.

(c) A proceeding commenced under this section may not be discontinued or settled without the court's approval. If the court determines that a proposed discontinuance or settlement will substantially affect the interest of the corporation's shareholders or a class of shareholders, the court shall direct that notice be given the shareholders affected.

(d) On termination of the proceeding the court may require the plaintiff to pay any defendant's reasonable expenses (including counsel fees) incurred in defending the proceeding if it finds that the proceeding was commenced without reasonable cause.

(e) For purposes of this section, "shareholder" includes a beneficial owner whose shares are held in a voting trust or held by a nominee on his behalf.

CHAPTER 8. DIRECTORS AND OFFICERS

Subchapter A. Board of Directors

§8.01. Requirement for and Duties of Board of Directors.—
(a) Except as provided in subsection (c), each corporation must have a board of directors.
(b) All corporate powers shall be exercised by or under the authority of, and the business and affairs of the corporation managed under the direction of, its board of directors, subject to any limitation set forth in the articles of incorporation.
(c) A corporation having 50 or fewer shareholders may dispense with or limit the authority of a board of directors by describing in its articles of incorporation who will perform some or all of the duties of a board of directors.

§8.02. Qualifications of Directors.—The articles of incorporation or bylaws may prescribe qualifications for directors. A director need not be a resident of this state or a shareholder of the corporation unless the articles of incorporation or bylaws so prescribe.

§8.03. Number and Election of Directors.—
(a) A board of directors must consist of one or more individuals, with the number specified in or fixed in accordance with the articles of incorporation or bylaws.
(b) If a board of directors has power to fix or change the number of directors, the board may increase or decrease by 30 percent or less the number of directors last approved by the shareholders, but only the shareholders may increase or decrease by more than 30 percent the number of directors last approved by the shareholders.
(c) The articles of incorporation or bylaws may establish a variable range for the size of the board of directors by fixing a minimum and maximum number of directors. If a variable range is established, the number of directors may be fixed or changed from time to time, within the minimum and maximum, by the shareholders or the board of directors. After shares are issued, only the shareholders may change the range for the size of the board or change from a fixed to a variable-range size board or vice versa.
(d) Directors are elected at the first annual shareholders' meeting and at each annual meeting thereafter unless their terms are staggered under section 8.06.

§8.04. Election of Directors by Certain Classes of Shareholders.— If the articles of incorporation authorize dividing the shares into classes, the articles may also authorize the election of all or a specified number of directors by the holders of one or more authorized classes of shares. A class (or classes) of shares entitled to elect one or more directors is a separate voting group for purposes of the election of directors.

§8.05. Terms of Directors Generally.—
(a) The terms of the initial directors of a corporation expire at the first shareholders' meeting at which directors are elected.
(b) The terms of all other directors expire at the next annual shareholders' meeting following their election unless their terms are staggered under section 8.06.
(c) A decrease in the number of directors does not shorten an incumbent director's term.
(d) The term of a director elected to fill a vacancy expires at the next shareholders' meeting at which directors are elected.
(e) Despite the expiration of a director's term, he continues to serve until his successor is elected and qualifies or until there is a decrease in the number of directors.

§8.06. Staggered Terms for Directors.—If there are nine or more directors, the articles of incorporation may provide for staggering their terms by dividing the total number of directors into two or three groups, with each group containing one half or one-third of the total, as near as may be. In that event, the terms of directors in the first group expire at the first annual shareholders' meeting after their election, the terms of the second group expire at the second annual shareholders' meeting after their election, and the terms of the third group, if any, expire at the third annual shareholders' meeting after their election. At each annual shareholders' meeting held thereafter, directors shall be chosen for a term of two years or three years, as the case may be, to succeed those whose terms expire.

§8.07. Resignation of Directors.—

(a) A director may resign at any time by delivering written notice to the board of directors, its chairman, or to the corporation.

(b) A resignation is effective when the notice is delivered unless the notice specifies a later effective date.

§8.08. Removal of Directors by Shareholders.—

(a) The shareholders may remove one or more directors with or without cause unless the articles of incorporation provide that directors may be removed only for cause.

(b) If a director is elected by a voting group of shareholders, only the shareholders of that voting group may participate in the vote to remove him.

(c) If cumulative voting is authorized, a director may not be removed if the number of votes sufficient to elect him under cumulative voting is voted against his removal. If cumulative voting is not authorized, a director may be removed only if the number of votes cast to remove him exceeds the number of votes cast not to remove him.

(d) A director may be removed by the shareholders only at a meeting called for the purpose of removing him and the meeting notice must state that the purpose, or one of the purposes, of the meeting is removal of the director.

§8.09. Removal of Directors by Judicial Proceeding.—

(a) The [name or describe] court of the county where a corporation's principal office (or, if none in this state, its registered office) is located may remove a director of the corporation from office in a proceeding commenced either by the corporation or by its shareholders holding at least 10 percent of the outstanding shares of any class if the court finds that (1) the director engaged in fraudulent or dishonest conduct, or gross abuse of authority or discretion, with respect to the corporation and (2) removal is in the best interest of the corporation.

(b) The court that removes a director may bar the director from reelection for a period prescribed by the court.

(c) If shareholders commence a proceeding under subsection (a), they shall make the corporation a party defendant.

§8.10. Vacancy on Board.—

(a) Unless the articles of incorporation provide otherwise, if a vacancy occurs on a board of directors, including a vacancy resulting from an increase in the number of directors:

> (1) the shareholders may fill the vacancy;
> (2) the board of directors may fill the vacancy; or
> (3) if the directors remaining in office constitute fewer than a quorum of the board, they may fill the vacancy by the affirmative vote of a majority of all the directors remaining in office.

(b) If the vacant office was held by a director elected by a voting group of shareholders, only the holders of shares of that voting group are entitled to vote to fill the vacancy if it is filled by the shareholders.

(c) A vacancy that will occur at a specific later date (by reason of a resignation effective at a later date under section 8.07(b) or otherwise) may be filled before the vacancy occurs but the new director may not take office until the vacancy occurs.

§8.11. Compensation of Directors.—Unless the articles of incorporation or bylaws provide otherwise, the board of directors may fix the compensation of directors.

Subchapter B. Meetings and Action of the Board

§8.20. Meetings.—
(a) The board of directors may hold regular or special meetings in or out of this state.
(b) Unless the articles of incorporation or bylaws provide otherwise, the board of directors may permit any or all directors to participate in a regular or special meeting by, or conduct the meeting through the use of, any means of communication by which all directors participating may simultaneously hear each other during the meeting. A director participating in a meeting by this means is deemed to be present in person at the meeting.

§8.21. Action Without Meeting.—
(a) Unless the articles of incorporation or bylaws provide otherwise, action required or permitted by this Act to be taken at a board of directors' meeting may be taken without a meeting if the action is taken by all members of the board. The action must be evidenced by one or more written consents describing the action taken, signed by each director, and included in the minutes or filed with the corporate records reflecting the action taken.
(b) Action taken under this section is effective when the last director signs the consent, unless the consent specifies a different effective date.
(c) A consent signed under this section has the effect of a meeting vote and may be described as such in any document.

§8.22. Notice of Meeting.—
(a) Unless the articles of incorporation or bylaws provide otherwise, regular meetings of the board of directors may be held without notice of the date, time, place, or purpose of the meeting.
(b) Unless the articles of incorporation or bylaws provide for a longer or shorter period, special meetings of the board of directors must be preceded by at least two days' notice of the date, time, and place of the meeting. The notice need not describe the purpose of the special meeting unless required by the articles of incorporation or bylaws.

§8.23. Waiver of Notice.—
(a) A director may waive any notice required by this Act, the articles of incorporation, or bylaws before or after the date and time stated in the notice. Except as provided by subsection (b), the waiver must be in writing, signed by the director entitled to the notice, and filed with the minutes or corporate records.
(b) A director's attendance at or participation in a meeting waives any required notice to him of the meeting unless the director at the beginning of the meeting (or promptly upon his arrival) objects to holding the meeting or transacting business at the meeting and does not thereafter vote for or assent to action taken at the meeting.

§8.24. Quorum and Voting.—
(a) Unless the articles of incorporation or bylaws require a greater number, a quorum of a board of directors consists of:

(1) a majority of the fixed number of directors if the corporation has a fixed board size; or

(2) a majority of the number of directors prescribed, or if no number is prescribed the number in office immediately before the meeting begins, if the corporation has a variable-range size board.

(b) The articles of incorporation or bylaws may authorize a quorum of a board of directors to consist of no fewer than one-third of the fixed or prescribed number of directors determined under subsection (a).

(c) If a quorum is present when a vote is taken, the affirmative vote of a majority of directors present is the act of the board of directors unless the articles of incorporation or bylaws require the vote of a greater number of directors.

(d) A director who is present at a meeting of the board of directors or a committee of the board of directors when corporate action is taken is deemed to have assented to the action taken unless: (1) he objects at the beginning of the meeting (or promptly upon his arrival) to holding it or transacting business at the meeting; (2) his dissent or abstention from the action taken is entered in the minutes of the meeting; or (3) he delivers written notice of his dissent or abstention to the presiding officer of the meeting before its adjournment or to the corporation immediately after adjournment of the meeting. The right of dissent or abstention is not available to a director who votes in favor of the action taken.

§8.25. Committees.—

(a) Unless the articles of incorporation or bylaws provide otherwise, a board of directors may create one or more committees and appoint members of the board of directors to serve on them. Each committee may have two or more members, who serve at the pleasure of the board of directors.

(b) The creation of a committee and appointment of members to it must be approved by the greater of (1) a majority of all the directors in office when the action is taken or (2) the number of directors required by the articles of incorporation or bylaws to take action under section 8.24.

(c) Sections 8.20 through 8.24, which govern meetings, action without meetings, notice and waiver of notice, and quorum and voting requirements of the board of directors, apply to committees and their members as well.

(d) To the extent specified by the board of directors or in the articles of incorporation or bylaws, each committee may exercise the authority of the board of directors under section 8.01.

(e) A committee may not, however:

(1) authorize distributions;

(2) approve or propose to shareholders action that this Act requires be approved by shareholders;

(3) fill vacancies on the board of directors or on any of its committees;

(4) amend articles of incorporation pursuant to section 10.02;

(5) adopt, amend, or repeal bylaws;

(6) approve a plan of merger not requiring shareholder approval;

(7) authorize or approve reacquisition of shares, except according to a formula or method prescribed by the board of directors; or

(8) authorize or approve the issuance or sale or contract for sale of shares, or determine the designation and relative rights, preferences, and limitations of a class or series of shares, except that the board of directors may authorize a committee (or a senior executive officer of the corporation) to do so within limits specifically prescribed by the board of directors.

(f) The creation of, delegation of authority to, or action by a committee does not alone constitute compliance by a director with the standards of conduct described in section 8.30.

Subchapter C. Standards of Conduct

§8.30. General Standards for Directors.—
(a) A director shall discharge his duties as a director, including his duties as a member of a committee:

(1) in good faith;
(2) with the care an ordinarily prudent person in a like position would exercise under similar circumstances; and
(3) in a manner he reasonably believes to be in the best interests of the corporation.

(b) In discharging his duties a director is entitled to rely on information, opinions, reports, or statements, including financial statements and other financial data, if prepared or presented by:

(1) one or more officers or employees of the corporation whom the director reasonably believes to be reliable and competent in the matters presented;
(2) legal counsel, public accountants, or other persons as to matters the director reasonably believes are within the person's professional or expert competence; or
(3) a committee of the board of directors of which he is not a member if the director reasonably believes the committee merits confidence.

(c) A director is not acting in good faith if he has knowledge concerning the matter in question that makes reliance otherwise permitted by subsection (b) unwarranted.
(d) A director is not liable for any action taken as a director, or any failure to take any action, if he performed the duties of his office in compliance with this section.

§8.31. Director Conflict of Interest.—
(a) A conflict of interest transaction is a transaction with the corporation in which a director of the corporation has a direct or indirect interest. A conflict of interest transaction is not voidable by the corporation solely because of the director's interest in the transaction if any one of the following is true:

(1) the material facts of the transaction and the director's interest were disclosed or known to the board of directors or a committee of the board of directors and the board of directors or committee authorized, approved, or ratified the transaction;
(2) the material facts of the transaction and the director's interest were disclosed or known to the shareholders entitled to vote and they authorized, approved, or ratified the transaction; or
(3) the transaction was fair to the corporation.

(b) For purposes of this section, a director of the corporation has an indirect interest in a transaction if (1) another entity in which he has a material financial interest or in which he is a general partner is a party to the transaction or (2) another entity of which he is a director, officer, or trustee is a party to the transaction and the transaction is or should be considered by the board of directors of the corporation.
(c) For purposes of subsection (a)(1), a conflict of interest transaction is authorized, approved, or ratified if it receives the affirmative vote of a majority of the directors on the board of directors (or on the committee) who have no direct or indirect interest in the transaction, but a transaction may not be authorized, approved, or ratified under this section by a single director. If a majority of the directors who have no direct or indirect interest in the transaction vote to authorize, approve, or ratify the transaction, a quorum is present for the purpose of taking action under this section. The presence of, or a vote cast by, a director with a direct or indirect

interest in the transaction does not affect the validity of any action taken under subsection (a)(1) if the transaction is otherwise authorized, approved, or ratified as provided in that subsection.

(d) For purposes of subsection (a)(22), a conflict of interest transaction is authorized, approved, or ratified if it receives the vote of a majority of the shares entitled to be counted under this subsection. Shares owned by or voted under the control of a director who has a direct or indirect interest in the transaction, and shares owned by or voted under the control of an entity described in subsection (b)(1), may not be counted in a vote of shareholders to determine whether to authorize, approve, or ratify a conflict of interest transaction under subsection (a)(2). The vote of those shares, however, is counted in determining whether the transaction is approved under other sections of this Act. A majority of the shares, whether or not present, that are entitled to be counted in a vote on the transaction under this subsection constitutes a quorum for the purpose of taking action under this section.

§8.32. Loans to Directors.—

(a) Except as provided by subsection (c), a corporation may not lend money to or guarantee the obligation of a director of the corporation unless:

> (1) the particular loan or guarantee is approved by a majority of the votes represented by the outstanding voting shares of all classes, voting as a single voting group, except the votes of shares owned by or voted under the control of the benefited director; or
>
> (2) the corporation's board of directors determines that the loan or guarantee benefits the corporation and either approves the specific loan or guarantee or a general plan authorizing loans and guarantees.

(b) The fact that a loan or guarantee is made in violation of this section does not affect the borrower's liability on the loan.

(c) This section does not apply to loans and guarantees authorized by statute regulating any special class of corporations.

§8.33. Liability for Unlawful Distributions.—

(a) Unless he complies with the applicable standards of conduct described in section 8.30, a director who votes for or assents to a distribution made in violation of this Act or the articles of incorporation is personally liable to the corporation for the amount of the distribution that exceeds what could have been distributed without violating this Act or the articles of incorporation.

(b) A director held liable for an unlawful distribution under subsection (a) is entitled to contribution:

> (1) from every other director who voted for or assented to the distribution without complying with the applicable standards of conduct described in section 8.30; and
>
> (2) from each shareholder for the amount the shareholder accepted knowing the distribution was made in violation of this Act or the articles of incorporation.

Subchapter D. Officers

§8.40. Required Officers.—

(a) A corporation has the officers described in its bylaws or appointed by the board of directors in accordance with the bylaws.

(b) A duly appointed officer may appoint one or more officers or assistant officers if authorized by the bylaws or the board of directors.

(c) The bylaws or the board of directors shall delegate to one of the officers responsibility for preparing minutes of the directors' and shareholders' meetings and for authenticating records of the corporation.

(d) The same individual may simultaneously hold more than one office in a corporation.

§8.41. Duties of Officers.—Each officer has the authority and shall perform the duties set forth in the bylaws or, to the extent consistent with the bylaws, the duties prescribed by the board of directors or by direction of an officer authorized by the board of directors to prescribe the duties of other officers.

§8.42. Standards of Conduct for Officers.—
(a) An officer with discretionary authority shall discharge his duties under that authority:

(1) in good faith;
(2) with the care an ordinarily prudent person in a like position would exercise under similar circumstances; and
(3) in a manner he reasonably believes to be in the best interests of the corporation.

(b) In discharging his duties an officer is entitled to rely on information, opinions, reports, or statements, including financial statements and other financial data, if prepared or presented by:

(1) one or more officers or employees of the corporation whom the officer reasonably believes to be reliable and competent in the matters presented; or
(2) legal counsel, public accountants, or other persons as to matters the officer reasonably believes are within the person's professional or expert competence.

(c) An officer is not acting in good faith if he has knowledge concerning the matter in question that makes reliance otherwise permitted by subsection (b) unwarranted.
(d) An officer is not liable for any action taken as an officer, or any failure to take any action, if he performed the duties of his office in compliance with this section.

§8.43. Resignation and Removal of Officers.—
(a) An officer may resign at any time by delivering notice to the corporation. A resignation is effective when the notice is delivered unless the notice specifies a later effective date. If a resignation is made effective at a later date and the corporation accepts the future effective date, its board of directors may fill the pending vacancy before the effective date if the board of directors provides that the successor does not take office until the effective date.
(b) A board of directors may remove any officer at any time with or without cause.

§8.44. Contract Rights of Officers.—
(a) The appointment of an officer does not itself create contract rights.
(b) An officer's removal does not affect the officer's contract rights, if any, with the corporation. An officer's resignation does not affect the corporation's contract rights, if any, with the officer.

Subchapter E. Indemnification

§8.50. Subchapter Definitions.—In this subchapter:
(1) "Corporation" includes any domestic or foreign predecessor entity of a corporation in a merger or other transaction in which the predecessor's existence ceased upon consummation of the transaction.
(2) "Director" means an individual who is or was a director of a corporation or an individual who, while a director of a corporation, is or was serving at the corporation's request as a director, officer, partner, trustee, employee, or agent of another foreign or domestic corporation, partnership, joint venture, trust, employee

benefit plan, or other enterprise. A director is considered to be serving an employee benefit plan at the corporation's request if his duties to the corporation also impose duties on, or otherwise involve services by, him to the plan or to participants in or beneficiaries of the plan. "Director" includes, unless the context requires otherwise, the estate or personal representative of a director.

(3) "Expenses" include counsel fees.

(4) "Liability" means the obligation to pay a judgment, settlement, penalty, fine (including an excise tax assessed with respect to an employee benefit plan), or reasonable expenses incurred with respect to a proceeding.

(5) "Official capacity" means: (i) when used with respect to a director, the office of director in a corporation; and (ii) when used with respect to an individual other than a director, as contemplated in section 8.56, the office in a corporation held by the officer or the employment or agency relationship undertaken by the employee or agent on behalf of the corporation. "Official capacity" does not include service for any other foreign or domestic corporation or any partnership, joint venture, trust, employee benefit plan, or other enterprise.

(6) "Party" includes an individual who was, is, or is threatened to be made a named defendant or respondent in a proceeding.

(7) "Proceeding" means any threatened, pending, or completed action, suit or proceeding, whether civil, criminal, administrative, or investigative and whether formal or informal.

§8.51. Authority to Indemnify.—

(a) Except as provided in subsection (d), a corporation may indemnify an individual made a party to a proceeding because he is or was a director against liability incurred in the proceeding if:

    (1) he conducted himself in good faith; and
    (2) he reasonably believed:
        (i) in the case of conduct in his official capacity with the corporation, that his conduct was in its best interests; and
        (ii) in all other cases, that his conduct was at least not opposed to its best interests; and
    (3) in the case of any criminal proceeding, he had no reasonable cause to believe his conduct was unlawful.

(b) A director's conduct with respect to an employee benefit plan for a purpose he reasonably believed to be in the interests of the participants in and beneficiaries of the plan is conduct that satisfies the requirement of subsection (a)(2)(ii).

(c) The termination of a proceeding by judgment, order, settlement, conviction, or upon a plea of nolo contendere or its equivalent is not, of itself, determinative that the director did not meet the standard of conduct described in this section.

(d) A corporation may not indemnify a director under this section:

    (1) in connection with a proceeding by or in the right of the corporation in which the director was adjudged liable to the corporation; or
    (2) in connection with any other proceeding charging improper personal benefit to him, whether or not involving action in his official capacity, in which he was adjudged liable on the basis that personal benefit was improperly received by him.

(e) Indemnification permitted under this section in connection with a proceeding by or in the right of the corporation is limited to reasonable expenses incurred in connection with the proceeding.

§8.52. Mandatory Indemnification.—

Unless limited by its articles of incorporation, a corporation shall indemnify a director who was wholly successful, on the merits or otherwise, in the defense of any proceeding to which he was a party because he is or was a director of the corporation against reasonable expenses incurred by him in connection with the proceeding.

§8.53. Advance for Expenses.—
(a) A corporation may pay for or reimburse the reasonable expenses incurred by a director who is a party to a proceeding in advance of final disposition of the proceeding if:

(1) the director furnishes the corporation a written affirmative of his good faith belief that he has met the standard of conduct described in section 8.51;
(2) the director furnishes the corporation a written undertaking, executed personally or on his behalf, to repay the advance if it is ultimately determined that he did not meet the standard of conduct; and
(3) a determination is made that the facts then known to those making the determination would not preclude indemnification under this subchapter.

(b) The undertaking required by subsection (a)(2) must be an unlimited general obligation of the director but need not be secured and may be accepted without reference to financial ability to make repayment.
(c) Determinations and authorizations of payments under this section shall be made in the manner specified in section 8.55.

§8.54. Court-Ordered Indemnification.—Unless a corporation's articles of incorporation provide otherwise, a director of the corporation who is a party to a proceeding may apply for indemnification to the court conducting the proceeding or to another court of competent jurisdiction. On receipt of an application, the court after giving any notice the court considers necessary may order indemnification if it determines:

(1) the director is entitled to mandatory indemnification under section 8.52, in which case the court shall also order the corporation to pay the director's reasonable expenses incurred to obtain court-ordered indemnification; or
(2) the director is fairly and reasonably entitled to indemnification in view of all the relevant circumstances, whether or not he met the standard of conduct set forth in section 8.51 or was adjudged liable as described in section 8.51(d), but if he was adjudged so liable his indemnification is limited to reasonable expenses incurred.

§8.55. Determination and Authorization of Indemnification.—
(a) A corporation may not indemnify a director under section 8.51 unless authorized in the specific case after a determination has been made that indemnification of the director is permissible in the circumstances because he has met the standard of conduct set forth in section 8.51.
(b) The determination shall be made:

(1) by the board of directors by majority vote of a quorum consisting of directors not at the time parties to the proceeding;
(2) if a quorum cannot be obtained under subdivision (1), by majority vote of a committee duly designated by the board of directors (in which designation directors who are parties may participate), consisting solely of two or more directors not at the time parties to the proceeding;
(3) by special legal counsel:
(i) selected by the board of directors or its committee in the manner prescribed in subdivision (1) or (2); or
(ii) if a quorum of the board of directors cannot be obtained under subdivision (1) and a committee cannot be designated under subdivision (2), selected by majority vote of the full board of directors (in which selection directors who are parties may participate); or

(4) by the shareholders, but shares owned by or voted under the control of directors who are at the time parties to the proceeding may not be voted on the determination.

(c) Authorization of indemnification and evaluation as to reasonableness of expenses shall be made in the same manner as the determination that indemnification is permissible, except that if the determination is made by special legal counsel, authorization of indemnification and evaluation as to reasonableness of expenses shall be made by those entitled under subsection (b)(3) to select counsel.

§8.56. Indemnification of Officers, Employees, and Agents.—Unless a corporation's articles of incorporation provide otherwise:
(1) An officer of the corporation who is not a director is entitled to mandatory indemnification under section 8.52, and is entitled to apply for court-ordered indemnification under section 8.54, in each case to the same extent as a director;
(2) the corporation may indemnify and advance expenses under this subchapter to an officer, employee, or agent of the corporation who is not a director to the same extent as to a director; and
(3) a corporation may also indemnify and advance expenses to an officer, employee, or agent who is not a director to the extent, consistent with public policy, that may be provided by its articles of incorporation, bylaws, general or specific action of its board of directors, or contract.

§8.57. Insurance.—A corporation may purchase and maintain insurance on behalf of an individual who is or was a director, officer, employee, or agent of the corporation, or who, while a director, officer, employee, or agent of the corporation, is or was serving at the request of the corporation as a director, officer, partner, trustee, employee, or agent of another foreign or domestic corporation, partnership, joint venture, trust, employee benefit plan, or other enterprise, against liability asserted against or incurred by him in that capacity or arising from his status as a director, officer, employee, or agent, whether or not the corporation would have power to indemnify him against the same liability under section 8.51 or 8.52.

§8.58. Application of Subchapter.—
(a) A provision treating a corporation's indemnification of or advance for expenses to directors that is contained in its articles of incorporation, bylaws, a resolution of its shareholders or board of directors, or in a contract or otherwise, is valid only if and to the extent the provision is consistent with this subchapter. If articles of incorporation limit indemnification or advance for expenses, indemnification and advance for expense are valid only to the extent consistent with the articles.
(b) This subchapter does not limit a corporation's power to pay or reimburse expenses incurred by a director in connection with his appearance as a witness in a proceeding at a time when he has not been made a named defendant or respondent to the proceeding.

CHAPTER 9. [Reserved]

CHAPTER 10. AMENDMENT OF ARTICLES OF INCORPORATION AND BYLAWS

Subchapter A. Amendment of Articles of Incorporation

§10.01. Authority To Amend.—
(a) A corporation may amend its articles of incorporation at any time to add or change a provision that is required or permitted in the articles of incorporation or to delete a provision not required in the articles of incorporation. Whether a

provision is required or permitted in the articles of incorporation is determined as of the effective date of the amendment.

(b) A shareholder of the corporation does not have a vested property right resulting from any provision in the articles of incorporation, including provisions relating to management, control, capital structure, dividend entitlement, or purpose or duration of the corporation.

§10.02. Amendment by Board of Directors. — Unless the articles of incorporation provide otherwise, a corporation's board of directors may adopt one or more amendments to the corporation's articles of incorporation without shareholder action:

(1) to extend the duration of the corporation if it was incorporation at a time when limited duration was required by law;

(2) to delete the names and addresses of the initial directors;

(3) to delete the name and address of the initial registered agent or registered office, if a statement of change is on file with the secretary of state;

(4) to change each issue and unissued authorized share of an outstanding class into a greater number of whole shares if the corporation has only shares of that class outstanding;

(5) to change the corporate name by substituting the word "corporation," "incorporated," "company," "limited," or the abbreviation "corp.,""inc.," "co.," or ltd.," for a similar word or abbreviation in the name, or by adding, deleting, or changing a geographical attribution for the name; or

(6) to make any other change expressly permitted by this Act to be made without shareholder action.

§10.03. Amendment by Board of Directors and Shareholders. —

(a) A corporation's board of directors may propose one or more amendments to the articles of incorporation for submission to the shareholders.

(b) For the amendment to be adopted:

(1) the board of directors must recommend the amendment to the shareholders unless the board of directors determines that because of conflict of interest or other special circumstances it should make no recommendation and communicates the basis for its determination to the shareholders with the amendment; and

(2) the shareholders entitled to vote on the amendment must approve the amendment as provided in subsection (e).

(c) The board of directors may condition its submission of the proposed amendment on any basis.

(d) The corporation shall notify each shareholder, whether or not entitled to vote, of the proposed shareholders' meeting in accordance with section 7.05. The notice of meeting must also state that the purpose, or one of the purposes, of the meeting is to consider the proposed amendment and contain or be accompanied by a copy or summary of the amendment.

(e) Unless this Act, the articles of incorporation, or the board of directors (acting pursuant to subsection (c)) require a greater vote or a vote by voting groups, the amendment to be adopted must be approved by:

(1) a majority of the votes entitled to be cast on the amendment by any voting group with respect to which the amendment would create dissenters' rights; and

(2) the votes required by section 7.25 and 7.26 by every other voting group entitled to vote on the amendment.

§10.04. Voting on Amendments by Voting Groups.—
(a) The holders of the outstanding shares of a class are entitled to vote as a separate voting group (if shareholder voting is otherwise required by this Act) on a proposed amendment if the amendment would:

(1) increase or decrease the aggregate number of authorized shares of the class;
(2) effect an exchange or reclassification of all or part of the shares of the class into shares of another class;
(3) effect an exchange or reclassification, or create the right of exchange, of all or part of the shares of another class into shares of the class;
(4) change the designation, rights, preferences, or limitations of all or part of the shares of the class;
(5) change the shares of all or part of the class into a different number of shares of the same class;
(6) create a new class of shares having rights or preferences with respect to distributions or to dissolution that are prior, superior, or substantially equal to the shares of the class;
(7) increase the rights, preferences, or number of authorized shares of any class that, after giving effect to the amendment, have rights or preferences with respect to distributions or to dissolution that are prior, superior, or substantially equal to the shares of the class;
(8) limit or deny an existing preemptive right of all or part of the shares of the class; or
(9) cancel or otherwise affect rights to distributions or dividends that have accumulated but not yet been declared on all or part of the shares of the class.

(b) If a proposed amendment would affect a series of a class of shares in one or more of the ways described in subsection (a), the shares of that series are entitled to vote as a separate voting group on the proposed amendment.
(c) If a proposed amendment that entitled two or more series of shares to vote as separate voting groups under this section would affect those two or more series in the same or a substantially similar way, the shares of all the series so affected must vote together as a single voting group on the proposed amendment.
(d) A class or series of shares is entitled to the voting rights granted by this section although the articles of incorporation provide that the shares are nonvoting shares.

§10.05. Amendment Before Issuance of Shares.—If a corporation has not yet issued shares, its incorporations or board of directors may adopt one or more amendments to the corporation's articles of incorporation.

§10.06. Articles of Amendment.—A corporation amending its articles of incorporation shall deliver to the secretary of state for filing articles of amendment setting forth:
(1) the name of the corporation;
(2) the text of each amendment adopted;
(3) if an amendment provides for an exchange, reclassification, or cancellation of issued shares, provisions for implementing the amendment if not contained in the amendment itself;
(4) the date of each amendment's adoption;
(5) if an amendment was adopted by the incorporators or board of directors without shareholder action, a statement to that effect and that shareholder action was not required;
(6) if an amendment was approved by the shareholders:
(i) the designation, number of outstanding shares, number of votes entitled to be cast by each voting group entitled to vote separately on the amendment, and number of votes of each voting group indisputably represented at the meeting;
(ii) either the total number of votes cast for and against the amendment by each voting group entitled to vote separately on the amendment or the total number

of undisputed votes cast for the amendment by each voting group and a statement that the number cast for the amendment by each voting group was sufficient for approval by that voting group.

§10.07. Restated Articles of Incorporation.—

(a) A corporation's board of directors may restate its articles of incorporation at any time with or without shareholder action.

(b) The restatement may include one or more amendments to the articles. If the restatement includes an amendment requiring shareholder approval, it must be adopted as provided in section 10.03.

(c) If the board of directors submits a restatement for shareholder action, the corporation shall notify each shareholder, whether or not entitled to vote, of the proposed shareholders' meeting in accordance with section 7.05. The notice must also state that the purpose, or one of the purposes, of the meeting is to consider the proposed restatement and contain or be accompanied by a copy of the restatement that identifies any amendment or other change it would make in the articles.

(d) A corporation restating its articles of incorporation shall deliver to the secretary of state for filing articles of restatement setting forth the name of the corporation and the text of the restated articles of incorporation together with a certificate setting forth:

> (1) whether the restatement contains an amendment to the articles requiring shareholder approval and, if it does not, that the board of directors adopted the restatement; or
>
> (2) if the restatement contains an amendment to the articles requiring shareholder approval, the information required by section 10.06.

(e) Duly adopted restated articles of incorporation supersede the original articles of incorporation and all amendments to them.

(f) The secretary of state may certify restated articles of incorporation, as the articles of incorporation currently in effect, without including the certificate information required by subsection (d).

§10.08. Amendment Pursuant to Reorganization.—

(a) A corporation's articles of incorporation may be amended without action by the board of directors or shareholders to carry out a plan of reorganization ordered or decreed by a court of competent jurisdiction under federal statute if the articles of incorporation after amendment contain only provisions required or permitted by section 2.02.

(b) The individual or individuals designed by the court shall deliver to the secretary of state for filing articles of amendment setting forth:

> (1) the name of the corporation;
>
> (2) the text of each amendment approved by the court;
>
> (3) the date of the court's order or decree approving the articles of amendment;
>
> (4) the title of the reorganization proceeding in which the order or decree was entered; and
>
> (5) a statement that the court had jurisdiction of the proceeding under federal statute.

(c) Shareholders of a corporation undergoing reorganization do not have dissenters' rights except as and to the extent provided in the reorganization plan.

(d) This section does not apply after entry of a final decree in the reorganization proceeding even though the court retains jurisdiction of the proceeding for limited purposes unrelated to consummation of the reorganization plan.

§10.09. Effect of Amendment.—An amendment to articles of incorporation does not affect a cause of action existing against or in favor of the corporation, a proceeding to which the corporation is a party, or the existing rights of persons other than shareholders of the corporation. An amendment changing a corporation's name does not abate a proceeding brought by or against the corporation in its former name.

Subchapter B. Amendment of Bylaws

§10.20. Amendment by Board of Directors of Shareholders.—
(a) A corporation's board of directors may amend or repeal the corporation's bylaws unless:

> (1) the articles of incorporation or this Act reserve this power exclusively to the shareholders in whole or part; or
> (2) the shareholders in amending or repealing a particular bylaw provide expressly that the board of directors may not amend or repeal that bylaw.

(b) A corporation's shareholders may amend or repeal the corporation's bylaws even though the bylaws may also be amended or repealed by its board of directors.

§10.21. Bylaw Increasing Quorum or Voting Requirement for Shareholders.—
(a) If authorized by the articles of incorporation, the shareholders may adopt or amend a bylaw that fixes a greater quorum or voting requirement for shareholders (or voting groups of shareholders) than is required by this Act. The adoption or amendment of a bylaw that adds, changes, or deletes a greater quorum or voting requirement for shareholders must meet the same quorum requirement and be adopted by the same vote and voting groups required to take action under the quorum and voting requirement then in effect or proposed to be adopted, whichever is greater.
(b) A bylaw that fixes a greater quorum or voting requirement for shareholders under subsection (a) may not be adopted, amended, or repealed by the board of directors.

§10.22. Bylaw Increasing Quorum or Voting Requirement for Directors.—
(a) A bylaw that fixes a greater quorum or voting requirement for the board of directors may be amended or repealed:

> (1) if originally adopted by the shareholders, only by the shareholders;
> (2) if originally adopted by the board of directors, either by the shareholders or by the board of directors.

(b) A bylaw adopted or amended by the shareholders that fixes a greater quorum or voting requirement for the board of directors may provide that it may be amended or repealed only by a specified vote of either the shareholders or the board of directors.
(c) Action by the board of directors under subsection (a)(2) to adopt or amend a bylaw that changes the quorum or voting requirement for the board of directors must meet the same quorum requirement and be adopted by the same vote required to take action under the quorum and voting requirement then in effect or proposed to be adopted, whichever is greater.

CHAPTER 11. MERGER AND SHARE EXCHANGE

§11.01. Merger.—
(a) One or more corporations may merge into another corporation if the board of directors of each corporation adopts and its shareholders (if required by section 11.03) approve a plan of merger.
(b) The plan of merger must set forth:

(1) the name of each corporation planning to merge and the name of the surviving corporation into which each other corporation plans to merge;

(2) the terms and conditions of the merger; and

(3) the manner and basis of converting the shares of each corporation into shares, obligations, or other securities of the surviving or any other corporation or into cash or other property in whole or part.

(c) The plan of merger may set forth:

(1) amendments to the articles of incorporation of the surviving corporation; and

(2) other provisions relating to the merger.

§11.02. Share Exchange.—

(a) A corporation may acquire all of the outstanding shares of one or more classes or series of another corporation if the board of directors of each corporation adopts and its shareholders (if required by section 11.03) approve the exchange.

(b) The plan of exchange must set forth:

(1) the name of the corporation whose shares will be acquired and the name of the acquiring corporation;

(2) the terms and conditions of the exchange;

(3) the manner and basis of exchanging the shares to be acquired for shares, obligations, or other securities of the acquiring or any other corporation or for cash or other property in whole or part.

(c) The plan of exchange may set forth other provisions relating to the exchange.

(d) This section does not limit the power of a corporation to acquire all or part of the shares of one or more classes or series of another corporation through a voluntary exchange or otherwise.

§11.03. Action on Plan.—

(a) After adopting a plan of merger or share exchange, the board of directors of each corporation party to the merger, and the board of directors of the corporation whose shares will be acquired in the share exchange, shall submit the plan of merger (except as provided in subsection (g)) or share exchange for approval by its shareholders.

(b) For plan of merger or share exchange to be approved:

(1) the board of directors must recommend the plan of merger or share exchange to the shareholders, unless the board of directors determines that because of conflict of interest or other special circumstances it should make no recommendation and communicates the basis for its determination to the shareholders with the plan; and

(2) the shareholders entitled to vote must approve the plan.

(c) The board of directors may condition its submission of the proposed merger or share exchange on any basis.

(d) The corporation shall notify each shareholder, whether or not entitled to vote, of the proposed shareholders' meeting in accordance with section 7.05. The notice must also state that the purpose, or one of the purposes, of the meeting is to consider the plan of merger or share exchange and contain or be accompanied by a copy or summary of the plan.

(e) Unless this Act, the articles of incorporation, or the board of directors (acting pursuant to subsection (c)) require a greater vote or a vote by voting groups, the plan of merger or share exchange to be authorized must be approved by each voting group entitled to vote separately on the plan by a majority of all the votes entitled to be cast on the plan by that voting group.

(f) Separate voting by voting groups is required:

(1) on a plan of merger if the plan contains a provision that, if contained in a proposed amendment to articles of incorporation, would require action by one or more separate voting groups on the proposed amendment under section 10.04;

(2) on a plan of share exchange by each class or series of shares included in the exchange, with each class or series constituting a separate voting group.

(g) Action by the shareholders of the surviving corporation on a plan of merger is not required if:

(1) the articles of incorporation of the surviving corporation will not differ (except for amendments enumerated in section 10.02) from its articles before the merger;

(2) each shareholder of the surviving corporation whose shares were outstanding immediately before the effective date of the merger will hold the same number of shares, with identical designations, preferences, limitations, and relative rights, immediately after;

(3) the number of voting shares outstanding immediately after the merger, plus the number of voting shares issuable as a result of the merger (either by the conversion of securities issued pursuant to the merger or the exercise of rights and warrants issued pursuant to the merger), will not exceed by more than 20 percent the total number of voting shares of the surviving corporation outstanding immediately before the merger; and

(4) the number of participating shares outstanding immediately after the merger, plus the number of participating shares issuable as a result of the merger (either by the conversion of securities issued pursuant to the merger or the exercise of rights and warrants issued pursuant to the merger), will not exceed by more than 20 percent the total number of participating shares outstanding immediately before the merger.

(h) As used in subsection (g):

(1) "Participating shares" means shares that entitle their holders to participate without limitation in distributions.

(2) "Voting shares" means shares that entitle their holders to vote unconditionally in elections of directors.

(i) After a merger or share exchange is authorized, and at any time before articles of merger or share exchange are filed, the planned merger or share exchange may be abandoned (subject to any contractual rights), without further shareholder action, in accordance with the procedure set forth in the plan of merger or share exchange or, if none is set forth, in the manner determined by the board of directors.

§11.04. Merger of Subsidiary.—

(a) A parent corporation owning at least 90 percent of the outstanding shares of each class of a subsidiary corporation may merge the subsidiary into itself without approval of the shareholders of the parent or subsidiary.

(b) The board of directors of the parent shall adopt a plan of merger that sets forth:

(1) the names of the parent and subsidiary; and

(2) the manner and basis of converting the shares of the subsidiary into shares, obligations, or other securities of the parent or any other corporation or into cash or other property in whole or part.

(c) The parent shall mail a copy or summary of the plan of merger to each shareholder of the subsidiary who does not waive the mailing requirement in writing.

(d) The parent may not deliver articles of merger to the secretary of state for filing until at least 30 days after the date it mailed a copy of the plan of merger to each shareholder of the subsidiary who did not waive the mailing requirement.

(e) Articles of merger under this section may not contain amendments to the articles of incorporation of the parent corporation (except for amendments enumerated in section 10.02).

§11.05. Articles of Merger or Share Exchange.—

(a) After a plan of merger or share exchange is approved by the shareholders, or adopted by the board of directors if shareholder approval is not required, the surviving or acquiring corporation shall deliver to the secretary of state for filing articles of merger or share exchange setting forth:

(1) the plan of merger or share exchange;
(2) if shareholder approval was not required, a statement to that effect;
(3) if approval of the shareholders of one or more corporations party to the merger or share exchange was required:
(i) the designation, number of outstanding shares, and number of votes entitled to be cast by each voting group entitled to vote separately on the plan as to each corporation; and
(ii) either the total number of votes cast for and against the plan by each voting group entitled to vote separately on the plan or the total number of undisputed votes cast for the plan separately by each voting group and a statement that the number cast for the plan by each voting group was sufficient for approval by that voting group.

(b) A merger or share exchange takes effect upon the effective date of the articles of merger or share exchange.

§11.06. Effect of Merger or Share Exchange.—

(a) When a merger takes effect:

(1) every other corporation party to the merger merges into the surviving corporation and the separate existence of every corporation except the surviving corporation ceases;
(2) the title to all real estate and other property owned by each corporation party to the merger is vested in the surviving corporation without reversion or impairment;
(3) the surviving corporation has all liabilities of each corporation party to the merger;
(4) a proceeding pending against any corporation party to the merger may be continued as if the merger did not occur or the surviving corporation may be substituted in the proceeding for the corporation whose existence ceased.
(5) the articles of incorporation of the surviving corporation are amended to the extent provided in the plan of merger; and
(6) the shares of each corporation party to the merger that are to be converted into shares, obligations, or other securities of the surviving or any other corporation or into cash or other property are converted, and the former holders of the shares are entitled only to the rights provided in the articles of merger or to their rights under chapter 13.

(b) When a share exchange takes effect, the shares of each acquired corporation are exchanged as provided in the plan, and the former holders of the shares are entitled only to the exchange rights provided in the articles of share exchange or to their rights under chapter 13.

§11.07. Merger or Share Exchange with Foreign Corporation.—

(a) One or more foreign corporations may merge or enter into a share exchange with one or more domestic corporations if:

(1) in a merger, the merger is permitted by the law of the state or country under whose law each foreign corporation is incorporated and each foreign corporation complies with that law in effecting the merger;

(2) in a share exchange, the corporation whose shares will be acquired is a domestic corporation, whether or not a share exchange is permitted by the law of the state or country under whose law the acquiring corporation is incorporated;

(3) the foreign corporation complies with section 11.05 if it is the surviving corporation of the merger or acquiring corporation of the share exchange, and

(4) each domestic corporation complies with the applicable provisions of sections 11.01 through 11.04 and, if it is the surviving corporation of the merger or acquiring corporation of the share exchange, with section 11.05.

(b) Upon the merger or share exchange taking effect, the surviving foreign corporation of a merger and the acquiring foreign corporation of a share exchange is deemed:

(1) to appoint the secretary of state as its agent for service of process in a proceeding to enforce any obligation or the rights of dissenting shareholders of each domestic corporation party to the merger or share exchange; and

(2) to agree that it will promptly pay to the dissenting shareholder of each domestic corporation party to the merger or share exchange the amount, if any, to which they are entitled under chapter 13.

(c) This section does not limit the power of a foreign corporation to acquire all or part of the shares of one or more classes or series of a domestic corporation through a voluntary exchange or otherwise.

CHAPTER 12. SALE OF ASSETS

§12.01. Sale of Assets in Regular Course of Business and Mortgage of Assets.—

(a) A corporation may, on the terms and conditions and for the consideration determined by the board of directors:

(1) sell, lease, exchange, or otherwise dispose of all, or substantially all, of its property in the usual and regular course of business;

(2) mortgage, pledge, dedicate to the repayment of indebtedness (whether with or without recourse), or otherwise encumber any or all of its property whether or not in the usual and regular course of business; or

(3) transfer any or all of its property to a corporation all the shares of which are owned by the corporation.

(b) Unless the articles of incorporation require it, approval by the shareholders of a transaction described in subsection (a) is not required.

§12.02. Sale of Assets Other Than in Regular Course of Business.—

(a) A corporation may sell, lease, exchange, or otherwise dispose of all, or substantially all, of its property (with or without the good will), otherwise than in the usual and regular course of business, on the terms and conditions and for the consideration determined by the corporation's board of directors, if the board of directors proposes and its shareholders approved the proposed transaction.

(b) For a transaction to be authorized:

(1) the board of directors must recommend the proposed transaction to the shareholders unless the board of directors determines that because of conflict of interest or other special circumstances it should make no recommendation and communicates the basis for its determination to the shareholders with the submission of the proposed transaction; and

(2) the shareholders entitled to vote must approve the transaction.

(c) The board of directors may condition its submission of the proposed transaction on any basis.

(d) The corporation shall notify each shareholder, whether or not entitled to vote, of the proposed shareholders' meeting in accordance with section 7.05. The notice must also state that the purpose, or one of the purposes, of the meeting is to consider the sale, lease, exchange, or other disposition of all, or substantially all, the property of the corporation and contain or be accompanied by a description of the transaction.

(e) Unless the articles of incorporation or the board of directors (acting pursuant to subsection (c)) require a greater vote or a vote by voting groups, the transaction to be authorized must be approved by a majority of all the votes entitled to be cast on the transaction.

(f) After a sale, lease, exchange, or other disposition of property is authorized, the transaction may be abandoned (subject to any contractual rights) without further shareholder action.

(g) A transaction that constitutes a distribution is governed by section 6.40 and not by this section.

CHAPTER 13. DISSENTERS' RIGHTS

Subchapter A. Right To Dissent and Obtain Payment for Shares

§13.01. Definitions.—In this chapter:

(1) "Corporation" means the issuer of the shares held by a dissenter before the corporate action, or the surviving or acquiring corporation by merger or share exchange of that issuer.

(2) "Dissenter" means a shareholder who is entitled to dissent from corporate action under section 13.02 and who exercises that right when and in the manner required by sections 13.20 through 13.28.

(3) "Fair value," with respect to a dissenter's shares, means the value of the shares immediately before the effectuation of the corporate action to which the dissenter objects, excluding any appreciation or depreciation in anticipation of the corporate action unless exclusion would be inequitable.

(4) "Interest" means interest from the effective date of the corporate action until the date of payment, at the average rate currently paid by the corporation on its principal bank loans or, if none, at a rate that is fair and equitable under all the circumstances.

(5) "Record shareholder" means the person in whose name shares are registered in the records of a corporation or the beneficial owner of shares to the extent of the rights granted by a nominee certificate on file with a corporation.

(6) "Beneficial shareholder" means the person who is a beneficial owner of shares held by a nominee as the record shareholder.

(7) "Shareholder" means the record shareholder or the beneficial shareholder.

§13.02. Right To Dissent.—

(a) A shareholder is entitled to dissent from, and obtain payment of the fair value of his shares in the event of, any of the following corporate actions:

(1) consummation of a plan of merger to which the corporation is a party (i) if shareholder approval is required for the merger by section 11.03 or the articles

of incorporation and the shareholder is entitled to vote on the merger or (ii) if the corporation is a subsidiary that is merged with its parent under section 11.04; (2) consummation of a plan of share exchange to which the corporation is a party as the corporation whose shares will be acquired, if the shareholder is entitled to vote on the plan;

(3) consummation of a sale or exchange of all, or substantially all, of the property of the corporation other than in the usual and regular course of business, if the shareholder is entitled to vote on the sale or exchange, including a sale in dissolution, but not including a sale pursuant to court order or a sale for cash pursuant to a plan by which all or substantially all of the net proceeds of the sale will be distributed to the shareholders within one year after the date of sale;

(4) an amendment of the articles of incorporation that materially and adversely affects rights in respect of a dissenter's shares because it:

(i) alters or abolishes a preferential right of the shares;

(ii) creates, alters, or abolishes a right in respect of redemption, including a provision respecting a sinking fund for the redemption or repurchase, of the shares;

(iii) alters or abolishes a preemptive right of the holder of the shares to acquire shares or other securities;

(iv) excludes or limits the right of the shares to vote on any matter, or to cumulate votes, other than a limitation by dilution through issuance of shares or other securities with similar voting rights; or

(v) reduces the number of shares owned by the shareholder to a fraction of a share if the fractional share so created is to be acquired for cash under section 6.04; or

(5) any corporate action taken pursuant to a shareholder vote to the extent the articles of incorporation, bylaws, or a resolution of the board of directors provides that voting or nonvoting shareholders are entitled to dissent and obtain payment for their shares.

(b) A shareholder entitled to dissent and obtain payment for his shares under this chapter may not challenge the corporate action creating his entitlement unless the action is unlawful or fraudulent with respect to the shareholder or the corporation.

§13.03. Dissent by Nominees and Beneficial Owners.—

(a) A record shareholder may assert dissenters' rights as to fewer than all the shares registered in his name only if he dissents with respect to all shares beneficially owned by any one person and notifies the corporation in writing of the name and address of each person on whose behalf he asserts dissenters' rights. The rights of a partial dissenter under this subsection are determined as if the shares as to which he dissents and his other shares were registered in the names of different shareholders.

(b) A beneficial shareholder may assert dissenters' rights as to shares held on his behalf only if:

(1) he submits to the corporation the record shareholder's written consent to the dissent not later than the time the beneficial shareholder asserts dissenters' rights; and

(2) he does so with respect to all shares of which he is the beneficial shareholder or over which he has power to direct the vote.

Subchapter B. Procedure for Exercise of Dissenters' Rights

§13.20. Notice of Dissenters' Rights.—

(a) If proposed corporate action creating dissenters' rights under section 13.02 is submitted to a vote at a shareholders' meeting, the meeting notice must state that shareholders are or may be entitled to assert dissenters' rights under this chapter and be accompanied by a copy of this chapter.

(b) If corporate action creating dissenters' rights under section 13.02 is taken without a vote of shareholders, the corporation shall notify in writing all shareholders entitled to assert dissenters' rights that the action was taken and send them the dissenters' notice described in section 13.22.

§13.21. Notice of Intent To Demand Payment.—

(a) If proposed corporate action creating dissenters' rights under section 13.02 is submitted to a vote at a shareholders' meeting, a shareholder who wishes to assert dissenters' rights (1) must deliver to the corporation before the vote is taken written notice of his intent to demand payment for his shares if the proposed action is effectuated and (2) must not vote his shares in favor of the proposed action.

(b) A shareholder who does not satisfy the requirements of subsection (a) is not entitled to payment for his shares under this chapter.

§13.22. Dissenters' Notice.—

(a) If proposed corporate action creating dissenters' rights under section 13.02 is authorized at a shareholders' meeting, the corporation shall deliver a written dissenters' notice to all shareholders who satisfied the requirements of section 13.21.

(b) The dissenters' notice must be sent no later than 10 days after the corporate action was taken, and must:

> (1) state where the payment demand must be sent and where and when certificates for certificated shares must be deposited;
> (2) inform holders of uncertificated shares to what extent transfer of the shares will be restricted after the payment demand is received;
> (3) supply a form for demanding payment that includes the date of the first announcement to news media or to shareholders of the terms of the proposed corporate action and requires that the person asserting dissenters' rights certify whether or not he acquired beneficial ownership of the shares before that date;
> (4) set a date by which the corporation must receive the payment demand, which date may not be fewer than 30 nor more than 60 days after the date the subsection (a) notice is delivered; and
> (5) be accompanied by a copy of this chapter.

§13.23. Duty To Demand Payment.—

(a) A shareholder sent a dissenter's notice described in section 13.22 must demand payment, certify whether he acquired beneficial ownership of the shares before the date required to be set forth in the dissenters' notice pursuant to section 13.22(b)(3), and deposit his certificates in accordance with the terms of the notice.

(b) The shareholder who demands payment and deposits his shares under section (a) retains all other rights of a shareholder until these rights are cancelled or modified by the taking of the proposed corporate action.

(c) A shareholder who does not demand payment or deposit his share certificates where required, each by the date set in the dissenters' notice, is not entitled to payment for his shares under this chapter.

§13.24. Share Restrictions.—

(a) The corporation may restrict the transfer of uncertificated shares from the date the demand for their payment is received until the proposed corporate action is taken or the restrictions released under section 13.26.

(b) The person for whom dissenters' rights are asserted as to uncertificated shares retains all other rights of a shareholder until these rights are cancelled or modified by the taking of the proposed corporate action.

§13.25. Payment.—

(a) Except as provided in section 13.27, as soon as the proposed corporate action is taken, or upon receipt of a payment demand, the corporation shall pay each dissenter who complied with section 13.23 the amount the corporation estimates to be the fair value of his shares, plus accrued interest.

(b) The payment must be accompanied by:

(1) the corporation's balance sheet as of the end of a fiscal year ending not more than 16 months before the date of payment, an income statement for that year, a statement of changes in shareholders' equity for that year, and the latest available interim financial statements, if any;

(2) a statement of the corporation's estimate of the fair value of the shares;

(3) an explanation of how the interest was calculated;

(4) a statement of the dissenter's right to demand payment under section 13.28; and

(5) a copy of this chapter.

§13.26. Failure To Take Action.—

(a) If the corporation does not take the proposed action within 60 days after the date set for demanding payment and depositing share certificates, the corporation shall return the deposited certificates and release the transfer restrictions imposed on uncertificated shares.

(b) If after returning deposited certificates and releasing transfer restrictions, the corporation takes the proposed action, it must send a new dissenters' notice under section 13.22 and repeat the payment demand procedure.

§13.27. After-acquired Shares.—

(a) A corporation may elect to withhold payment required by section 13.25 from a dissenter unless he was the beneficial owner of the shares before the date set forth in the dissenters' notice as the date of the first announcement to news media or to shareholders of the terms of the proposed corporate action.

(b) To the extent the corporation elects to withhold payment under subsection (a), after taking the proposed corporate action, it shall estimate the fair value of the shares, plus accrued interest, and shall pay this amount to each dissenter who agrees to accept it in full satisfaction of his demand. The corporation shall send with its offer a statement of its estimate of the fair value of the shares, an explanation of how the interest was calculated, and a statement of the dissenter's right to demand payment under section 13.28.

§13.28. Procedure if Shareholder Dissatisfied with Payment or Offer.—

(a) A dissenter may notify the corporation in writing of his own estimate of the fair value of his shares and amount of interest due, and demand payment of his estimate (less any payment under section 13.25), or reject the corporation's offer under section 13.27 and demand payment of the fair value of his shares and interest due, if:

(1) the dissenter believes that the amount paid under section 13.25 or offered under section 13.27 is less than the fair value of his shares or that the interest due is incorrectly calculated;

(2) the corporation fails to make payment under section 13.25 within 60 days after the date set for demanding payment; or

(3) the corporation, having failed to take the proposed action, does not return the deposited certificates or release the transfer restrictions imposed on uncertificated shares within 60 days after the date set for demanding payment.

(b) A dissenter waives his right to demand payment under this section unless he notifies the corporation of his demand in writing under subsection (a) within 30 days after the corporation made or offered payment for his shares.

Subchapter C. Judicial Appraisal of Shares

§13.30. Court Action.—
(a) If a demand for payment under section 13.28 remains unsettled, the corporation shall commence a proceeding within 60 days after receiving the payment demand and petition the court to determine the fair value of the shares and accrued interest. If the corporation does not commence the proceeding within the 60-day period, it shall pay each dissenter whose demand remains unsettled the amount demanded.

(b) The corporation shall commence the proceeding in the [name or describe] court of the county where a corporation's principal office (or, if none in this state, its registered office) is located. If the corporation is a foreign corporation without a registered office in this state, it shall commence the proceeding in the county in this state where the registered office of the domestic corporation merged with or whose shares were acquired by the foreign corporation was located.

(c) The corporation shall make all dissenters (whether or not residents of this state) whose demands remain unsettled parties to the proceeding as in an action against their shares and all parties must be served with a copy of the petition. Nonresidents may be served by registered or certified mail or by publication as proved by law.

(d) The jurisdiction of the court in which the proceeding is commenced under subsection (b) is plenary and exclusive. The court may appoint one or more persons as appraisers to receive evidence and recommend decision on the question of fair value. The appraisers have the powers described in the order appointing them, or in any amendment to it. The dissenters are entitled to the same discovery rights as parties in other civil proceedings.

(e) Each dissenter made a party to the proceeding is entitled to judgment (1) for the amount, if any, by which the court finds the fair value of his shares, plus interest, exceeds the amount paid by the corporation or (2) for the fair value, plus accrued interest, of his after-acquired shares for which the corporation elected to withhold payment under section 13.27.

§13.31. Court Costs and Counsel Fees.—
(a) The court in an appraisal proceeding commenced under section 13.30 shall determine all costs of the proceeding, including the reasonable compensation and expenses of appraisers appointed by the court. The court shall assess the costs against the corporation, except that the court may assess costs against all or some of the dissenters, in amounts the court finds equitable, to the extent the court finds the dissenters acted arbitrarily, vexatiously, or not in good faith in demanding payment under section 13.28.

(b) The court may also assess the fees and expenses of counsel and experts for the respective parties, in amounts the court finds equitable:

(1) against the corporation and in favor of any or all dissenters if the court finds the corporation did not substantially comply with the requirements of sections 13.20 through 13.28; or

(2) against either the corporation or a dissenter, in favor of any other party, if the court finds that the party against whom the fees and expenses are assessed acted arbitrarily, vexatiously, or not in good faith with respect to the rights provided by this chapter.

(c) If the court finds that the services of counsel for any dissenter were of substantial benefit to other dissenters similarly situated, and that the fees for those services should not be assessed against the corporation, the court may award to these counsel reasonable fees to be paid out of the amounts awarded the dissenters who were benefited.

CHAPTER 14. DISSOLUTION

Subchapter A. Voluntary Dissolution

§14.01. Dissolution by Incorporators or Initial Directors.—A majority of the incorporators or initial directors of a corporation that has not issued shares or has not commenced business may dissolve the corporation by delivering to the secretary of state for filing articles of dissolution that set forth:

(1) the name of the corporation;
(2) the date of its incorporation;
(3) either (i) that none of the corporation's shares has been issued or (ii) that the corporation has not commenced business;
(4) that no debt of the corporation remains unpaid;
(5) that the net assets of the corporation remaining after winding up have been distributed to the shareholders, if shares were issued; and
(6) that a majority of the incorporators or initial directors authorized the dissolution.

§14.02. Dissolution by Board of Directors and Shareholders.—
(a) A corporation's board of directors may propose dissolution for submission to the shareholders.
(b) For a proposal to dissolve to be adopted:

(1) the board of directors must recommend dissolution to the shareholders unless the board of directors determines that because of conflict of interest or other special circumstances it should make no recommendation and communicates the basis for its determination to the shareholders; and
(2) the shareholders entitled to vote must approve the proposal to dissolve as provided in subsection (e).

(c) The board of directors may condition its submission of the proposal for dissolution on any basis.
(d) The corporation shall notify each shareholder, whether or not entitled to vote, of the proposed shareholders' meeting in accordance with section 7.05. The notice must also state that the purpose, or one of the purposes, of the meeting is to consider dissolving the corporation.
(e) Unless the articles of incorporation or the board of directors (acting pursuant to subsection (c)) require a greater vote or a vote by voting groups, the proposal to dissolve to be adopted must be approved by a majority of all the votes entitled to be cast on that proposal.

§14.03. Articles of Dissolution.—
(a) At any time after dissolution is authorized, the corporation may dissolve by delivering to the secretary of state for filing articles of dissolution setting forth:

(1) the name of the corporation;
(2) the date dissolution was authorized;
(3) if dissolution was approved by the shareholders:
　(i) the number of votes entitled to be cast on the proposal to dissolve; and
　(ii) either the total number of votes cast for and against dissolution or the total number of undisputed votes cast for dissolution and a statement that the number cast for dissolution was sufficient for approval.
(4) If voting by voting groups was required, the information required by subparagraph (3) must be separately provided for each voting group entitled to vote separately on the plan to dissolve.

(b) A corporation is dissolved upon the effective date of its articles of dissolution.

§14.04. Revocation of Dissolution.—
(a) A corporation may revoke its dissolution within 120 days of its effective date.
(b) Revocation of dissolution must be authorized in the same manner as the dissolution was authorized unless that authorization permitted revocation by action of the board of directors alone, in which event the board of directors may revoke the dissolution without shareholder action.
(c) After the revocation of dissolution is authorized, the corporation may revoke the dissolution by delivering to the secretary of state for filing articles of revocation of dissolution, together with a copy of its articles of dissolution, that set forth:

(1) the name of the corporation;
(2) the effective date of the dissolution that was revoked;
(3) the date that the revocation of dissolution was authorized;
(4) if the corporation's board of directors (or incorporators) revoked the dissolution, a statement to that effect;
(5) if the corporation's board of directors revoked a dissolution authorized by the shareholders, a statement that revocation was permitted by action by the board of directors alone pursuant to that authorization; and
(6) if shareholder action was required to revoke the dissolution, the information required by section 14.03(a)(3) or (4).

(d) Revocation of dissolution is effective upon the effective date of the articles of revocation of dissolution.
(e) When the revocation of dissolution is effective, it relates back to and takes effect as of the effective date of the dissolution and the corporation resumes carrying on its business as if dissolution had never occurred.

§14.05. Effect of Dissolution.—
(a) A dissolved corporation continues its corporate existence but may not carry on any business except that appropriate to wind up and liquidate its business and affairs, including:

(1) collecting its assets;
(2) disposing of its properties that will not be distributed in kind to its shareholders;
(3) discharging or making provision for discharging its liabilities;
(4) distributing its remaining property among its shareholders according to their interests; and
(5) doing every other act necessary to wind up and liquidate its business and affairs.

(b) Dissolution of a corporation does not:

(1) transfer title to the corporation's property;
(2) prevent transfer of its shares or securities, although the authorization to dissolve may provide for closing the corporation's share transfer records;
(3) subject its directors or officers to standards of conduct different from those prescribed in chapter 8;
(4) change quorum or voting requirements for its board of directors or shareholders; change provisions for selection, resignation, or removal of its directors or officers or both; or change provisions for amending its bylaws;
(5) prevent commencement of a proceeding by or against the corporation in its corporate name;
(6) abate or suspend a proceeding pending by or against the corporation on the effective date of dissolution; or
(7) terminate the authority of the registered agent of the corporation.

§14.06. Known Claims Against Dissolved Corporation.—
(a) A dissolved corporation may dispose of the known claims against it by following the procedure described in this section.
(b) The dissolved corporation shall notify its known claimants in writing of the dissolution at any time after its effective date. The written notice must:

(1) describe information that must be included in a claim;
(2) provide a mailing address where a claim may be sent;
(3) state the deadline, which may not be fewer than 120 days from the effective date of the written notice, by which the dissolved corporation must receive the claim; and
(4) state that the claim will be barred if not received by the deadline.

(c) A claim against the dissolved corporation is barred:

(1) if a claimant who was given written notice under subsection (b) does not deliver the claim to the dissolved corporation by the deadline;
(2) if a claimant whose claim was rejected by the dissolved corporation does not commence a proceeding to enforce the claim within 90 days from the effective date of the rejection notice.

(d) For purposes of this section, "claim" does not include a contingent liability or a claim based on an event occurring after the effective date of dissolution.

§14.07. Unknown Claims Against Dissolved Corporation.—
(a) A dissolved corporation may also publish notice of its dissolution and request that persons with claims against the corporation present them in accordance with the notice.
(b) The notice must:

(1) be published one time in a newspaper of general circulation in the county where the dissolved corporation's principal office (or, if none in this state, its registered office) is or was last located;
(2) describe the information that must be included in a claim and provide a mailing address where the claim may be sent; and
(3) state that a claim against the corporation will be barred unless a proceeding to enforce the claim is commenced within five years after the publication of the notice.

(c) If the dissolved corporation publishes a newspaper notice in accordance with subsection (b), the claim of each of the following claimants is barred unless the claimant commences a proceeding to enforce the claim against the dissolved corporation within five years after the publication date of the newspaper notice:

(1) a claimant who did not receive written notice under section 14.06;
(2) a claimant whose claim was timely sent to the dissolved corporation but not acted on;
(3) a claimant whose claim is contingent or based on an event occurring after the effective date of dissolution.

(d) A claim may be enforced under this section:

(1) against the dissolved corporation, to the extent of its undistributed assets; or
(2) if the assets have been distributed in liquidation, against a shareholder of the dissolved corporation to the extent of his pro rata share of the claim or the corporate assets distributed to him in liquidation, whichever is less, but a shareholder's total liability for all claims under this section may not exceed the total amount of assets distributed to him.

436

Subchapter B. Administrative Dissolution

§14.20. Grounds for Administrative Dissolution.—The secretary of state may commence a proceeding under section 14.21 to administratively dissolve a corporation if:

(1) the corporation does not pay within 60 days after they are due any franchise taxes or penalties imposed by this Act or other law;

(2) the corporation does not deliver its annual report to the secretary of state within 60 days after it is due;

(3) the corporation is without a registered agent or registered office in this state for 60 days or more;

(4) the corporation does not notify the secretary of state within 60 days that its registered agent or registered office has been changed, that its registered agent has resigned, or that its registered office has been discontinued; or

(5) the corporation's period of duration stated in its articles of incorporation expires.

§14.21. Procedure for and Effect of Administrative Dissolution.—

(a) If the secretary of state determines that one or more grounds exist under section 14.20 for dissolving a corporation, he shall serve the corporation with written notice of his determination under section 5.04.

(b) If the corporation does not correct each ground for dissolution or demonstrate to the reasonable satisfaction of the secretary of state that each ground determined by the secretary of state does not exist within 60 days after service of the notice is perfected under section 5.04, the secretary of state shall administratively dissolve the corporation by signing a certificate of dissolution that recites the ground or grounds for dissolution and its effective date. The secretary of state shall file the original of the certificate and serve a copy on the corporation under section 5.04.

(c) A corporation administratively dissolved continues its corporate existence but may not carry on any business except that necessary to wind up and liquidate its business and affairs under section 14.05 and notify claimants under sections 14.06 and 14.07.

(d) The administrative dissolution of a corporation does not terminate the authority of its registered agent.

§14.22. Reinstatement Following Administrative Dissolution.—

(a) A corporation administratively dissolved under section 14.21 may apply to the secretary of state for reinstatement within two years after the effective date of dissolution. The application must:

(1) recite the name of the corporation and the effective date of its administrative dissolution;

(2) state that the ground or grounds for dissolution either did not exist or have been eliminated;

(3) state that the corporation's name satisfied the requirements of section 4.01; and

(4) contain a certificate from the [taxing authority] reciting that all taxes owed by the corporation have been paid.

(b) If the secretary of state determines that the application contains the information required by subsection (a) and that the information is correct, he shall cancel the certificate of dissolution and prepare a certificate of reinstatement that recites his determination and the effective date of reinstatement, file the original of the certificate, and serve a copy on the corporation under section 5.04.

(c) When the reinstatement is effective, it relates back to and takes effect as of the effective date of the administrative dissolution and the corporation resumes carrying on its business as if the administrative dissolution had never occurred.

§14.23. Appeal From Denial of Reinstatement.—

(a) If the secretary of state denies a corporation's application for reinstatement following administrative dissolution, he shall serve the corporation under section 5.04 with a written notice that explains the reason or reasons for denial.

(b) The corporation may appeal the denial of reinstatement to the [name or describe] court within 30 days after service of the notice of denial is perfected. The corporation appeals by petitioning the court to set aside the dissolution and attaching to the petition copies of the secretary of state's certificate of dissolution, the corporation's application for reinstatement, and the secretary of state's notice of denial.

(c) The court may summarily order the secretary of state to reinstate the dissolved corporation or may take other action the court considers appropriate.

(d) The court's final decision may be appealed as in other civil proceedings.

Subchapter C. Judicial Dissolution

§14.30. Grounds for Judicial Dissolution.—The [name or describe court or courts] may dissolve a corporation:

(1) in a proceeding by the attorney general if it is established that:

(i) the corporation obtained its articles of incorporation through fraud; or

(ii) the corporation has continued to exceed or abuse the authority conferred upon it by law;

(2) in a proceeding by a shareholder if it is established that:

(i) the directors are deadlocked in the management of the corporate affairs, the shareholders are unable to break the deadlock, and irreparable injury to the corporation is threatened or being suffered, or the business and affairs of the corporation can no longer be conducted to the advantage of the shareholders generally, because of the deadlock;

(ii) the directors or those in control of the corporation have acted, are acting, or will act in a manner that is illegal, oppressive, or fraudulent;

(iii) the shareholders are deadlocked in voting power and have failed, for a period that includes at least two consecutive annual meeting dates, to elect successors to directors whose terms have expired; or

(iv) the corporate assets are being misapplied or wasted;

(3) in a proceeding by a creditor if it is established that:

(i) the creditor's claim has been reduced to judgment, the execution on the judgment returned unsatisfied, and the corporation is insolvent; or

(ii) the corporation has admitted in writing that the creditor's claim is due and owing and the corporation is insolvent; or

(4) in a proceeding by the corporation to have its voluntary dissolution continued under court supervision.

§14.31. Procedure for Judicial Dissolution.—

(a) Venue for a proceeding by the attorney general to dissolve a corporation lies in [name the county or counties]. Venue for a proceeding brought by any other party named in section 14.30 lies in the county where a corporation's principal office (or, if none in this state, its registered office) is or was last located.

(b) It is not necessary to make shareholders parties to a proceeding to dissolve a corporation unless relief is sought against them individually.

(c) A court in a proceeding brought to dissolve a corporation may issue injunctions, appoint a receiver or custodian pendente lite with all powers and duties the court directs, take other action required to preserve the corporate assets wherever located, and carry on the business of the corporation until a full hearing can be held.

§14.32. Receivership or Custodianship.—

(a) A court in a judicial proceeding brought to dissolve a corporation may appoint one or more receivers to wind up and liquidate, or one or more custodians to manage, the business and affairs of the corporation. The court shall hold a hearing, after notifying all parties to the proceeding and any interested persons designated by the court, before appointing a receiver or custodian. The court appointing a receiver or custodian has exclusive jurisdiction over the corporation and all of its property wherever located.

(b) The court may appoint an individual or a domestic or foreign corporation (authorized to transact business in this state) as a receiver or custodian. The court may require the receiver or custodian to post bond, with or without sureties, in an amount the court directs.

(c) The court shall describe the powers and duties of the receiver or custodian in its appointing order, which may be amended from time to time. Among other powers:

(1) the receiver (i) may dispose of all or any part of the assets of the corporation wherever located, at a public or private sale, if authorized by the court; and (ii) may sue and defend in his own name as receiver of the corporation in all courts of this state;

(2) the custodian may exercise all of the powers of the corporation, through or in place of its board of directors or officers, to the extent necessary to manage the affairs of the corporation in the best interests of its shareholders and creditors.

(d) The court during a receivership may redesignate the receiver a custodian, and during a custodianship may redesignate the custodian a receiver, if doing so is in the best interests of the corporation, its shareholders, and creditors.

(e) The court from time to time during the receivership or custodianship may order compensation paid and expense disbursements or reimbursements made to the receiver or custodian and his counsel from the assets of the corporation or proceeds from the sale of the assets.

§14.33. Decree of Dissolution.—

(a) If after a hearing the court determines that one or more grounds for judicial dissolution described in section 14.30 exist, it may enter a decree dissolving the corporation and specifying the effective date of the dissolution, and the clerk of the court shall deliver a certified copy of the decree to the secretary of state, who shall file it.

(b) After entering the decree of dissolution, the court shall direct the winding up and liquidation of the corporation's business and affairs in accordance with section 14.05 and the notification of claimants in accordance with sections 14.06 and 14.07.

Subchapter D. Miscellaneous

§14.40 Deposit With State Treasurer.—Assets of a dissolved corporation that should be transferred to a creditor, claimant, or shareholder of the corporation who cannot be found or who is not competent to receive them shall be reduced to cash and deposited with the state treasurer or other appropriate state official for safekeeping. When the creditor, claimant, or shareholder furnishes satisfactory proof of entitlement to the amount deposited, the state treasurer or other appropriate state official shall pay him or his representative that amount.

CHAPTER 15. FOREIGN CORPORATIONS

Subchapter A. Certificate of Authority

§15.01. Authority To Transact Business Required.—

(a) A foreign corporation may not transact business in this state until it obtains a certificate of authority from the secretary of state.

(b) The following activities, among others, do not constitute transacting business within the meaning of subsection (a):

(1) maintaining, defending, or settling any proceeding;

(2) holding meetings of the board of directors or shareholders or carrying on other activities concerning internal corporate affairs;

(3) maintaining bank accounts;

(4) maintaining offices or agencies for the transfer, exchange, and registration of the corporation's own securities or maintaining trustees or depositaries with respect to those securities;

(5) selling through independent contractors;

(6) soliciting or obtaining orders, whether by mail or through employees or agents or otherwise, if the orders require acceptance outside this state before they become contracts;

(7) creating or acquiring indebtedness, mortgages, and security interests in real or personal property;

(8) securing or collecting debts or enforcing mortgages and security interests in property securing the debts;

(9) owning, without more, real or personal property;

(10) conducting an isolated transaction that is completed within 30 days and that is not one in the course of repeated transactions of a like nature;

(11) transacting business in interstate commerce.

(c) The list of activities in subsection (b) is not exhaustive.

§15.02. Consequences of Transacting Business Without Authority.—

(a) A foreign corporation transacting business in this state without a certificate of authority may not maintain a proceeding in any court in this state until it obtains a certificate of authority.

(b) The successor to a foreign corporation that transacted business in this state without a certificate of authority and the assignee of a cause of action arising out of that business may not maintain a proceeding based on that cause of action in any court in this state until the foreign corporation or its successor obtains a certificate of authority.

(c) A court may stay a proceeding commenced by a foreign corporation, its successor, or assignee until it determines whether the foreign corporation or its successor requires a certificate of authority. If it so determines, the court may further stay the proceeding until the foreign corporation or its successor obtains the certificate.

(d) A foreign corporation is liable for a civil penalty of $_____ for each day, but not to exceed a total of $_____ for each year, it transacts business in this state without a certificate of authority. The attorney general may collect all penalties due under this subsection.

(e) Notwithstanding subsections (a) and (b), the failure of a foreign corporation to obtain a certificate of authority does not impair the validity of its corporate acts or prevent it from defending any proceeding in this state.

§15.03. Application for Certificate of Authority.—

(a) A foreign corporation may apply for a certificate of authority to transact business in this state by delivering an application to the secretary of state for filing. The application must set forth:

(1) the name of the foreign corporation or, if its name is unavailable for use in this state, a corporate name that satisfies the requirements of section 15.06;

(2) the name of the state or country under whose law it is incorporated;

(3) its date of incorporation and period of duration;

(4) the street address of its principal office;

(5) the address of its registered office in this state and the name of its registered agent at that office; and

(6) the names and usual business addresses of its current directors and officers.

(b) The foreign corporation shall deliver with the completed application a certificate of existence (or a document of similar import) duly authenticated by the secretary of state or other official having custody of corporate records in the state or country under whose law it is incorporated.

§15.04. Amended Certificate of Authority.—

(a) A foreign corporation authorized to transact business in this state must obtain an amended certificate of authority from the secretary of state if it changes:

(1) its corporate name;
(2) the period of its duration; or
(3) the state or country of its incorporation.

(b) The requirements of section 15.03 for obtaining an original certificate of authority apply to obtaining an amended certificate under this section.

§15.05. Effect of Certificate of Authority.—

(a) A certificate of authority authorizes the foreign corporation to which it is issued to transact business in this state subject, however, to the right of the state to revoke the certificate as provided in this Act.
(b) A foreign corporation with a valid certificate of authority has the same but no greater rights and has the same but no greater privileges as, and except as otherwise provided by this Act is subject to the same duties, restrictions, penalties, and liabilities now or later imposed on, a domestic corporation of like character.
(c) This Act does not authorize this state to regulate the organization or internal affairs of a foreign corporation authorized to transact business in this state.

§15.06. Corporate Name of Foreign Corporation.—

(a) If the corporate name of a foreign corporation does not satisfy the requirements of section 4.01, the foreign corporation to obtain or maintain a certificate of authority to transact business in this state:

(1) may add the word "corporation," "incorporated," "company," or "limited," or the abbreviation "corp.," "inc.," "co.," or "ltd.," to its corporate name for use in this state; or
(2) may use a fictitious name to transact business in this state if its real name is unavailable and it delivers to the secretary of state for filing a copy of the resolution of its board of directors, certified by its secretary, adopting the fictitious name.

(b) Except as authorized by subsections (c) and (d), the corporate name (including a fictitious name of a foreign corporation must be distinguishable upon the records of the secretary of state from:

(1) the corporate name of a corporation incorporated or authorized to transact business in this state;
(2) a corporate name reserved or registered under section 4.02 or 4.03;
(3) the fictitious name of another foreign corporation authorized to transact business in this state; and
(4) the corporate name of a not-for-profit corporation incorporated or authorized to transact business in this state.

(c) A foreign corporation may apply to the secretary of state for authorization to use in this state the name of another corporation (incorporated or authorized to transact business in this state) that is not distinguishable upon his records from the name applied for. The secretary of state shall authorize use of the name applied for if:

(1) the other corporation consents to the use in writing and submits an undertaking in form satisfactory to the secretary of state to change its name to a name that is distinguishable upon the records of the secretary of state from the name of the applying corporation; or

(2) the applicant delivers to the secretary of state a certified copy of a final judgment of a court of competent jurisdiction establishing the applicant's right to use the name applied for in this state.

(d) A foreign corporation may use in this state the name (including the fictitious name) of another domestic or foreign corporation that is used in this state if the other corporation is incorporated or authorized to transact business in this state and the foreign corporation:

(1) has merged with the other corporation;

(2) has been formed by reorganization of the other corporation; or

(3) has acquired all or substantially all of the assets, including the corporate name, of the other corporation.

(e) If a foreign corporation authorized to transact business in this state changes its corporate name to one that does not satisfy the requirements of section 4.01, it may not transact business in this state under the changed name until it adopts a name satisfying the requirements of section 4.01 and obtains an amended certificate of authority under section 15.04.

§15.07. Registered Office and Registered Agent of Foreign Corporation.—Each foreign corporation authorized to transact business in this state must continuously maintain in this state:

(1) a registered office that may be the same as any of its places of business; and

(2) a registered agent, who may be:

(i) an individual who resides in this state and whose business office is identical with the registered office;

(ii) a domestic corporation or not-for-profit domestic corporation whose business office is identical with the registered office; or

(iii) a foreign corporation or foreign not-for-profit corporation authorized to transact business in this state whose business office is identical with the registered office.

§15.08. Change of Registered Office or Registered Agent of Foreign Corporation.— (a) A foreign corporation authorized to transact business in this state may change its registered office or registered agent by delivering to the secretary of state for filing a statement of change that sets forth:

(1) its name;

(2) the street addresses of its current registered office;

(3) if the current registered office is to be changed, the street address of its new registered office;

(4) the name of its current registered agent;

(5) if the current registered agent is to be changed, the name of its new registered agent and the new agent's written consent (either on the statement or attached to it) to the appointment; and

(6) that after the change or changes are made, the street addresses of its registered office and the business office of its registered agent will be identical.

(b) If a registered agent changes the street address of his business office, he may change the street address of the registered office of any foreign corporation for which he is the registered agent by notifying the corporation in writing of the change and signing (either manually or in facsimile) and delivering to the secretary of state for filing a statement of change that complies with the requirements of subsection (a) and recites that the corporation has been notified of the change.

§15.09. Resignation of Registered Agent of Foreign Corporation.—

(a) The registered agent of a foreign corporation may resign his agency appointment by signing and delivering to the secretary of state for filing the original and two exact or conformed copies of a statement of resignation. The statement of resignation may include a statement that the registered office is also discontinued.

(b) After filing the statement, the secretary of state shall attach the filing receipt to one copy and mail the copy and receipt to the registered office if not discontinued. The secretary of state shall mail the other copy to the foreign corporation at its principal office address shown in its most recent annual report.

(c) The agency appointment is terminated, and the registered office discontinued if so provided, on the 31st day after the date on which the statement was filed.

§15.10. Service on Foreign Corporation.—

(a) The registered agent of a foreign corporation authorized to transact business in this state is the corporation's agent for service of process, notice, or demand required or permitted by law to be served on the foreign corporation.

(b) A foreign corporation may be served by registered or certified mail, return receipt requested, addressed to the secretary of the foreign corporation at its principal office shown in its application for a certificate of authority or in its most recent annual report if the foreign corporation:

> (1) has no registered agent or its registered agent cannot with reasonable diligence be served;
> (2) has withdrawn from transacting business in this state under section 15.20; or
> (3) has had its certificate of authority revoked under section 15.31.

(c) Service is perfected under subsection (b) at the earliest of:

> (1) the date the foreign corporation receives the mail;
> (2) the date shown on the return receipt, if signed on behalf of the foreign corporation; or
> (3) five days after its deposit in the United States Mail, as evidenced by the postmark if mailed postpaid and correctly addressed.

(d) This section does not prescribe the only means, or necessarily the required means, of serving a foreign corporation.

Subchapter B. Withdrawal

§15.20. Withdrawal of Foreign Corporation.—

(a) A foreign corporation authorized to transact business in this state may not withdraw from this state until it obtains a certificate of withdrawal from the secretary of state.

(b) A foreign corporation authorized to transact business in this state may apply for a certificate of withdrawal by delivering an application to the secretary of state for filing. The application must set forth:

> (1) the name of the foreign corporation and the name of the state or country under whose law it is incorporated;
> (2) that it is not transacting business in this state and that it surrenders its authority to transact business in this state;
> (3) that it revokes the authority of its registered agent to accept service on its behalf and appoints the secretary of state as its agent for service of process in any proceeding based on a cause of action arising during the time it was authorized to transact business in this state;

(4) a mailing address to which the secretary of state may mail a copy of any process served on him under subdivision (3); and

(5) a commitment to notify the secretary of state in the future of any change in its mailing address.

(c) After the withdrawal of the corporation is effective, service of process on the secretary of state under this section is service on the foreign corporation. Upon receipt of process, the secretary of state shall mail a copy of the process to the foreign corporation at the mailing address set forth under subsection (b).

Subchapter C. Revocation of Certificate of Authority

§15.30. Grounds for Revocation.—The secretary of state may commence a proceeding under section 15.31 to revoke the certificate of authority of a foreign corporation authorized to transact business in this state if:

(1) the foreign corporation does not deliver its annual report to the secretary of state within 60 days after it is due;

(2) the foreign corporation does not pay within 60 days after they are due any franchise taxes or penalties imposed by this Act or other law;

(3) the foreign corporation is without a registered agent or registered office in this state for 60 days or more;

(4) the foreign corporation does not inform the secretary of state under section 15.08 or 15.09 that its registered agent or registered office has changed, that its registered agent has resigned, or that its registered office has been discontinued within 60 days of the change, resignation, or discontinuance;

(5) an incorporator, director, officer, or agent of the foreign corporation signed a document he knew was false in any material respect with intent that the document be delivered to the secretary of state for filing;

(6) the secretary of state receives a duly authenticated certificate from the secretary of state or other official having custody of corporate records in the state or country under whose law the foreign corporation is incorporated stating that it has been dissolved or disappeared as the result of a merger.

§15.31. Procedure for and Effect of Revocation.—

(a) If the secretary of state determines that one or more grounds exist under section 15.30 for revocation of a certificate of authority, he shall serve the foreign corporation with written notice of his determination under section 15.10.

(b) If the foreign corporation does not correct each ground for revocation or demonstrate to the reasonable satisfaction of the secretary of state that each ground determined by the secretary of state does not exist within 60 days after service of the notice is perfected under section 15.10, the secretary of state may revoke the foreign corporation's certificate of authority by signing a certificate of revocation that recites the ground or grounds for revocation and its effective date. The secretary of state shall file the original of the certificate and serve a copy on the foreign corporation under section 15.10.

(c) The authority of a foreign corporation to transact business in this state ceases on the date shown on the certificate revoking its certificate of authority.

(d) The secretary of state's revocation of a foreign corporation's certificate of authority appoints the secretary of state the foreign corporation's agent for service of process in any proceeding based on a cause of action which arose during the time the foreign corporation was authorized to transact business in this state. Service of process on the secretary of state under this subsection is service on the foreign corporation. Upon receipt of process, the secretary of state shall mail a copy of the process to the secretary of the foreign corporation at its principal office shown in its most recent annual report or in any subsequent communication received from the corporation stating the current mailing address of its principal office, or, if none are on file, in its application for a certificate of authority.

(e) Revocation of a foreign corporation's certificate of authority does not terminate the authority of the registered agent of the corporation.

§15.32. Appeal From Revocation.—
(a) A foreign corporation may appeal the secretary of state's revocation of its certificate of authority to the [name or describe] court within 30 days after service of the certificate of revocation is perfected under section 15.10. The foreign corporation appeals by petitioning the court to set aside the revocation and attaching to the petition copies of its certificate of authority and the secretary of state's certificate of revocation.
(b) The court may summarily order the secretary of state to reinstate the certificate of authority or may take any other action the court considers appropriate.
(c) The court's final decision may be appealed as in other civil proceedings.

CHAPTER 16. RECORDS AND REPORTS

Subchapter A. Records

§16.01. Corporate Records.—
(a) A corporation shall keep as permanent records minutes of all meetings of its shareholders and board of directors, a record of all actions taken by the shareholders or board of directors without a meeting, and a record of all actions taken by a committee of the board of directors in place of the board of directors on behalf of the corporation.
(b) A corporation shall maintain appropriate accounting records.
(c) A corporation or its agent shall maintain a record of its shareholders, in a form that permits preparation of a list of the names and addresses of all shareholders, in alphabetical order by class of shares showing the number and class of shares held by each.
(d) A corporation shall maintain its records in written form or in another form capable of conversion into written form within a reasonable time.
(e) A corporation shall keep a copy of the following records at its principal office:

(1) its articles or restated articles of incorporation and all amendments to them currently in effect;
(2) its bylaws or restated bylaws and all amendments to them currently in effect;
(3) resolutions adopted by its board of directors creating one or more classes or series of shares, and fixing their relative rights, preferences, and limitations, if shares issued pursuant to those resolutions are outstanding;
(4) the minutes of all shareholders' meetings, and records of all action taken by shareholders without a meeting, for the past three years;
(5) all written communications to shareholders generally within the past three years, including the financial statements furnished for the past three years under section 16.20;
(6) a list of the names and business addresses of its current directors and officers; and
(7) its most recent annual report delivered to the secretary of state under section 16.22.

§16.02. Inspection of Records by Shareholders.—
(a) A shareholder of a corporation is entitled to inspect and copy, during regular business hours at the corporation's principal office, any of the records of the corporation described in section 16.01(e) if he gives the corporation written notice of his demand at least five business days before the date on which he wishes to inspect and copy.
(b) A shareholder of a corporation is entitled to inspect and copy, during regular business hours at a reasonable location specified by the corporation, any of the

following records of the corporation if the shareholder meets the requirements of subsection (c) and gives the corporation written notice of his demand at least five business days before the date on which he wishes to inspect and copy:

(1) excerpts from minutes of any meeting of the board of directors, records of any action of a committee of the board of directors while acting in place of the board of directors on behalf of the corporation, minutes of any meeting of the shareholders, and records of action taken by the shareholders or board of directors without a meeting, to the extent not subject to inspection under section 16.02(a);
(2) accounting records of the corporation; and
(3) the record of shareholders.

(c) A shareholder may inspect and copy the records described in subsection (b) only if:

(1) his demand is made in good faith and for a proper purpose;
(2) he describes with reasonable particularity his purpose and the records he desires to inspect; and
(3) the records are directly connected with his purpose.

(d) The right of inspection granted by this section may not be abolished or limited by a corporation's articles of incorporation or bylaws.
(e) This section does not affect:

(1) the right of a shareholder to inspect records under section 7.20 or, if the shareholder is in litigation with the corporation, to the same extent as any other litigant;
(2) the power of a court, independently of this Act, to compel the production of corporate records for examination.

§16.03. Scope of Inspection Right.—
(a) A shareholder's agent or attorney has the same inspection and copying rights as the shareholder he represents.
(b) The right to copy records under section 16.02 includes, if reasonable, the right to receive copies made by photographic, xerographic, or other means.
(c) The corporation may impose a reasonable charge, covering the costs of labor and material, for copies of any documents provided to the shareholder. The charge may not exceed the estimated cost of production or reproduction of the records.
(d) The corporation may comply with a shareholder's demand to inspect the record of shareholders under section 16.02(b)(3) by providing him with a list of its shareholders that was compiled no earlier than the date of the shareholder's demand.

§16.04. Court-ordered Inspection.—
(a) If a corporation does not allow a shareholder who complies with section 16.02(a) to inspect and copy any records required by that subsection to be available for inspection, the [name or describe court] of the county where the corporation's principal office (or, if none in this state, its registered office) is located may summarily order inspection and copying of the records demanded at the corporation's expense upon application of the shareholder.
(b) If a corporation does not within a reasonable time allow a shareholder to inspect and copy and other record, the shareholder who complies with section 16.02(b) and (c) may apply to the [name or describe court] in the county where the corporation's principal office (or, if none in this state, its registered office) is located for an order to permit inspection and copying of the records demanded. The court shall dispose of an application under this subsection on an expedited basis.

(c) If the court orders inspection and copying of the records demanded, it shall also order the corporation to pay the shareholder's costs (including reasonable counsel fees) incurred to obtain the order unless the corporation proves that it refused inspection in good faith because it had a reasonable basis for doubt about the right of the shareholder to inspect the records demanded.

(d) If the court orders inspection and copying of the records demanded, it may impose reasonable restrictions on the use or distribution of the records by the demanding shareholder.

Subchapter B. Reports

§16.20. Financial Statements for Shareholders.—

(a) A corporation shall furnish its shareholders annual financial statements, which may be consolidated or combined statements of the corporation and one or more of its subsidiaries, as appropriate, that include a balance sheet as of the end of the fiscal year, an income statement for that year, and a statement of changes in shareholders' equity for the year unless that information appears elsewhere in the financial statements. If financial statements are prepared for the corporation on the basis of generally accepted accounting principles, the annual financial statements must also be prepared on that basis.

(b) If the annual financial statements are reported upon by a public accountant, his report must accompany them. If not, the statements must be accompanied by a statement of the president or the person responsible for the corporation's accounting records:

> (1) stating his reasonable belief whether the statements were prepared on the basis of generally accepted accounting principles and, if not, describing the basis of preparation; and
> (2) describing any respects in which the statements were not prepared on a basis of accounting consistent with the statements prepared for the preceding year.

(c) A corporation shall mail the annual financial statements to each shareholder within 120 days after the close of each fiscal year. Thereafter, on written request from a shareholder who was not mailed the statements, the corporation shall mail him the latest financial statements.

§16.21. Other Reports to Shareholders.—

(a) If a corporation indemnifies or advances expenses to a director under section 8.51, 8.52, 8.53, or 8.54 in connection with a proceeding by or in the right of the corporation, the corporation shall report the indemnification or advance in writing to the shareholders with or before the notice of the next shareholders' meeting.

(b) If a corporation issues or authorizes the issuance of shares for promissory notes or for promises to render services in the future, the corporation shall report in writing to the shareholders the number of shares authorized or issued, and the consideration received by the corporation, with or before the notice of the next shareholders' meeting.

§16.22. Annual Report for Secretary of State.—

(a) Each domestic corporation, and each foreign corporation authorized to transact business in this state, shall deliver to the secretary of state for filing an annual report that sets forth:

> (1) the name of the corporation and the state or country under whose law it is incorporated;
> (2) the address of its registered office and the name of its registered agent at that office in this state;
> (3) the address of its principal office;
> (4) the names and business addresses of its directors and principal officers;

(5) a brief description of the nature of its business;

(6) the total number of authorized shares, itemized by class and series, if any, within each class; and

(7) the total number of issued and outstanding shares, itemized by class and series, if any, within each class.

(b) Information in the annual report must be current as of the date the annual report is executed on behalf of the corporation.

(c) The first annual report must be delivered to the secretary of state between January 1 and April 1 of the year following the calendar year in which a domestic corporation was incorporated or a foreign corporation was authorized to transact business. Subsequent annual reports must be delivered to the secretary of state between January 1 and April 1 of the following calendar years.

(d) If an annual report does not contain the information required by this section, the secretary of state shall promptly notify the reporting domestic or foreign corporation in writing and return the report to it for correction. If the report is corrected to contain the information required by this section and delivered to the secretary of state within 30 days after the effective date of notice, it is deemed to be timely filed.

CHAPTER 17. TRANSITION PROVISIONS

§17.01. Application to Existing Domestic Corporations.— This Act applies to all domestic corporations in existence on its effective date that were incorporated under any general statute of this state providing for incorporation of corporations for profit if power to amend or repeal the statute under which the corporation was incorporated was reserved.

§17.02. Application to Qualified Foreign Corporations.— A foreign corporation authorized to transact business in this state on the effective date of this Act is subject to this Act but is not required to obtain a new certificate of authority to transact business under this Act.

§17.03. Saving Provisions.—

(a) Except as provided in subsection (b), the repeal of a statute by this Act does not affect:

(1) the operation of the statute or any action taken under it before its repeal;

(2) any ratification, right, remedy, privilege, obligation, or liability acquired, accrued, or incurred under the statute before its repeal;

(3) any violation of the statute, or any penalty, forfeiture, or punishment incurred because of the violation, before its repeal;

(4) any proceeding, reorganization, or dissolution commenced under the statute before its repeal, and the proceeding, reorganization, or dissolution may be completed in accordance with the statute as if it had not been repealed.

(b) If a penalty or punishment imposed for violation of a statute repealed by this Act is reduced by this Act, the penalty or punishment if not already imposed shall be imposed in accordance with this Act.

§17.04. Severability.— If any provision of this Act or its application to any person or circumstance is held invalid by a court of competent jurisdiction, the invalidity does not affect other provisions or applications of the Act that can be given effect without the invalid provision or application, and to this end the provisions of the Act are severable.

§17.05. Repeal.—The following laws and parts of laws are repealed: [to be inserted].

§17.06. Effective Date.—This Act takes effect _____.

APPENDIX II

Glossary

Accounts Payable   An obligation to pay an amount to a creditor.

Accounts Receivable   Amounts owed to the corporation on open account usually from customers in the ordinary course of business.

Acknowledgment   The act of signing a paper under oath before a public official such as a notary public; also known as notarization.

Administrator   The personal representative of a decedent who dies without a will.

Affidavit   A formal legal document signed with an acknowledgment.

Affidavit of Mailing   A statement under oath made by a person as to the time of depositing an item in the mails.

Agreed Valuation   A method for establishment of price, found in some shareholders' agreements, which fixes a specified dollar purchase price based on the parties' agreement.

Allocation Formula   A specified method for dividing a sum among different parties or things.

American Arbitration Association   A private organization which makes available individuals who agree to serve on a panel to decide a disagreement arising under a contract. The arbitration is a private way to expedite the resolving of disputes outside of the judicial system.

Annual Meeting   The regular meeting of the shareholders of the corporation required by statute and held each year for election of directors.

Antidilution Provision   A provision in options or agreements for sale of stock designed to prevent the purchaser from having a proportionate stock interest reduced by stock dividends, stock splits, other sales of stock, etc.

Arbitration   A method of settling controversies through a private forum rather than litigation in court.

Articles of Amendment   The formal document which modifies the articles of incorporation when properly filed with the state.

Articles of Incorporation   The formal document which creates a corporation when properly filed in accordance with the laws of a state; also known as corporate charter.

Asset   Something of value.

Assigns   Persons to whom rights or title to assets have been transferred.

Attestation   The act of formally witnessing the execution of a document by another person.

Attorney-in-Fact   A person who has been granted a power of attorney by another person to act on a matter for the first person as fully as the first person could act directly.

Authorized Capital   The total number of shares of all classes of stock of a corporation authorized for issuance in its articles of incorporation.

Authorized Stock   The total number of shares of stock authorized by a corporation in its articles of incorporation (see authorized capital).

Balance Sheet   A financial statement setting forth, in dollar terms, the assets and liabilities of a person or entity as of a given point in time.

Ballot   A writing which exercises the right to vote on a matter.

Bank Resolutions   The resolutions adopted by the board of directors of a corporation authorizing a bank account and establishing which persons will have authority to sign for the corporation with respect to the account.

Bankruptcy   A formal judicial proceeding in which a person whose debts exceed assets can restructure his or her debts or be discharged from debts by a pro-rata distribution of assets to creditors.

Bearer   One in possession of an instrument.

Blue Sky Laws   State securities laws.

Board of Directors   The group of individuals which collectively has the legal responsibility of exercising control over and managing the affairs of a corporation.

"Boilerplate" Provisions   Standard provisions repeatedly appearing in agreements or other documents.

Bona Fide Offer   An offer in writing by a person who is ready, willing, and able to buy and who has no external constraint to buy.

Bonds   Secured indebtedness evidenced in writing.

Book Value   The historical cost to a corporation of an asset.

Book Value Per Share   An amount equal to the net assets (gross assets less liabilities) of the corporation divided by the number of outstanding shares of stock of the corporation.

Business Corporations   Corporations which operate for a profit.

Bylaws The standards and procedures for the legal organization of a corporation adopted by the corporation in compliance with corporate statutes and the articles of incorporation.

Capital Stock or Franchise Taxes The special tax levied on corporations by a state. These taxes are frequently based on the number of shares which a corporation is authorized to issue, the authorized capital of these shares, or some similar factors, and may be a one-time tax payable upon incorporation or an annual franchise tax or both.

Capital Surplus The entire surplus of a corporation other than its earned surplus; also known as paid-in surplus.

Cause of Action A set of facts which is asserted by a plaintiff and which, if proven, is sufficient to support a valid claim in a lawsuit.

Certificate of Authority or Qualification The document issued by a state which acknowledges that a foreign corporation is entitled to transact business within the state.

Certificate of Incorporation A formal document issued by the state acknowledging incorporation and stating the date of incorporation.

Certificate of Withdrawal A formal document issued by a state acknowledging termination of a certificate of authority of a foreign corporation.

Certificates Pieces of paper evidencing shares in a corporation.

Certified or Audited Statements Financial statements which have been reviewed by an accountant who has performed such independent tests as are appropriate to verify the accuracy of the corporation's books and records.

Classes of Stock The designation of different categories of shares, such as common stock and preferred stock.

Classification of Directors A method whereby some corporations provide for election of only a portion of the board of directors each year.

Clearance Certificate A formal acknowledgment from the various state taxing departments that all fees and franchise taxes have been paid.

"Close" Corporation A corporation with few shareholders formed under special state provisions allowing greater managerial flexibility by shareholders.

Closely Held Corporation A corporation which has only a few shareholders.

Closing the Transfer Books A procedure whereby a corporation freezes the list of shareholders entitled to vote at a meeting or receive dividends by suspending the ability to transfer stock on the corporate books.

Collateral Asset which secures a debt so that, if a debtor defaults, the creditor may obtain the asset.

Common Stock A class of shares which is created when the articles of incorporation provide for a class without any special features which represents the residual equity of a corporation.

Confession of Judgment A procedure now often disfavored by courts pursuant to which the holder of an obligation, without obtaining the obligor's consent or approval, may obtain an immediate judgment from a court against the obligor and enforce the judgment by levy and execution on the obligor's property in accordance with state law.

Consideration Value received for a promise to perform an act.

Consolidated Financial Statements A combination of the financial statements of the company and its subsidiaries.

Consolidation The combination of two or more corporations to create an entirely new corporation which is different from any of the absorbed corporations.

Contempt Willful disobedience of a direct court order.

Conversion The process of exchanging one class of securities for another class of the same corporation.

Conversion Rate The formula which determines the amount of one class of securities that can be exchanged for another class of the same corporation.

Corporate Kit The corporate seal, minute book, and stock certificate book of the corporation.

Corporate Marriage A slang term for a merger or consolidation or other combination of several corporations.

Corporate Seal The official imprint to be affixed to documents by a corporation.

Corporation A legal entity which is a creature of the state of incorporation separate and apart from its owners.

Creditor A person who is owned money by another person.

Cumulative Dividends Dividends on preferred stock which have accrued over time but have not been paid and must be paid before any dividends can be paid on common stock.

Cumulative Voting The right of a shareholder, voting in the election of directors, to multiply the number of votes to which the shareholder is entitled by the number of directors to be elected and to cast the whole number of such votes for one candidate or to distribute them among any two or more candidates.

Damages A court award of money compensation to a litigant.

Debentures Unsecured debt evidenced by a formal written document.

Debt Security A formal written document evidencing a corporation's obligation.

Debtor A person who owes money to another.

Default An act of a borrower which violates the terms of a loan agreement.

Defendant A person against whom a court action is commenced.

Demand Note A written promise to pay money entitling the holder to require the payment of the principal at any time upon making demand to the obligor for payment.

DGCL Delaware General Corporation Law.

Dissolution The formal termination of corporate existence pursuant to statutory procedures of the state of incorporation.

Distribution of Assets The transfer of cash or property by a corporation to its creditors or shareholders.

Dividend A pro-rata distribution of profits by a corporation in cash, stock, or property to shareholders with respect to its shares.

Dividend Arrearage A distribution on a cumulative preferred stock which has been scheduled to be paid to shareholders but has not been timely paid.

Dividend Rights The specific terms setting forth circumstances under which a class of stock shall receive a distribution from the corporation.

Division A part of the corporation's operations which is segregated for corporate and financial purposes by product, location, function, or some other logical basis of differentiation.

Document of Public Record A document which may be inspected by any person at the official office where the document is filed.

"Doing Business" The acts of a foreign corporation in a specific state sufficient to require it to obtain a certificate of authority in that state.

Domestic Corporation A corporation that is incorporated in a specific state is a domestic corporation with respect to that state.

Double Taxation   The concept that a corporation's income is taxed at the corporate level and again at the shareholders' level when it is received as dividends.

Draw   A payment of money as an advance against future commissions earned by an employee.

Earned Surplus   The sum total of a corporation's net profits, gains, or losses from the date of incorporation, less distributions to shareholders and transfers to stated capital and capital surplus; also known as retained earnings.

Earnings and Profits   The income tax calculation of the accumulation of all profits of the corporation during its existence reduced by losses and distributions to shareholders; different from earned surplus.

Earnings Multiples   A formula used to fix the purchase price of stock which provides that the value of the corporation for purposes of determining the purchase price is the product obtained by multiplying the net income of the corporation by an arbitrary fixed number, such as 3 times earnings or 10 times earnings.

Employment Agreement   A formal written agreement between a corporation and an employee setting forth the terms and conditions of the employment relationship.

Equity "Kicker"   An agreement with a lender to permit it to acquire an interest in the stock of the corporation. It is designed to make the loan more attractive to the lender.

Equity Securities   Generally, the classes of stock of a corporation.

ERISA   Employee Retirement Income Security Act of 1974.

Execution   The act of formally signing a document.

Executor   The personal representative of a decedent named in the will.

Fair Market Value   The price which would be paid by a willing buyer to a willing seller.

Family Transferees   Members of the family of a shareholder to whom the shareholder may transfer stock pursuant to a shareholders' agreement.

Fictitious Name   Any assumed name, style, or designation other than the proper corporate name of the corporation using such name.

Fiduciary   A person in a position of trust with respect to another person, such as the relationship of a director or officer to the corporation. The law imposes certain obligations on the fiduciary.

Financing Statements   Documents which are filed to evidence a security interest of a creditor in personal property of the debtor.

Fiscal Year The twelve consecutive calendar months which a corporation elects as its accounting and financial reporting year.

Fringe Benefits Compensation to an employee of an indirect nature rather than wages or salary, such as health insurance, pension plans, life insurance, etc.

Fully Paid and Nonassessable Stock on which the corporation can demand no further money because the original purchaser paid in the agreed amount.

Good-Faith Purchaser for Value A person who bought stock (or other assets) in an arm's-length transaction without any knowledge or reason to know of any problem of the seller with respect to the title to the stock or asset.

Group Life Insurance A life insurance program which covers all employees or all employees of a specific class; a type of fringe benefit.

Incentive Compensation A method of determining employee compensation that ties the amount earned to the productivity of the employee in the employment.

Incorporation The procedures to be followed in forming the corporation.

Incorporator The person or entity who forms the corporation and signs the articles of incorporation which are filed with the state.

Indemnification of Officers and Directors Payment by a corporation for losses incurred by a director or officer for actions on behalf of the corporation.

Informal Shareholder Action With Less Than Unanimous Consent A procedure permitted by some corporate statutes pursuant to which written consent of fewer than all shareholders is adequate for effective action.

Injunction A direct court order to a person to refrain from an action or risk jail for contempt of court.

Insolvency The inability of a person or corporation to pay debts as they become due in the usual course of its business, or the existence of more debts than assets.

Interest Charge assessed by a creditor for the use of money in a loan transaction.

Inter vivos Between or among living persons.

Inventory Collectively, the raw materials, work in process, and finished goods of a business which are manufactured and sold to customers in the ordinary course of business.

IRC The United States Internal Revenue Code of 1954, as amended.

Issued Shares Shares that have been sold by proper corporate action to a shareholder for value.

Joinder of Spouses The uniting of a husband or wife to an agreement to insure that he or she will be bound thereby even though otherwise not directly a party to the subject matter of the agreement.

Joint Tenancy A method of ownership by two or more persons where, when one owner dies, the survivor(s) get the decedent's share directly rather than having the property pass through the estate of the decedent.

Judges of Election Persons selected at a shareholders meeting to tally the voting on an impartial basis.

Key-Person Life Insurance A policy specifically on the life of a valuable individual employee to provide funds to the corporation in the event of the employee's death.

Legend A statement on the face of a stock certificate indicating the existence of special rights or limitations.

Liability An obligation to pay money.

License Fee A special tax to which a corporation may be subject, especially as a foreign corporation.

Limited Liability The limitation of the obligation of a shareholder of a corporation to the amount invested or agreed to be invested in the corporation.

Liquid Assets Property of the corporation which is cash or which is easily convertible into cash, such as government bonds.

Liquidation The paying off of the debts of the corporation, winding up of its affairs, and distribution of the remaining assets among the shareholders of the corporation.

Liquidation Rights The respective claims related to a corporation in the event of its liquidation.

Litigant A party to a lawsuit.

Mandatory Purchase The right of one person to compel another to purchase an asset owned by the first person; also known as a "put."

Mandatory Sale The right of one person to compel another to sell an asset to the first person; also known as a "call."

Matching Offers A requirement that a person with a right of first refusal pay the amount offered by a third party.

MBCA   The Model Business Corporation Act, as revised.

Merger   A formal combination of two or more corporations where one corporation is absorbed by another, the latter of which is called the surviving corporation.

Minute Book   A book containing the written legal history of a corporation, the written notes of proceedings at corporate shareholder and director meetings, and official corporate documents.

Minutes   A summary of the proceedings of a corporate meeting including formal resolutions.

Mortgage   A written grant by a debtor to a creditor of a collateral interest in real estate owned by the debtor.

Mortgagee   The creditor in a mortgage relationship.

Mortgagor   The debtor in a mortgage relationship.

Name-Holding Corporation   A corporation created in a state whose only purpose is to protect the availability of a name for future use.

Net Assets   The dollar value difference between assets and liabilities of a corporation.

Net Worth   The balancing figure between assets and liabilities; also known as "net assets," "shareholders equity," or "capital."

Nominal Directors   Persons who are designated directors only for the purpose of forming a corporation as required by some state laws and who will immediately resign in favor of the directors who will make business decisions.

Nonassessable Stock   Stock which has been issued for not less than par value, if any, or for the agreed consideration if of no par value, on which the owner cannot be charged any further amount.

Noncumulative Preferred Stock   Preferred stock, the shareholders of which are not entitled to receive at a future time any dividends which were not previously paid at the scheduled time.

Notary Public   A public officer authorized to administer oaths, witness documents, and take acknowledgments.

Note   The simplest form of written promise to pay money.

Notice   The providing of advance information of a future event such as a corporate meeting.

Obligor   A debtor.

Ordinary and Necessary Expenses Generally, those costs which are deductible from revenues in computing taxable income because such expenses are those usually incurred by a business of that type.

Organization Meeting The first meeting of the board of directors after incorporation at which initial actions are taken.

Outstanding Shares Shares of stock which have been issued and are in the hands of shareholders other than the corporation itself; also, issued shares less treasury shares.

Par Value The minimum amount that may legally be paid in for stock upon issuance to render it fully paid and nonassessable.

Parent A corporation which owns all or a majority portion of the shares of another corporation.

Parliamentary Procedure The formal rules of order used at a corporate meeting.

Partnership An arrangement between two or more persons to carry on a business together, and to share profits and losses therefrom, where the individuals have personal liability.

Payment Date The day on which a dividend which has been declared on stock is actually distributed to shareholders.

PBCL Pennsylvania Business Corporation Law.

Perfection of the Security Interest The filing of a financing statement or taking possession of the collateral.

Perpetual Existence The designation of an unlimited life of a corporation in its articles of incorporation.

Personal Liability The availability of the personal assets of an individual to business creditors for satisfaction of the obligations of the business.

Personal Property All non-real estate assets, whether tangible or intangible.

Personal Representative The individual who administers the estate of a decedent who dies without a will or who carries out the will of the decedent.

Plaintiff A person who commences a court action against another.

Pledge The granting of a security interest in personal property by delivering physical possession of the collateral to the creditor.

Power of Attorney A writing which authorizes a person to act for and on behalf of the person signing the writing as described in the writing (see attorney-in-fact).

Preemptive Rights   The right of a shareholder to purchase a pro-rata share of a new issue of common stock or security convertible into common stock which the corporation proposes to issue before any nonshareholder may be offered such security by the corporation.

Preferred Stock   A class of stock entitled to prior rights over another class of stock of the corporation with respect to dividends or the distribution of assets in the event of liquidation; also known as preference stock.

Preincorporation Subscription   An agreement by a person before a corporation has been formed to buy stock of a corporation upon its incorporation.

Prime Rate   The rate of interest charged by a bank to its most creditworthy borrowers for short-term unsecured debts.

Proof of Publication   A certificate of a newspaper that a legal notice has been published on a specific date.

Prothonotary   The head clerk of county courts in some states.

Proxy   A written authorization by a shareholder of record to another person to vote shares at a shareholders' meeting with the same effect as if the holder of the shares were present in person at the meeting.

Proxy Statement   A document that public companies mail with a request for a proxy to their shareholders which describes the actions to be taken at the meeting.

Public Market   Generally, the ability of the stock of a publicly held corporation to be bought and sold by the public at large through stockbrokers.

Public Offering   A sale of securities, such as stock or bonds, to the general public in accordance with applicable federal and state laws.

Publicly Held Corporation   Corporation, the stock of which is owned by a large number of persons, such as Xerox, General Motors, and IBM.

Qualification   The acquisition by a foreign corporation of a certificate of authority.

Quorum   The minimum number of people prescribed by statute or bylaws that must be present at a meeting in order to transact business.

Ratification   The process of confirming and adopting an act already performed on behalf of a corporation.

Record Date   A day set by the board of directors as the time for determination of those shareholders of record entitled to notice, dividends, or other shareholder rights.

Record Shareholders The owners of stock of a corporation as reflected in its stock transfer books.

Registered Office The location of a corporation designated in its articles of incorporation or certificate of authority where legal documents may be served.

Registry Statement A document filed with the articles of incorporation, containing information about the officers and other corporate matters, which is used by the corporate taxing bureau for its purposes.

Regular Meeting A periodically scheduled shareholders' or directors' meeting at which any corporate business may be conducted.

Resolution A formal written statement of the shareholders or directors of a corporation designating (a) an action that the corporation may take and (b) those persons who may effectuate the action on its behalf.

Restated Articles of Incorporation An amendment to the articles of incorporation which consolidates into one document all previous amendments of the articles.

Restrictive Covenant In an agreement a clause which restricts the future employment or engagement in a business by a person.

Reverse Stock Split A combination of the issued shares of any class of stock of a corporation so that fewer shares remain issued after the reverse stock split than before it; opposite of stock split.

Right of First Refusal The option of a person to decide whether to buy or refuse to buy an asset before the asset can be sold by another to anyone else.

Right of Redemption The right of a corporation to require the holders of a class of securities to sell all or a part of their securities to the corporation at a specified price.

/S/ The symbol which conforms a copy of a manually executed document to indicate that it is a true and correct copy of the executed document.

Sealed Instrument An agreement which, in many states, is enforceable even without consideration to the person against whom it is enforceable.

Section 1244 Stock Stock issued by a corporation in compliance with Section 1244 of the IRC which may confer tax benefits on purchasers of stock in the event of a loss on the disposition of the stock.

Secured Debt An obligation for which the holder has a specific claim against designated collateral of a debtor in the event of failure to repay the debt at maturity.

Secured Party A creditor that has obtained collateral for repayment of the debt.

Security Agreement A contract between a debtor and a creditor which designates collateral to assure payment of the debt and designates the respective rights of the parties with respect to the collateral.

Security Interest A collateral interest in real or personal property (such as a mortgage) which secures the payment of an obligation.

Series Preferred Stock Preferred stock which may be authorized for issuance from time to time by the board of directors where state law permits and the articles of incorporation authorize the class of preferred stock.

Severability Clause A boilerplate provision in an agreement stating that if a court finds another provision invalid or unenforceable, the remainder of the agreement shall be interpreted as if the invalid provision was not in the agreement.

Shareholder One who is a holder of one or more shares of stock of a corporation; also known as stockholder.

Shareholders' Agreement A written agreement entered into among two or more shareholders of a corporation with a small number of shareholders restricting transfers of stock by the parties to the agreement.

Shareholders List A list of all shareholders of a corporation at a specific date.

Shares The units into which the proprietary interests in a corporation are divided.

Sinking Fund A required periodic payment for the purpose of (a) the redemption of a specified number of shares of preferred stock (or reduction of an indebtedness) each year or of (b) the future retirement of the preferred stock (or debt) at a specified date.

Sole Proprietorship A form of business which is conducted by one person who has personal liability for the business debts.

Special Meeting A meeting of shareholders or directors called for a specific purpose.

Specific Performance A direct court order to a person to do a specific act or risk jail for contempt of court.

Stated Capital The sum of the par value of all shares having a par value and the consideration received by a corporation for shares without par value.

Statement of Cancellation A document required to be filed with some states when a corporation formally cancels treasury stock.

Stock Shares of a corporation.

APPENDIX III

Suggested readings/sources on computer use in the practice of law

American Bar Association. *Access 1989-1990: A resource guide to legal automation.* [750 N. Lake Shore Drive, Chicago IL 60611. A clearinghouse of information and practical pointers that show where to get help about technology and how a legal professional can learn more about computers and software. Listing of periodicals, books, user groups, seminars, training resources, vendor listings related to legal automation.]

American Bar Association. *American Bar Association journal.* [Address above. Provides periodic supplements dealing with computer issues.]

American Bar Association. *LOCATE: A directory of law office computer software vendors.* [Address above. A compilation of articles, vendor names, software descriptions designed to assist the legal professional in selecting the appropriate software. Lists micro, mini, and mainframe computer vendors.]

Computer counsel: The leading edge of law office automation. [150 N. Wacker Drive, Suite 1870, Chicago IL 60606-6846. A monthly newsletter that provides reviews of software and hardware suitable for law practice. Includes articles by technical specialists, attorneys, and paralegals.]

Law office technology review. [P.O. Box 24032, Oakland CA 94623-1032. A monthly newsletter that provides reviews of software and hardware suitable for law practice.]

The lawyer's PC: A newsletter for lawyers using personal computers. [Shepard's/McGraw Hill, P.O. Box 1235, Colorado Springs CO 80901-9843. A bimonthly newsletter that gives valuable insight into what the computerized law office is really like. Reviews of software and hardware actually used by legal professionals.]

Legal software review. [Lawyer's Library, 12761 New Halls Ferry Road, Florissant, MO 63033. A compilation of legal software reviews. Gives in-depth description of leading software of interest to legal professionals. Review programs designed for MS-DOS, Macintosh, Unix, DEC, Data General, Altos, and Wang Systems.

Robbins, Richard, Esq. *The automated law firm: A complete guide to systems and software.* Englewood Cliffs, NJ: Prentice Hall Law and Business.

SUBJECT INDEX

Periodic reporting under the,
342–43
Proxy rules, 344–46
Purpose of, 331, 340
Section 10 (antifraud provisions)
of the, 349
Section 16 (beneficial ownership
reporting requirements) of
the, 346–47
Section 16 (short-swing profits
recovery rules) of the, 347–48

SERVICE OF PROCESS, 71

SHAREHOLDERS
See also, Meetings, shareholder
Amending articles of
incorporation, 10, 81–83
Cumulative voting by, 39–41
Definition of, 9
Dissenters' rights and, 364–66
Dividend rights of holders of
common stock, 159, 162
Dividend rights of holders of
preferred stock, 164–67
Informal action of, 41
Liability, 10–11, 160
Liquidation rights of holders of
common stock, 160
Liquidation rights of holders of
preferred stock, 167–68
Management by, 14
Mergers and approval from,
358–59
Preemptive rights, 38–39
Preemptive rights of holders of
common stock, 159
Redemption rights of holders of
preferred stock, 168–71
Rights of, 9–11
Voting rights of holders of
common stock, 158–59,
161–62
Voting rights of holders of
preferred stock, 172–74

SHAREHOLDERS' AGREEMENTS
Authorization of, 277–78
Boilerplate clauses, 278–79
Call, 257
Covenants not to compete,
274–75
Death of shareholder, 260–62
Definition of, 251
Dilution of stock interests, 274
Duration of, 277
Insurance funding, need for, 262
Interfamily transfers, 276

Management of business
provisions, 272–75
Mandatory sales/purchases,
256–59
Multiple classes of shares,
275–76
Other names for, 251
Parties to, 253
Purchase price of stock, 263–71
Purpose of, 251–52
Put, 256
Restrictions for two or more
groups of shareholders,
259–60
Right of first refusal, 254–56
Transfer restrictions for, 252–60
Voting trusts, 273–74

SHARES
See also, Stock
Agreed values for, 265
Amendments to articles of
incorporation prior to
issuance of, 85–86
Authorized, 12–13, 155
Book/appraisal value for, 266–68
Class and series, 151–52
Death of shareholder and
disposition of, 260–62
Definition of, 152
Earnings multiple formula for
purchasing, 268–69
Fully paid and nonassessable,
156–58
Interfamily transfers of, 276
Issued and not outstanding, 155
Issued and outstanding, 155
Matching offers for, 264
Multiple classes of, 275–76
Purchase by corporation of its
own, 323–24
Selling of, 155–56
Tender offers, 366–68
Terms of payment for, 270–71
Treasury, 155, 324

SHERMAN ANTITRUST ACT,
361–62

SHORT-SWING RULES, 347–48

SINKING FUND
Debt securities and, 196
Preferred stock and, 175–76

FORMS INDEX